gh School

Host Club

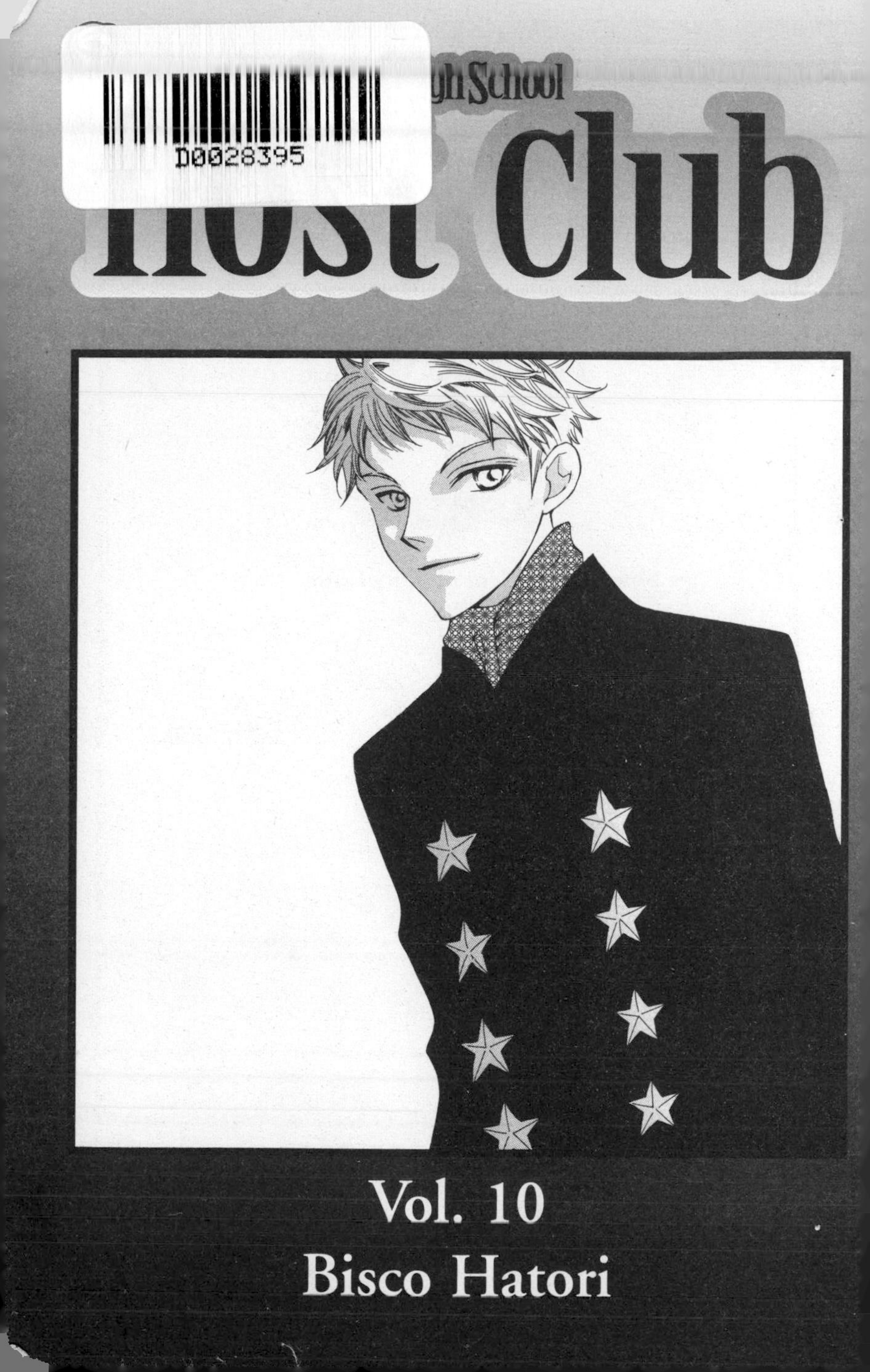

Vol. 10

Bisco Hatori

Ouran High School

Host Club

Vol. 10

CONTENTS

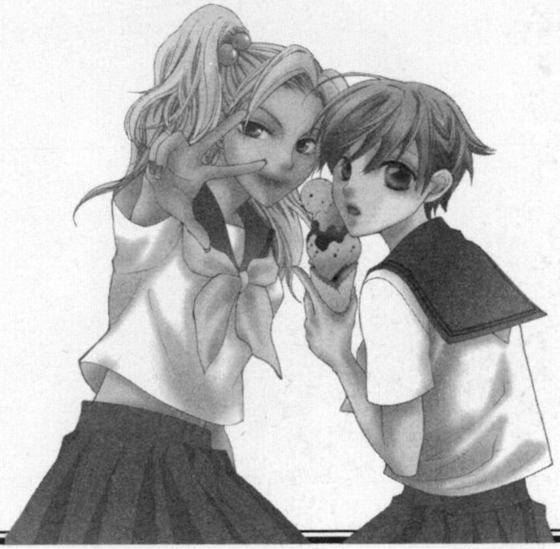

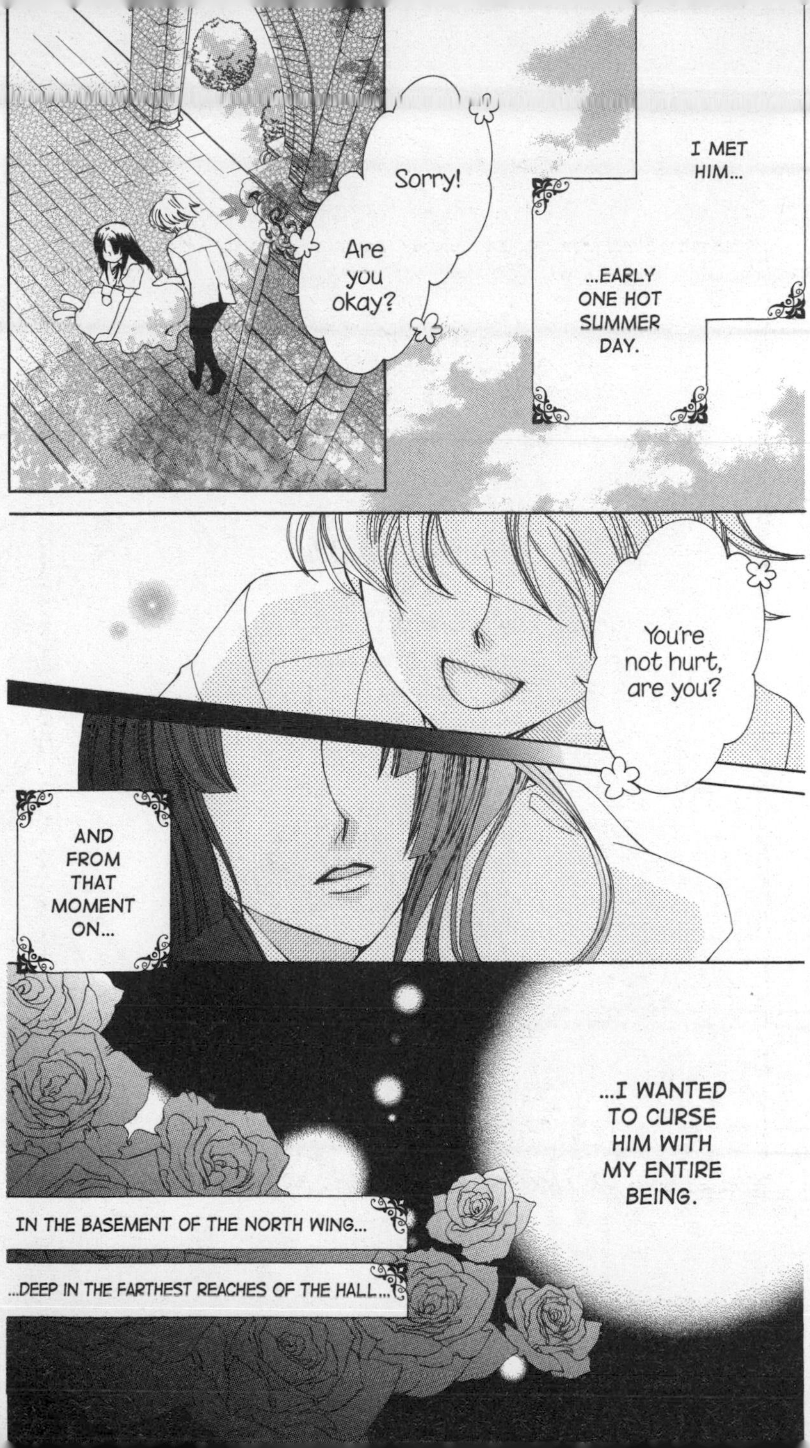
I MET HIM...
...EARLY ONE HOT SUMMER DAY.
Sorry!
Are you okay?
You're not hurt, are you?
AND FROM THAT MOMENT ON...
...I WANTED TO CURSE HIM WITH MY ENTIRE BEING.
IN THE BASEMENT OF THE NORTH WING...
...DEEP IN THE FARTHEST REACHES OF THE HALL...

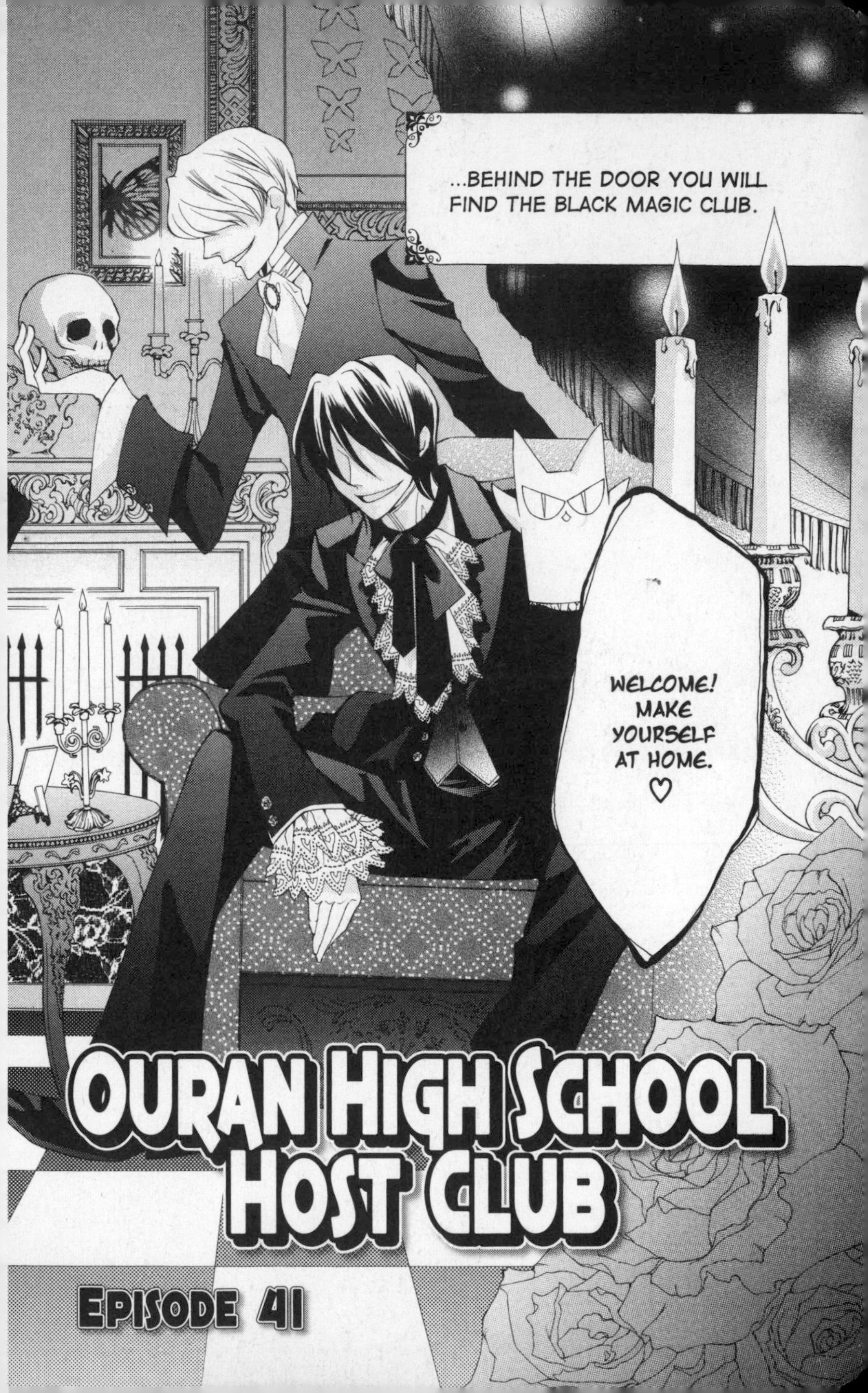
...BEHIND THE DOOR YOU WILL FIND THE BLACK MAGIC CLUB.
WELCOME! MAKE YOURSELF AT HOME. ♡
OURAN HIGH SCHOOL HOST CLUB
EPISODE 41

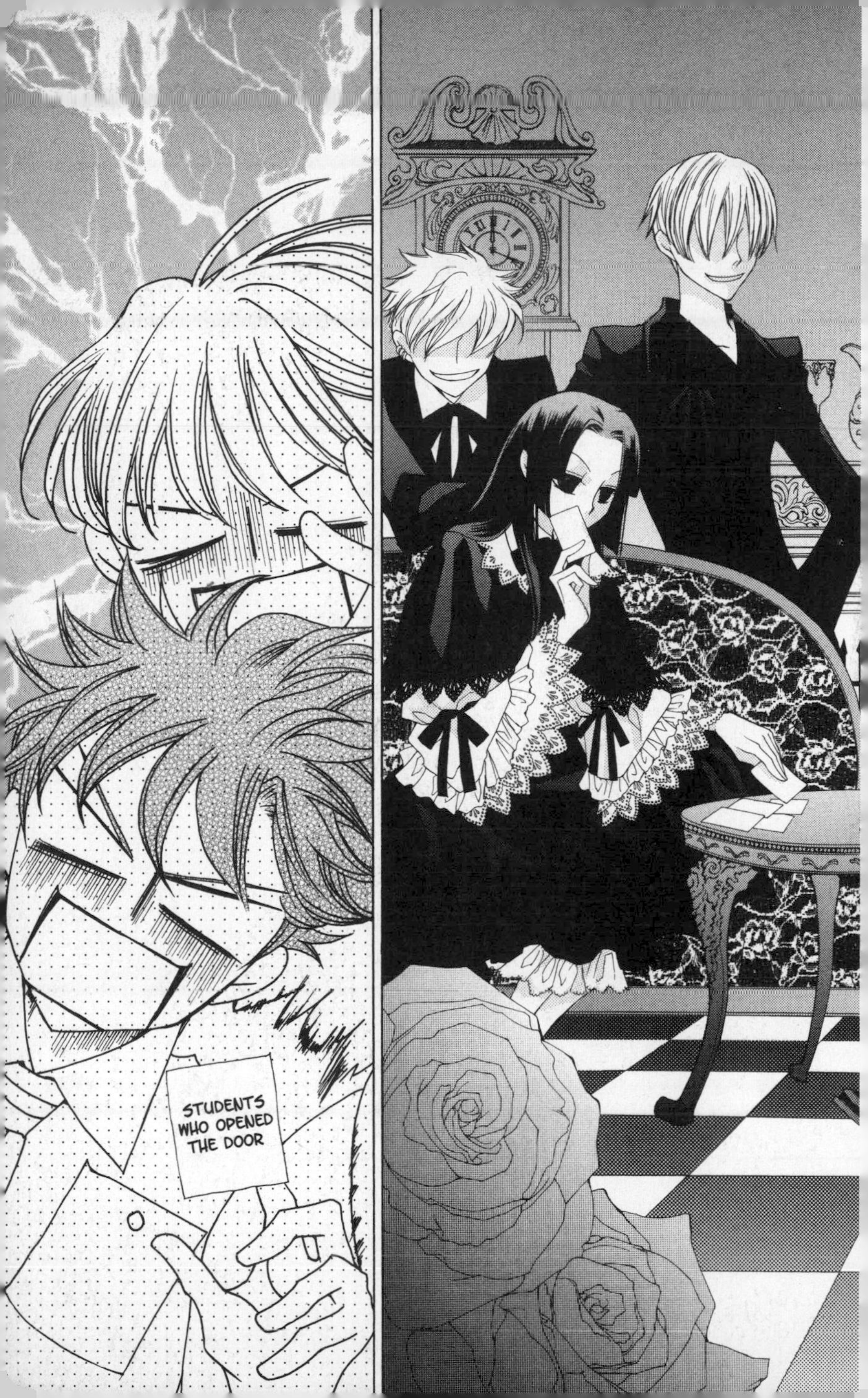
STUDENTS WHO OPENED THE DOOR

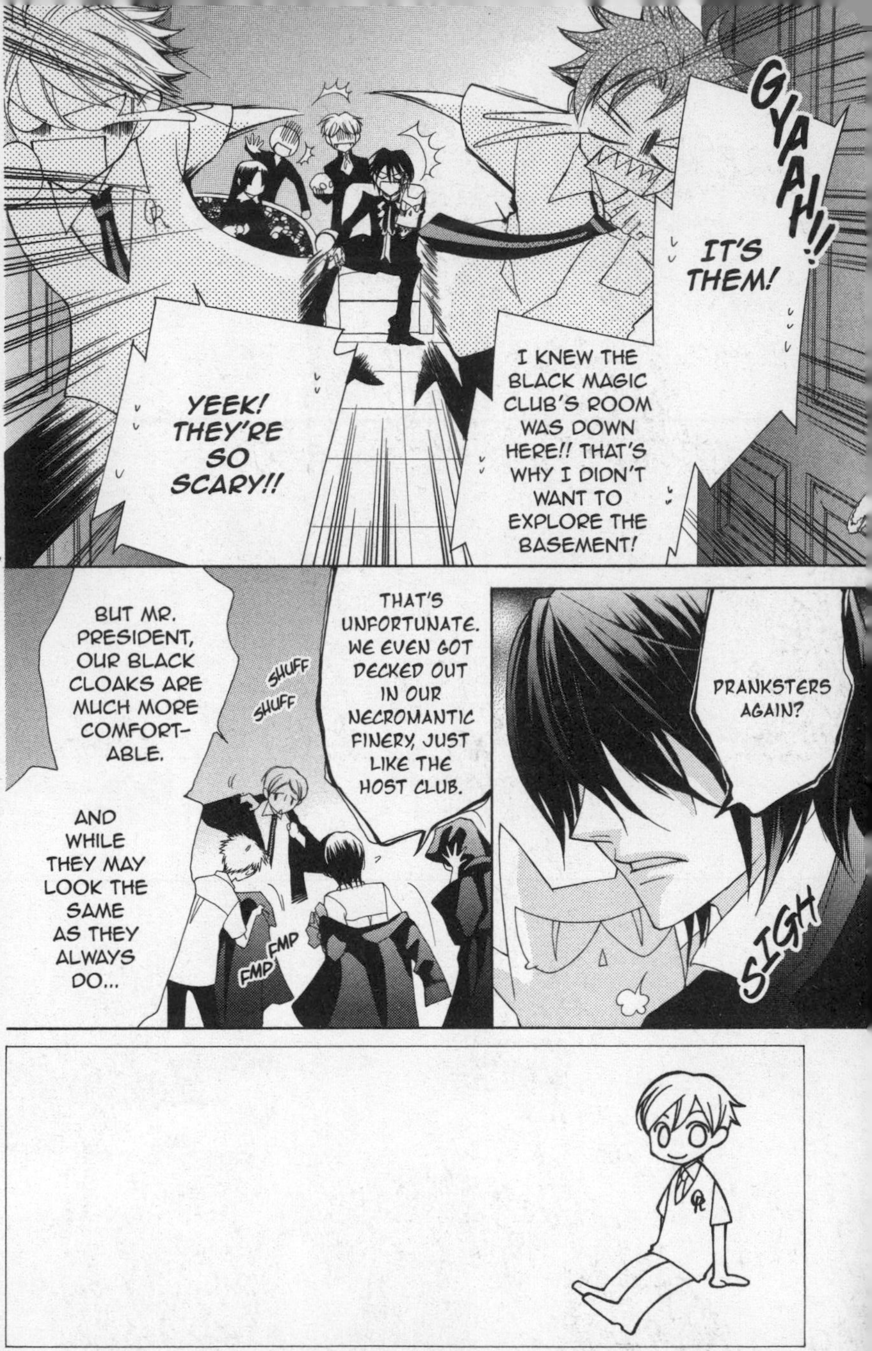
GYAAH!!
IT'S THEM!
I KNEW THE BLACK MAGIC CLUB'S ROOM WAS DOWN HERE!! THAT'S WHY I DIDN'T WANT TO EXPLORE THE BASEMENT!
YEEK! THEY'RE SO SCARY!!
PRANKSTERS AGAIN?
SIGH
THAT'S UNFORTUNATE. WE EVEN GOT DECKED OUT IN OUR NECROMANTIC FINERY, JUST LIKE THE HOST CLUB.
SHUFF
SHUFF
BUT MR. PRESIDENT, OUR BLACK CLOAKS ARE MUCH MORE COMFORT-ABLE.
AND WHILE THEY MAY LOOK THE SAME AS THEY ALWAYS DO...
FMP
FMP

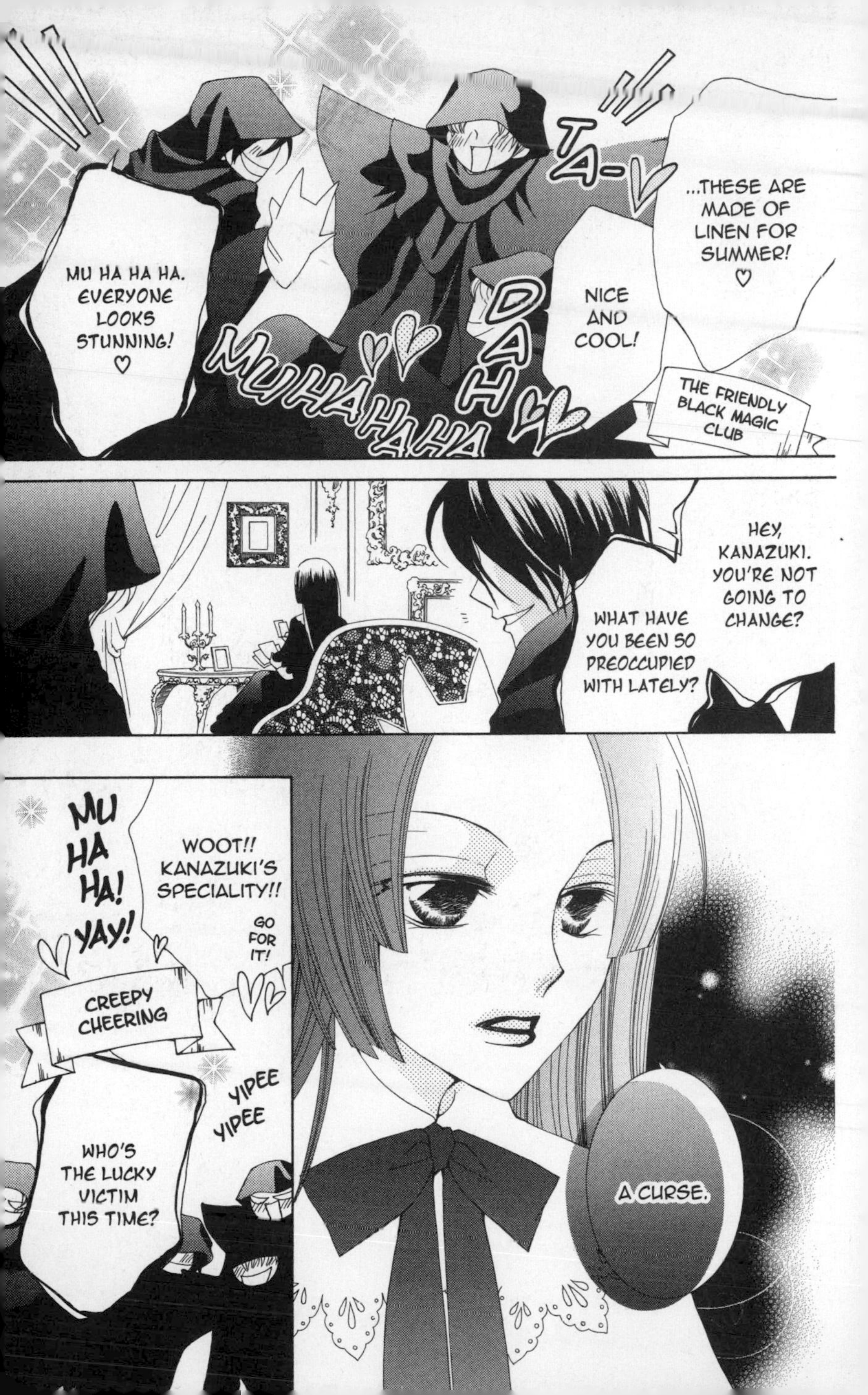
TA-
...THESE ARE MADE OF LINEN FOR SUMMER! ♡
NICE AND COOL!
DAH
THE FRIENDLY BLACK MAGIC CLUB
MUHAHAHAHA
MU HA HA HA. EVERYONE LOOKS STUNNING! ♡
HEY, KANAZUKI. YOU'RE NOT GOING TO CHANGE?
WHAT HAVE YOU BEEN SO PREOCCUPIED WITH LATELY?
A CURSE.
WOOT!! KANAZUKI'S SPECIALITY!!
MU HA HA! YAY!
GO FOR IT!
CREEPY CHEERING
YIPEE YIPEE
WHO'S THE LUCKY VICTIM THIS TIME?

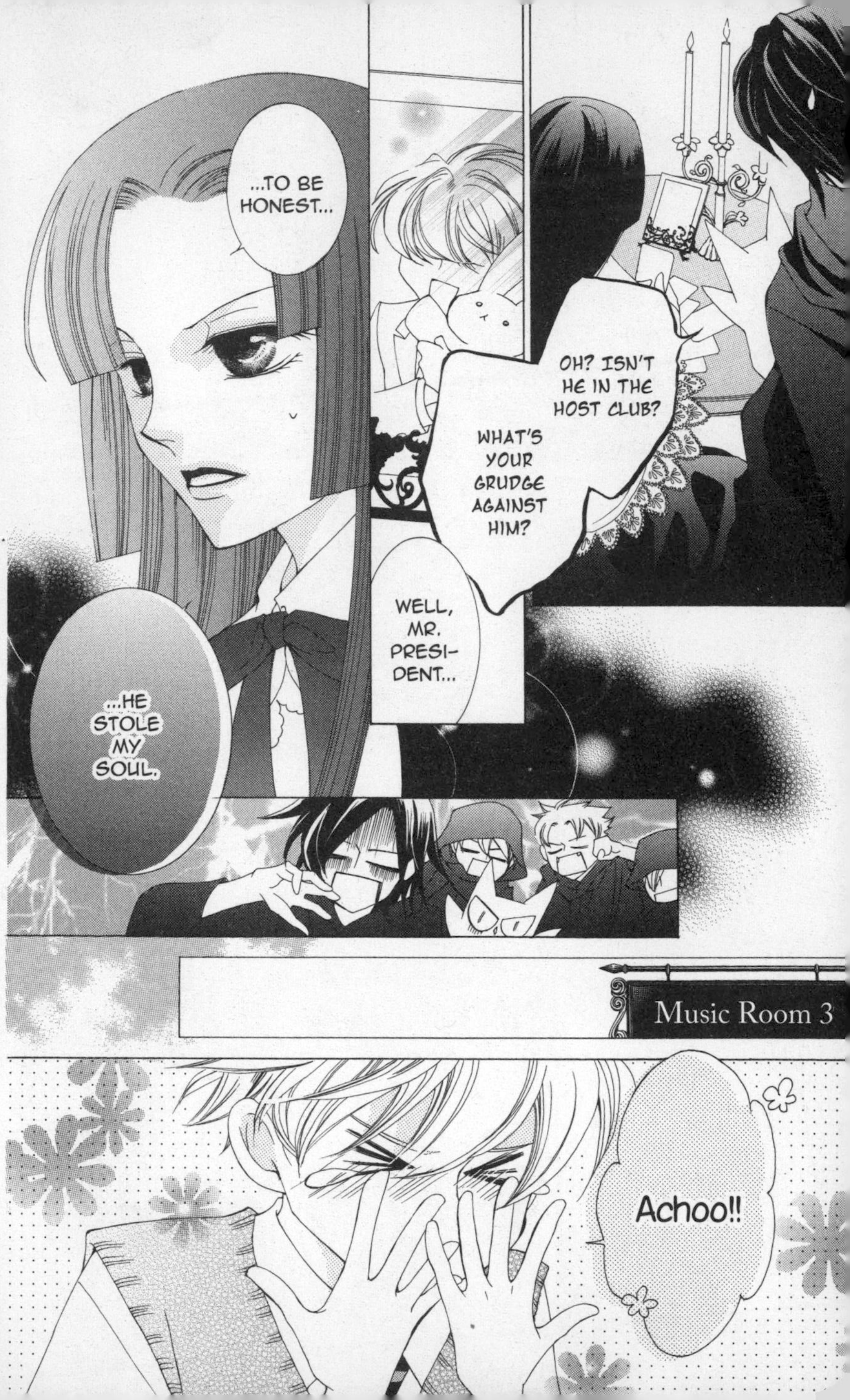
OH? ISN'T HE IN THE HOST CLUB?
WHAT'S YOUR GRUDGE AGAINST HIM?
WELL, MR. PRESIDENT...
...TO BE HONEST...
...HE STOLE MY SOUL.
Music Room 3
Achoo!!

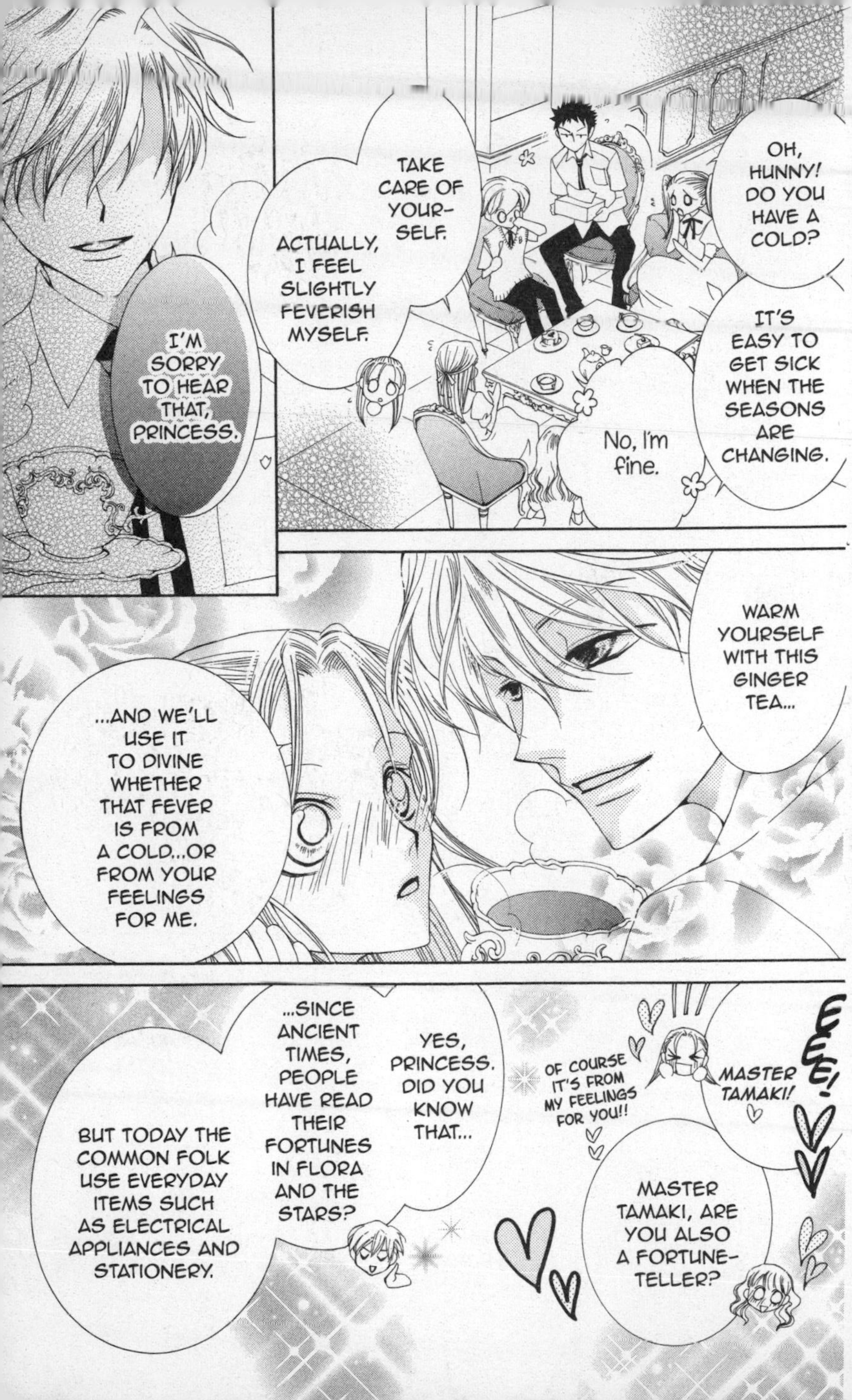
OH, HUNNY! DO YOU HAVE A COLD?
IT'S EASY TO GET SICK WHEN THE SEASONS ARE CHANGING.
No, I'm fine.
TAKE CARE OF YOUR-SELF.
ACTUALLY, I FEEL SLIGHTLY FEVERISH MYSELF.
I'M SORRY TO HEAR THAT, PRINCESS.
WARM YOURSELF WITH THIS GINGER TEA...
...AND WE'LL USE IT TO DIVINE WHETHER THAT FEVER IS FROM A COLD...OR FROM YOUR FEELINGS FOR ME.
EEE!
MASTER TAMAKI!
OF COURSE IT'S FROM MY FEELINGS FOR YOU!!
MASTER TAMAKI, ARE YOU ALSO A FORTUNE-TELLER?
YES, PRINCESS. DID YOU KNOW THAT...
...SINCE ANCIENT TIMES, PEOPLE HAVE READ THEIR FORTUNES IN FLORA AND THE STARS?
BUT TODAY THE COMMON FOLK USE EVERYDAY ITEMS SUCH AS ELECTRICAL APPLIANCES AND STATIONERY.

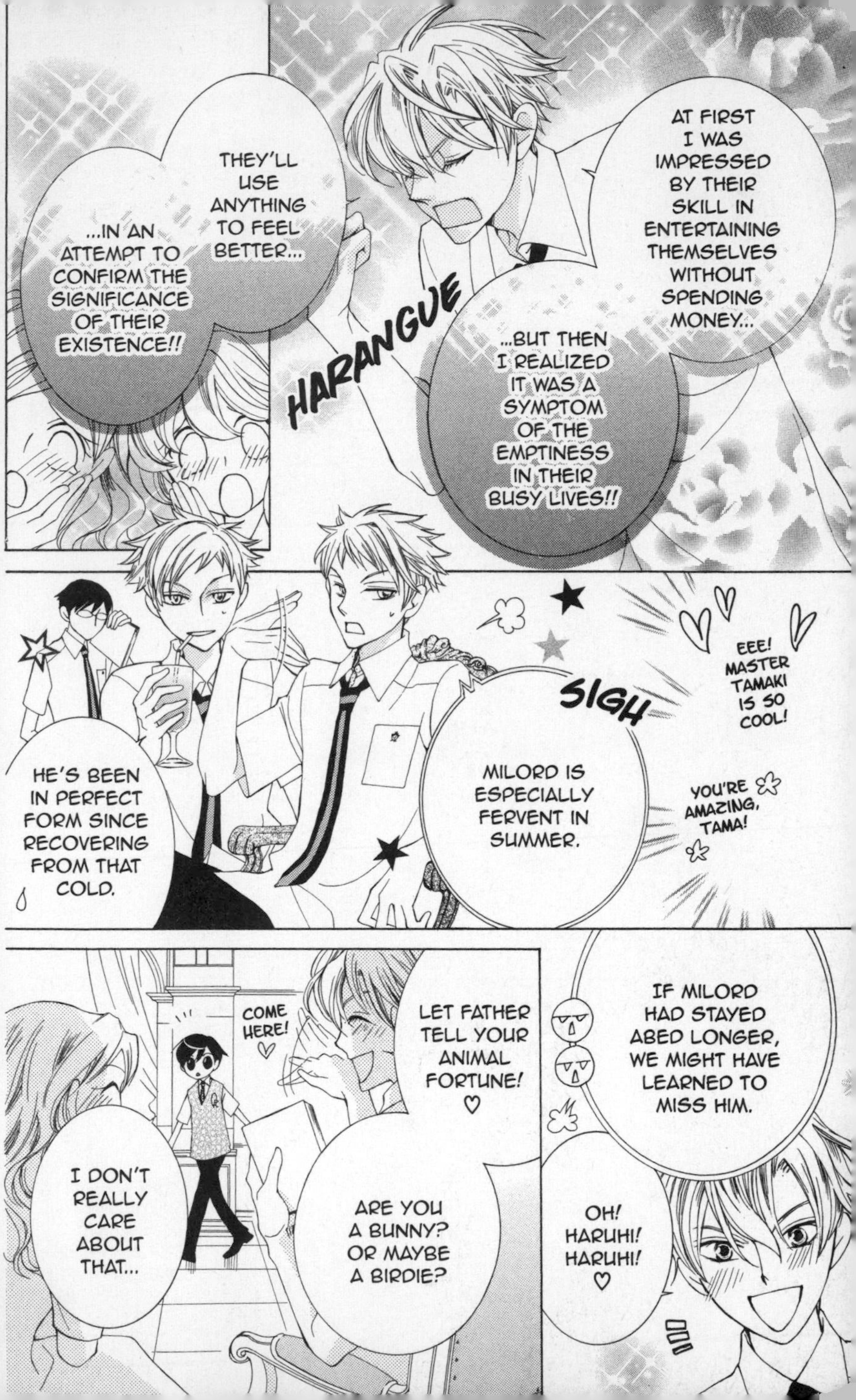
AT FIRST I WAS IMPRESSED BY THEIR SKILL IN ENTERTAINING THEMSELVES WITHOUT SPENDING MONEY...
...BUT THEN I REALIZED IT WAS A SYMPTOM OF THE EMPTINESS IN THEIR BUSY LIVES!!
HARANGUE
THEY'LL USE ANYTHING TO FEEL BETTER...
...IN AN ATTEMPT TO CONFIRM THE SIGNIFICANCE OF THEIR EXISTENCE!!
EEE! MASTER TAMAKI IS SO COOL!
YOU'RE AMAZING, TAMA!
SIGH
MILORD IS ESPECIALLY FERVENT IN SUMMER.
HE'S BEEN IN PERFECT FORM SINCE RECOVERING FROM THAT COLD.
IF MILORD HAD STAYED ABED LONGER, WE MIGHT HAVE LEARNED TO MISS HIM.
OH! HARUHI! HARUHI! ♡
LET FATHER TELL YOUR ANIMAL FORTUNE! ♡
COME HERE! ♡
ARE YOU A BUNNY? OR MAYBE A BIRDIE?
I DON'T REALLY CARE ABOUT THAT...

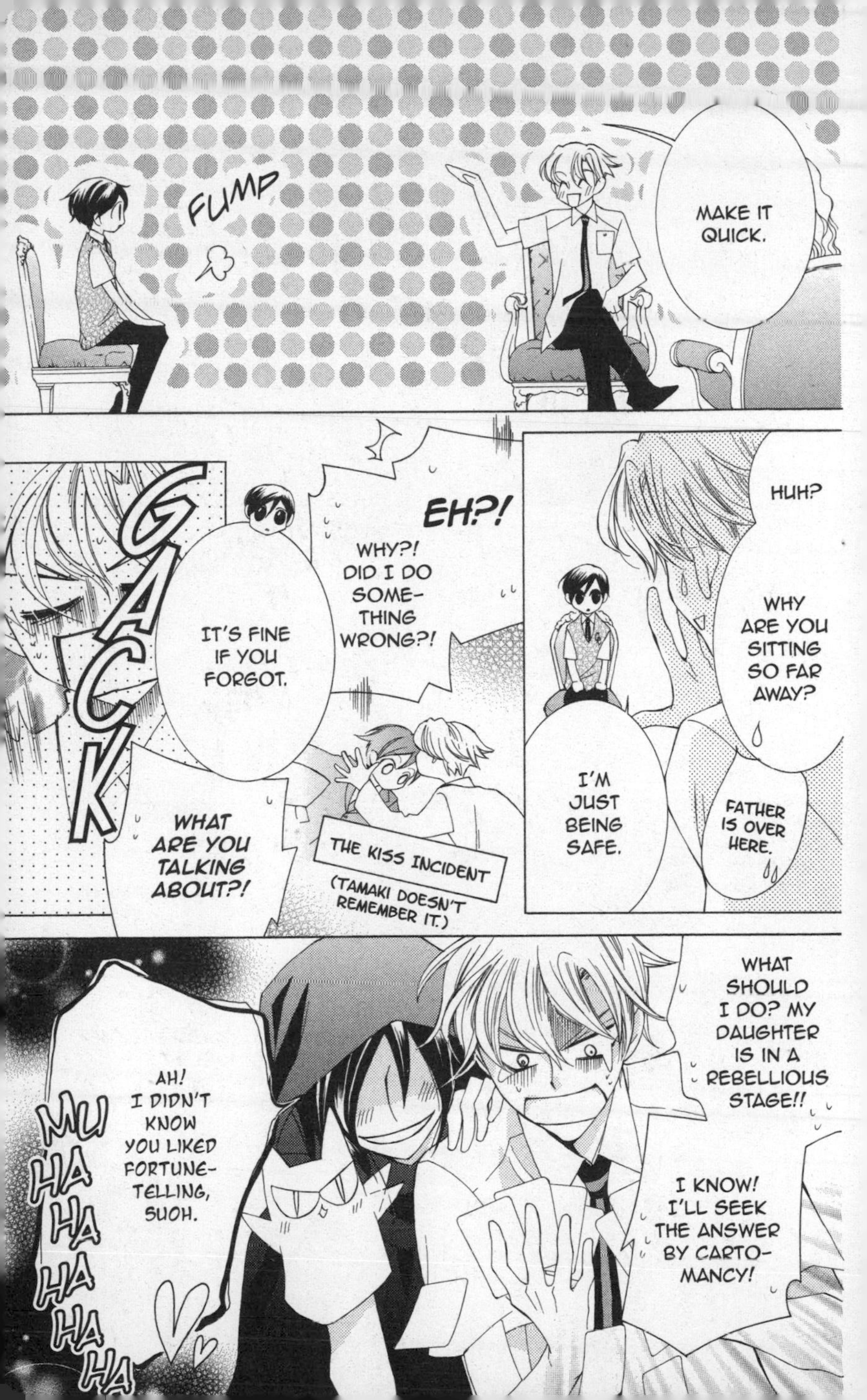
MAKE IT QUICK.
FUMP
HUH?
WHY ARE YOU SITTING SO FAR AWAY?
FATHER IS OVER HERE.
I'M JUST BEING SAFE.
EH?!
WHY?! DID I DO SOME-THING WRONG?!
IT'S FINE IF YOU FORGOT.
GACK
WHAT ARE YOU TALKING ABOUT?!
THE KISS INCIDENT
(TAMAKI DOESN'T REMEMBER IT.)
WHAT SHOULD I DO? MY DAUGHTER IS IN A REBELLIOUS STAGE!!
I KNOW! I'LL SEEK THE ANSWER BY CARTO-MANCY!
AH! I DIDN'T KNOW YOU LIKED FORTUNE-TELLING, SUOH.
MU HA HA HA HA HA HA

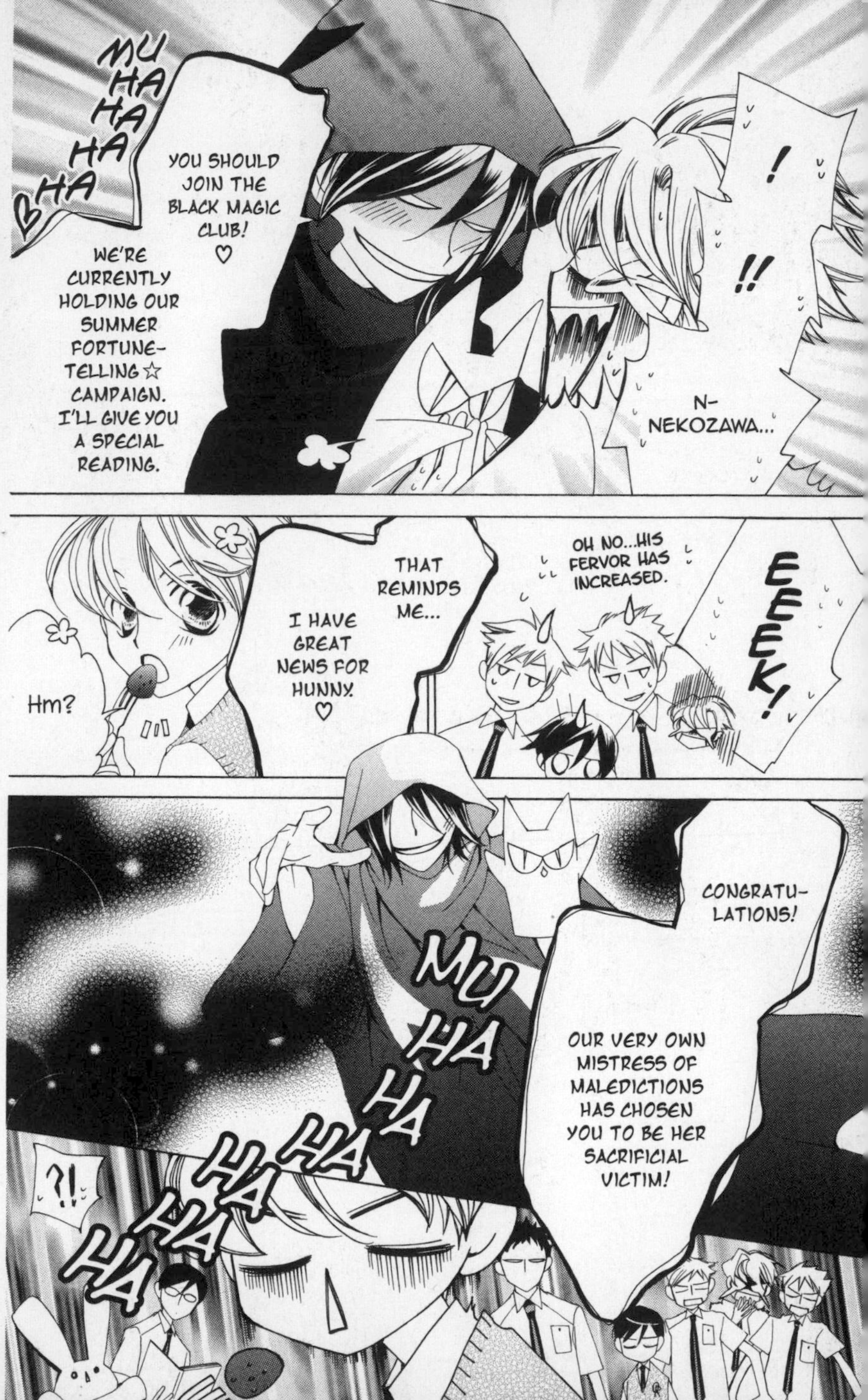
!
!!
N-NEKOZAWA...
YOU SHOULD JOIN THE BLACK MAGIC CLUB! ♡
MUHAHAHAHA ♡
WE'RE CURRENTLY HOLDING OUR SUMMER FORTUNE-TELLING☆CAMPAIGN. I'LL GIVE YOU A SPECIAL READING.
EEEEK!
OH NO...HIS FERVOR HAS INCREASED.
THAT REMINDS ME...
I HAVE GREAT NEWS FOR HUNNY. ♡
Hm?
CONGRATU-LATIONS!
OUR VERY OWN MISTRESS OF MALEDICTIONS HAS CHOSEN YOU TO BE HER SACRIFICIAL VICTIM!
MUHAHAHAHAHAHA
?!

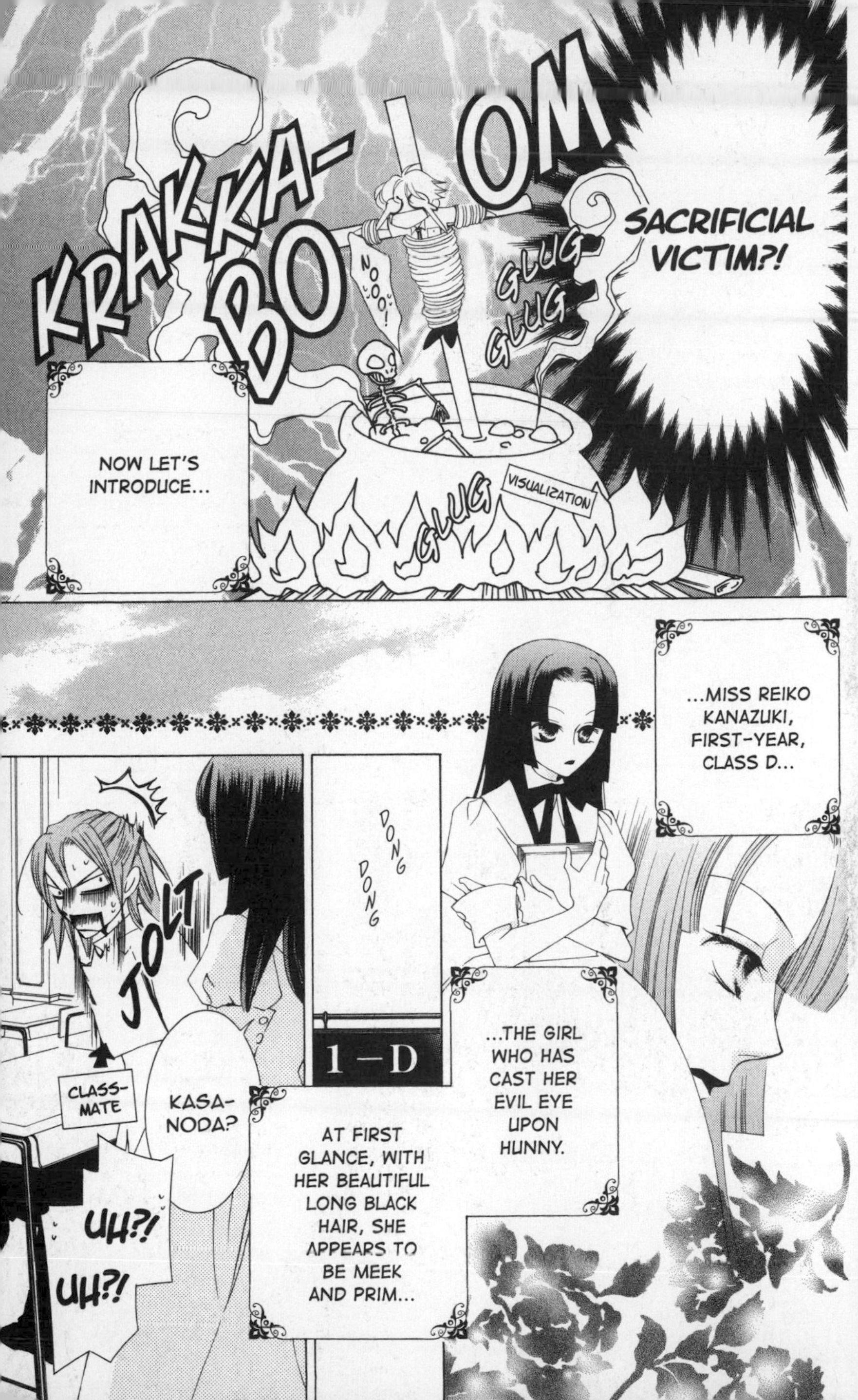
SACRIFICIAL VICTIM?!
KRAKKA-BOOM
GLUG GLUG
NOOOO!
NOW LET'S INTRODUCE...
VISUALIZATION
GLUG
...MISS REIKO KANAZUKI, FIRST-YEAR, CLASS D...
...THE GIRL WHO HAS CAST HER EVIL EYE UPON HUNNY.
AT FIRST GLANCE, WITH HER BEAUTIFUL LONG BLACK HAIR, SHE APPEARS TO BE MEEK AND PRIM...
DONG DONG
1-D
JOLT
KASA-NODA?
CLASSMATE
UH?!
UH?!

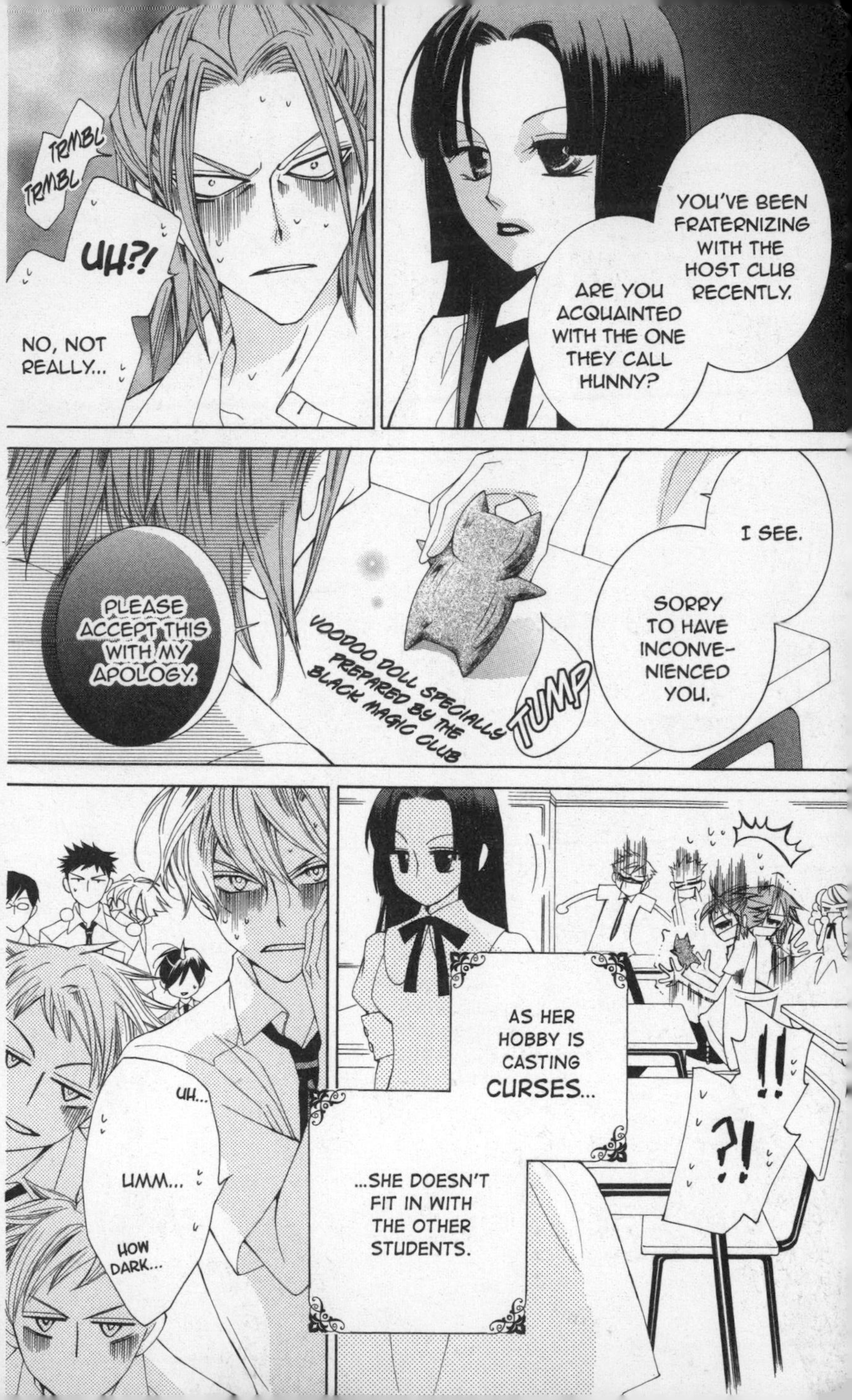
YOU'VE BEEN FRATERNIZING WITH THE HOST CLUB RECENTLY.
ARE YOU ACQUAINTED WITH THE ONE THEY CALL HUNNY?
TRMBL TRMBL
UH?!
NO, NOT REALLY...
I SEE.
SORRY TO HAVE INCONVENIENCED YOU.
TUMP
VOODOO DOLL SPECIALLY PREPARED BY THE BLACK MAGIC CLUB
PLEASE ACCEPT THIS WITH MY APOLOGY.
!!
?!
AS HER HOBBY IS CASTING CURSES...
...SHE DOESN'T FIT IN WITH THE OTHER STUDENTS.
UH...
UMM...
HOW DARK...

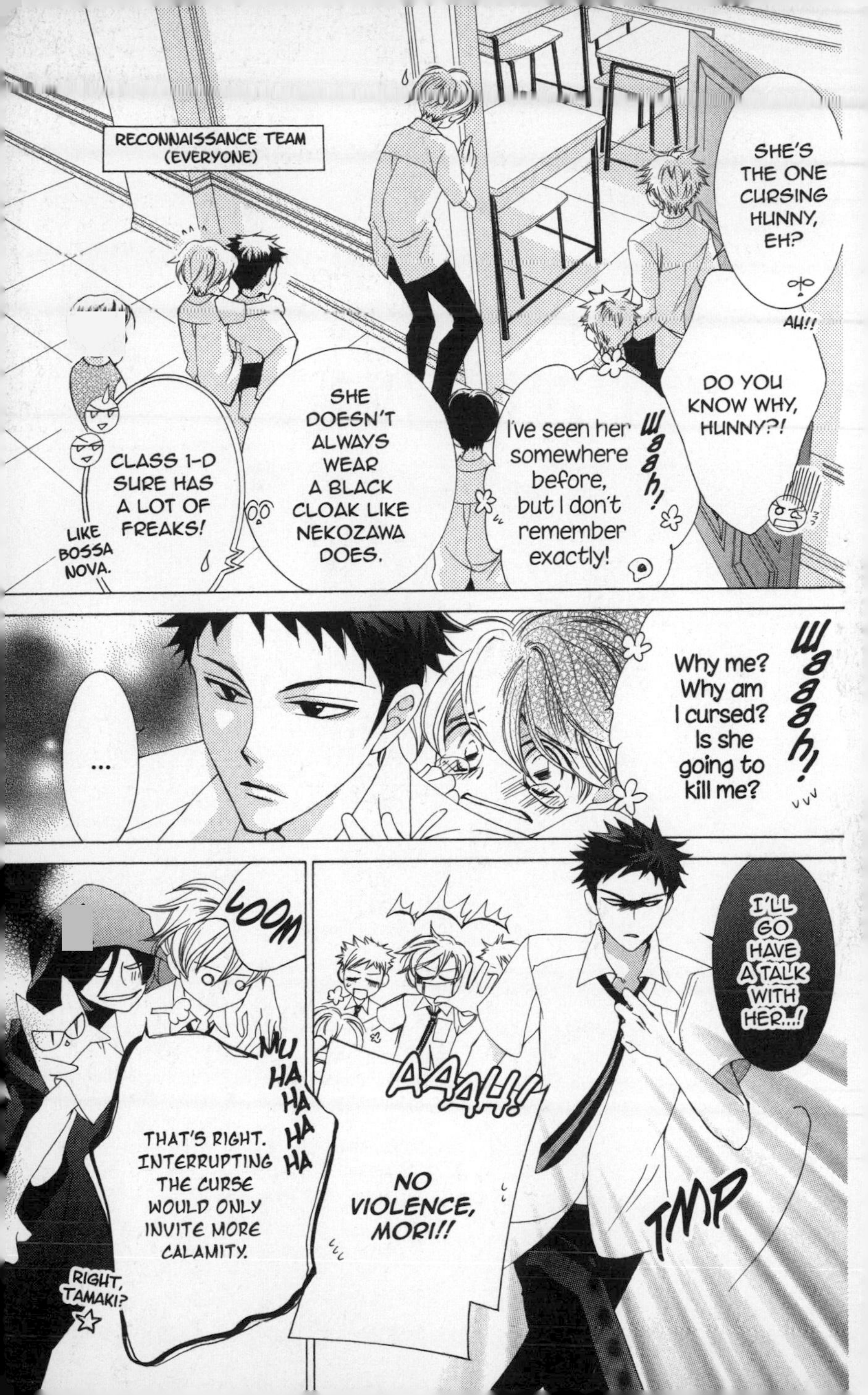
RECONNAISSANCE TEAM (EVERYONE)
SHE'S THE ONE CURSING HUNNY, EH?
AH!!
DO YOU KNOW WHY, HUNNY?!
Waah!
I've seen her somewhere before, but I don't remember exactly!
SHE DOESN'T ALWAYS WEAR A BLACK CLOAK LIKE NEKOZAWA DOES.
CLASS 1-D SURE HAS A LOT OF FREAKS!
LIKE BOSSA NOVA.
Waaah!
Why me? Why am I cursed? Is she going to kill me?
...
I'LL GO HAVE A TALK WITH HER...!
AAAH!
NO VIOLENCE, MORI!!
TMP
LOOM
MU HA HA HA HA
THAT'S RIGHT. INTERRUPTING THE CURSE WOULD ONLY INVITE MORE CALAMITY.
RIGHT, TAMAKI?

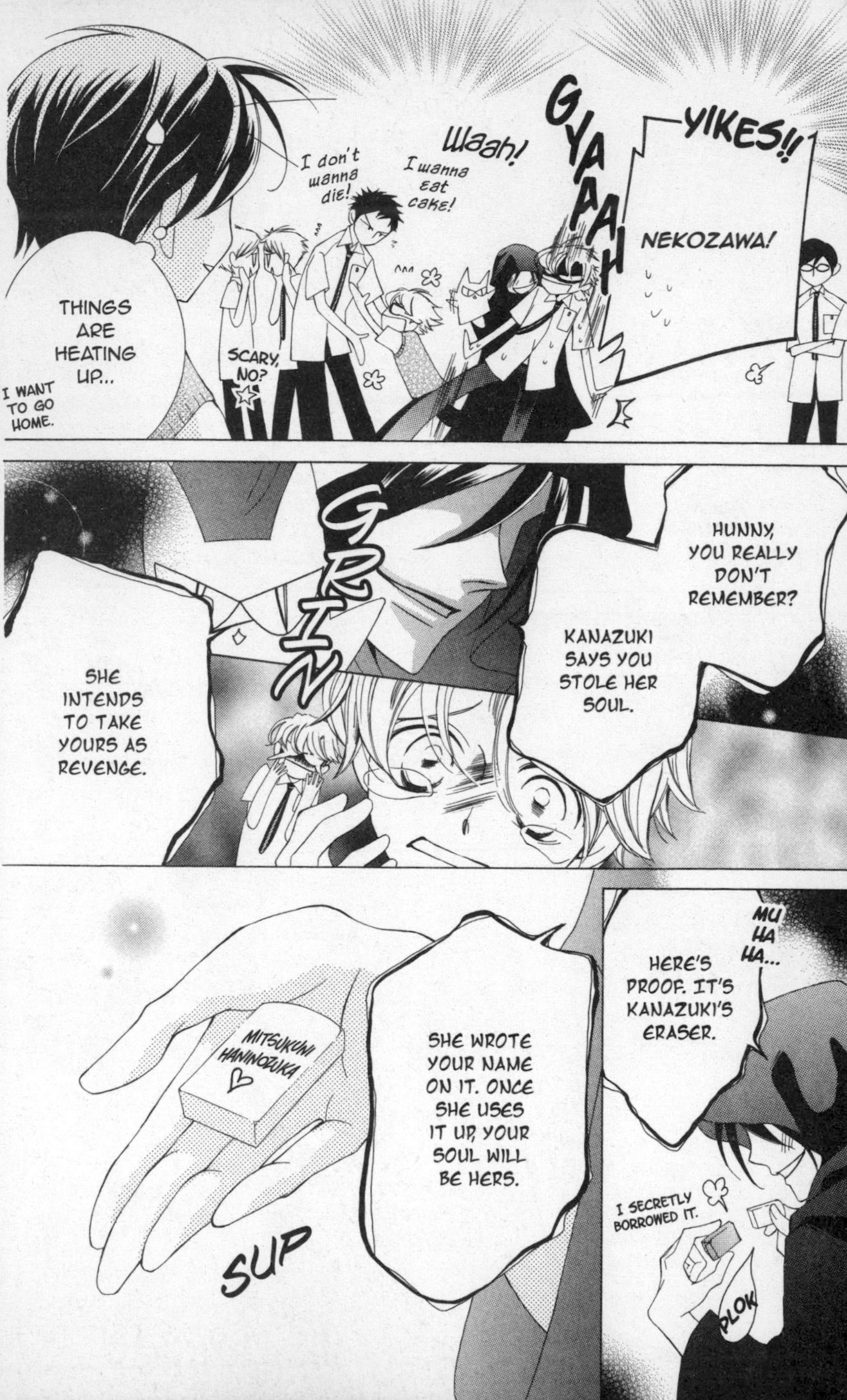
YIKES!!
NEKOZAWA!
GYAAAH!
Waah! I wanna eat cake!
I don't wanna die!
SCARY, NO?
THINGS ARE HEATING UP...
I WANT TO GO HOME.
HUNNY, YOU REALLY DON'T REMEMBER?
KANAZUKI SAYS YOU STOLE HER SOUL.
GRIN
SHE INTENDS TO TAKE YOURS AS REVENGE.
MU HA HA...
HERE'S PROOF. IT'S KANAZUKI'S ERASER.
I SECRETLY BORROWED IT.
PLOK
SHE WROTE YOUR NAME ON IT. ONCE SHE USES IT UP, YOUR SOUL WILL BE HERS.
MITSUKUNI HANINOZUKA ♥
SUP

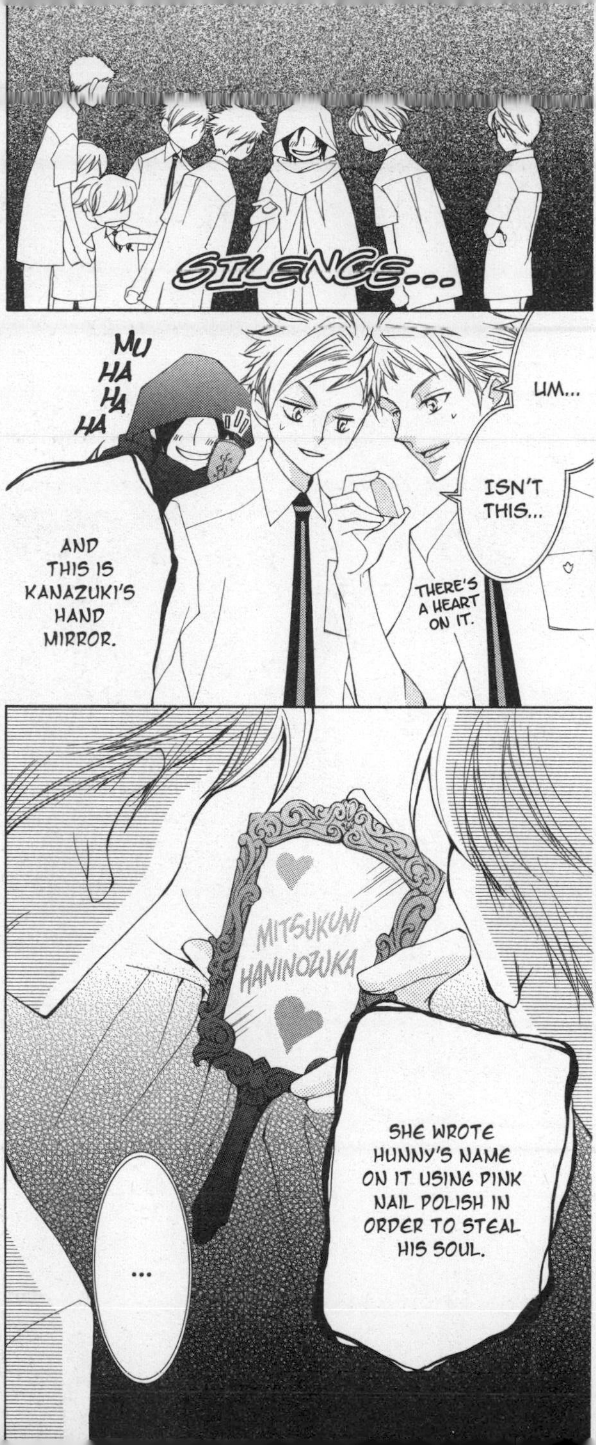
SILENCE...
UM...
ISN'T THIS...
THERE'S A HEART ON IT.
AND THIS IS KANAZUKI'S HAND MIRROR.
MU HA HA HA
MITSUKUNI HANINOZUKA
SHE WROTE HUNNY'S NAME ON IT USING PINK NAIL POLISH IN ORDER TO STEAL HIS SOUL.
...

I

✿ HELLO!! HOW HAS EVERYONE BEEN?

HATORI, HERE. THESE DAYS I'VE BEEN GETTING A LOT OF WONDERFUL LETTERS FROM PEOPLE WHO SAY THEY READ *HOST CLUB* TOGETHER WITH THEIR PARENTS ♡ OR BROTHERS. ♡ AND SINCE THE ANIME STARTED, I'VE BEEN GETTING MORE LETTERS FROM HOUSEWIVES AND MEN. THIS MAKES ME REALLY HAPPY!!

THE STORY OF *HOST CLUB* HAS BEEN PROGRESSING AT A LEISURELY PACE, BUT NOW IT'S STARTING TO GET MORE ROMANTIC! IN THE BEGINNING I COULDN'T WAIT TO START DRAWING THE ROMANTIC STUFF, BUT NOW THAT I'M TEN VOLUMES IN, I WONDER IF I'LL BE ABLE TO INTRODUCE CHANGE IN THE CHARACTERS' RELATIONSHIPS AND TIE EVERYTHING TOGETHER NICELY. I'M REALLY SCARED!!

ALSO, NOTICE HOW THE SEASONS HAVE STARTED TO SLOW DOWN...

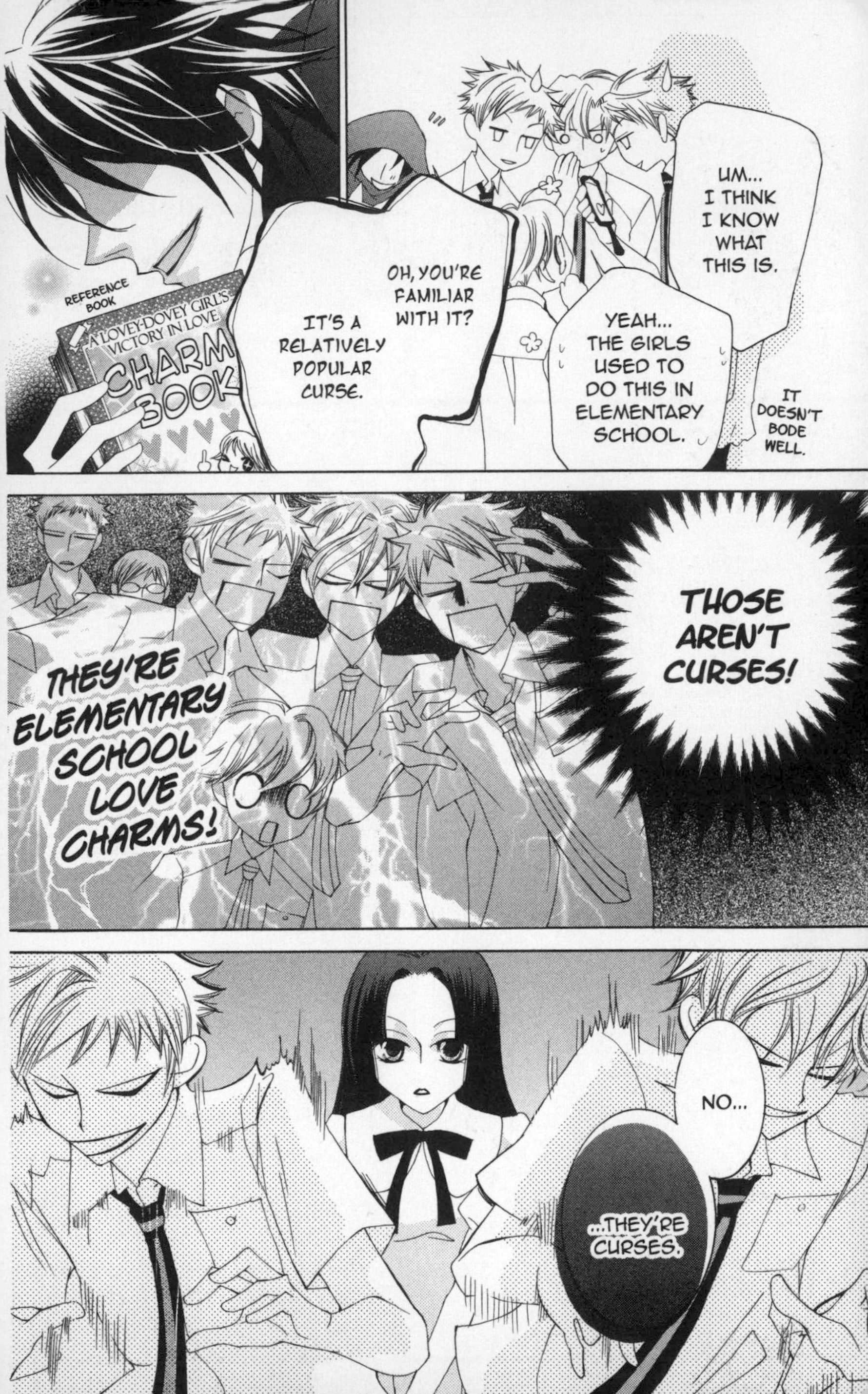
UM... I THINK I KNOW WHAT THIS IS.
IT DOESN'T BODE WELL.
YEAH... THE GIRLS USED TO DO THIS IN ELEMENTARY SCHOOL.
OH, YOU'RE FAMILIAR WITH IT?
IT'S A RELATIVELY POPULAR CURSE.
REFERENCE BOOK
A LOVEY-DOVEY GIRL'S VICTORY IN LOVE
CHARM BOOK
THOSE AREN'T CURSES!
THEY'RE ELEMENTARY SCHOOL LOVE CHARMS!
NO...
...THEY'RE CURSES.

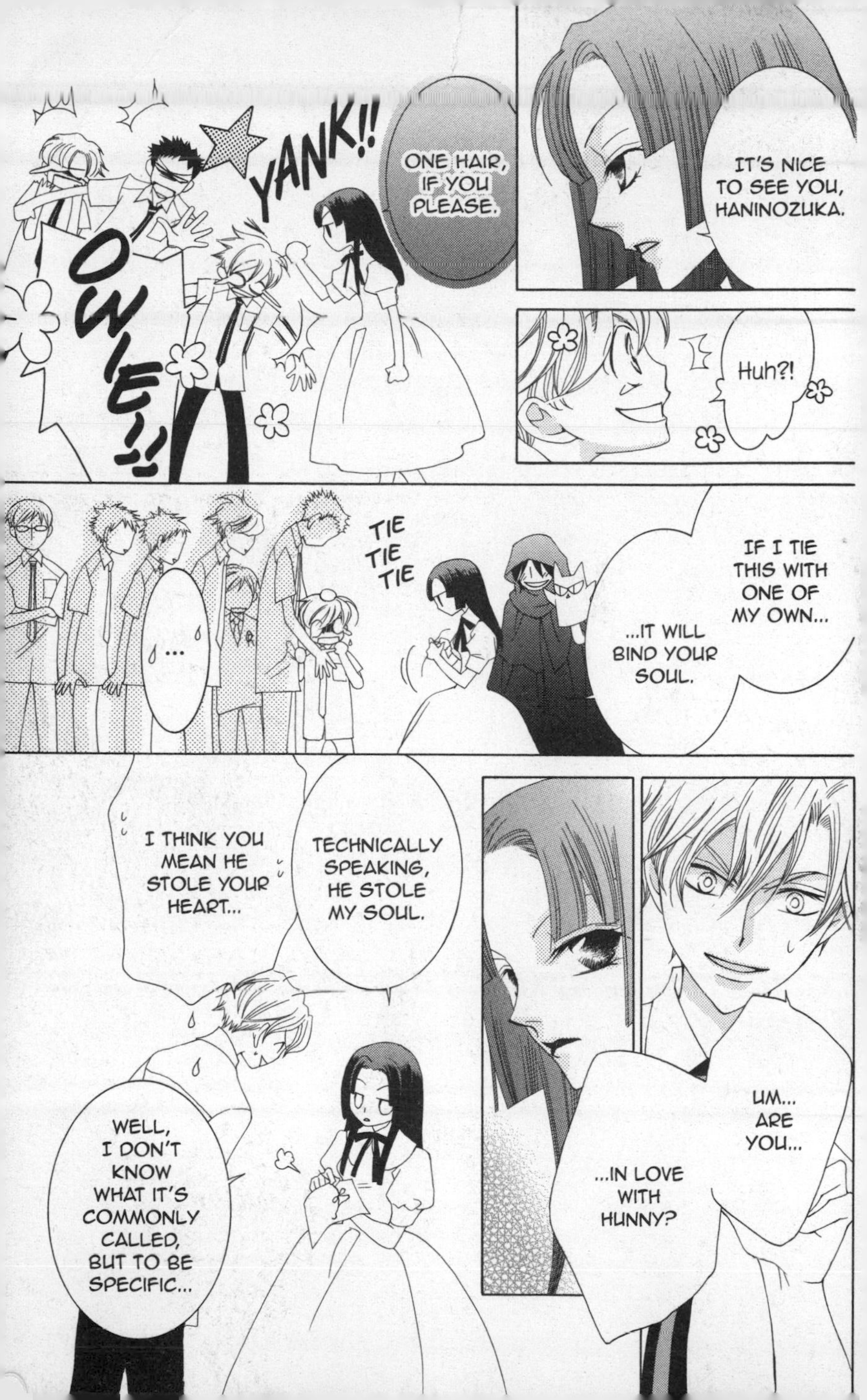
IT'S NICE TO SEE YOU, HANINOZUKA.
Huh?!
ONE HAIR, IF YOU PLEASE.
YANK!!
OWIE!!
IF I TIE THIS WITH ONE OF MY OWN...
...IT WILL BIND YOUR SOUL.
TIE TIE TIE
...
UM... ARE YOU...
...IN LOVE WITH HUNNY?
WELL, I DON'T KNOW WHAT IT'S COMMONLY CALLED, BUT TO BE SPECIFIC...
TECHNICALLY SPEAKING, HE STOLE MY SOUL.
I THINK YOU MEAN HE STOLE YOUR HEART...

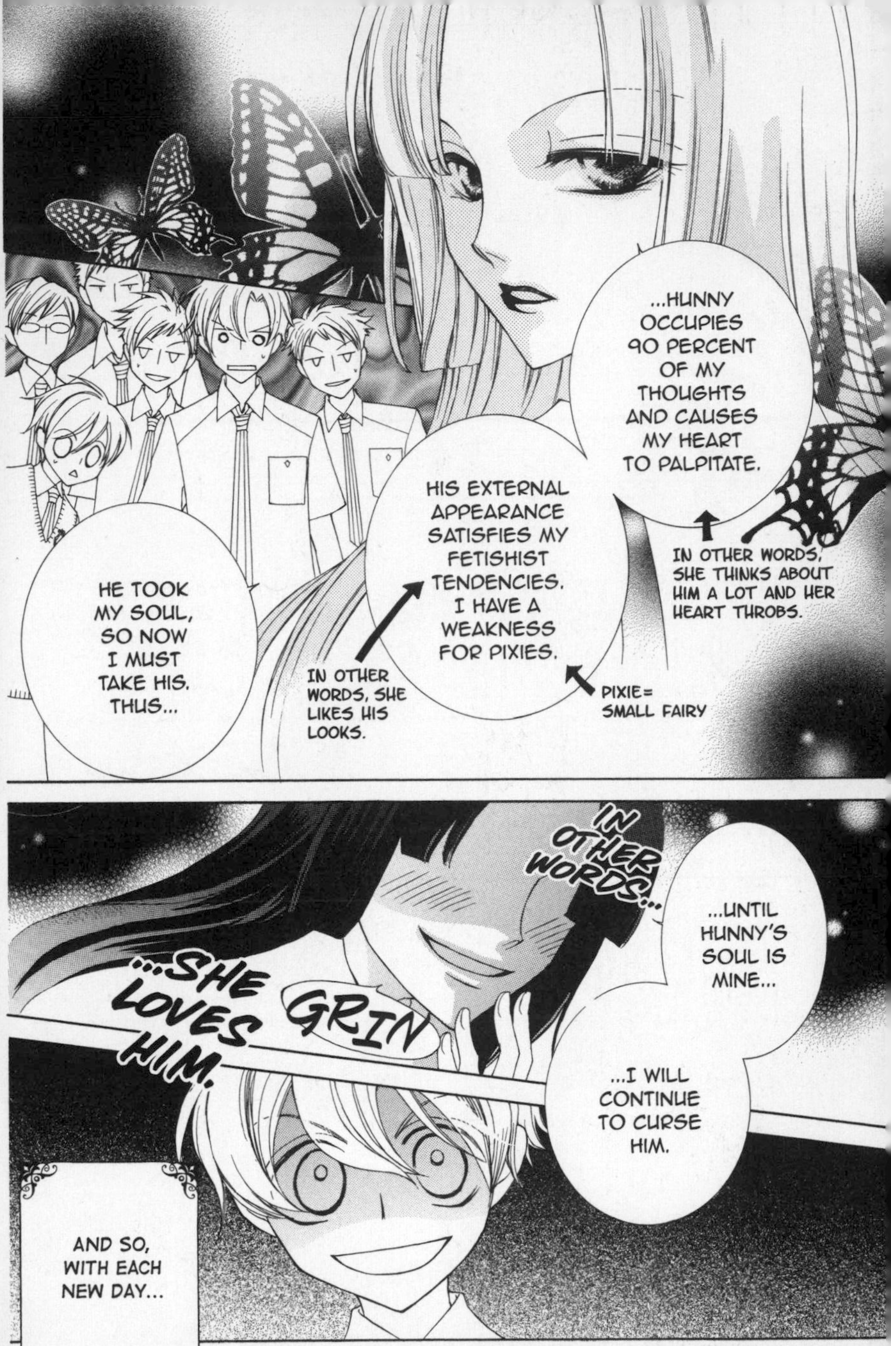
...HUNNY OCCUPIES 90 PERCENT OF MY THOUGHTS AND CAUSES MY HEART TO PALPITATE.
IN OTHER WORDS, SHE THINKS ABOUT HIM A LOT AND HER HEART THROBS.
HIS EXTERNAL APPEARANCE SATISFIES MY FETISHIST TENDENCIES. I HAVE A WEAKNESS FOR PIXIES.
PIXIE= SMALL FAIRY
IN OTHER WORDS, SHE LIKES HIS LOOKS.
HE TOOK MY SOUL, SO NOW I MUST TAKE HIS. THUS...
...UNTIL HUNNY'S SOUL IS MINE...
IN OTHER WORDS...
...SHE LOVES HIM.
GRIN
...I WILL CONTINUE TO CURSE HIM.
AND SO, WITH EACH NEW DAY...

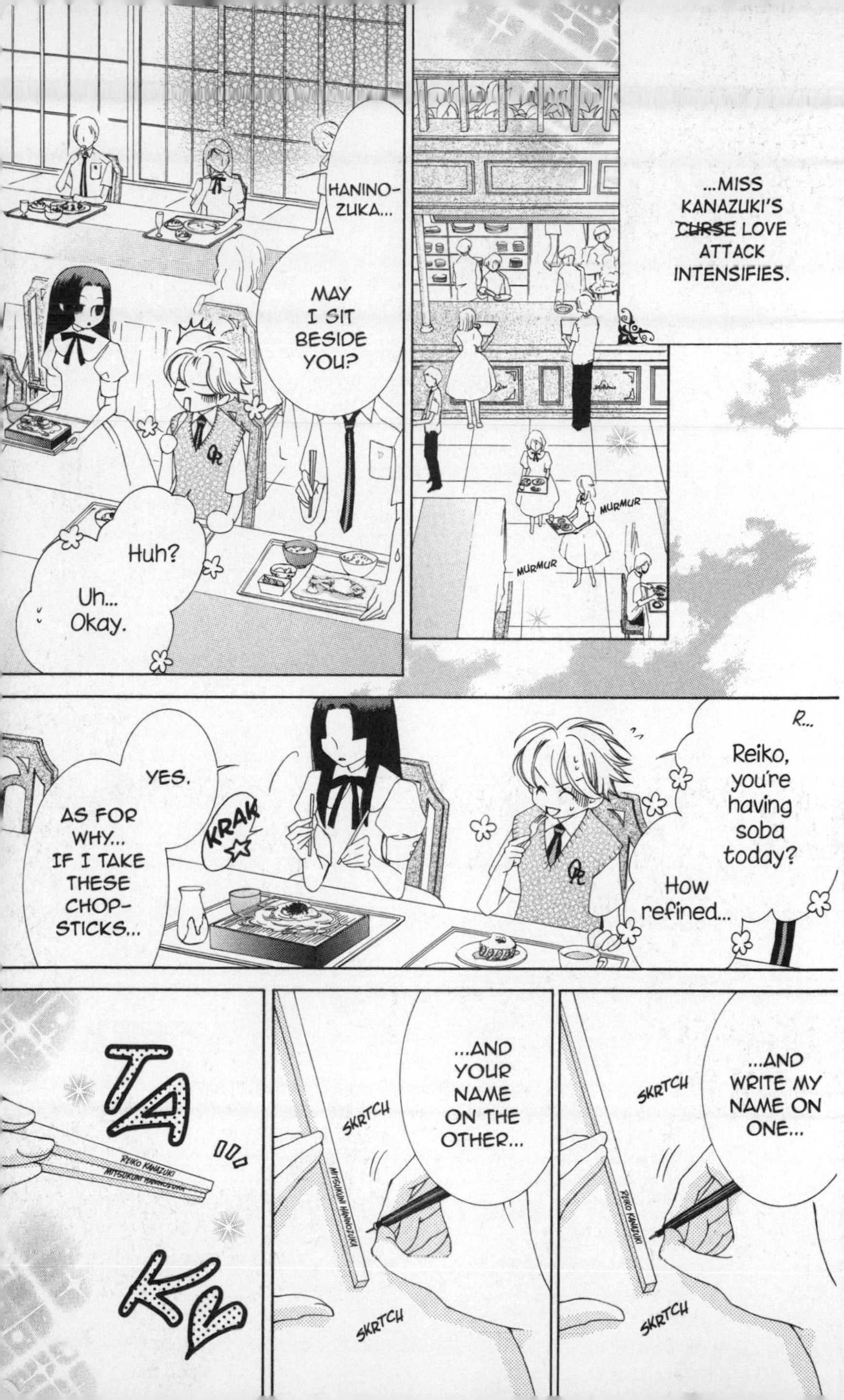
...MISS KANAZUKI'S ~~CURSE~~ LOVE ATTACK INTENSIFIES.
MURMUR
MURMUR
HANINOZUKA...
MAY I SIT BESIDE YOU?
Huh?
Uh... Okay.
R...
Reiko, you're having soba today?
How refined...
KRAK
YES.
AS FOR WHY... IF I TAKE THESE CHOPSTICKS...
...AND WRITE MY NAME ON ONE...
SKRTCH
REIKO KANAZUKI
SKRTCH
...AND YOUR NAME ON THE OTHER...
SKRTCH
MITSUKUNI HANINOZUKA
SKRTCH
TA
REIKO KANAZUKI
MITSUKUNI HANINOZUKA

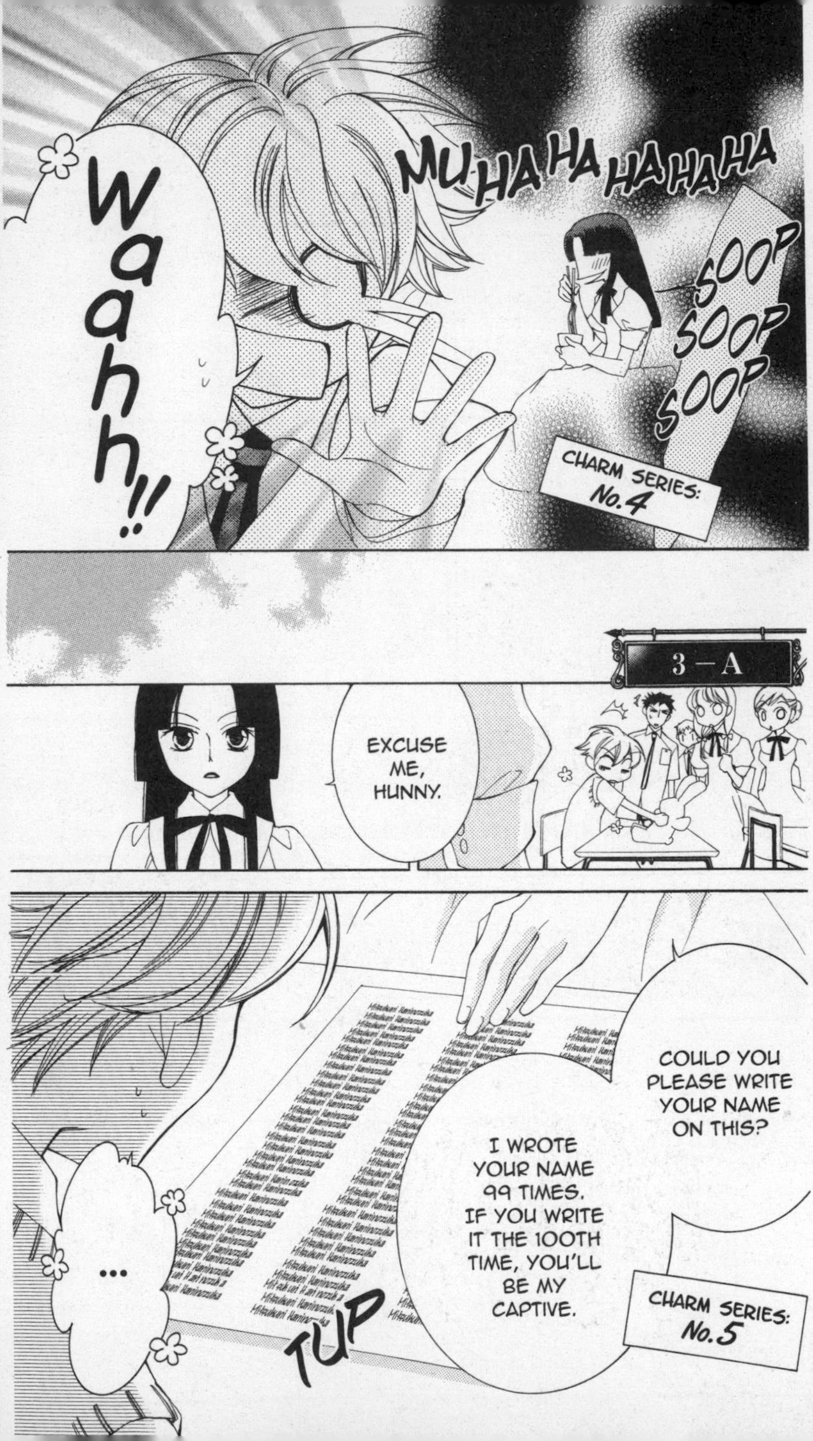
MU HA HA HA HA HA
SOOP SOOP SOOP
CHARM SERIES: No.4
Waahh!!
3—A
EXCUSE ME, HUNNY.
COULD YOU PLEASE WRITE YOUR NAME ON THIS?
I WROTE YOUR NAME 99 TIMES. IF YOU WRITE IT THE 100TH TIME, YOU'LL BE MY CAPTIVE.
CHARM SERIES: No.5
TUP
...

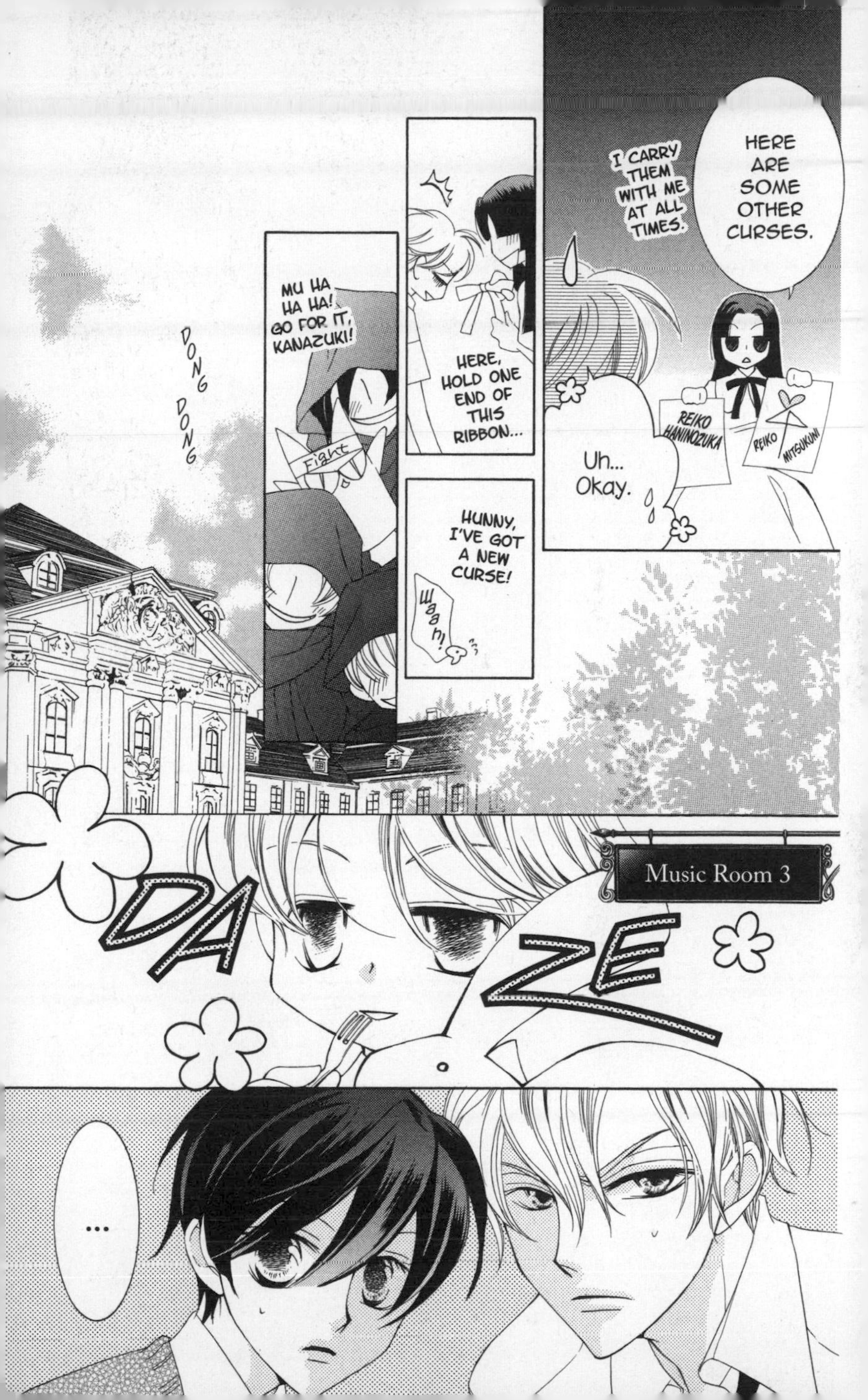
HERE ARE SOME OTHER CURSES.
I CARRY THEM WITH ME AT ALL TIMES.
REIKO HANINOZUKA
REIKO MITSUKUNI
Uh... Okay.
HERE, HOLD ONE END OF THIS RIBBON...
HUNNY, I'VE GOT A NEW CURSE!
Waah!
MU HA HA HA! GO FOR IT, KANAZUKI!
Fight
DONG DONG
Music Room 3
DA ZE
...

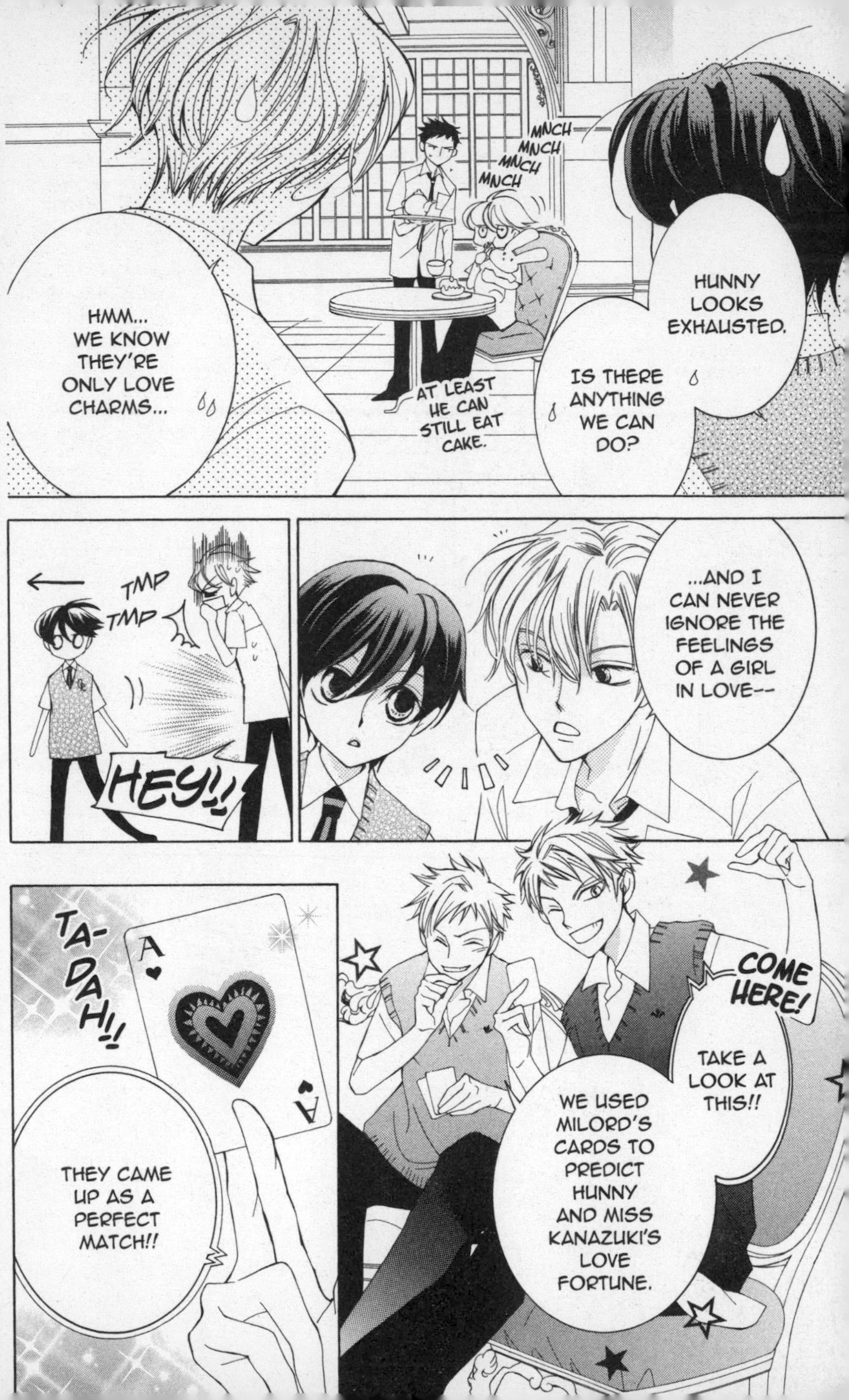
HUNNY LOOKS EXHAUSTED.
IS THERE ANYTHING WE CAN DO?
MNCH MNCH MNCH MNCH
AT LEAST HE CAN STILL EAT CAKE.
HMM... WE KNOW THEY'RE ONLY LOVE CHARMS...
...AND I CAN NEVER IGNORE THE FEELINGS OF A GIRL IN LOVE--
TMP TMP
HEY!!
COME HERE!
TAKE A LOOK AT THIS!!
WE USED MILORD'S CARDS TO PREDICT HUNNY AND MISS KANAZUKI'S LOVE FORTUNE.
TA-DAH!!
THEY CAME UP AS A PERFECT MATCH!!

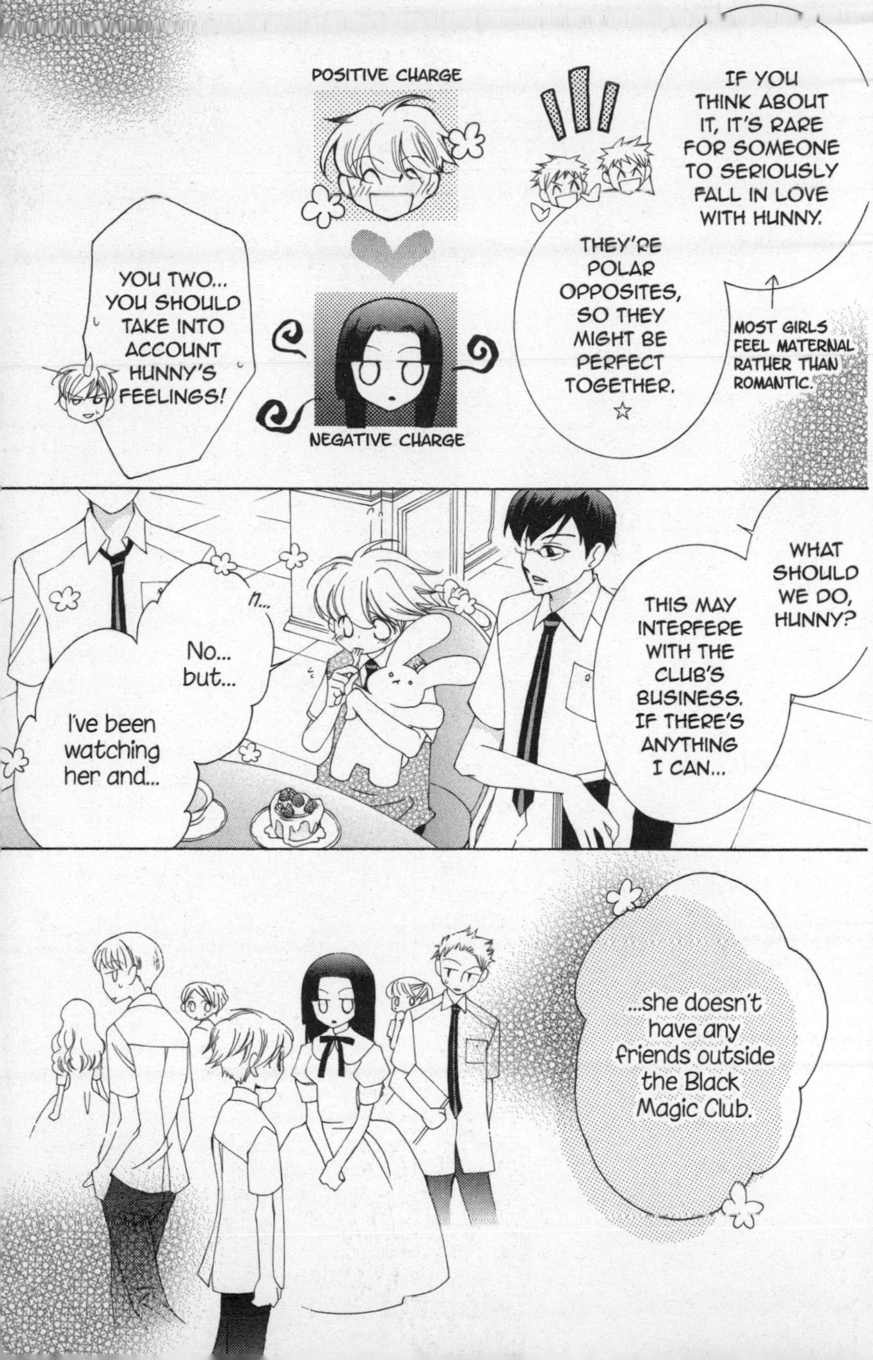

IF YOU THINK ABOUT IT, IT'S RARE FOR SOMEONE TO SERIOUSLY FALL IN LOVE WITH HUNNY.
MOST GIRLS FEEL MATERNAL RATHER THAN ROMANTIC.
THEY'RE POLAR OPPOSITES, SO THEY MIGHT BE PERFECT TOGETHER. ☆
POSITIVE CHARGE
NEGATIVE CHARGE
YOU TWO... YOU SHOULD TAKE INTO ACCOUNT HUNNY'S FEELINGS!
WHAT SHOULD WE DO, HUNNY?
THIS MAY INTERFERE WITH THE CLUB'S BUSINESS. IF THERE'S ANYTHING I CAN...
n...
No... but...
I've been watching her and...
...she doesn't have any friends outside the Black Magic Club.

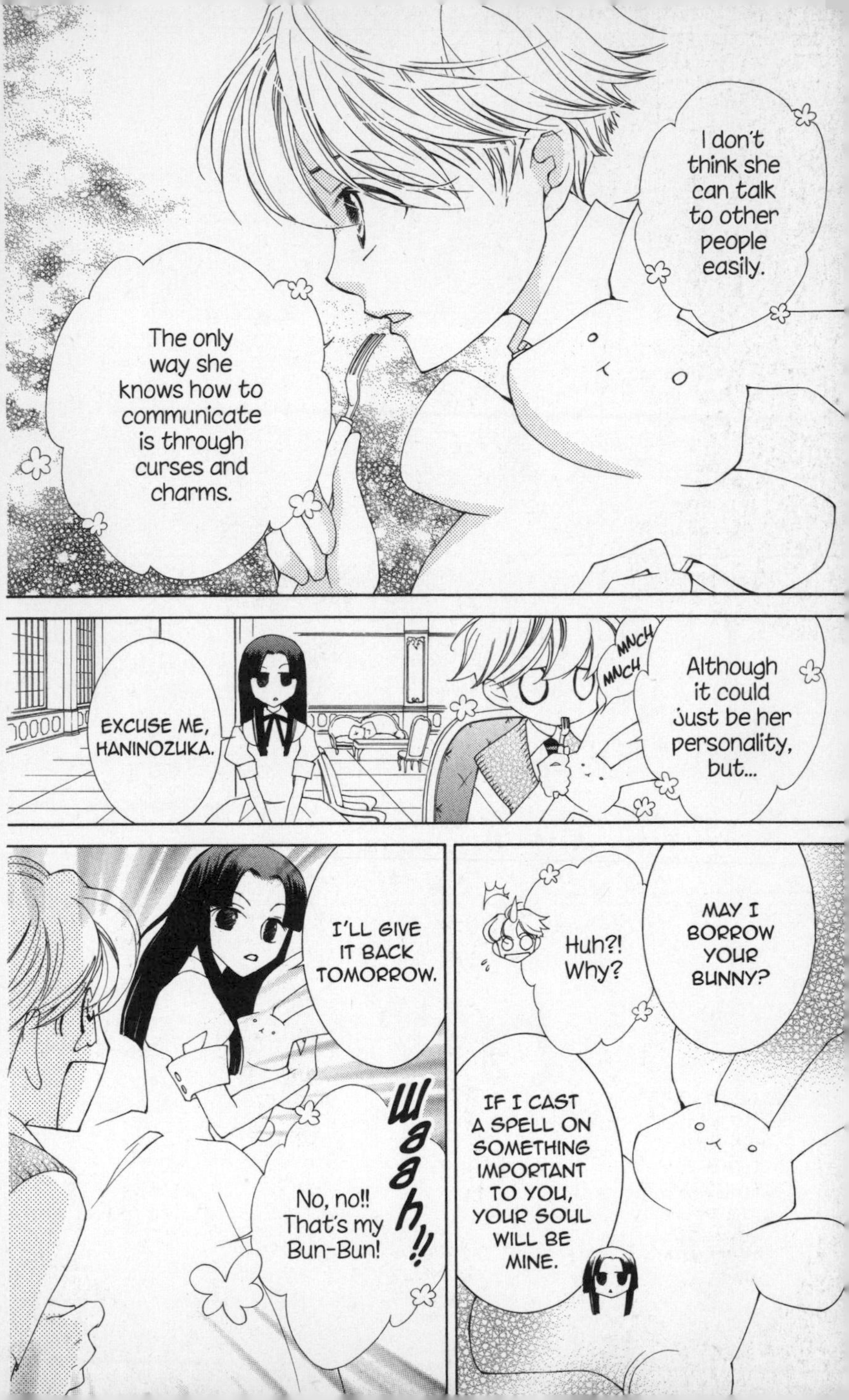
I don't think she can talk to other people easily.
The only way she knows how to communicate is through curses and charms.
MNCH MNCH
Although it could just be her personality, but...
EXCUSE ME, HANINOZUKA.
MAY I BORROW YOUR BUNNY?
Huh?! Why?
IF I CAST A SPELL ON SOMETHING IMPORTANT TO YOU, YOUR SOUL WILL BE MINE.
I'LL GIVE IT BACK TOMORROW.
Waah!!
No, no!! That's my Bun-Bun!

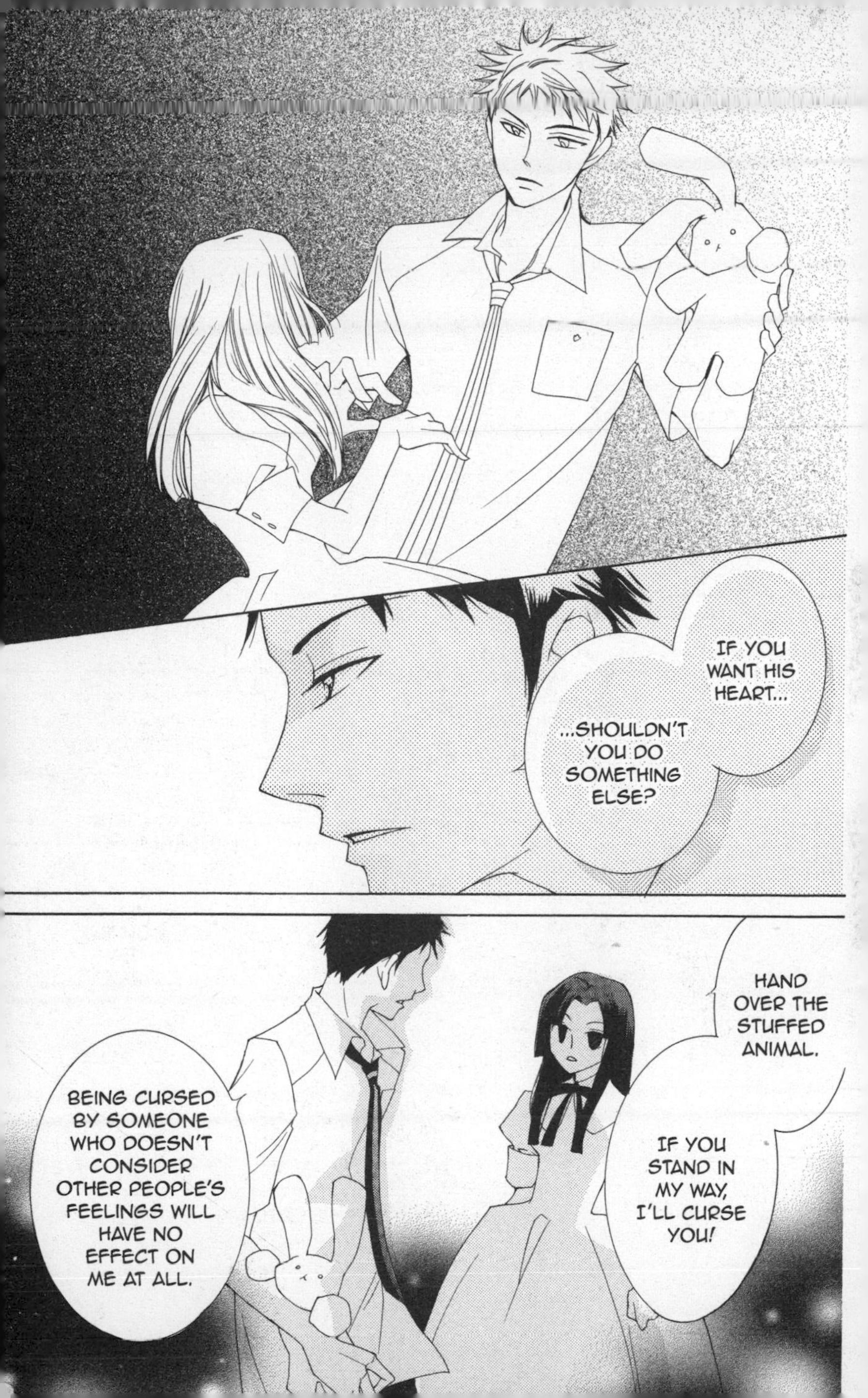
IF YOU WANT HIS HEART...
...SHOULDN'T YOU DO SOMETHING ELSE?
HAND OVER THE STUFFED ANIMAL.
IF YOU STAND IN MY WAY, I'LL CURSE YOU!
BEING CURSED BY SOMEONE WHO DOESN'T CONSIDER OTHER PEOPLE'S FEELINGS WILL HAVE NO EFFECT ON ME AT ALL.

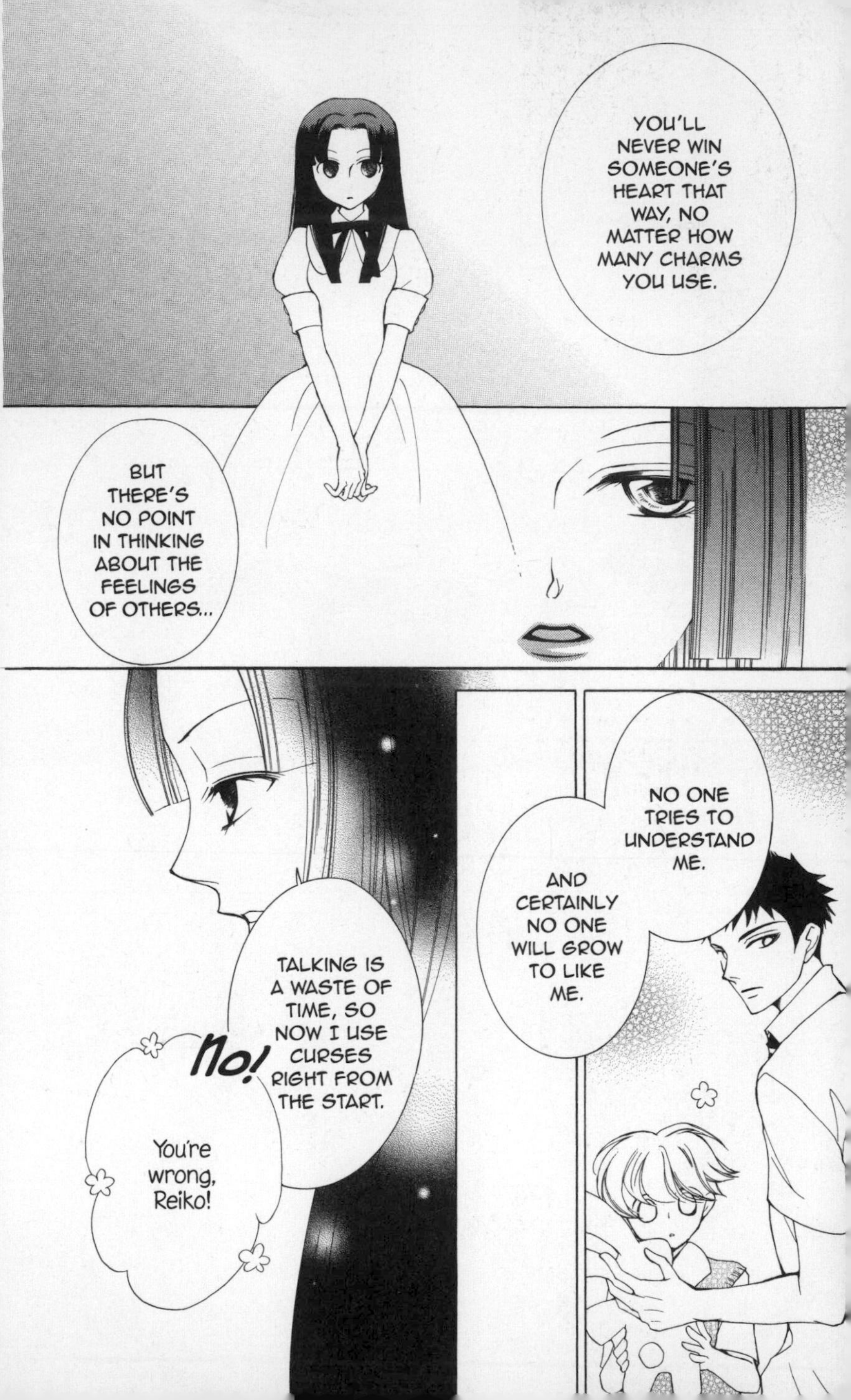

YOU'LL NEVER WIN SOMEONE'S HEART THAT WAY, NO MATTER HOW MANY CHARMS YOU USE.
BUT THERE'S NO POINT IN THINKING ABOUT THE FEELINGS OF OTHERS...
NO ONE TRIES TO UNDERSTAND ME.
AND CERTAINLY NO ONE WILL GROW TO LIKE ME.
TALKING IS A WASTE OF TIME, SO NOW I USE CURSES RIGHT FROM THE START.
No!
You're wrong, Reiko!

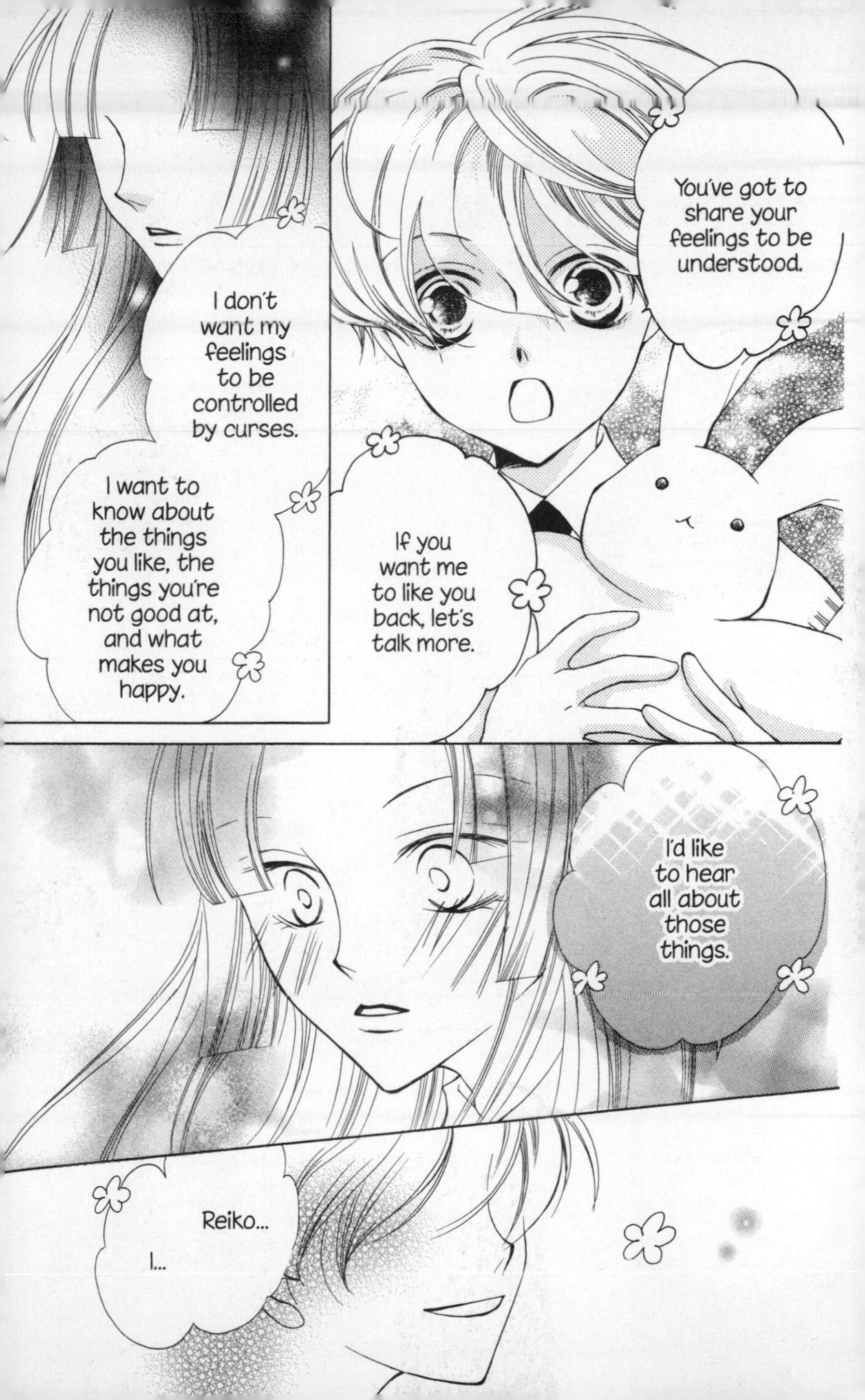

You've got to share your feelings to be understood.
If you want me to like you back, let's talk more.
I don't want my feelings to be controlled by curses.
I want to know about the things you like, the things you're not good at, and what makes you happy.
I'd like to hear all about those things.
Reiko...
I...

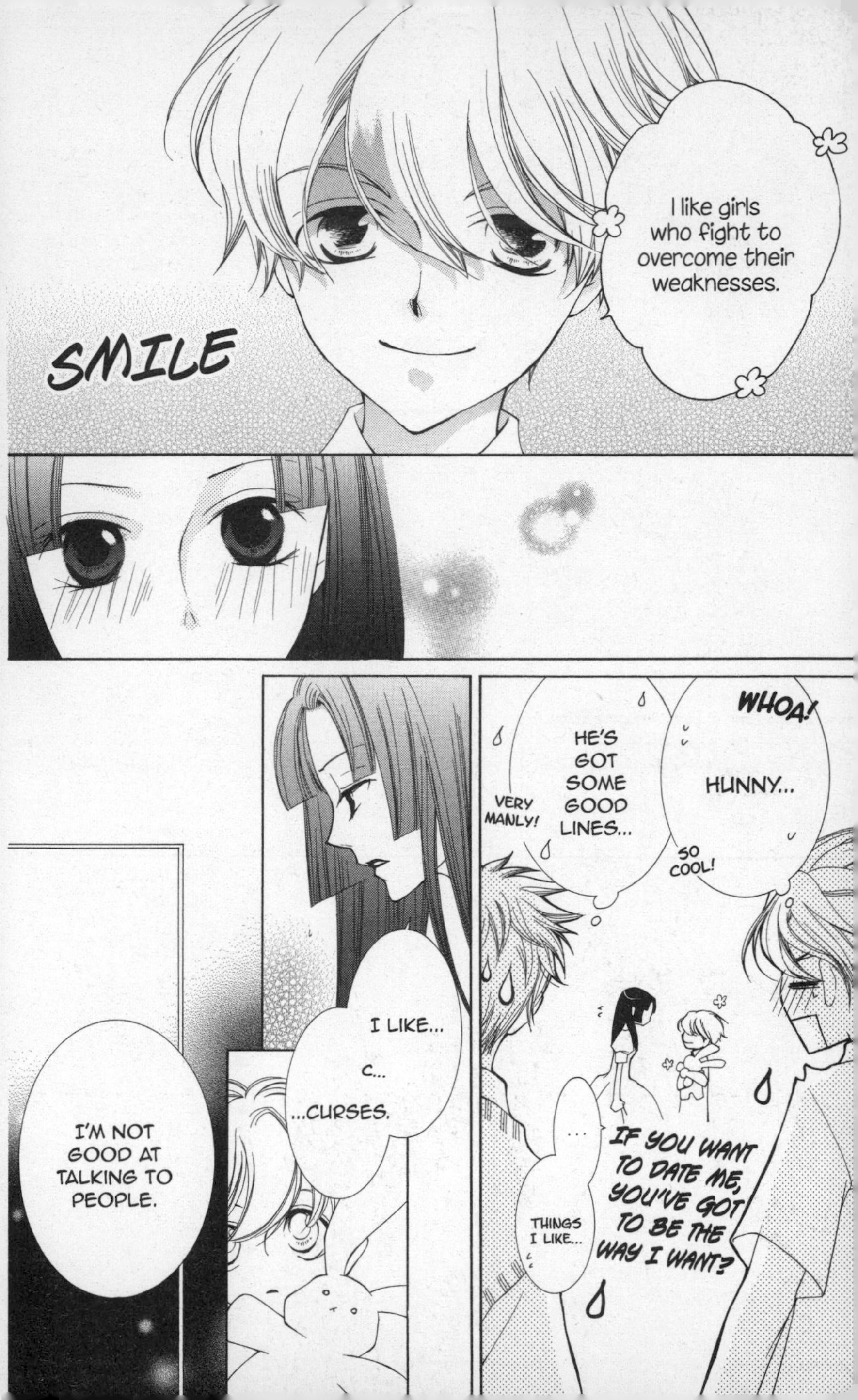
I like girls who fight to overcome their weaknesses.
SMILE
WHOA!
HUNNY...
SO COOL!
HE'S GOT SOME GOOD LINES...
VERY MANLY!
IF YOU WANT TO DATE ME, YOU'VE GOT TO BE THE WAY I WANT?
...
THINGS I LIKE...
I LIKE...
C...
...CURSES.
I'M NOT GOOD AT TALKING TO PEOPLE.

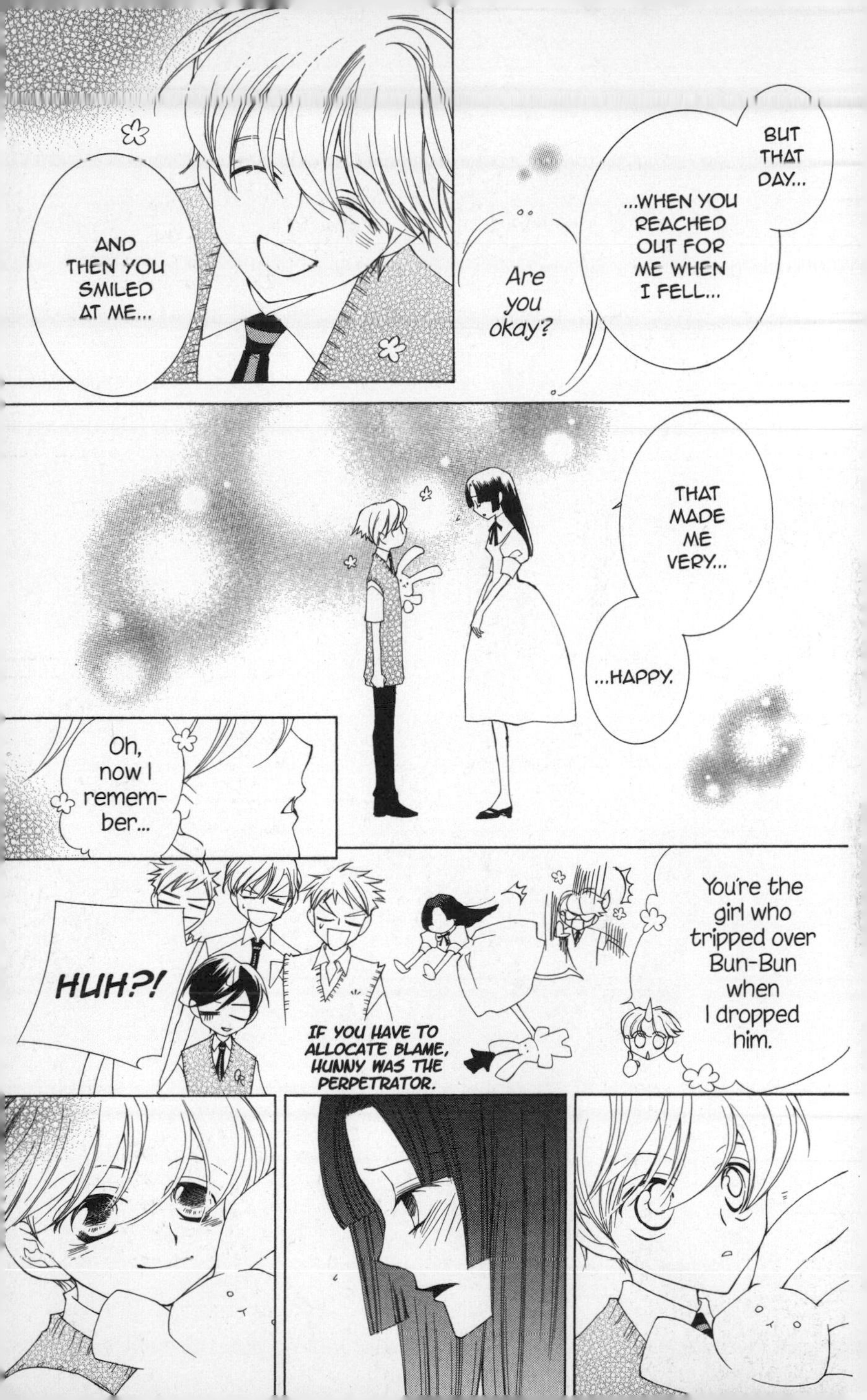
BUT THAT DAY...
...WHEN YOU REACHED OUT FOR ME WHEN I FELL...
Are you okay?
AND THEN YOU SMILED AT ME...
THAT MADE ME VERY...
...HAPPY.
Oh, now I remember...
You're the girl who tripped over Bun-Bun when I dropped him.
IF YOU HAVE TO ALLOCATE BLAME, HUNNY WAS THE PERPETRATOR.
HUH?!

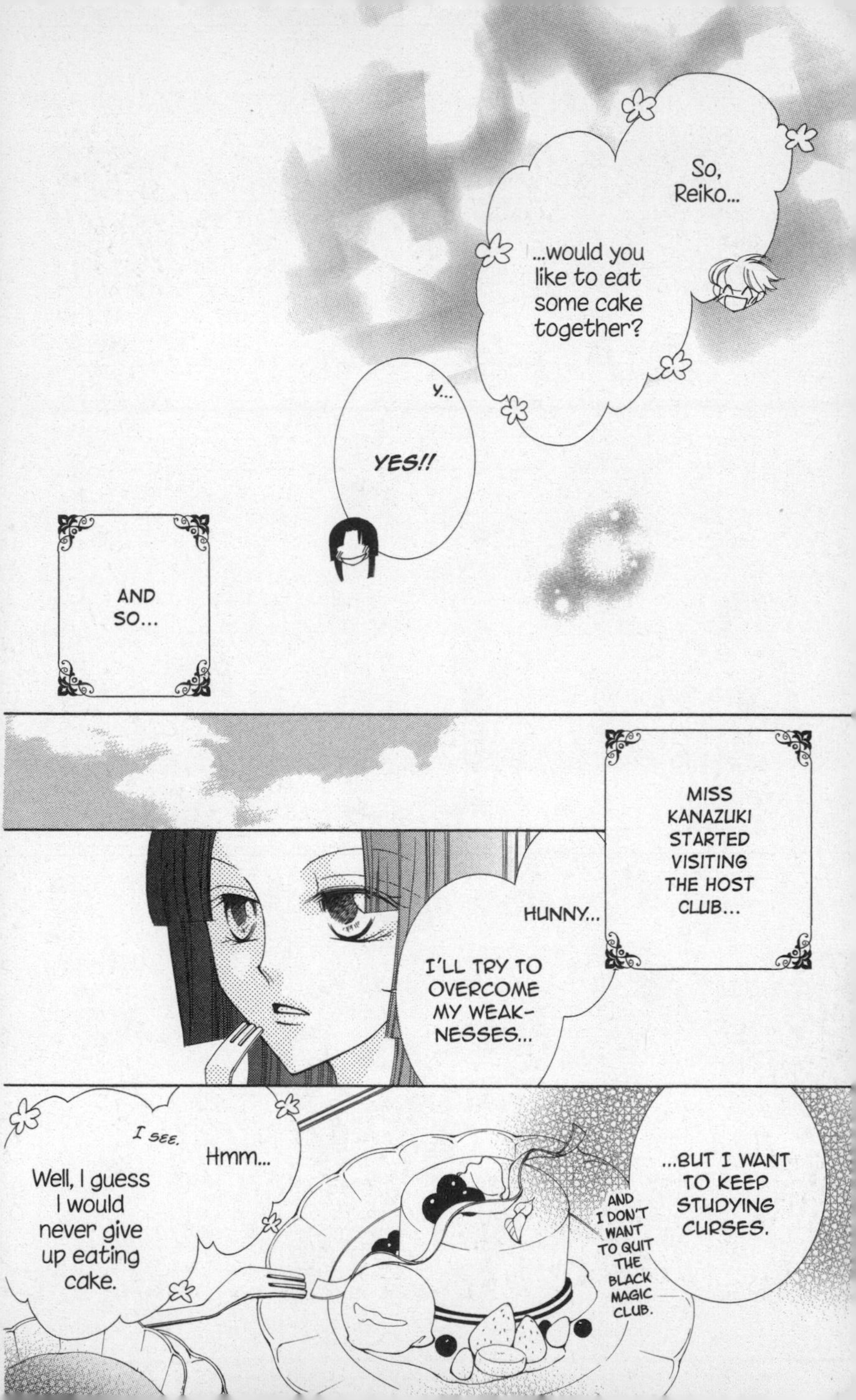
So, Reiko...
...would you like to eat some cake together?
Y...
YES!!
AND SO...
MISS KANAZUKI STARTED VISITING THE HOST CLUB...
HUNNY...
I'LL TRY TO OVERCOME MY WEAK-NESSES...
...BUT I WANT TO KEEP STUDYING CURSES.
AND I DON'T WANT TO QUIT THE BLACK MAGIC CLUB.
I SEE.
Hmm...
Well, I guess I would never give up eating cake.

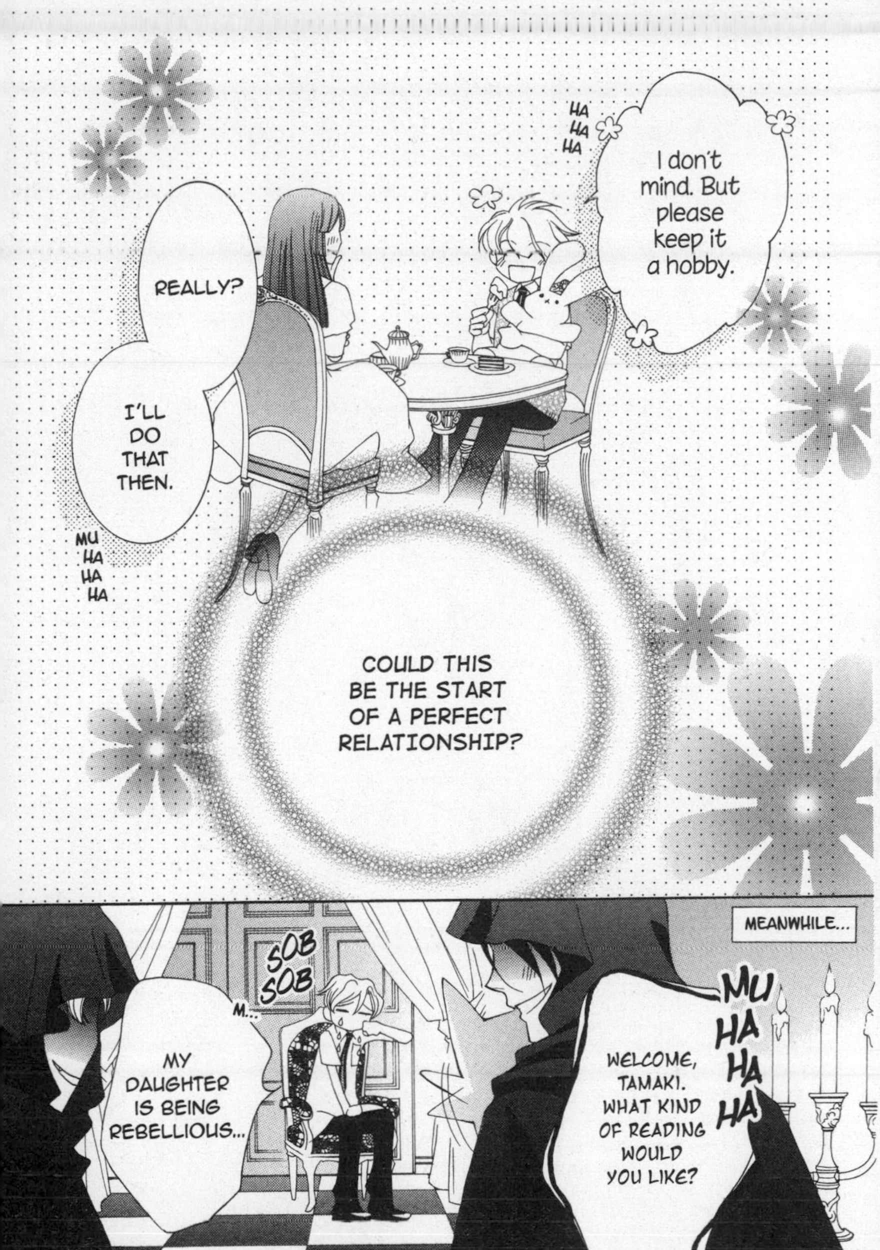
HA HA HA
I don't mind. But please keep it a hobby.
REALLY?
I'LL DO THAT THEN.
MU HA HA HA
COULD THIS BE THE START OF A PERFECT RELATIONSHIP?
MEANWHILE...
MU HA HA HA
WELCOME, TAMAKI. WHAT KIND OF READING WOULD YOU LIKE?
SOB SOB
M...
MY DAUGHTER IS BEING REBELLIOUS...

GUEST ROOM: FAXES ①

SPECIAL THANKS TO
TONAMI YAMASHIRO!!

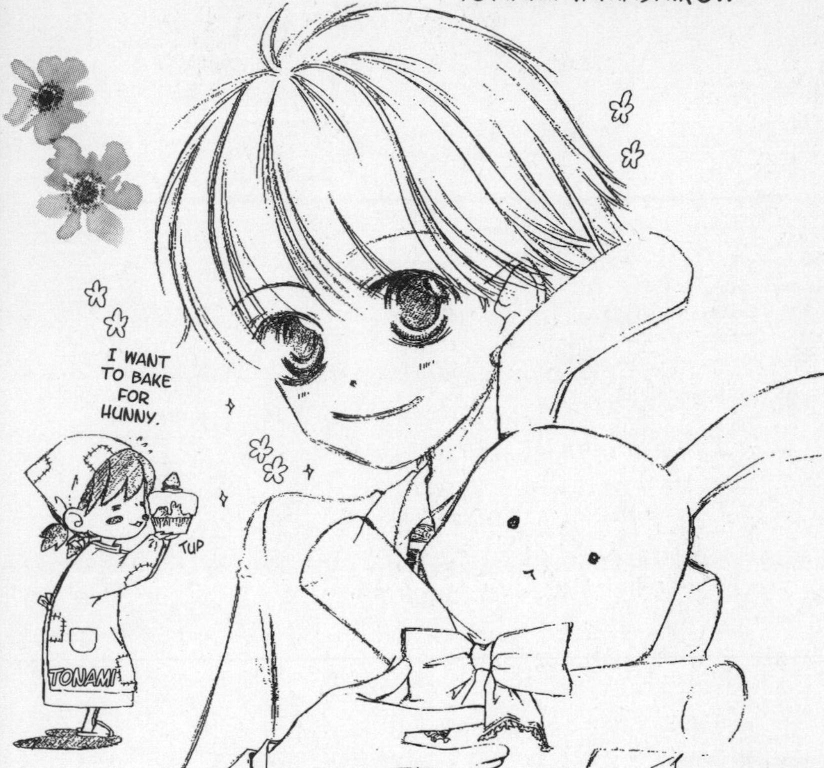
I WANT TO BAKE FOR HUNNY.
TUP
TONAMI

WE DEBUTED AT DIFFERENT TIMES, BUT I'VE ALWAYS THOUGHT OF TONAMI AS A KINDRED SPIRIT. SHE SENT ME A VERY CUTE DRAWING OF HUNNY. SHE SAYS, "I REALIZED MY HUNNY DOESN'T LOOK LIKE THE REAL ONE BECAUSE MINE DOESN'T LOOK AS NAUGHTY."
WHICH MEANS...YOU KNOW. MY HUNNY LOOKS...WELL, I THINK YOU UNDERSTAND. HA HA HA!! THANKS, TONAMI!
ALL TONAMI'S WORK IS EXTREMELY WELL THOUGHT-OUT, SO I REALLY WANT AS MANY PEOPLE AS POSSIBLE TO READ HER MANGA. READ *LALA DX*!!

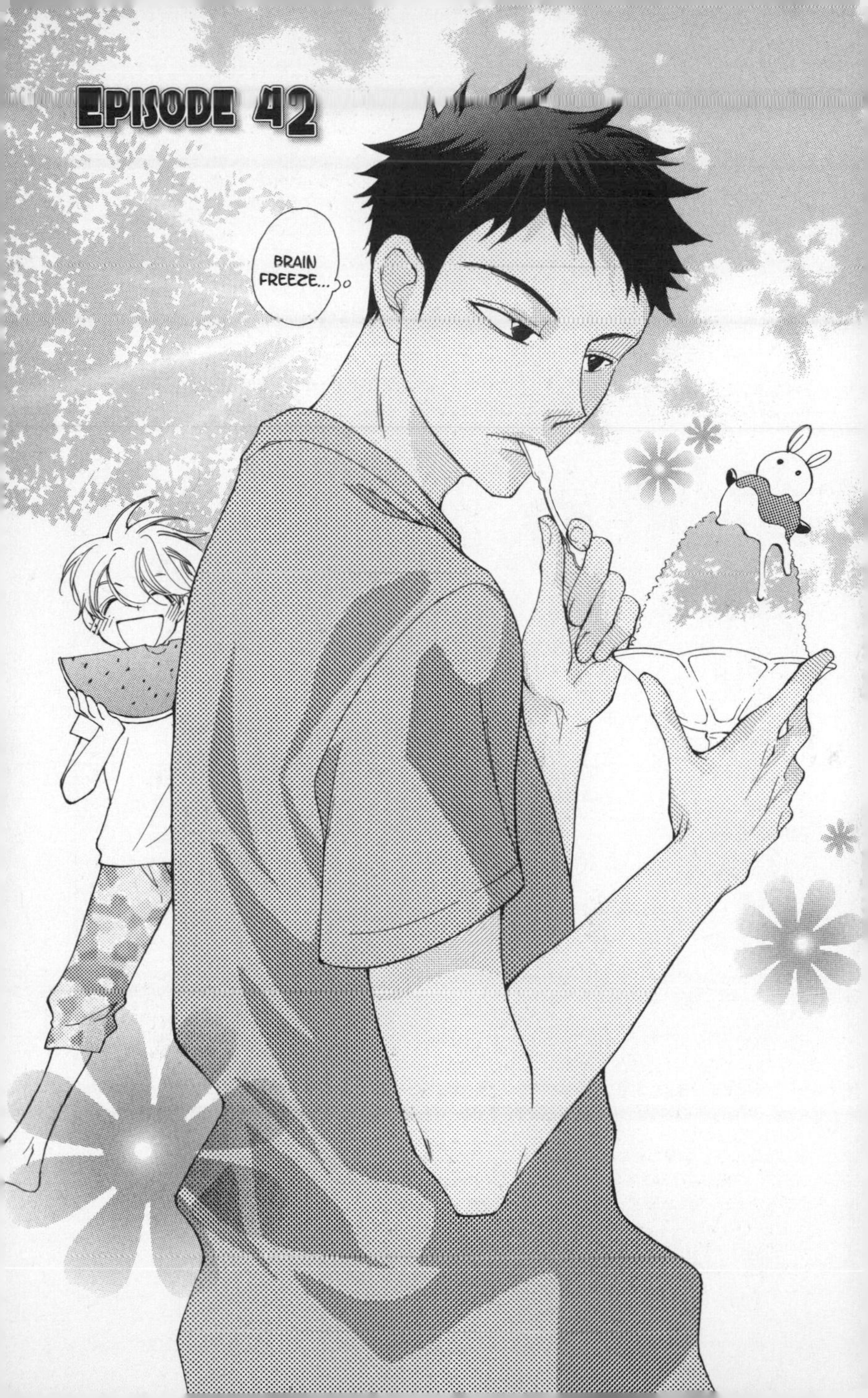
EPISODE 42
BRAIN FREEZE...

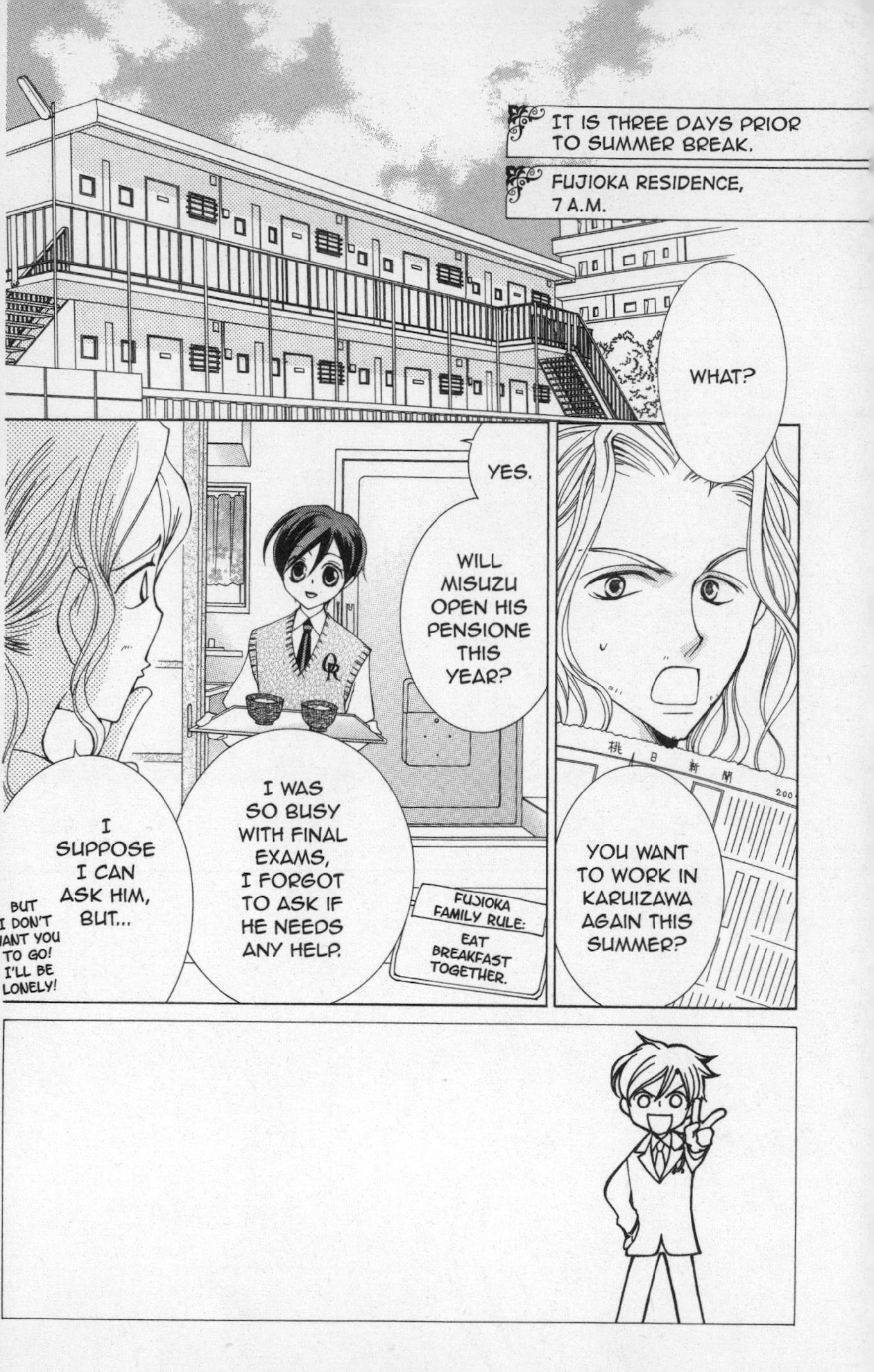
IT IS THREE DAYS PRIOR TO SUMMER BREAK.
FUJIOKA RESIDENCE, 7 A.M.
WHAT?
YOU WANT TO WORK IN KARUIZAWA AGAIN THIS SUMMER?
YES.
WILL MISUZU OPEN HIS PENSIONE THIS YEAR?
I WAS SO BUSY WITH FINAL EXAMS, I FORGOT TO ASK IF HE NEEDS ANY HELP.
FUJIOKA FAMILY RULE: EAT BREAKFAST TOGETHER.
I SUPPOSE I CAN ASK HIM, BUT...
BUT I DON'T WANT YOU TO GO! I'LL BE LONELY!

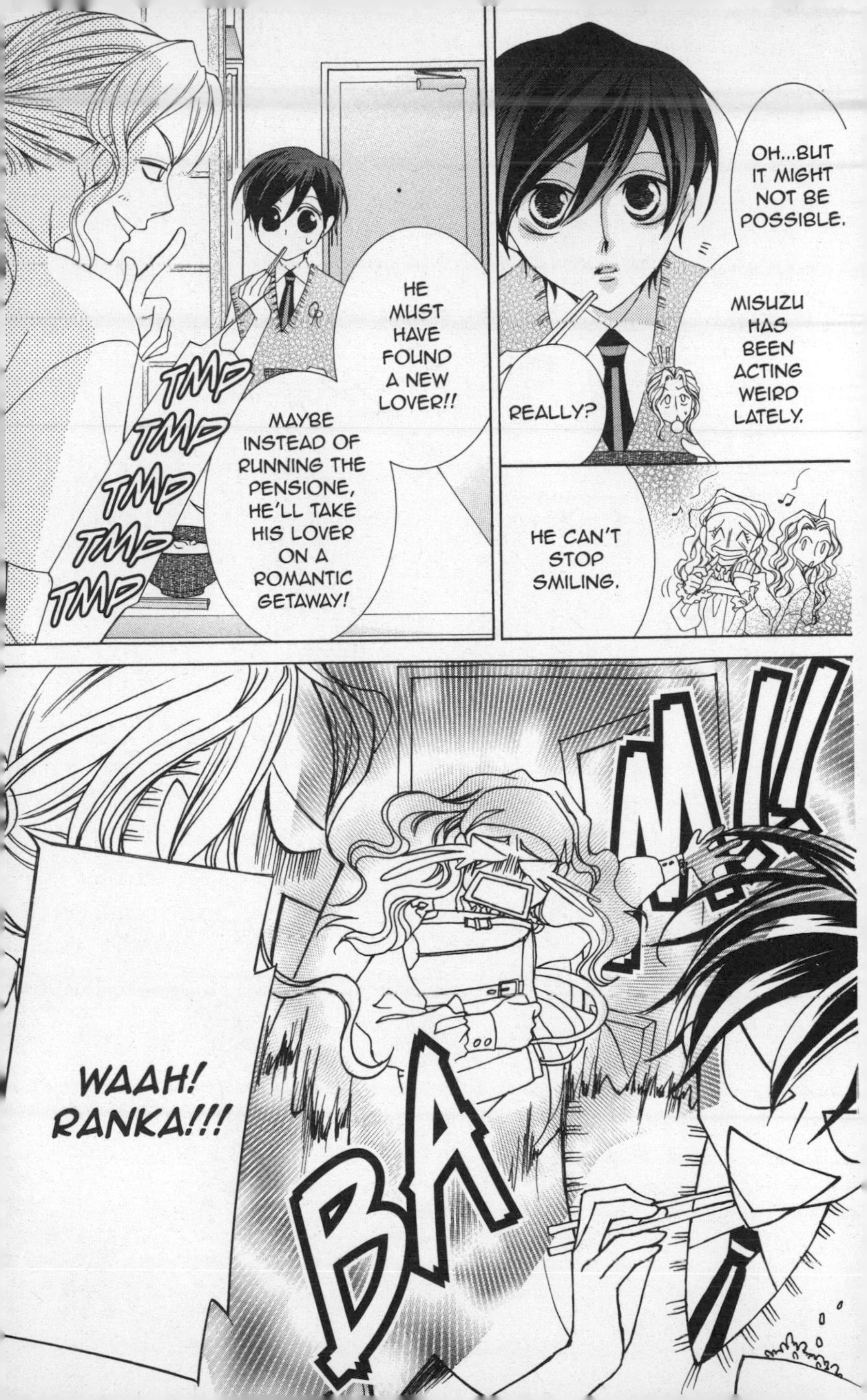
OH...BUT IT MIGHT NOT BE POSSIBLE.
MISUZU HAS BEEN ACTING WEIRD LATELY.
REALLY?
HE CAN'T STOP SMILING.
HE MUST HAVE FOUND A NEW LOVER!!
MAYBE INSTEAD OF RUNNING THE PENSIONE, HE'LL TAKE HIS LOVER ON A ROMANTIC GETAWAY!
TMP TMP TMP TMP TMP
BAM!!
WAAH! RANKA!!!

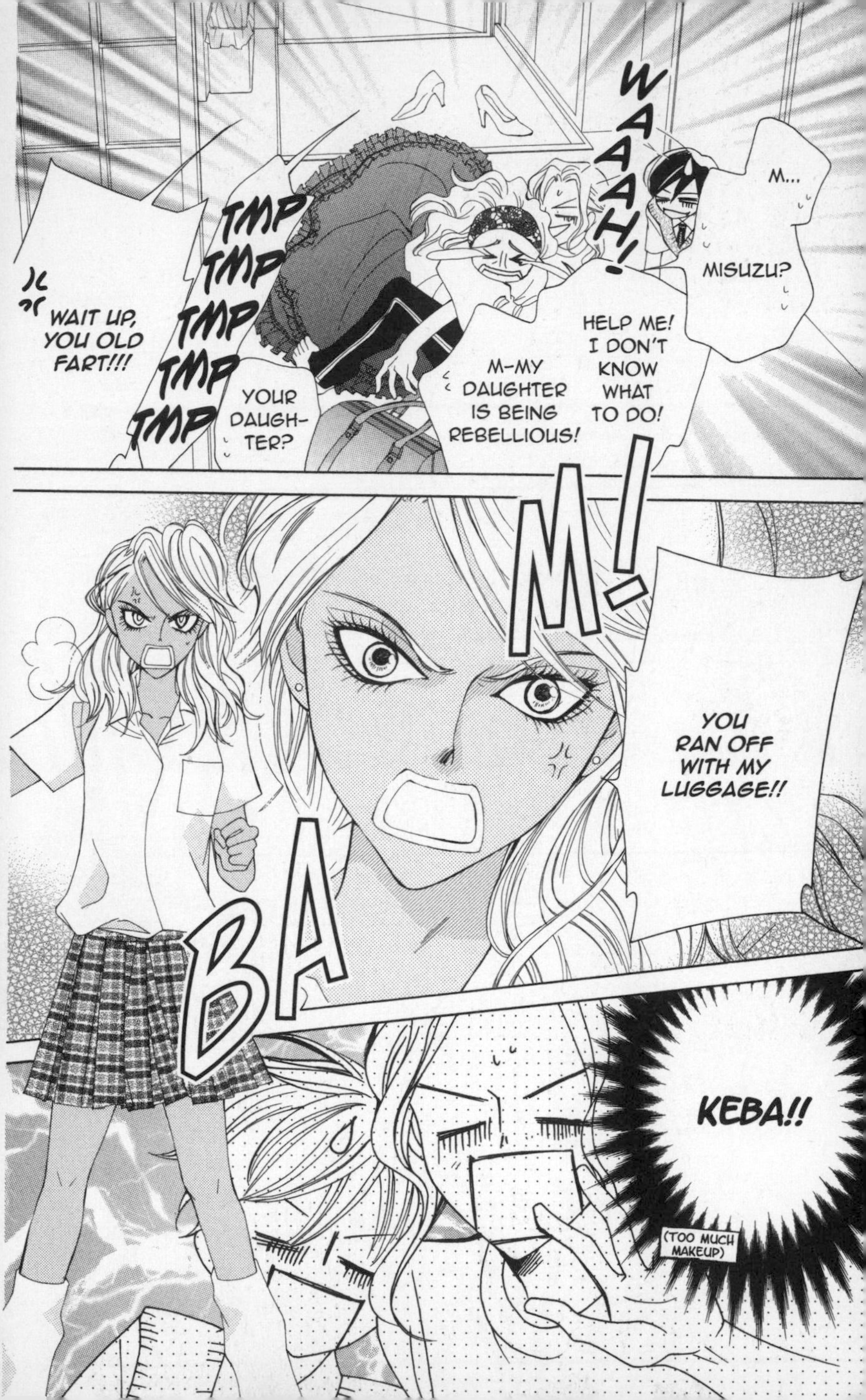
M...
MISUZU?
WAAAAH!
HELP ME! I DON'T KNOW WHAT TO DO!
M-MY DAUGHTER IS BEING REBELLIOUS!
YOUR DAUGHTER?
TMP TMP TMP TMP TMP
WAIT UP, YOU OLD FART!!!
BAM!
YOU RAN OFF WITH MY LUGGAGE!!
KEBA!!
(TOO MUCH MAKEUP)

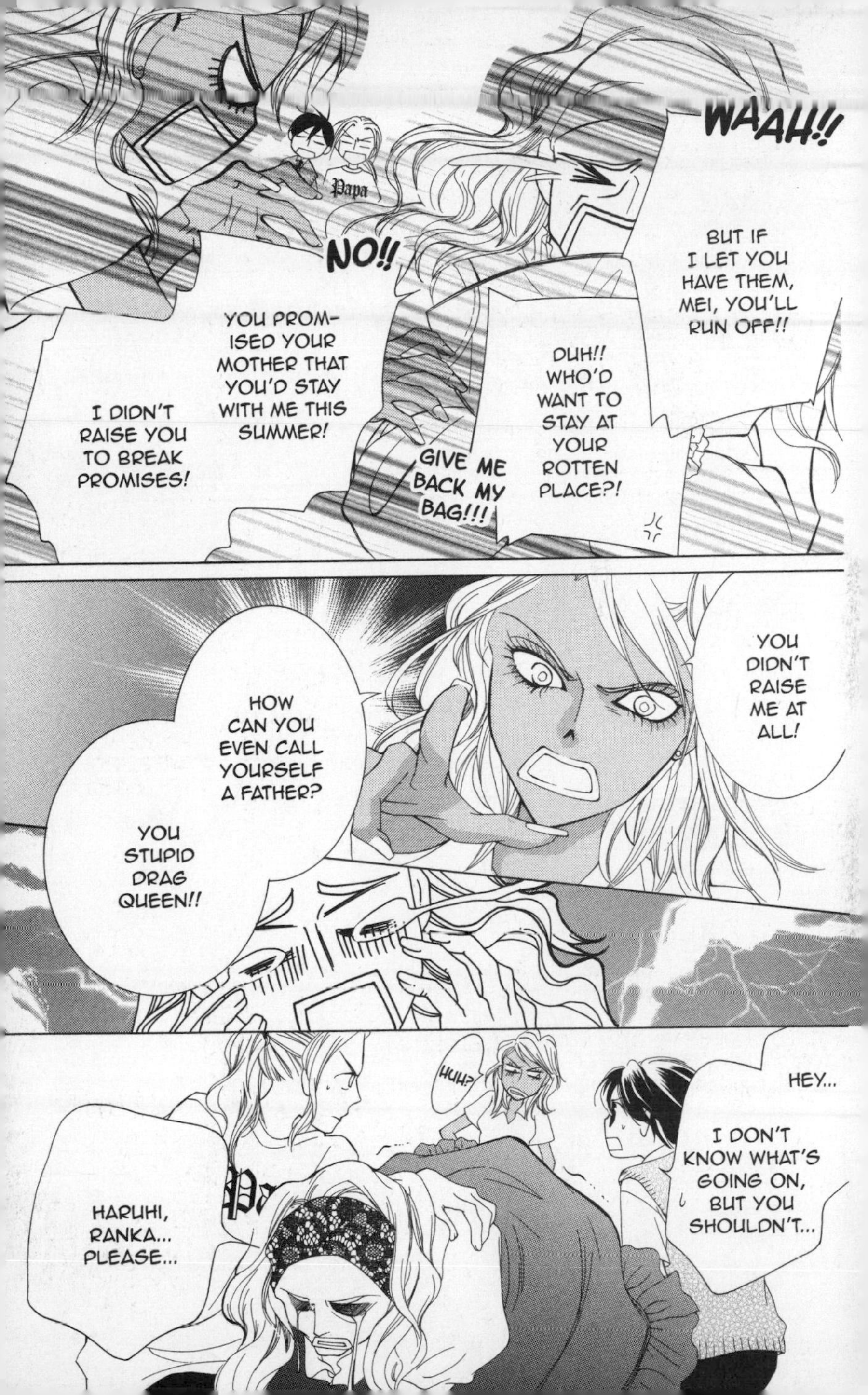
WAAH!!
BUT IF I LET YOU HAVE THEM, MEI, YOU'LL RUN OFF!!
DUH!! WHO'D WANT TO STAY AT YOUR ROTTEN PLACE?!
GIVE ME BACK MY BAG!!!
NO!!
Papa
YOU PROMISED YOUR MOTHER THAT YOU'D STAY WITH ME THIS SUMMER!
I DIDN'T RAISE YOU TO BREAK PROMISES!
YOU DIDN'T RAISE ME AT ALL!
HOW CAN YOU EVEN CALL YOURSELF A FATHER?
YOU STUPID DRAG QUEEN!!
HEY...
I DON'T KNOW WHAT'S GOING ON, BUT YOU SHOULDN'T...
HUH?
HARUHI, RANKA... PLEASE...

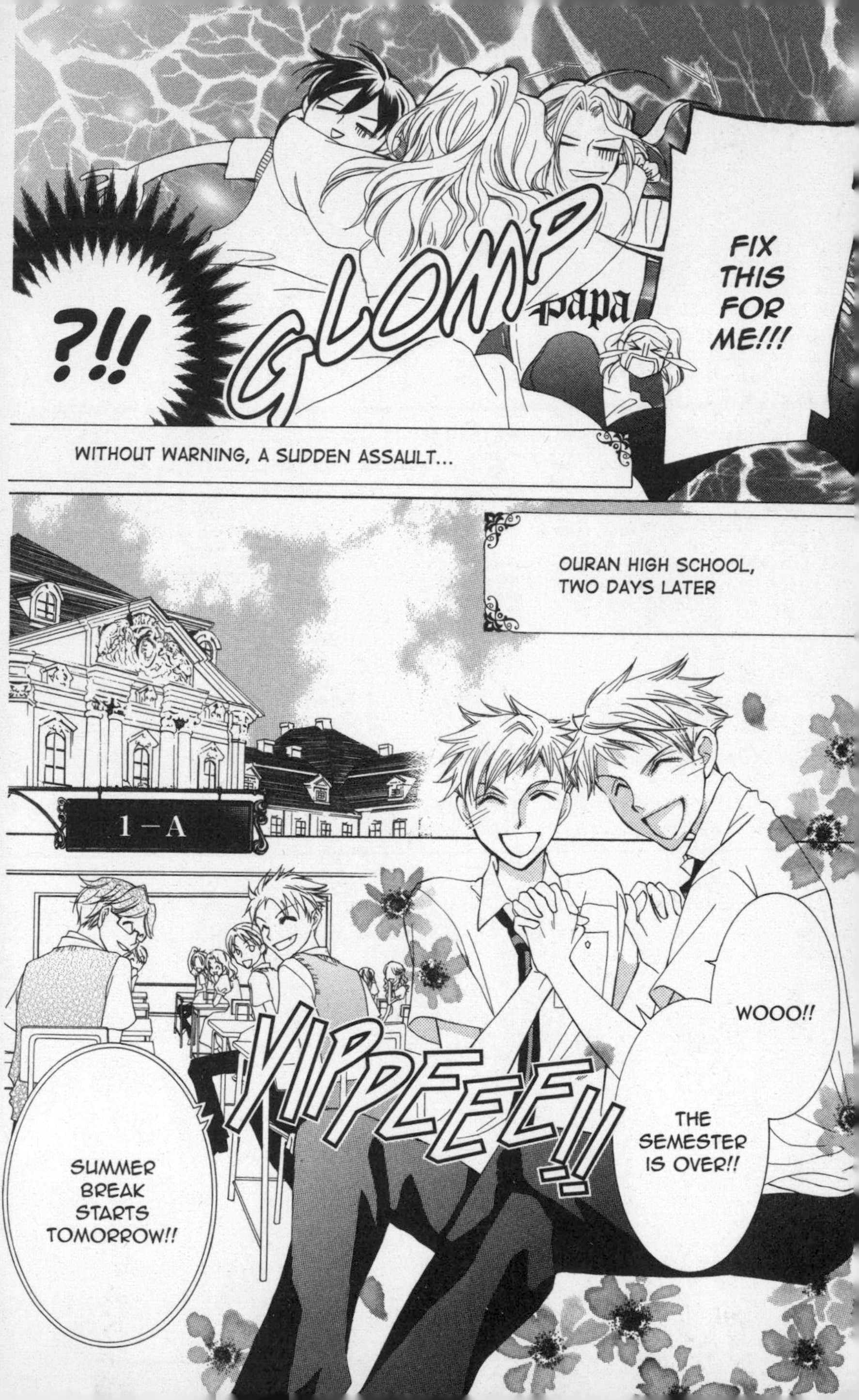
FIX THIS FOR ME!!!
papa
GLOMP
?!!
WITHOUT WARNING, A SUDDEN ASSAULT...
OURAN HIGH SCHOOL, TWO DAYS LATER
1-A
WOOO!!
THE SEMESTER IS OVER!!
YIPPEEE!!
SUMMER BREAK STARTS TOMORROW!!

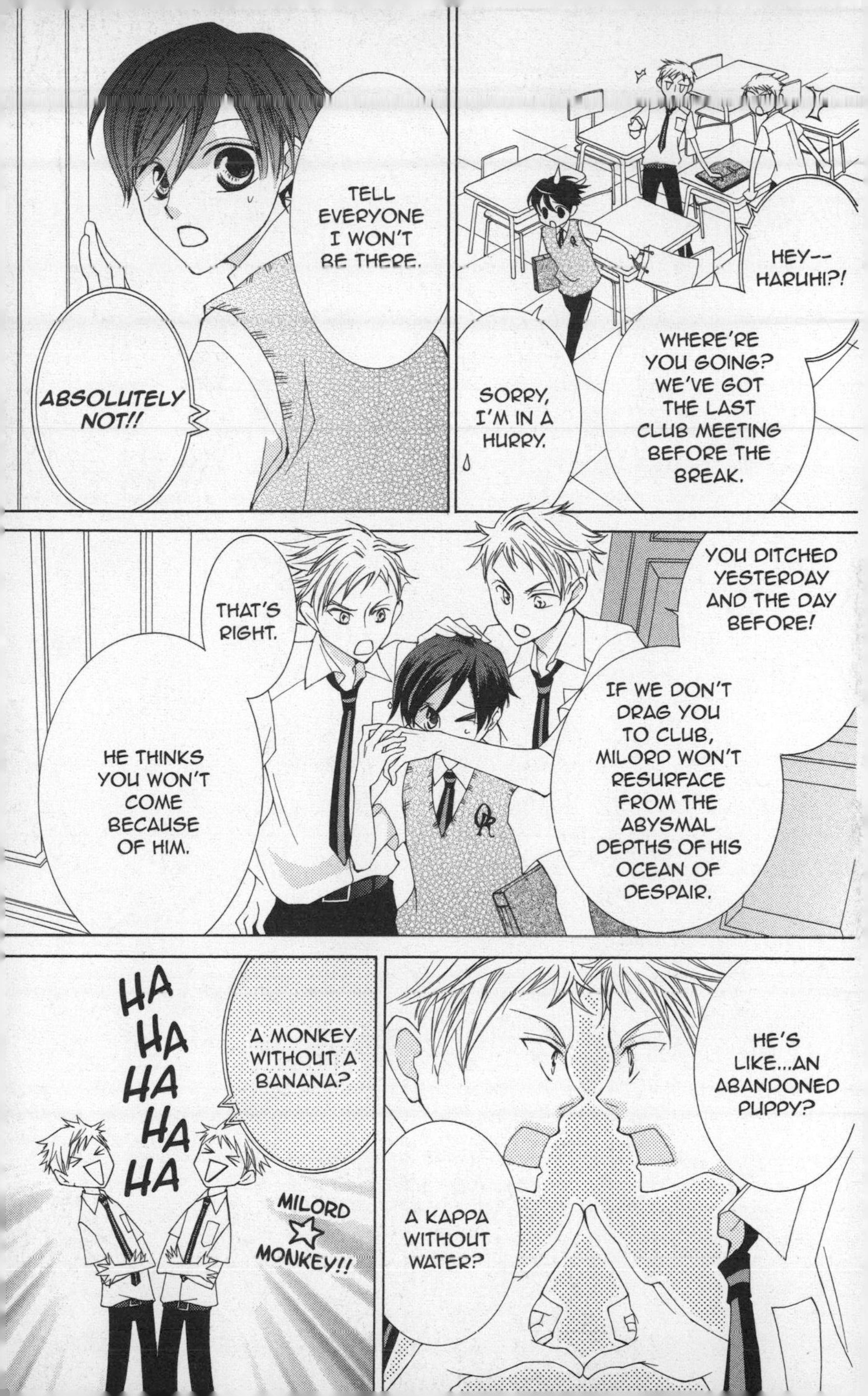
HEY-- HARUHI?!
WHERE'RE YOU GOING? WE'VE GOT THE LAST CLUB MEETING BEFORE THE BREAK.
SORRY, I'M IN A HURRY.
TELL EVERYONE I WON'T BE THERE.
ABSOLUTELY NOT!!
YOU DITCHED YESTERDAY AND THE DAY BEFORE!
IF WE DON'T DRAG YOU TO CLUB, MILORD WON'T RESURFACE FROM THE ABYSMAL DEPTHS OF HIS OCEAN OF DESPAIR.
THAT'S RIGHT.
HE THINKS YOU WON'T COME BECAUSE OF HIM.
HE'S LIKE...AN ABANDONED PUPPY?
A KAPPA WITHOUT WATER?
A MONKEY WITHOUT A BANANA?
HA HA HA HA HA
MILORD ☆ MONKEY!!

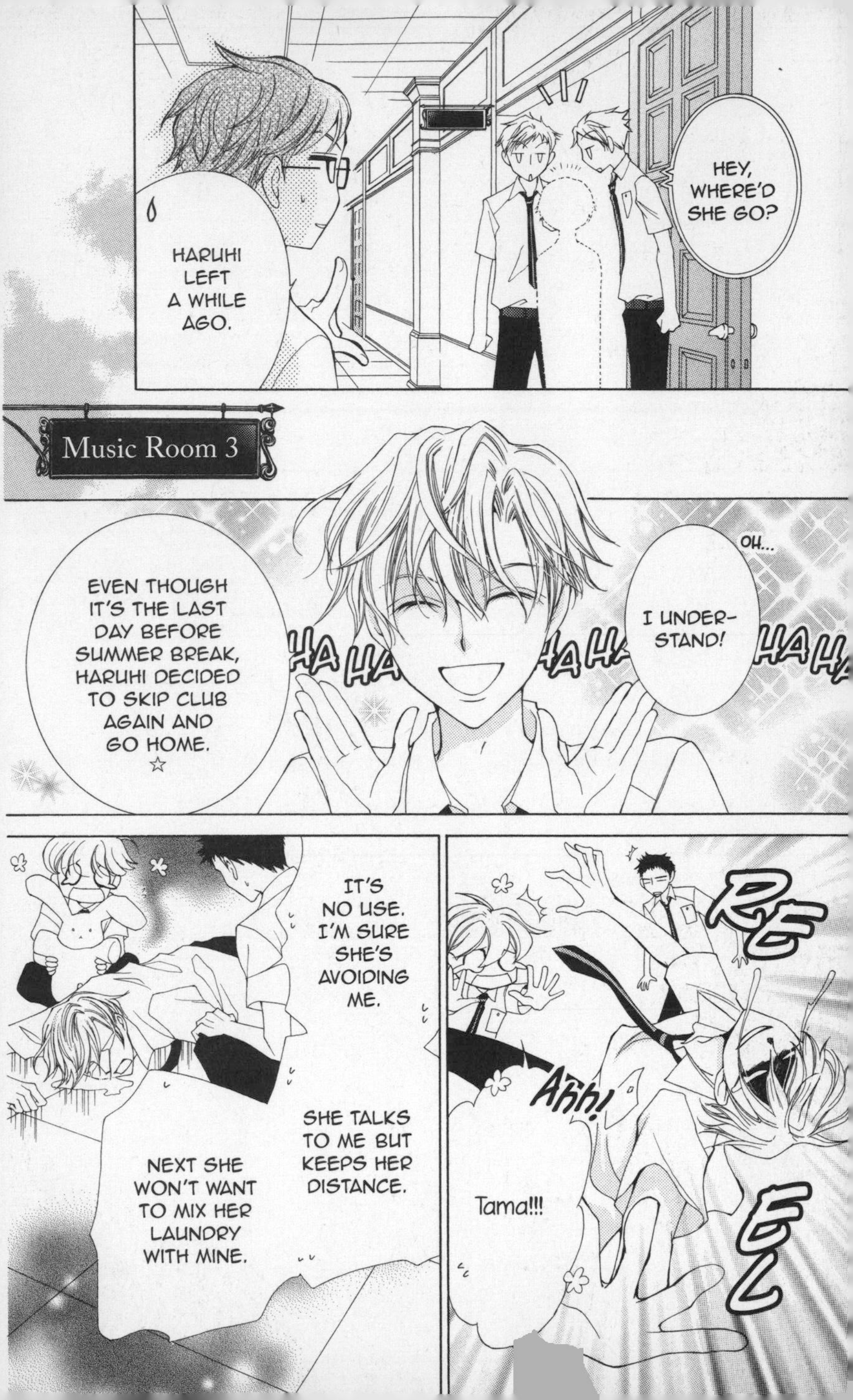
HEY, WHERE'D SHE GO?
HARUHI LEFT A WHILE AGO.
Music Room 3
OH...
I UNDER-STAND!
HA HA HA HA HA HA
EVEN THOUGH IT'S THE LAST DAY BEFORE SUMMER BREAK, HARUHI DECIDED TO SKIP CLUB AGAIN AND GO HOME. ☆
RE
EL
Ahh!
Tama!!!
IT'S NO USE. I'M SURE SHE'S AVOIDING ME.
SHE TALKS TO ME BUT KEEPS HER DISTANCE.
NEXT SHE WON'T WANT TO MIX HER LAUNDRY WITH MINE.

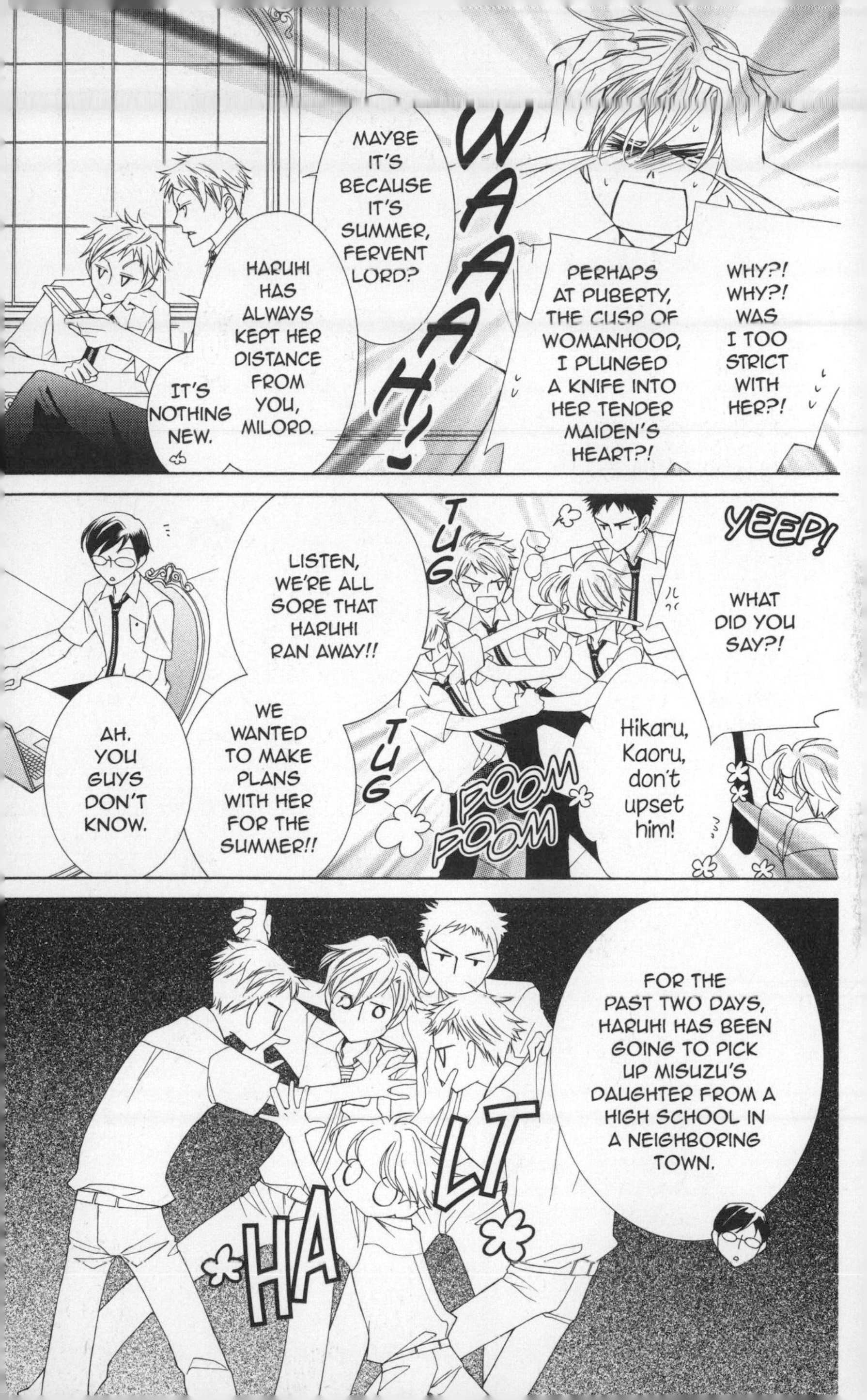
WHY?! WHY?! WAS I TOO STRICT WITH HER?!
PERHAPS AT PUBERTY, THE CUSP OF WOMANHOOD, I PLUNGED A KNIFE INTO HER TENDER MAIDEN'S HEART?!
WAAAH!
MAYBE IT'S BECAUSE IT'S SUMMER, FERVENT LORD?
HARUHI HAS ALWAYS KEPT HER DISTANCE FROM YOU, MILORD.
IT'S NOTHING NEW.
YEEP!
WHAT DID YOU SAY?!
Hikaru, Kaoru, don't upset him!
POOM POOM
TUG
TUG
LISTEN, WE'RE ALL SORE THAT HARUHI RAN AWAY!!
WE WANTED TO MAKE PLANS WITH HER FOR THE SUMMER!!
AH. YOU GUYS DON'T KNOW.
FOR THE PAST TWO DAYS, HARUHI HAS BEEN GOING TO PICK UP MISUZU'S DAUGHTER FROM A HIGH SCHOOL IN A NEIGHBORING TOWN.
HALT

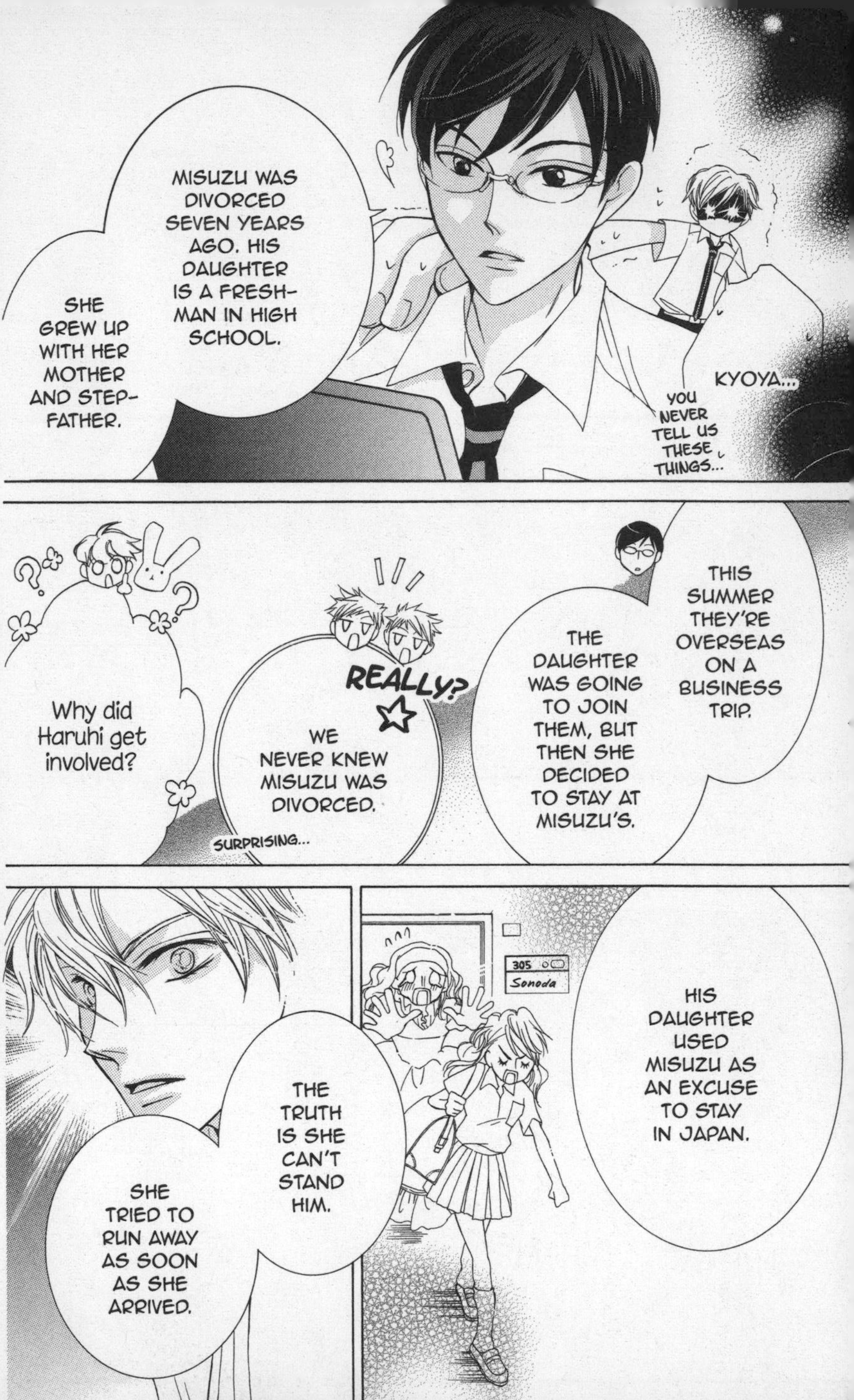
KYOYA...
YOU NEVER TELL US THESE THINGS...
MISUZU WAS DIVORCED SEVEN YEARS AGO. HIS DAUGHTER IS A FRESHMAN IN HIGH SCHOOL.
SHE GREW UP WITH HER MOTHER AND STEPFATHER.
THIS SUMMER THEY'RE OVERSEAS ON A BUSINESS TRIP.
THE DAUGHTER WAS GOING TO JOIN THEM, BUT THEN SHE DECIDED TO STAY AT MISUZU'S.
REALLY?
WE NEVER KNEW MISUZU WAS DIVORCED.
SURPRISING...
Why did Haruhi get involved?
HIS DAUGHTER USED MISUZU AS AN EXCUSE TO STAY IN JAPAN.
305
Sonoda
THE TRUTH IS SHE CAN'T STAND HIM.
SHE TRIED TO RUN AWAY AS SOON AS SHE ARRIVED.

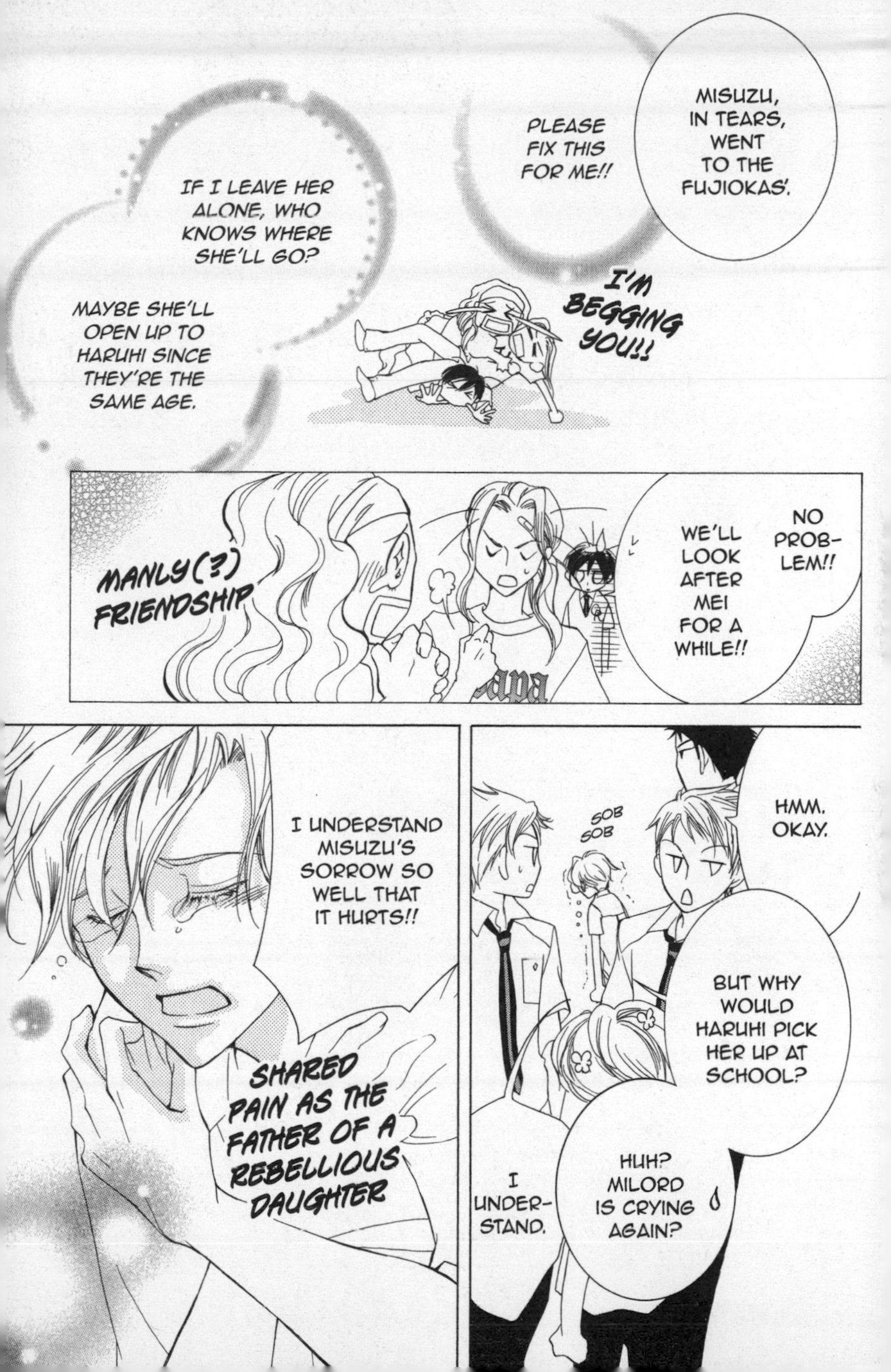
MISUZU, IN TEARS, WENT TO THE FUJIOKAS'.
PLEASE FIX THIS FOR ME!!
I'M BEGGING YOU!!
IF I LEAVE HER ALONE, WHO KNOWS WHERE SHE'LL GO?
MAYBE SHE'LL OPEN UP TO HARUHI SINCE THEY'RE THE SAME AGE.
NO PROB-LEM!!
WE'LL LOOK AFTER MEI FOR A WHILE!!
MANLY(?) FRIENDSHIP
HMM. OKAY.
BUT WHY WOULD HARUHI PICK HER UP AT SCHOOL?
SOB SOB
HUH? MILORD IS CRYING AGAIN?
I UNDER-STAND.
I UNDERSTAND MISUZU'S SORROW SO WELL THAT IT HURTS!!
SHARED PAIN AS THE FATHER OF A REBELLIOUS DAUGHTER

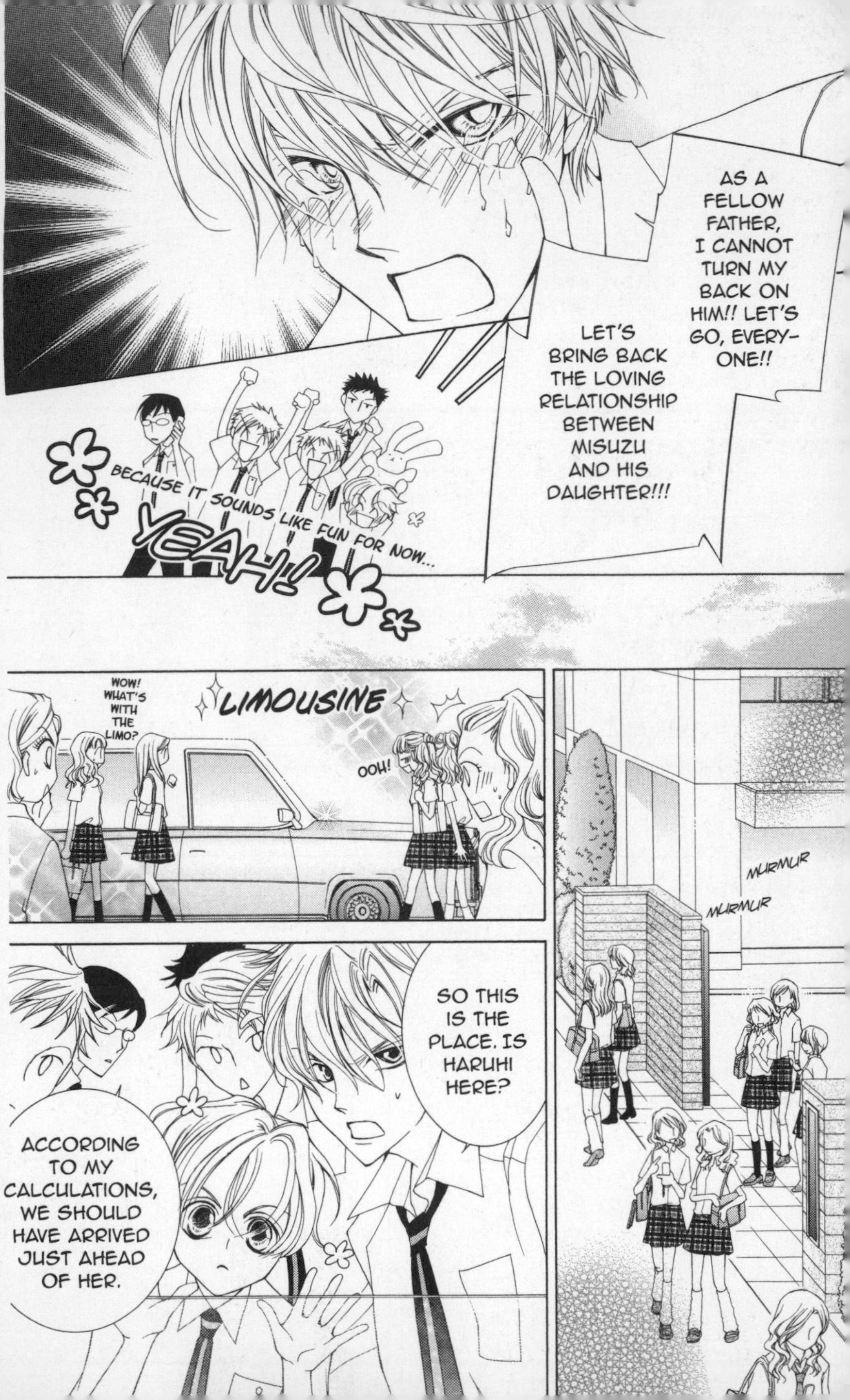
AS A FELLOW FATHER, I CANNOT TURN MY BACK ON HIM!! LET'S GO, EVERYONE!!
LET'S BRING BACK THE LOVING RELATIONSHIP BETWEEN MISUZU AND HIS DAUGHTER!!!
BECAUSE IT SOUNDS LIKE FUN FOR NOW...
YEAH!
MURMUR
MURMUR
OOH!
LIMOUSINE
WOW! WHAT'S WITH THE LIMO?
SO THIS IS THE PLACE. IS HARUHI HERE?
ACCORDING TO MY CALCULATIONS, WE SHOULD HAVE ARRIVED JUST AHEAD OF HER.

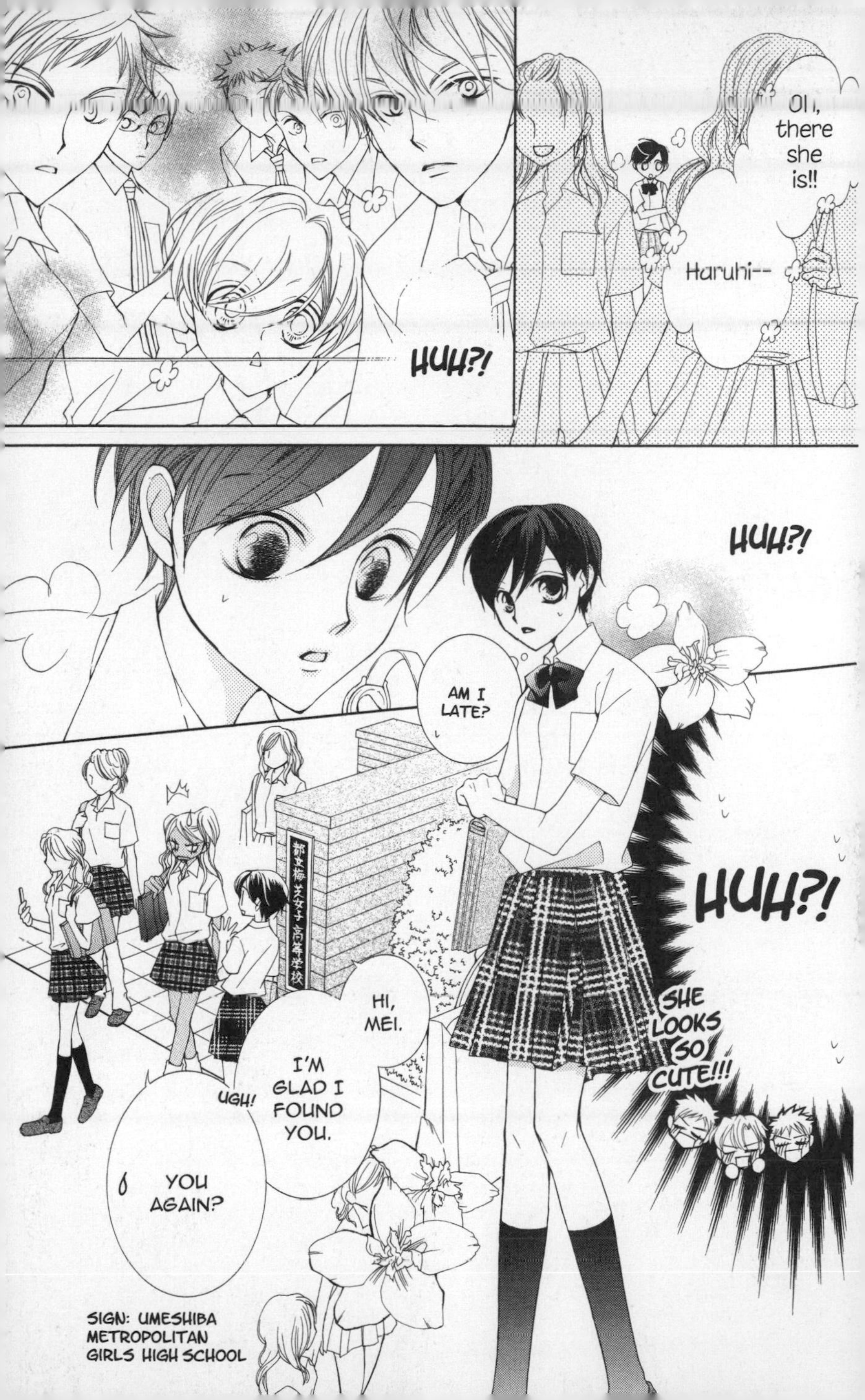
Oh, there she is!!
Haruhi--
HUH?!
HUH?!
AM I LATE?
HUH?!
SHE LOOKS SO CUTE!!!
HI, MEI.
I'M GLAD I FOUND YOU.
UGH!
YOU AGAIN?
SIGN: UMESHIBA METROPOLITAN GIRLS HIGH SCHOOL

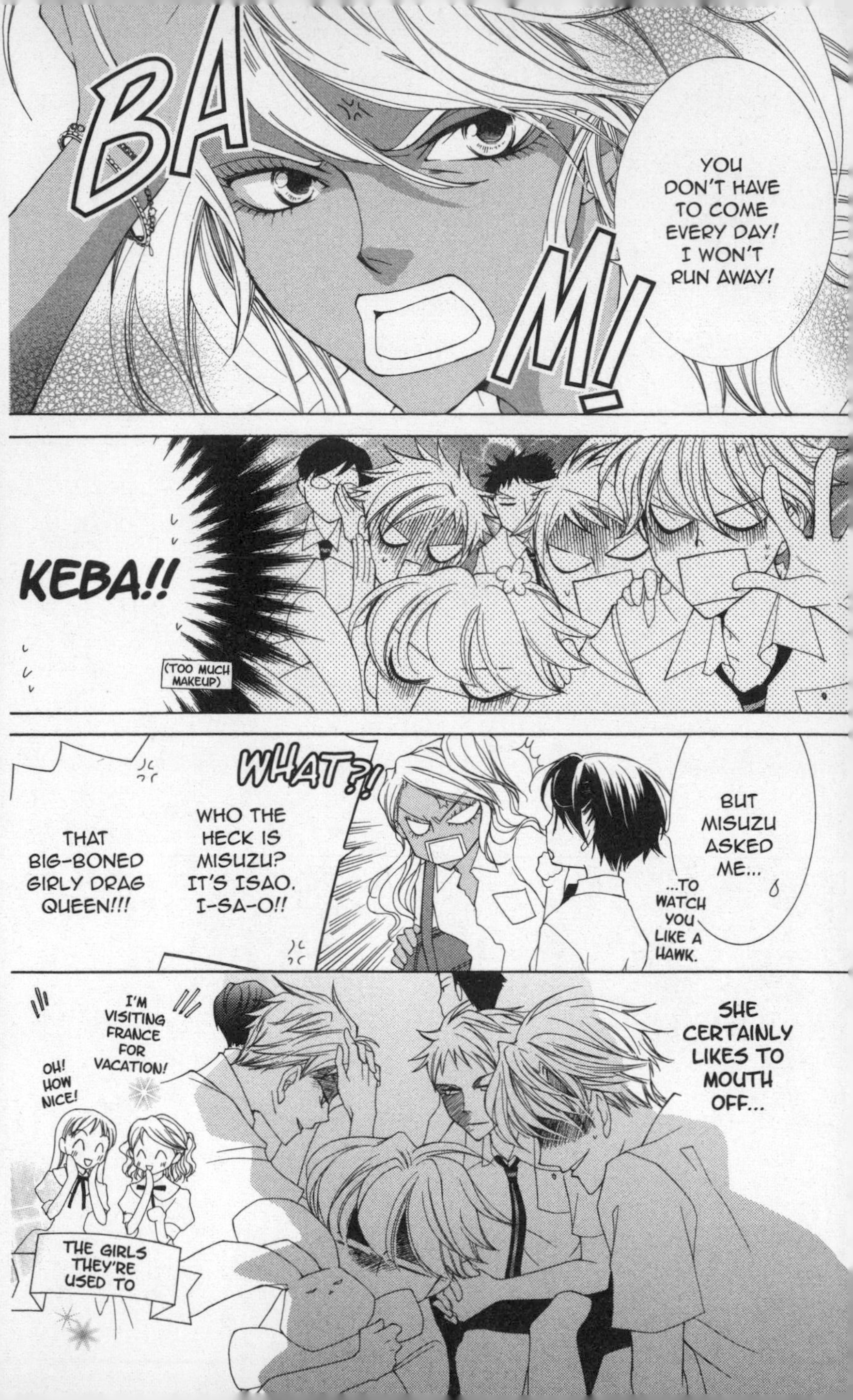
BAMM!
YOU DON'T HAVE TO COME EVERY DAY! I WON'T RUN AWAY!
KEBA!!
(TOO MUCH MAKEUP)
BUT MISUZU ASKED ME...
...TO WATCH YOU LIKE A HAWK.
WHAT?!
WHO THE HECK IS MISUZU? IT'S ISAO. I-SA-O!!
THAT BIG-BONED GIRLY DRAG QUEEN!!!
SHE CERTAINLY LIKES TO MOUTH OFF...
I'M VISITING FRANCE FOR VACATION!
OH! HOW NICE!
THE GIRLS THEY'RE USED TO

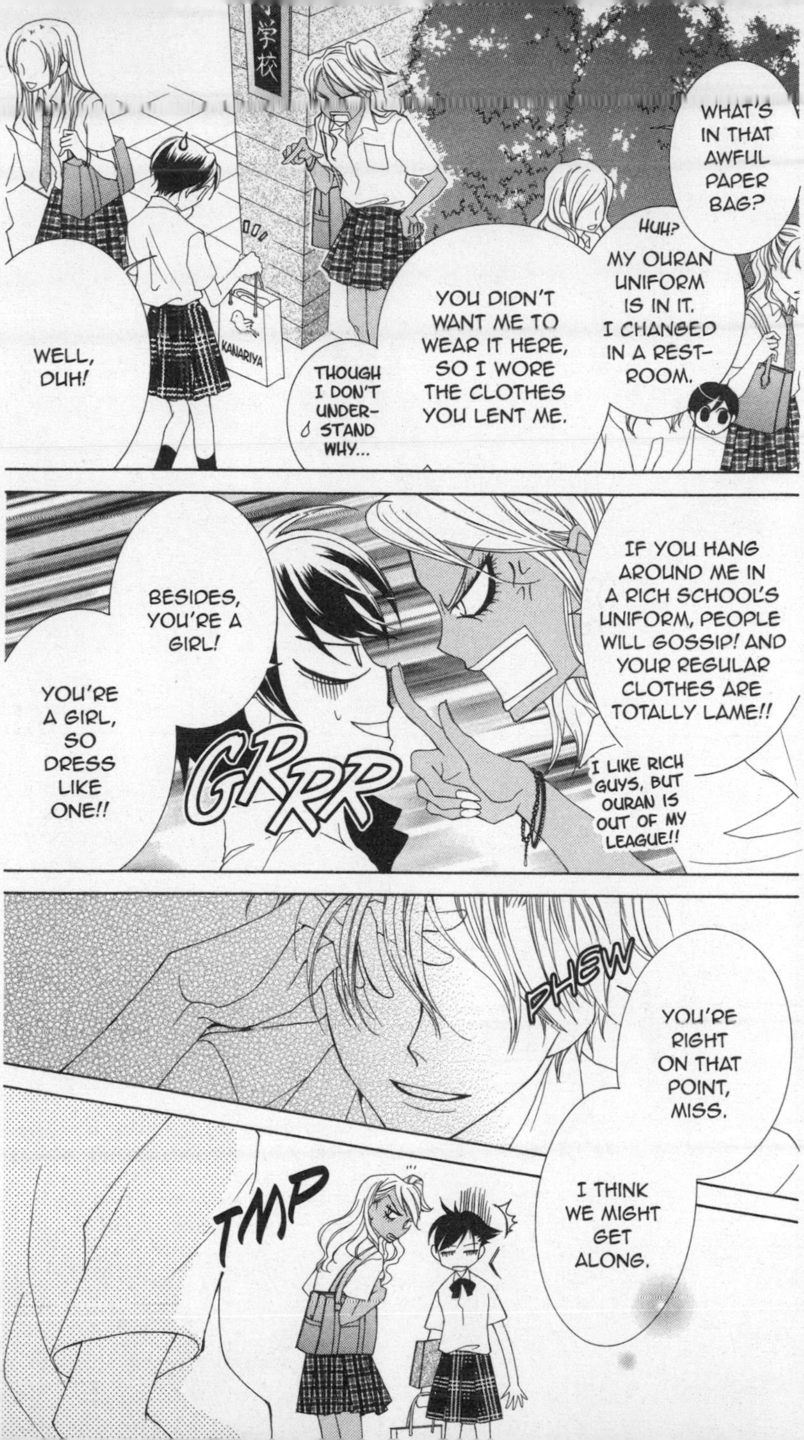
学校
WHAT'S IN THAT AWFUL PAPER BAG?
HUH?
MY OURAN UNIFORM IS IN IT. I CHANGED IN A REST-ROOM.
YOU DIDN'T WANT ME TO WEAR IT HERE, SO I WORE THE CLOTHES YOU LENT ME.
THOUGH I DON'T UNDER-STAND WHY...
KANARIYA
WELL, DUH!
IF YOU HANG AROUND ME IN A RICH SCHOOL'S UNIFORM, PEOPLE WILL GOSSIP! AND YOUR REGULAR CLOTHES ARE TOTALLY LAME!!
I LIKE RICH GUYS, BUT OURAN IS OUT OF MY LEAGUE!!
BESIDES, YOU'RE A GIRL!
YOU'RE A GIRL, SO DRESS LIKE ONE!!
GRRR
PHEW
YOU'RE RIGHT ON THAT POINT, MISS.
I THINK WE MIGHT GET ALONG.
TMP

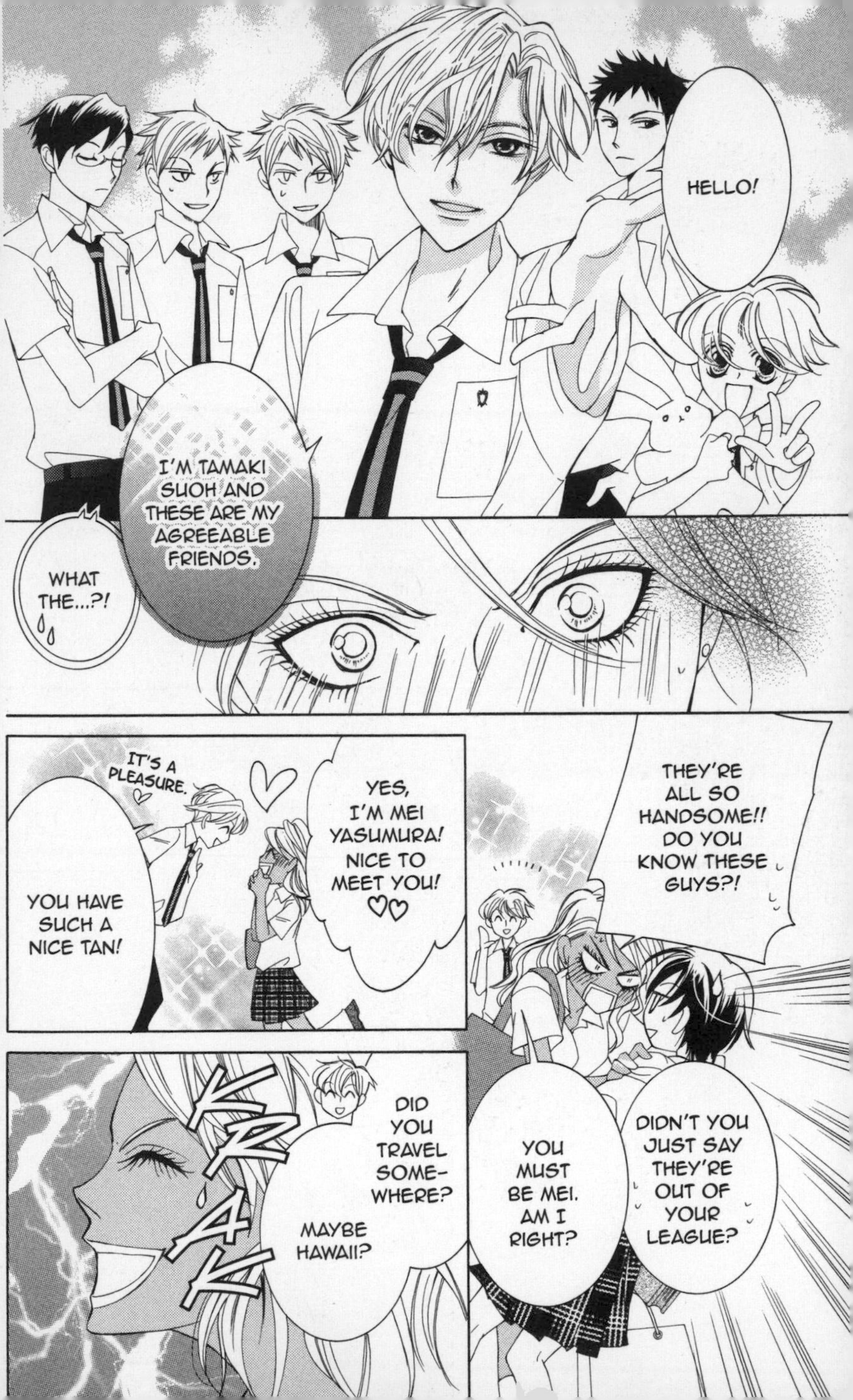
HELLO!
I'M TAMAKI SUOH AND THESE ARE MY AGREEABLE FRIENDS.
WHAT THE...?!
THEY'RE ALL SO HANDSOME!! DO YOU KNOW THESE GUYS?!
YES, I'M MEI YASUMURA! NICE TO MEET YOU! ♡♡
IT'S A PLEASURE. ♡
YOU HAVE SUCH A NICE TAN!
DIDN'T YOU JUST SAY THEY'RE OUT OF YOUR LEAGUE?
YOU MUST BE MEI. AM I RIGHT?
DID YOU TRAVEL SOME-WHERE?
MAYBE HAWAII?
KRAK

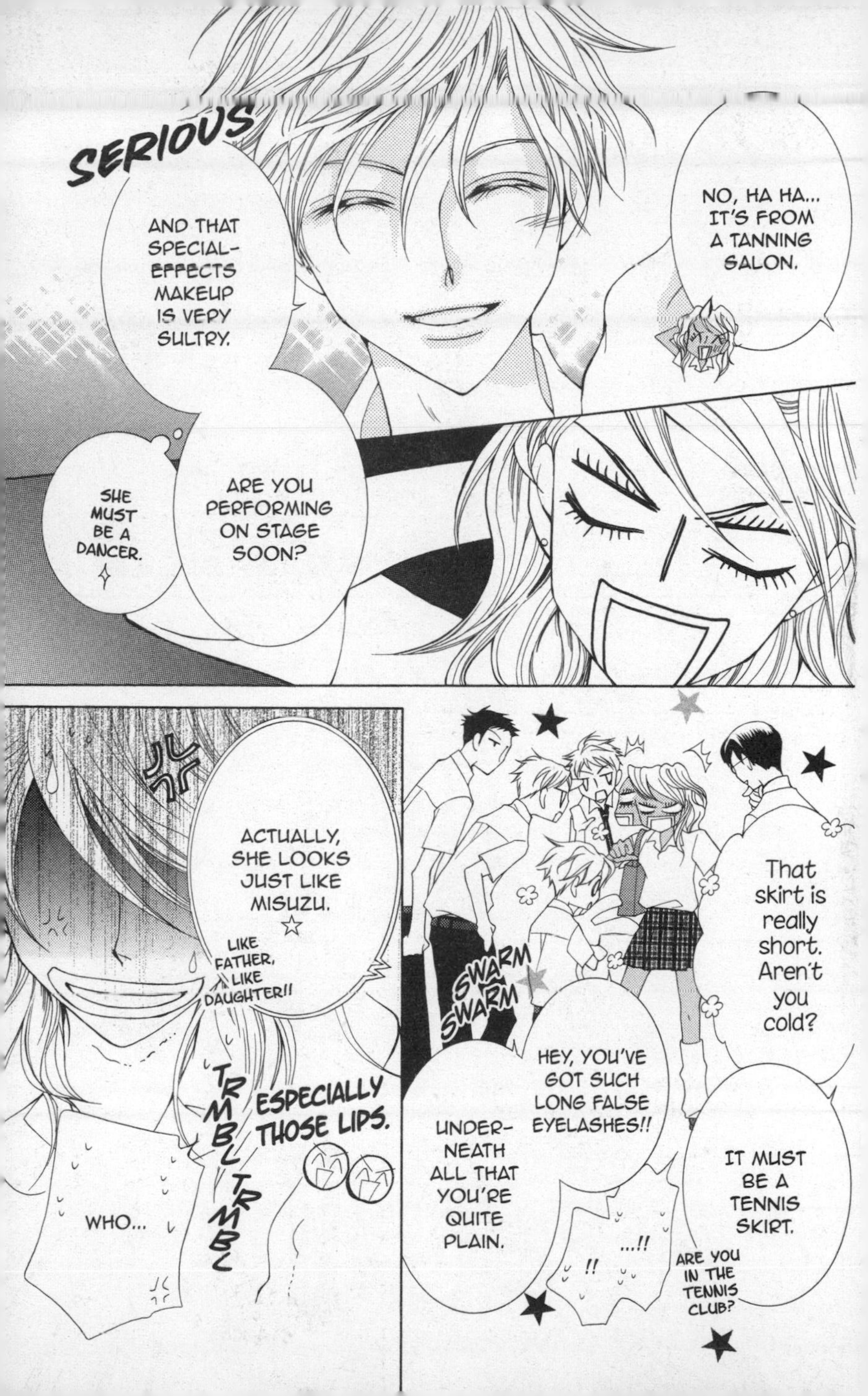
NO, HA HA... IT'S FROM A TANNING SALON.
SERIOUS
AND THAT SPECIAL-EFFECTS MAKEUP IS VERY SULTRY.
ARE YOU PERFORMING ON STAGE SOON?
SHE MUST BE A DANCER.
That skirt is really short. Aren't you cold?
IT MUST BE A TENNIS SKIRT.
ARE YOU IN THE TENNIS CLUB?
HEY, YOU'VE GOT SUCH LONG FALSE EYELASHES!!
SWARM SWARM
...!!
!!
UNDER-NEATH ALL THAT YOU'RE QUITE PLAIN.
ACTUALLY, SHE LOOKS JUST LIKE MISUZU.
LIKE FATHER, LIKE DAUGHTER!!
ESPECIALLY THOSE LIPS.
TRMBL TRMBL
WHO...

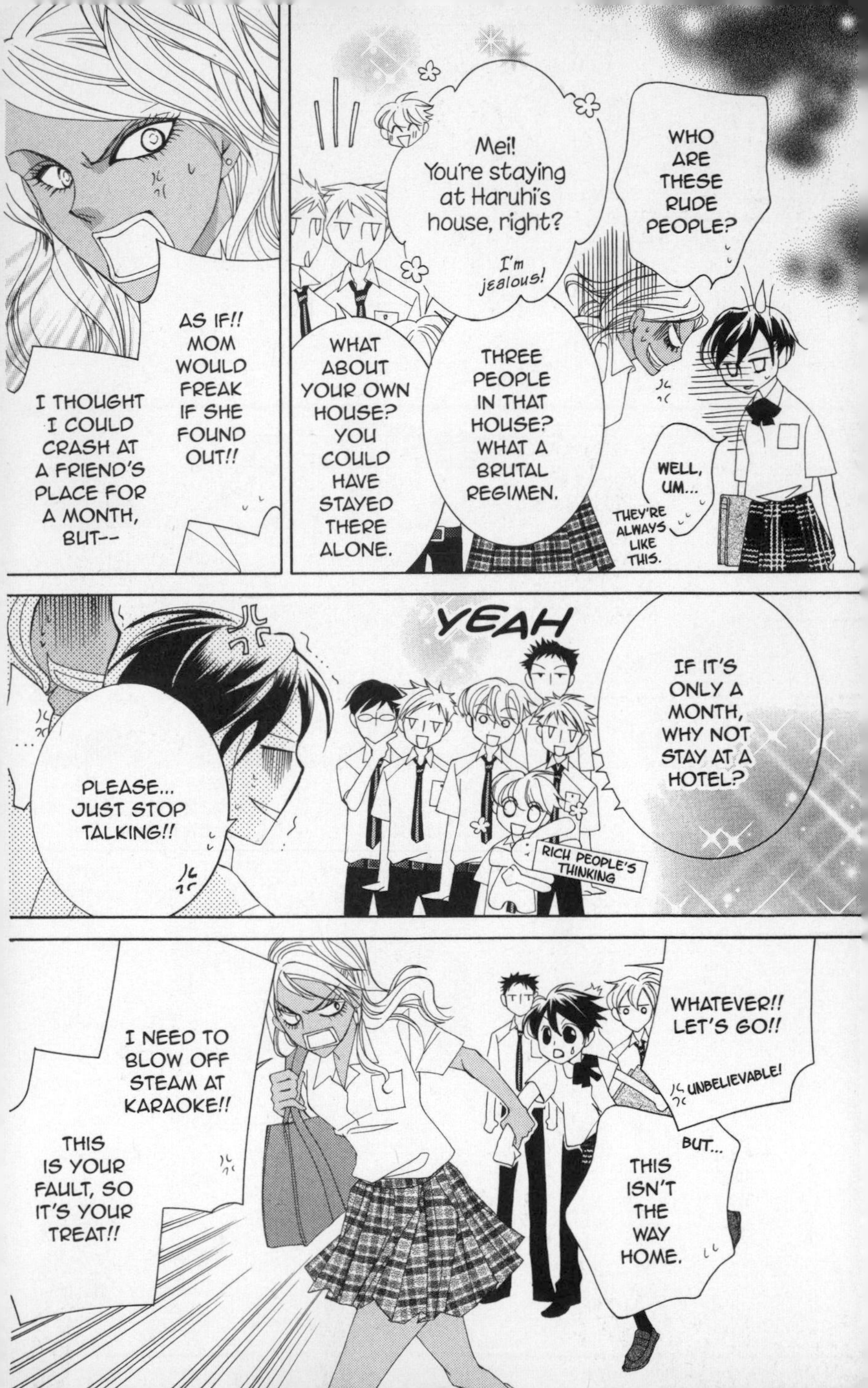
WHO ARE THESE RUDE PEOPLE?
Mei! You're staying at Haruhi's house, right?
I'm jealous!
WELL, UM...
THEY'RE ALWAYS LIKE THIS.
THREE PEOPLE IN THAT HOUSE? WHAT A BRUTAL REGIMEN.
WHAT ABOUT YOUR OWN HOUSE? YOU COULD HAVE STAYED THERE ALONE.
AS IF!! MOM WOULD FREAK IF SHE FOUND OUT!!
I THOUGHT I COULD CRASH AT A FRIEND'S PLACE FOR A MONTH, BUT--
IF IT'S ONLY A MONTH, WHY NOT STAY AT A HOTEL?
YEAH
RICH PEOPLE'S THINKING
PLEASE... JUST STOP TALKING!!
WHATEVER!! LET'S GO!!
UNBELIEVABLE!
BUT...
THIS ISN'T THE WAY HOME.
I NEED TO BLOW OFF STEAM AT KARAOKE!!
THIS IS YOUR FAULT, SO IT'S YOUR TREAT!!

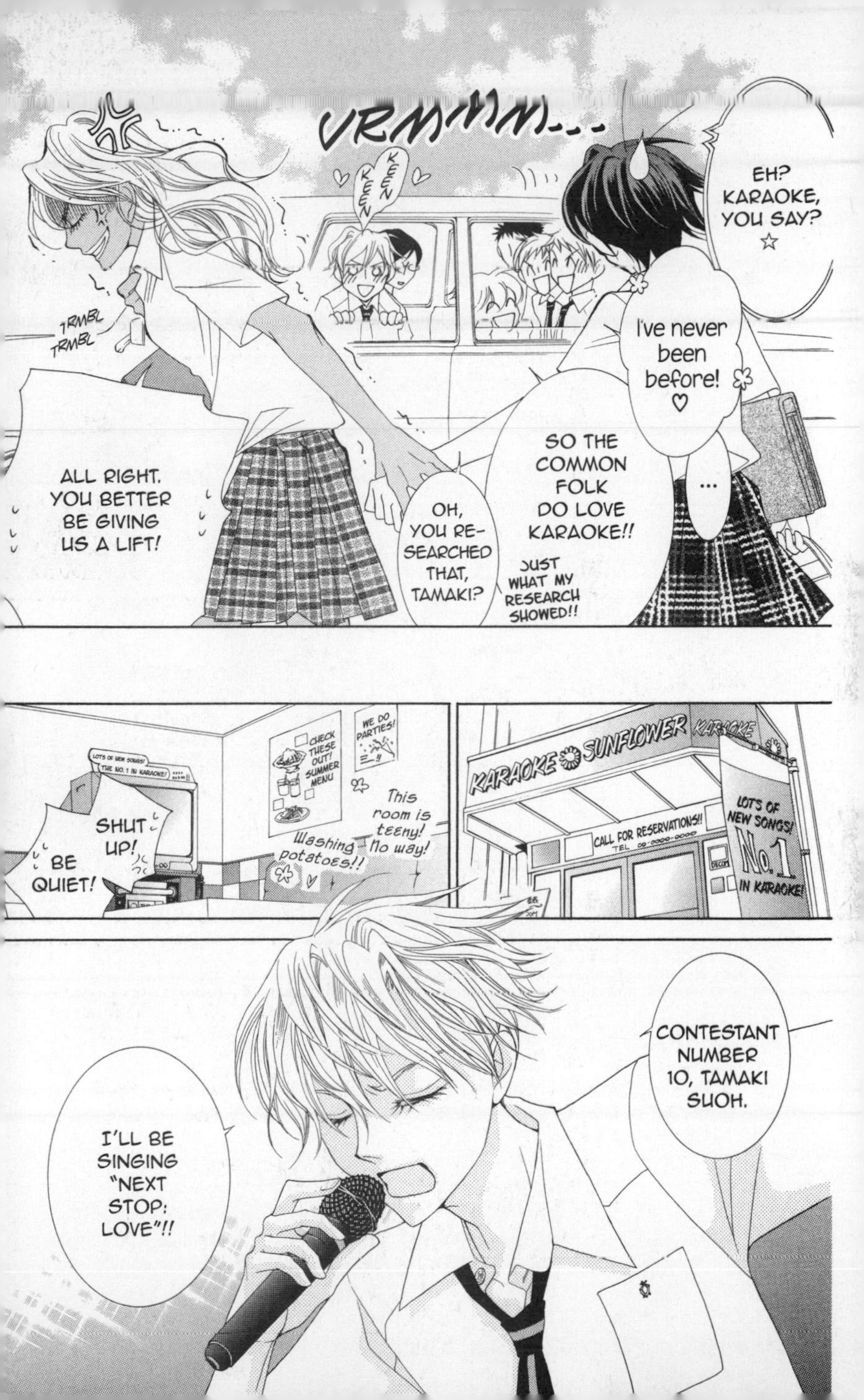
VRMMM...
EH? KARAOKE, YOU SAY? ☆
I've never been before! ♡
...
KEEN KEEN
SO THE COMMON FOLK DO LOVE KARAOKE!!
JUST WHAT MY RESEARCH SHOWED!!
OH, YOU RE-SEARCHED THAT, TAMAKI?
ALL RIGHT. YOU BETTER BE GIVING US A LIFT!
TRMBL TRMBL
KARAOKE SUNFLOWER KARAOKE
LOTS OF NEW SONGS! No. 1 IN KARAOKE!
CALL FOR RESERVATIONS!!
TEL 00-0000-0000
This room is teeny! No way!
Washing potatoes!!
WE DO PARTIES!
CHECK THESE OUT! SUMMER MENU
LOTS OF NEW SONGS!
THE NO. 1 IN KARAOKE!
SHUT UP!
BE QUIET!
CONTESTANT NUMBER 10, TAMAKI SUOH.
I'LL BE SINGING "NEXT STOP: LOVE"!!

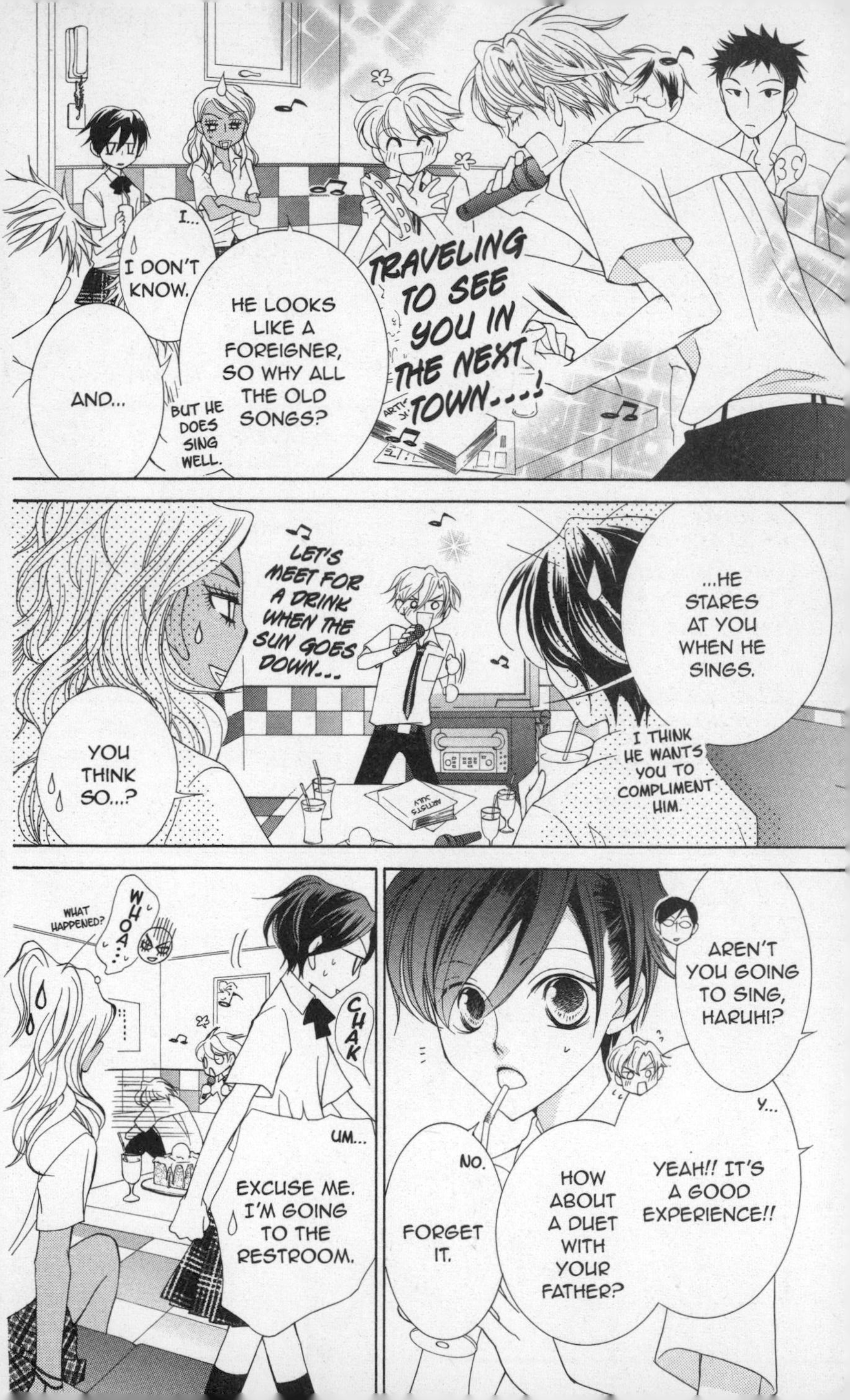
TRAVELING TO SEE YOU IN THE NEXT TOWN...!
HE LOOKS LIKE A FOREIGNER, SO WHY ALL THE OLD SONGS?
BUT HE DOES SING WELL.
I...
I DON'T KNOW.
AND...
...HE STARES AT YOU WHEN HE SINGS.
I THINK HE WANTS YOU TO COMPLIMENT HIM.
LET'S MEET FOR A DRINK WHEN THE SUN GOES DOWN...
YOU THINK SO...?
AREN'T YOU GOING TO SING, HARUHI?
Y...
YEAH!! IT'S A GOOD EXPERIENCE!!
HOW ABOUT A DUET WITH YOUR FATHER?
NO.
FORGET IT.
UM...
EXCUSE ME. I'M GOING TO THE RESTROOM.
CHAK
WHOA...
WHAT HAPPENED?

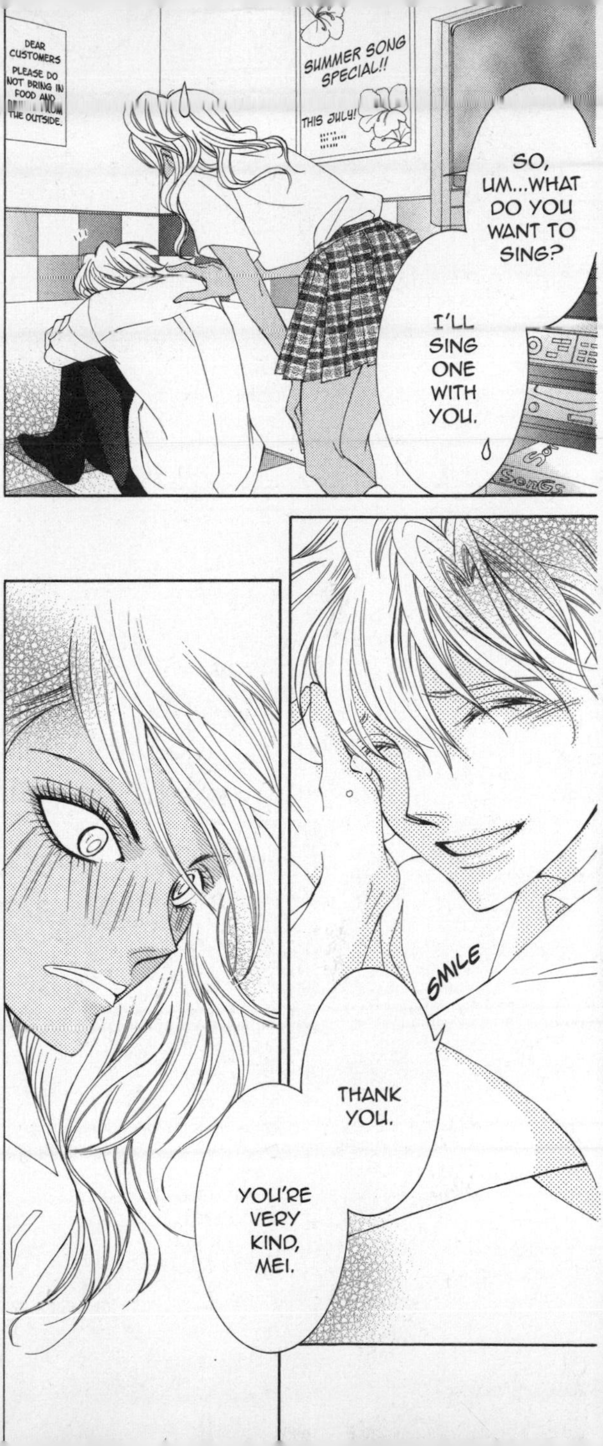
SUMMER SONG SPECIAL!!
THIS JULY!
DEAR CUSTOMERS
PLEASE DO NOT BRING IN FOOD AND
THE OUTSIDE.
SO, UM...WHAT DO YOU WANT TO SING?
I'LL SING ONE WITH YOU.
SONGS
SMILE
THANK YOU.
YOU'RE VERY KIND, MEI.

2

✿ THE STORY HAS REALLY TAKEN OFF, AND I'M PREPARED TO SEE IT THROUGH TO THE END. I'D BE OVERJOYED IF YOU KEEP READING THROUGH THIS LAST LONG (NO, PERHAPS NOT THAT LONG...) STRETCH. ✿✿

✿ WHEN YOU BOUGHT THIS VOLUME, DID YOU WONDER WHO WAS ON THE COVER? IT'S MEI, WHO APPEARS FOR THE FIRST TIME IN THIS VOLUME. SHE JUST MIGHT BE MY FAVORITE CHARACTER SO FAR IN THE *HOST CLUB* SERIES. IT FEELS GREAT DRAWING HER AND CONVEYING HER PERSONALITY.

I LIKE KANAZUKI TOO. AT FIRST I THOUGHT ABOUT HAVING HER FALL IN LOVE WITH NEKOZAWA. THEN I REALIZED THAT SHE WAS A BETTER MATCH FOR HUNNY AND I CHANGED EVERYTHING AT THE LAST MINUTE. (THIS KIND OF THING HAPPENS A LOT...)

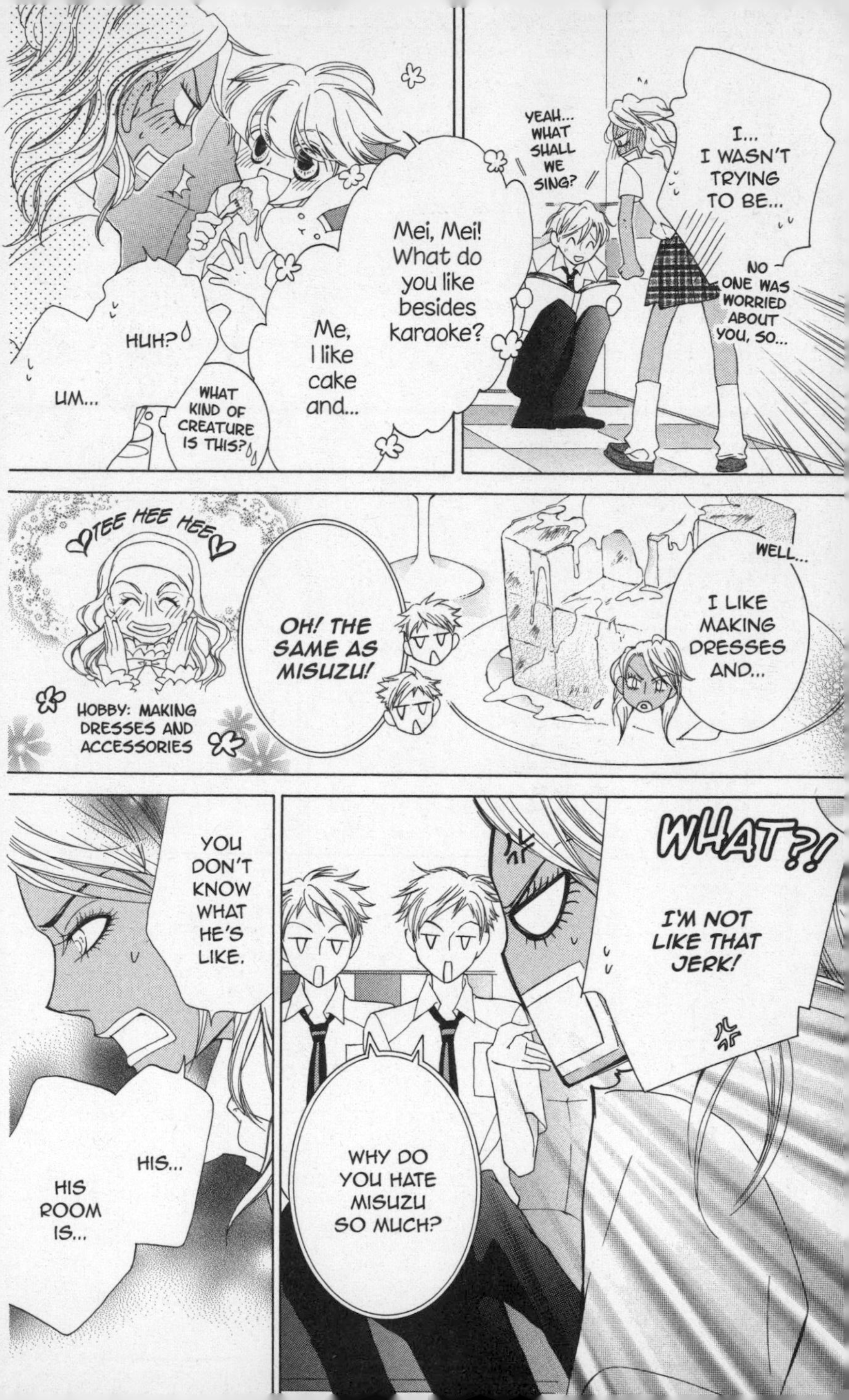
I... I WASN'T TRYING TO BE...
NO ONE WAS WORRIED ABOUT YOU, SO...
YEAH... WHAT SHALL WE SING?
Mei, Mei! What do you like besides karaoke?
Me, I like cake and...
HUH?
WHAT KIND OF CREATURE IS THIS?
UM...
WELL...
I LIKE MAKING DRESSES AND...
OH! THE SAME AS MISUZU!
TEE HEE HEE
HOBBY: MAKING DRESSES AND ACCESSORIES
WHAT?!
I'M NOT LIKE THAT JERK!
WHY DO YOU HATE MISUZU SO MUCH?
YOU DON'T KNOW WHAT HE'S LIKE.
HIS...
HIS ROOM IS...

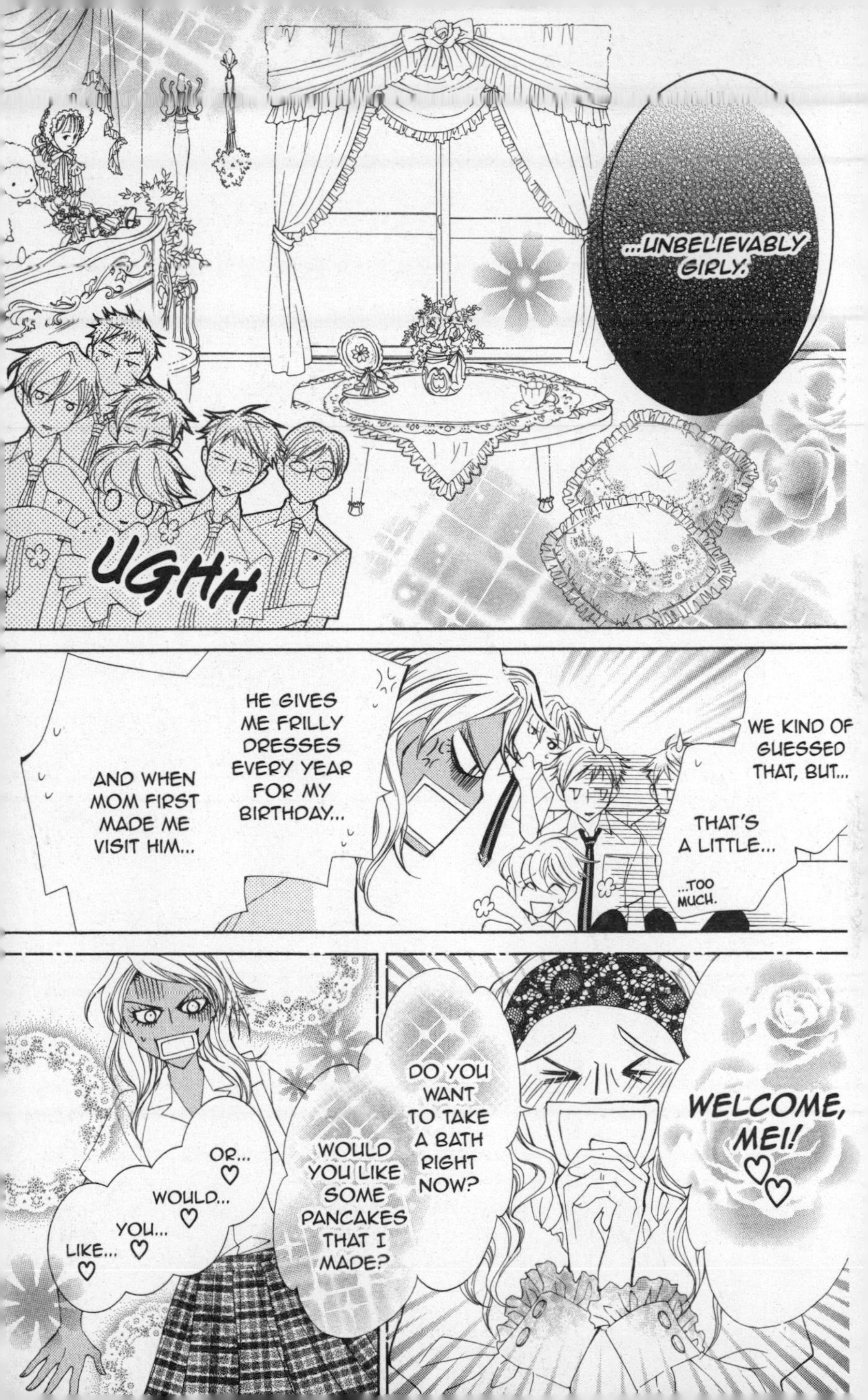
...UNBELIEVABLY GIRLY.
UGHH
WE KIND OF GUESSED THAT, BUT...
THAT'S A LITTLE...
...TOO MUCH.
HE GIVES ME FRILLY DRESSES EVERY YEAR FOR MY BIRTHDAY...
AND WHEN MOM FIRST MADE ME VISIT HIM...
WELCOME, MEI! ♥ ♥
DO YOU WANT TO TAKE A BATH RIGHT NOW?
WOULD YOU LIKE SOME PANCAKES THAT I MADE?
OR... ♥ WOULD... ♥ YOU... ♥ LIKE... ♥

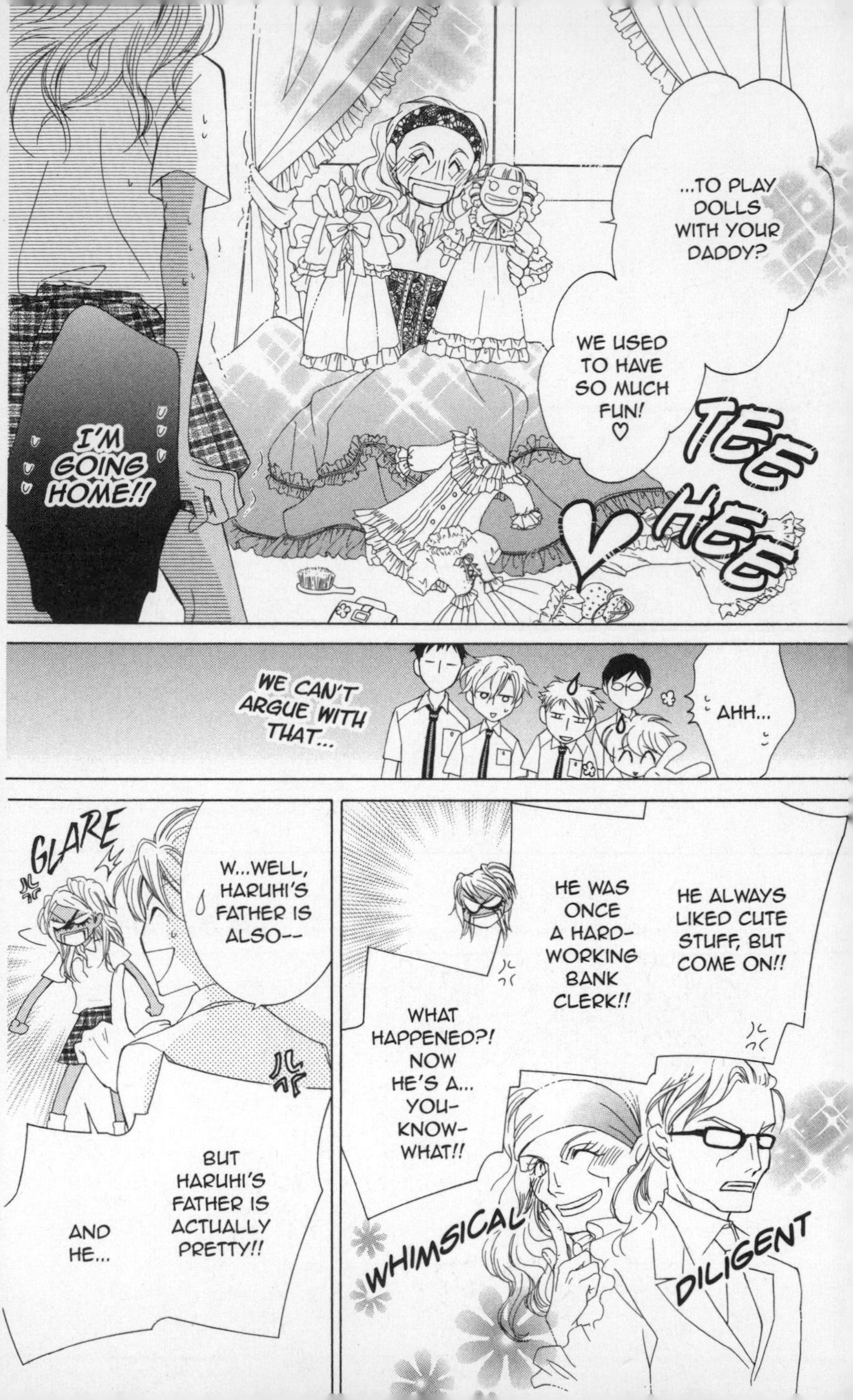
...TO PLAY DOLLS WITH YOUR DADDY?
WE USED TO HAVE SO MUCH FUN! ♡
TEE HEE ♡
I'M GOING HOME!!
AHH...
WE CAN'T ARGUE WITH THAT...
HE ALWAYS LIKED CUTE STUFF, BUT COME ON!!
HE WAS ONCE A HARD-WORKING BANK CLERK!!
WHAT HAPPENED?! NOW HE'S A... YOU-KNOW-WHAT!!
DILIGENT
WHIMSICAL
W...WELL, HARUHI'S FATHER IS ALSO--
GLARE
BUT HARUHI'S FATHER IS ACTUALLY PRETTY!!
AND HE...

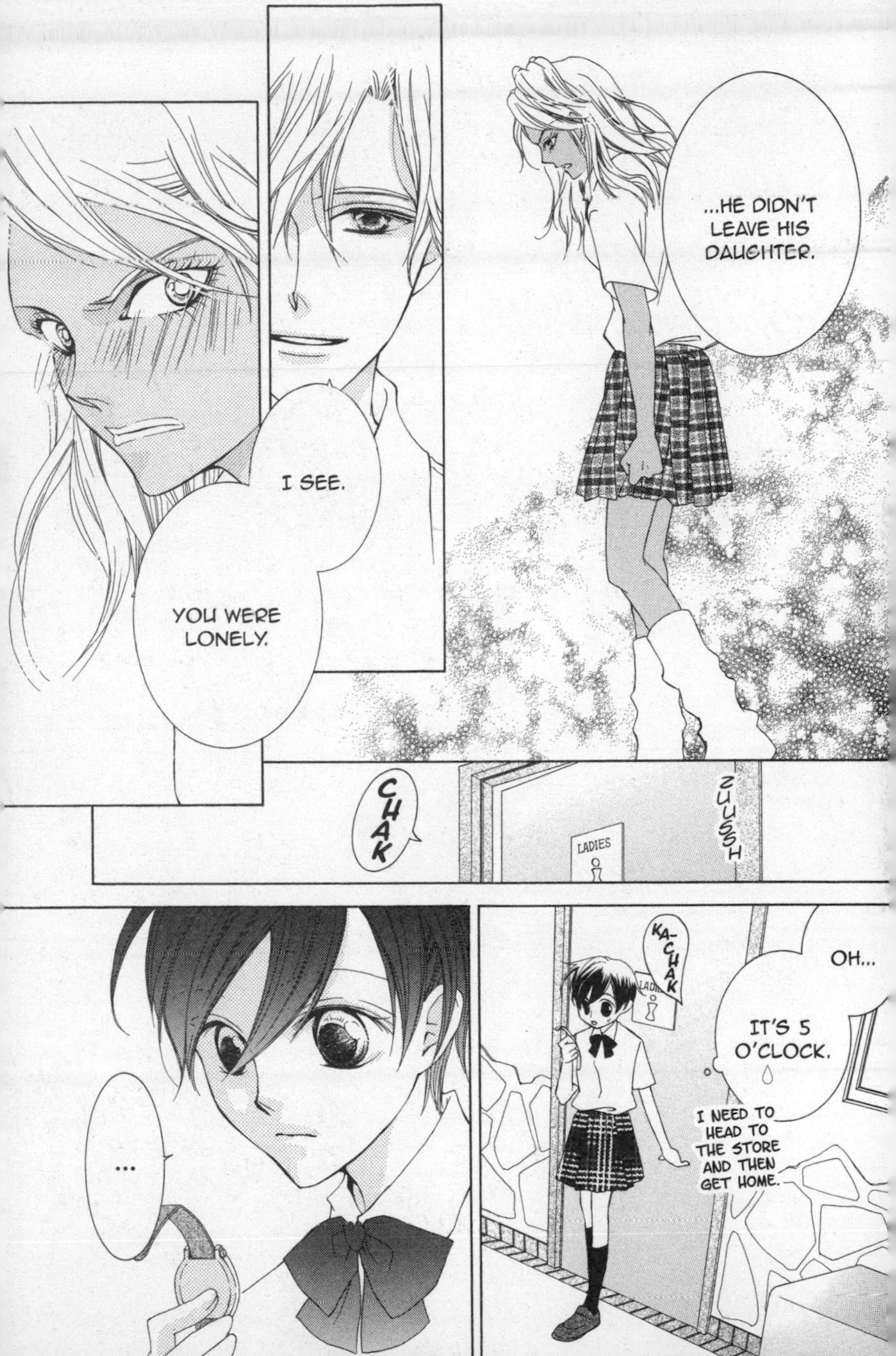
...HE DIDN'T LEAVE HIS DAUGHTER.
I SEE.
YOU WERE LONELY.
ZUUSH
LADIES
CHAK
KA-CHAK
LADIES
OH...
IT'S 5 O'CLOCK.
I NEED TO HEAD TO THE STORE AND THEN GET HOME.
...

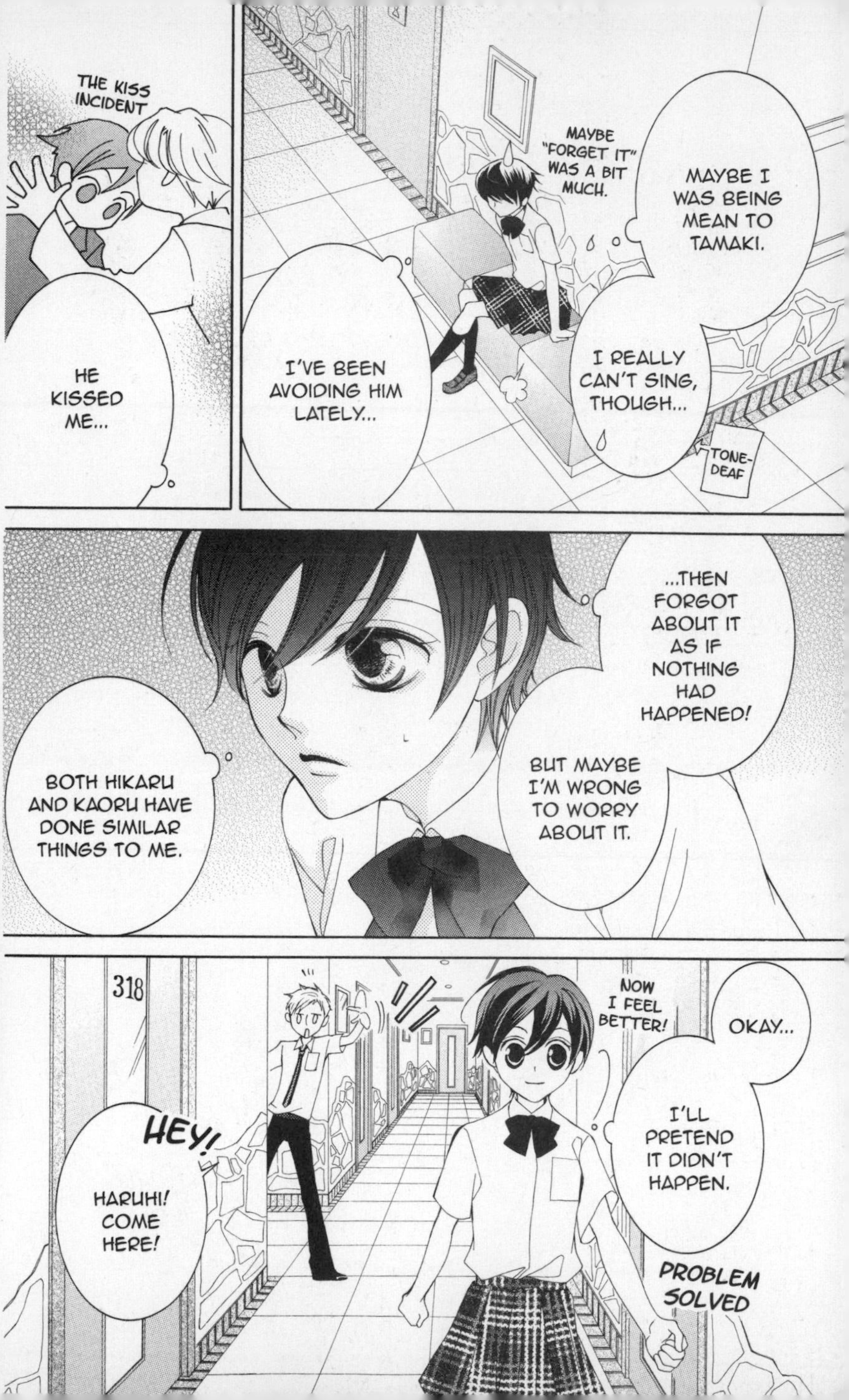
MAYBE I WAS BEING MEAN TO TAMAKI.
MAYBE "FORGET IT" WAS A BIT MUCH.
I REALLY CAN'T SING, THOUGH...
TONE-DEAF
I'VE BEEN AVOIDING HIM LATELY...
THE KISS INCIDENT
HE KISSED ME...
...THEN FORGOT ABOUT IT AS IF NOTHING HAD HAPPENED!
BUT MAYBE I'M WRONG TO WORRY ABOUT IT.
BOTH HIKARU AND KAORU HAVE DONE SIMILAR THINGS TO ME.
OKAY...
NOW I FEEL BETTER!
I'LL PRETEND IT DIDN'T HAPPEN.
PROBLEM SOLVED
318
HEY!
HARUHI! COME HERE!

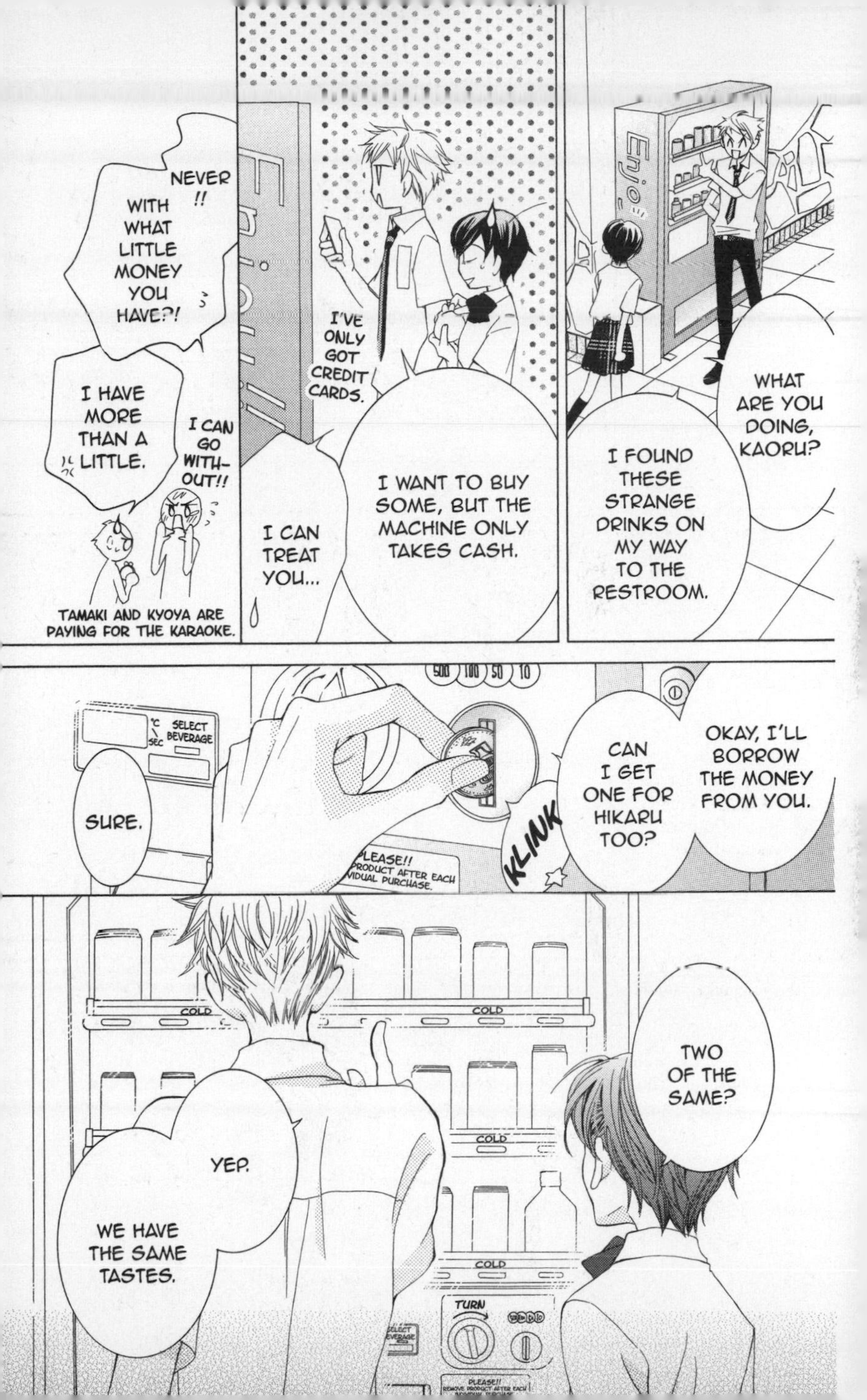
WHAT ARE YOU DOING, KAORU?
I FOUND THESE STRANGE DRINKS ON MY WAY TO THE RESTROOM.
I WANT TO BUY SOME, BUT THE MACHINE ONLY TAKES CASH.
I'VE ONLY GOT CREDIT CARDS.
I CAN TREAT YOU...
NEVER!!
WITH WHAT LITTLE MONEY YOU HAVE?!
I HAVE MORE THAN A LITTLE.
I CAN GO WITHOUT!!
TAMAKI AND KYOYA ARE PAYING FOR THE KARAOKE.
500 100 50 10
OKAY, I'LL BORROW THE MONEY FROM YOU.
CAN I GET ONE FOR HIKARU TOO?
KLINK
SELECT BEVERAGE
PLEASE!!
SURE.
COLD
TWO OF THE SAME?
YEP.
WE HAVE THE SAME TASTES.
TURN

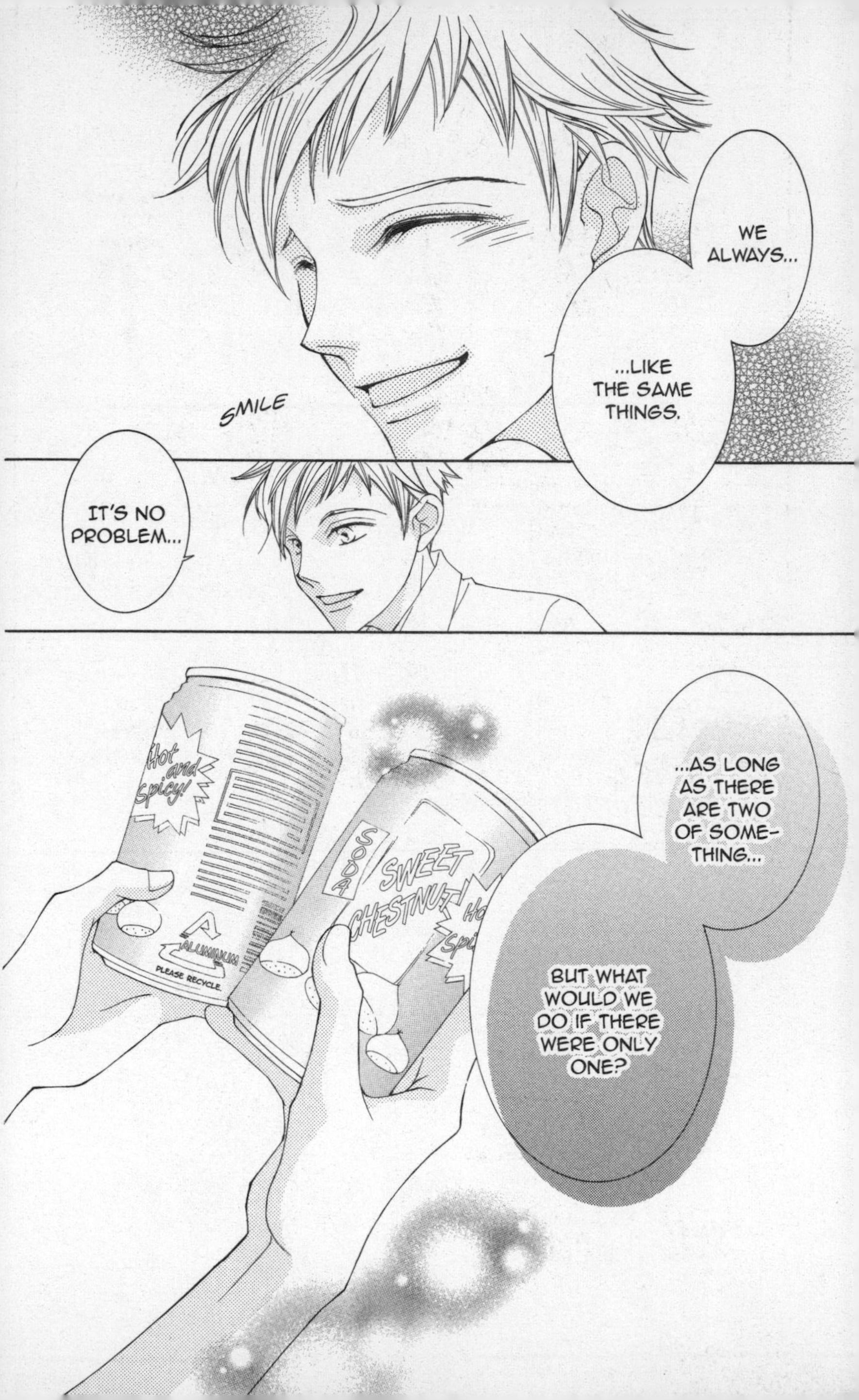
WE ALWAYS...
...LIKE THE SAME THINGS.
SMILE
IT'S NO PROBLEM...
...AS LONG AS THERE ARE TWO OF SOME-THING...
BUT WHAT WOULD WE DO IF THERE WERE ONLY ONE?
Hot and Spicy!
ALUMINUM
PLEASE RECYCLE
SODA
SWEET CHESTNUT!

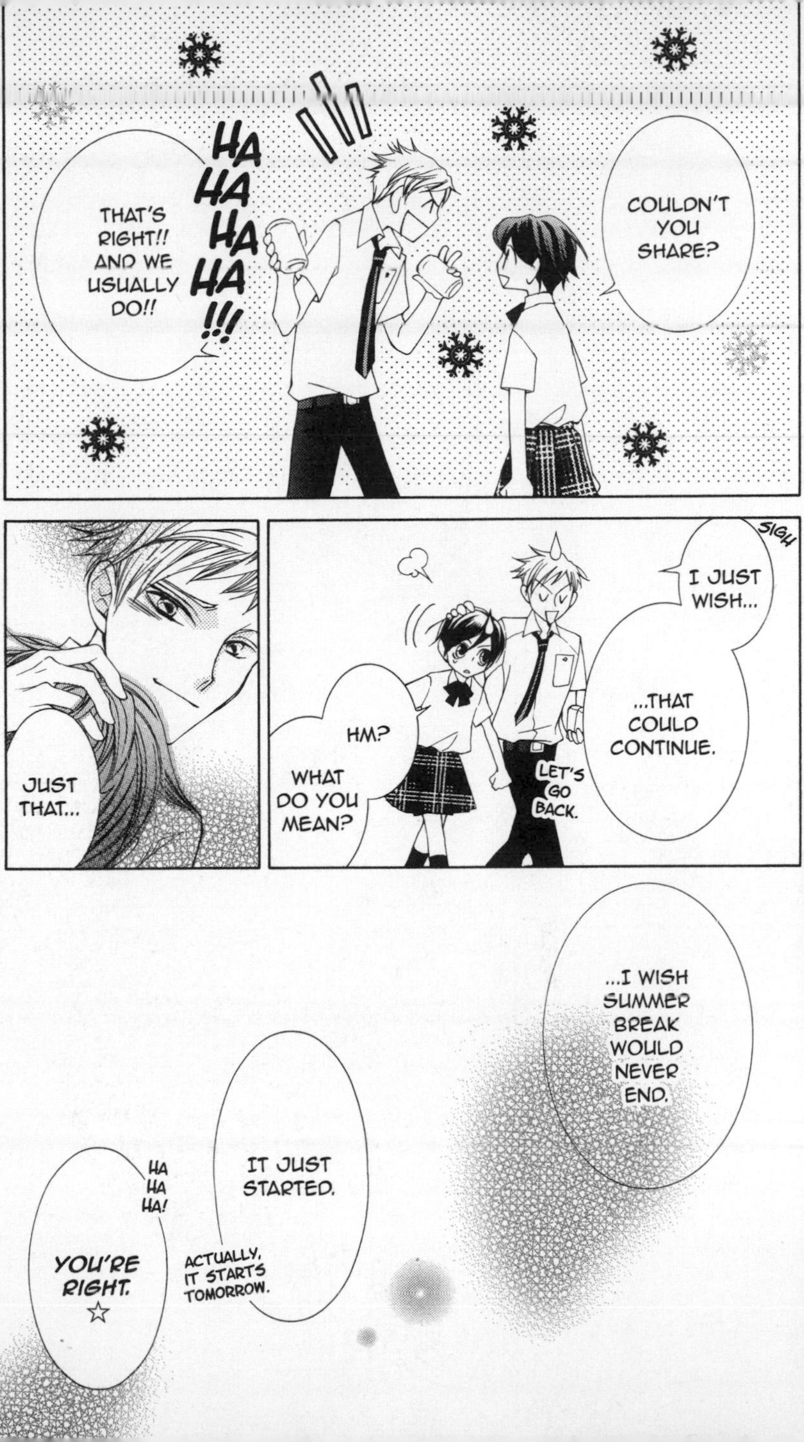
COULDN'T YOU SHARE?
HA HA HA HA HA!!!
THAT'S RIGHT!! AND WE USUALLY DO!!
SIGH
I JUST WISH...
...THAT COULD CONTINUE.
LET'S GO BACK.
HM? WHAT DO YOU MEAN?
JUST THAT...
...I WISH SUMMER BREAK WOULD NEVER END.
IT JUST STARTED.
ACTUALLY, IT STARTS TOMORROW.
HA HA HA!
YOU'RE RIGHT. ☆

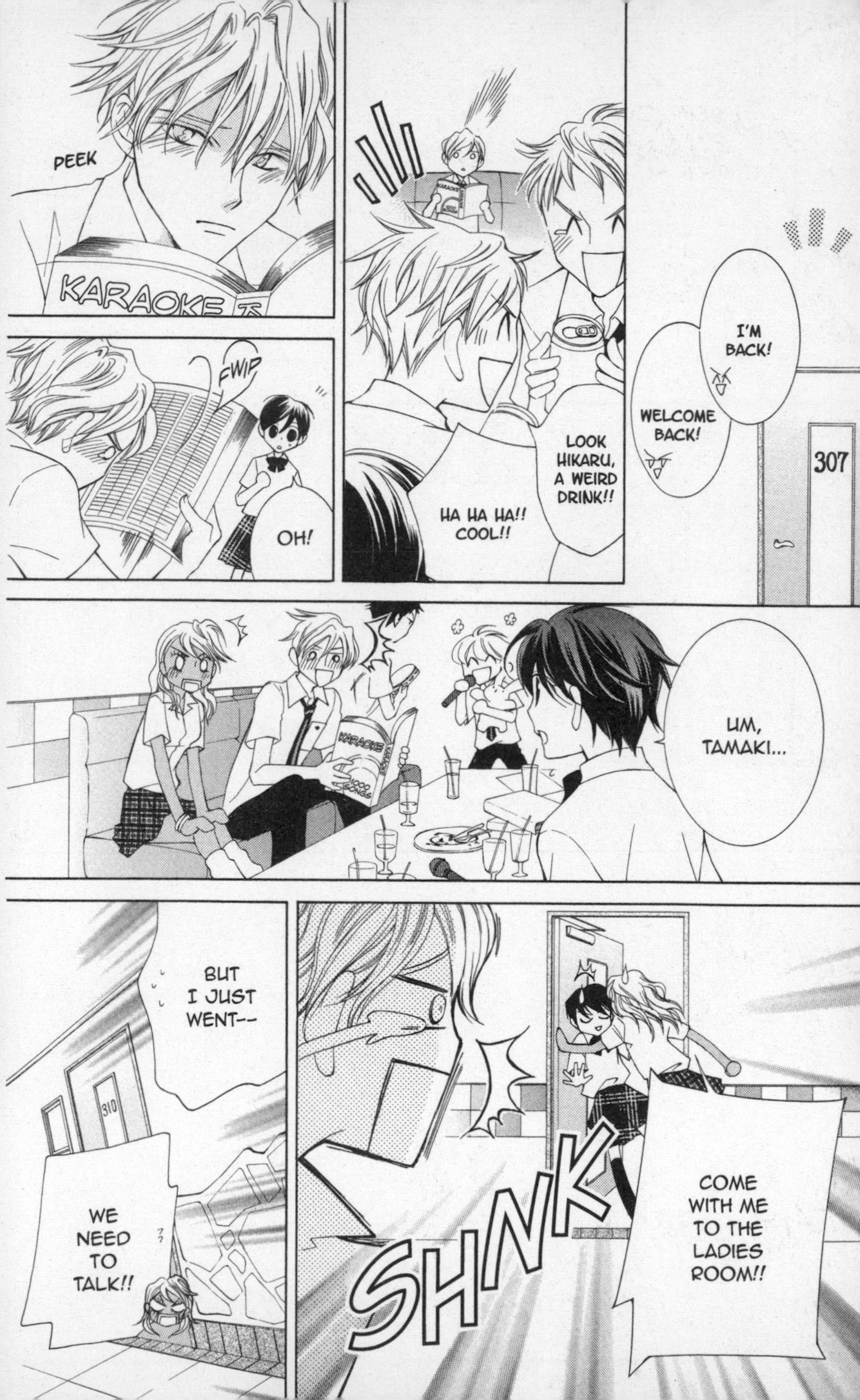
I'M BACK!
WELCOME BACK!
LOOK HIKARU, A WEIRD DRINK!!
HA HA HA!! COOL!!
PEEK
KARAOKE
FWIP
OH!
UM, TAMAKI...
KARAOKE
1000 SONGS
COME WITH ME TO THE LADIES ROOM!!
SHNK
BUT I JUST WENT--
WE NEED TO TALK!!

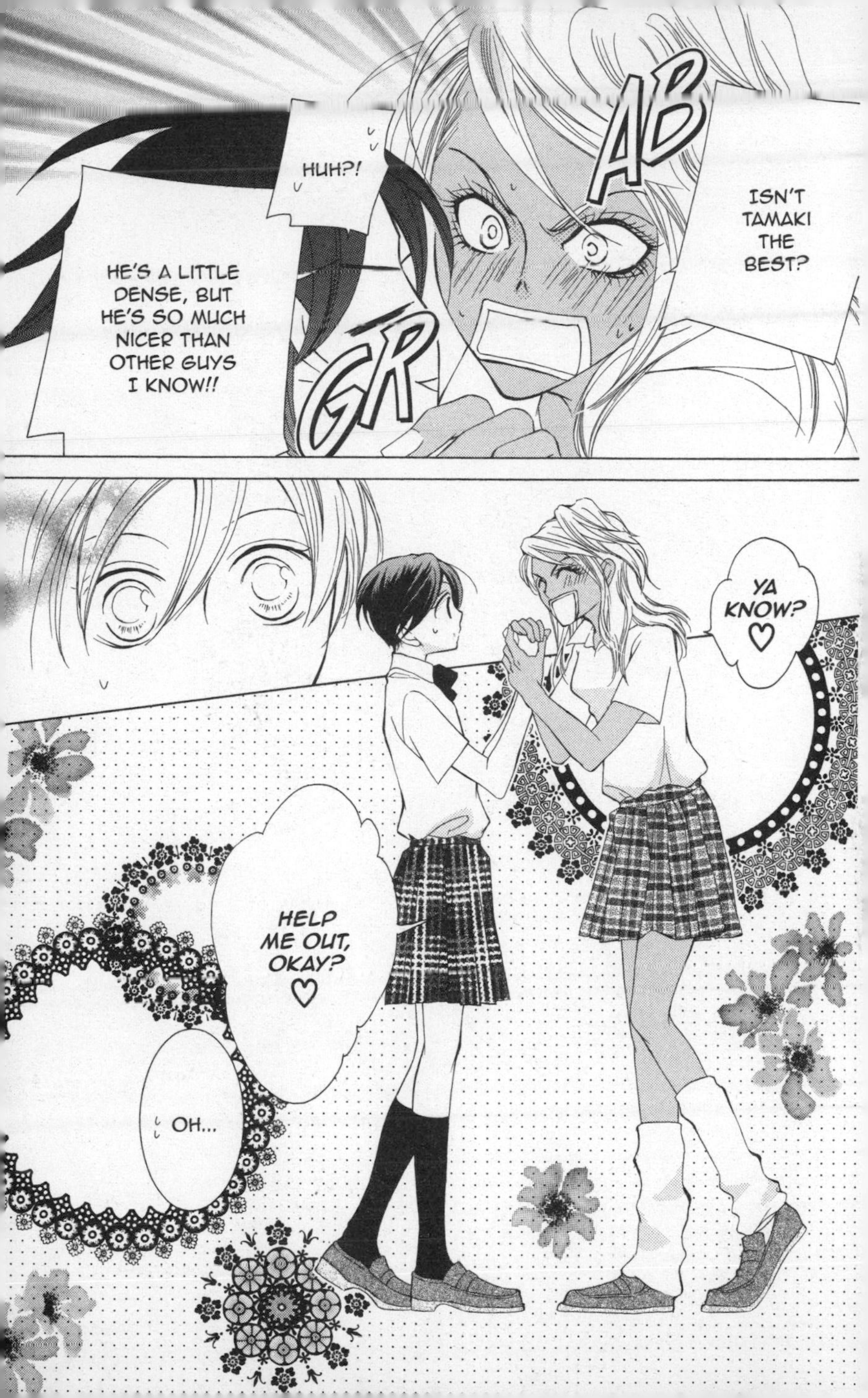
AB
ISN'T TAMAKI THE BEST?
HUH?!
HE'S A LITTLE DENSE, BUT HE'S SO MUCH NICER THAN OTHER GUYS I KNOW!!
GR
YA KNOW? ♡
HELP ME OUT, OKAY? ♡
OH...

GUEST ROOM: FAXES ②

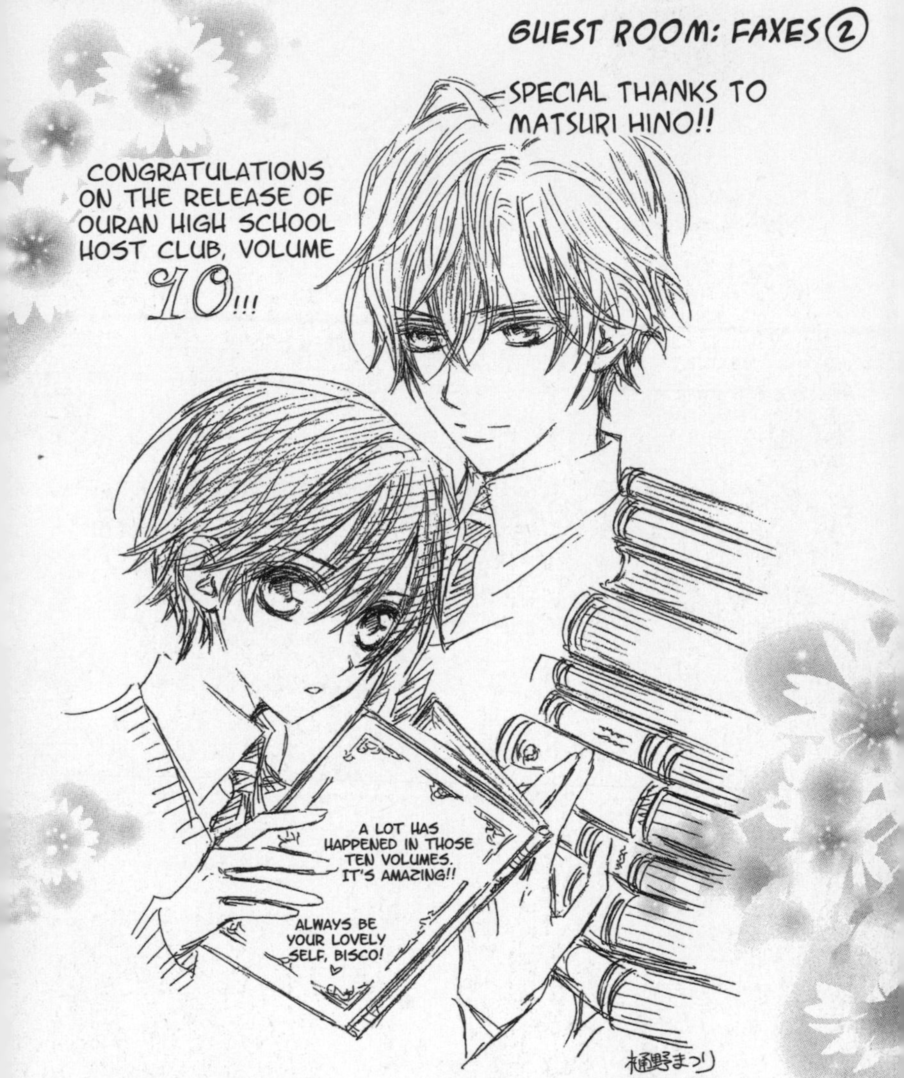

SPECIAL THANKS TO MATSURI HINO!!
CONGRATULATIONS ON THE RELEASE OF OURAN HIGH SCHOOL HOST CLUB, VOLUME 10!!!
A LOT HAS HAPPENED IN THOSE TEN VOLUMES. IT'S AMAZING!!
ALWAYS BE YOUR LOVELY SELF, BISCO! ♡
樋野まつり
MATSURI HINO

WHEN I GOT THIS FAX, I WOULDN'T HAVE MINDED DYING RIGHT THEN. I COULD CRY EVEN NOW. MAY I? I ABSOLUTELY LOVE THIS!! FROM NOW ON, I WANT EVERYONE TO CHANGE MY TAMAKI TO THIS ONE IN THEIR HEAD WHEN THEY READ *HOST CLUB*. SQUEE! HE'S SO COOL! (TEARS) I HIGHLY RESPECT MATSURI-SAN AS A SENPAI MANGAKA, AND AS A PERSON. SHE GAVE ME SOME WONDERFUL ADVICE ONCE WHEN I WAS IN TROUBLE. I'M ALWAYS GRATEFUL, MATSURI-SAN!! I'M A BIG FAN!!

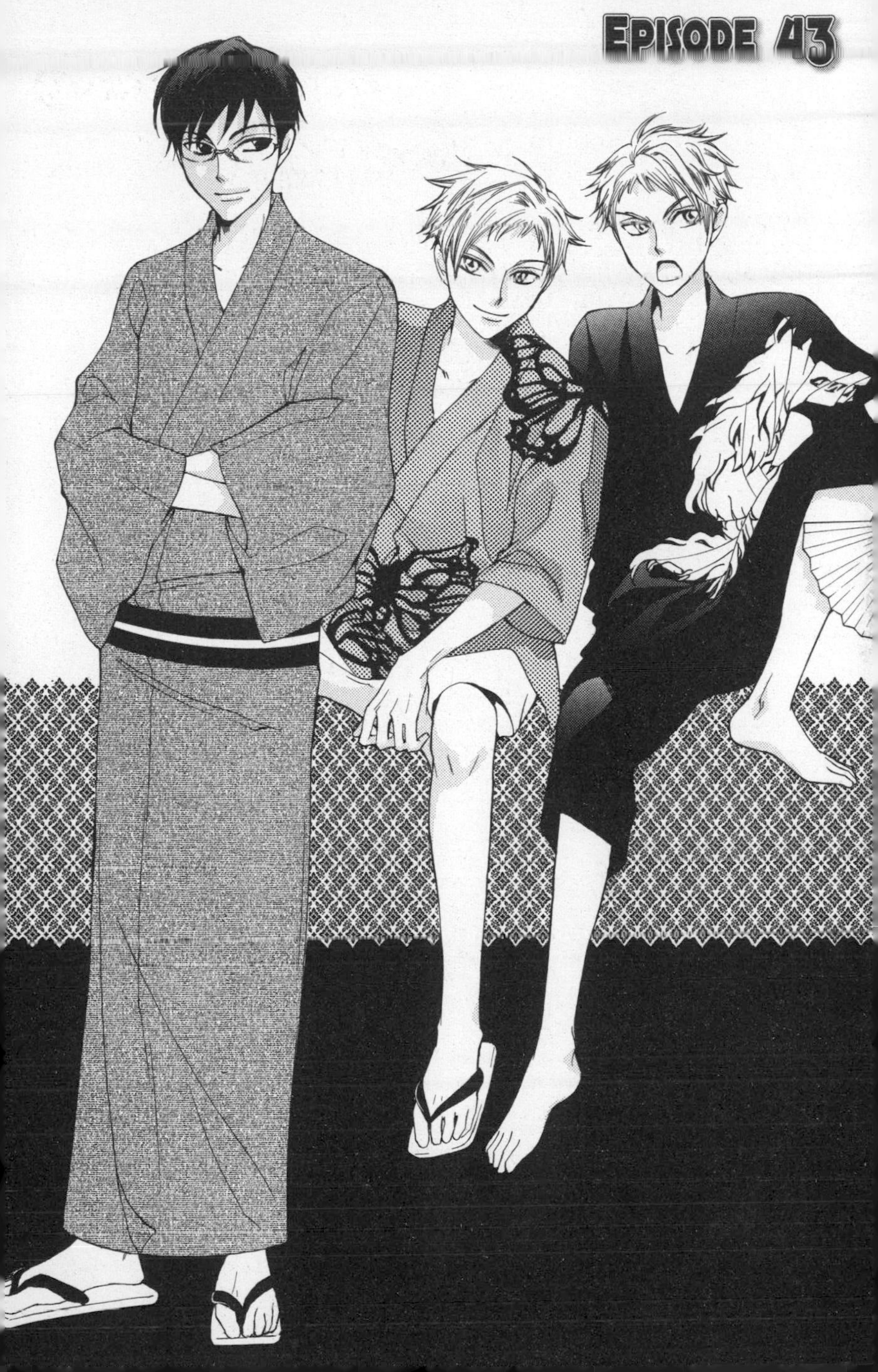
EPISODE 43

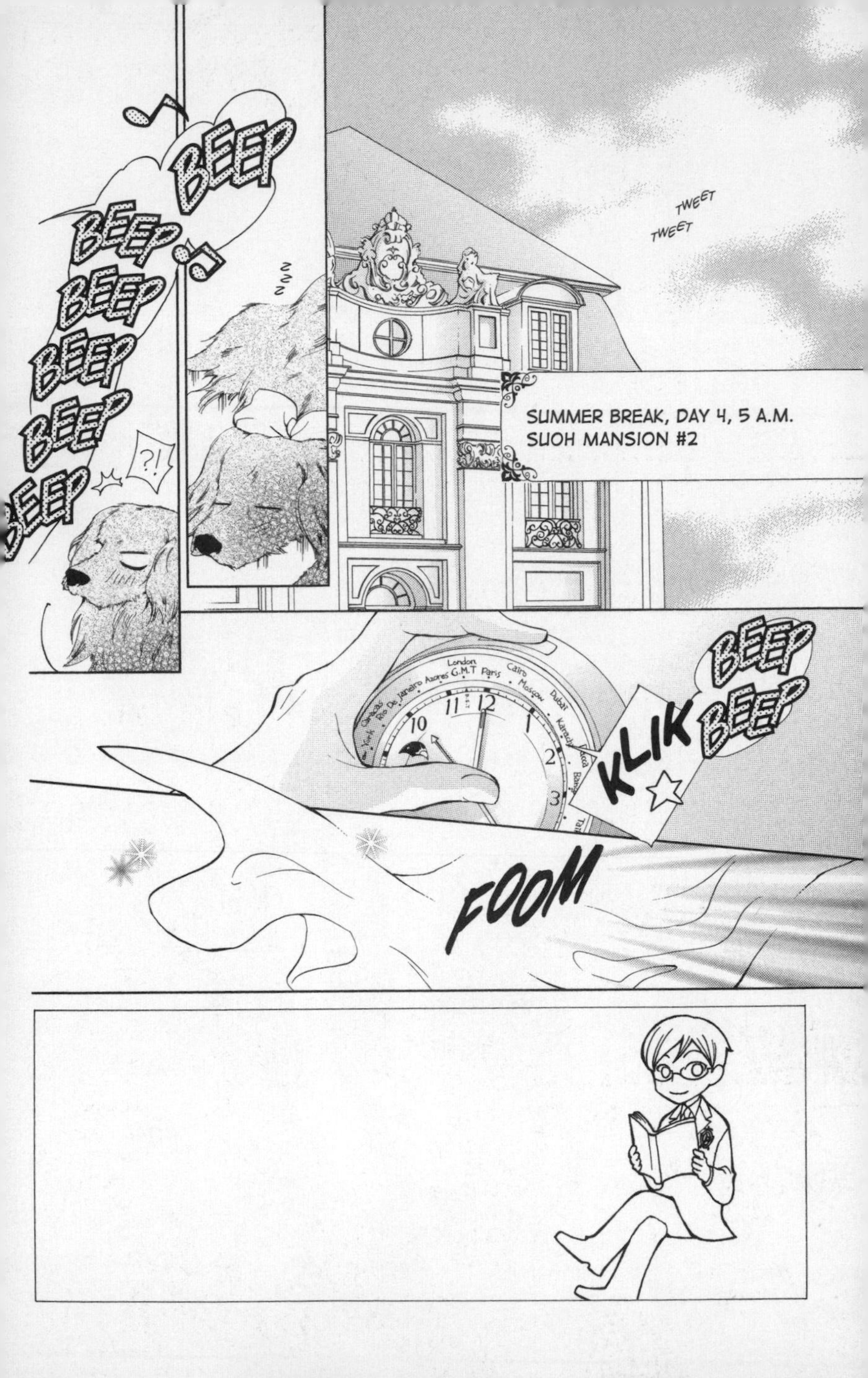
TWEET
TWEET
SUMMER BREAK, DAY 4, 5 A.M.
SUOH MANSION #2
ZZZ
BEEP
BEEP
BEEP
BEEP
BEEP
BEEP
?!
BEEP
BEEP
KLIK
London
G.M.T
Paris
Cairo
Moscow
Dubai
Azores
Rio De Janeiro
Caracas
FOOM

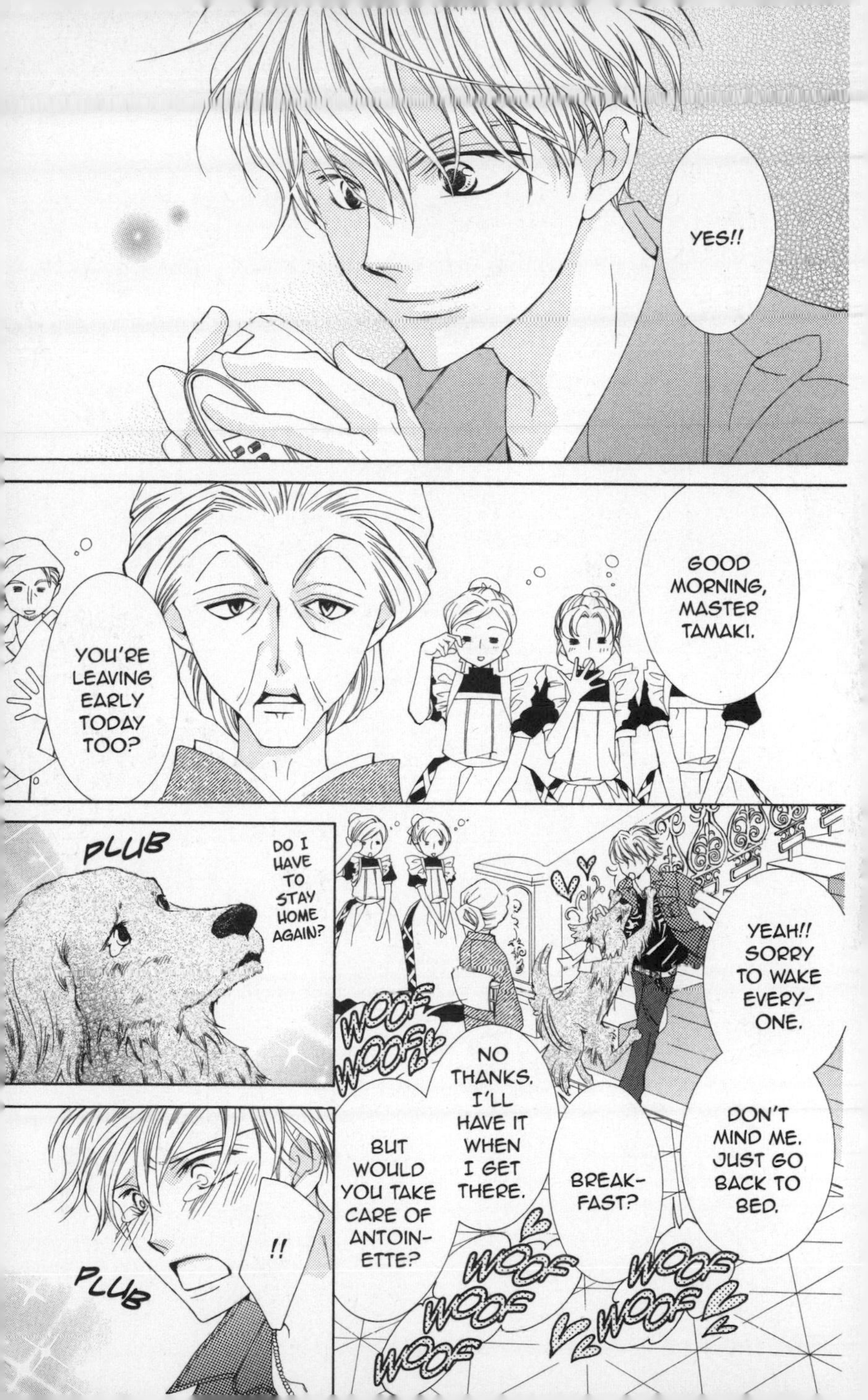
YES!!
GOOD MORNING, MASTER TAMAKI.
YOU'RE LEAVING EARLY TODAY TOO?
YEAH!! SORRY TO WAKE EVERY-ONE.
DON'T MIND ME. JUST GO BACK TO BED.
BREAK-FAST?
NO THANKS. I'LL HAVE IT WHEN I GET THERE.
BUT WOULD YOU TAKE CARE OF ANTOIN-ETTE?
WOOF WOOF
WOOF WOOF
WOOF WOOF WOOF
WOOF WOOF
PLUB
DO I HAVE TO STAY HOME AGAIN?
!!
PLUB

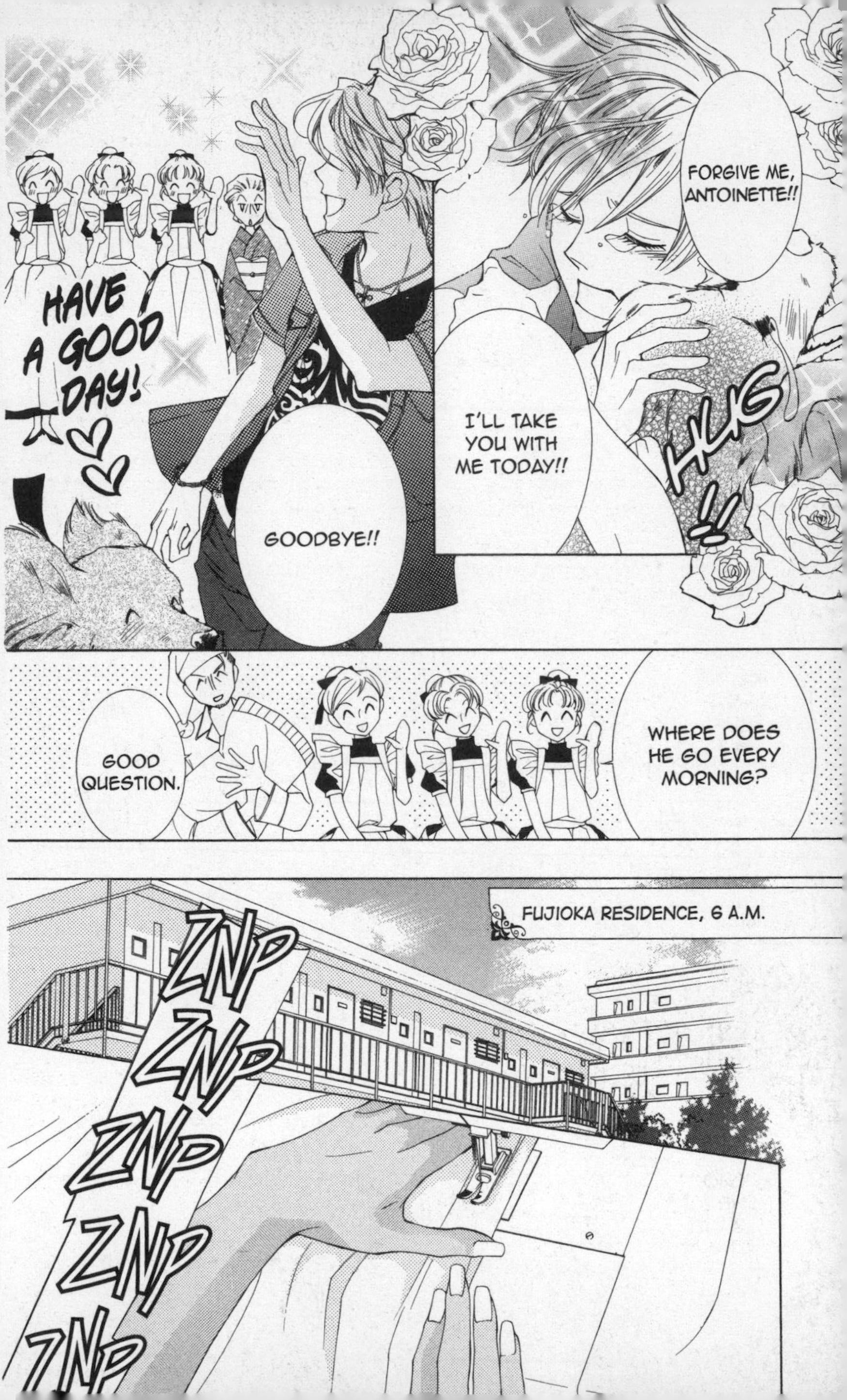
FORGIVE ME, ANTOINETTE!!
I'LL TAKE YOU WITH ME TODAY!!
HUG!!
GOODBYE!!
HAVE A GOOD DAY!
WHERE DOES HE GO EVERY MORNING?
GOOD QUESTION.
FUJIOKA RESIDENCE, 6 A.M.
ZNP ZNP ZNP ZNP ZNP ZNP

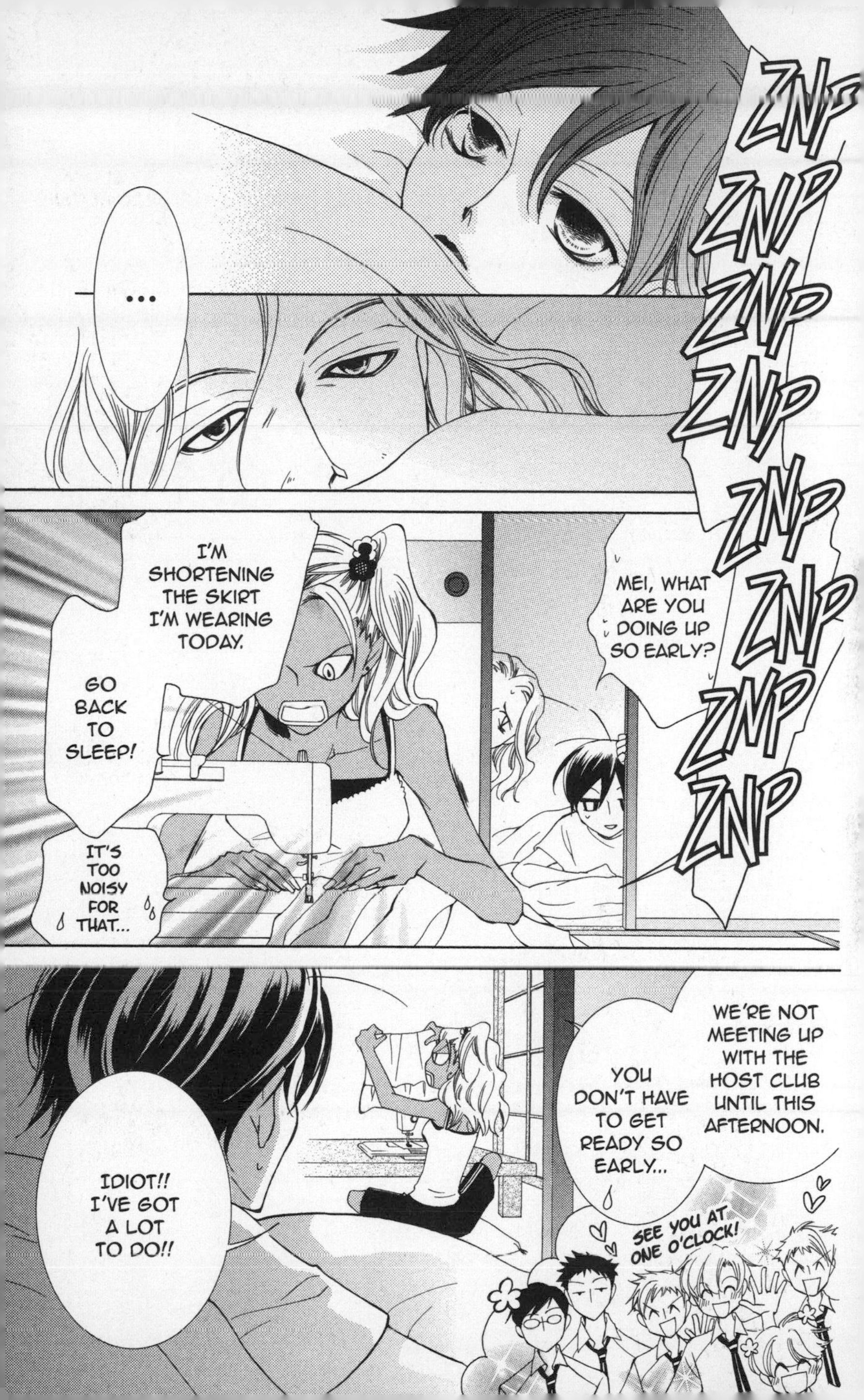
ZNP ZNP ZNP ZNP ZNP ZNP ZNP ZNP
...
MEI, WHAT ARE YOU DOING UP SO EARLY?
I'M SHORTENING THE SKIRT I'M WEARING TODAY.
GO BACK TO SLEEP!
IT'S TOO NOISY FOR THAT...
WE'RE NOT MEETING UP WITH THE HOST CLUB UNTIL THIS AFTERNOON.
YOU DON'T HAVE TO GET READY SO EARLY...
SEE YOU AT ONE O'CLOCK!
IDIOT!! I'VE GOT A LOT TO DO!!

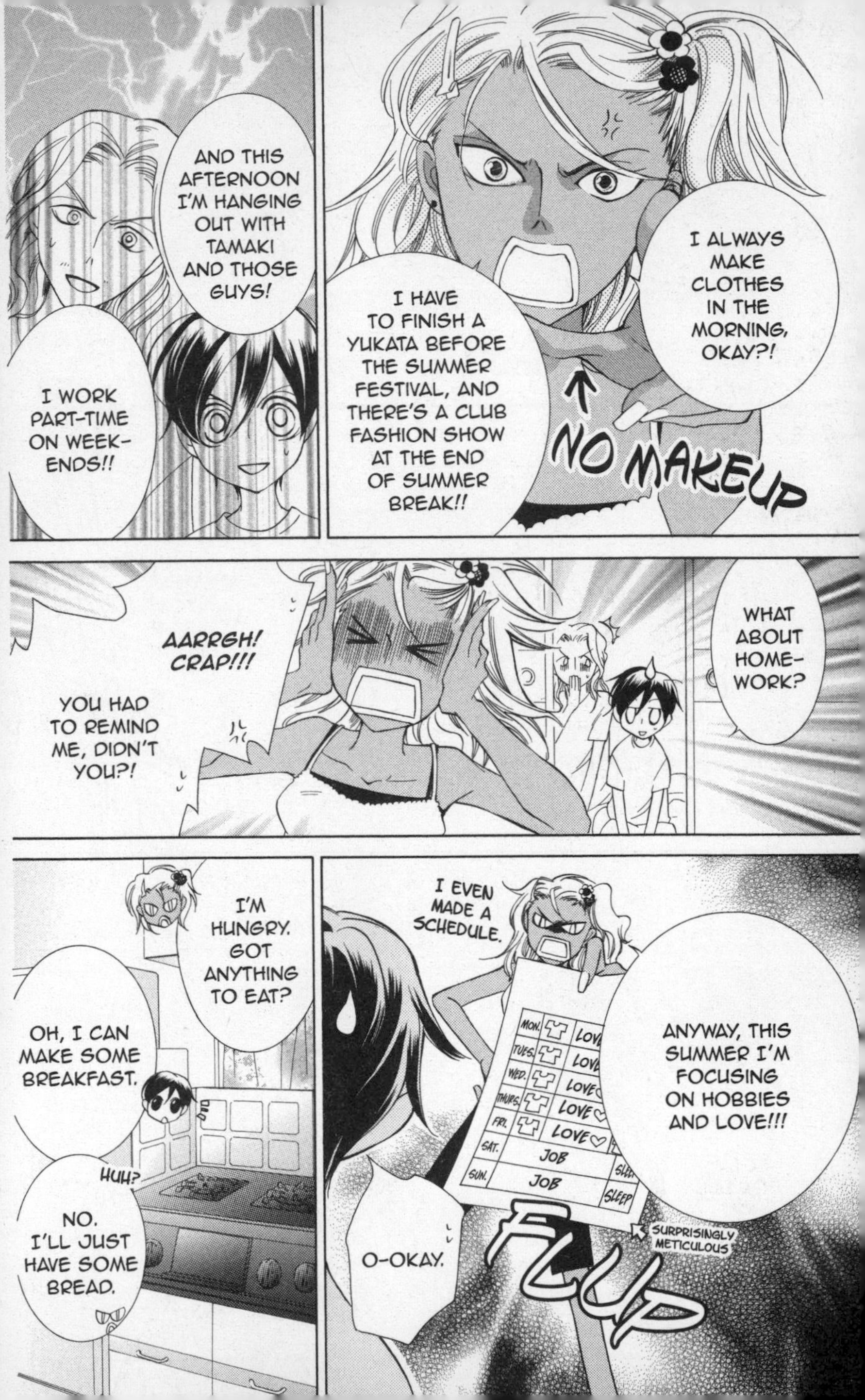
I ALWAYS MAKE CLOTHES IN THE MORNING, OKAY?!
I HAVE TO FINISH A YUKATA BEFORE THE SUMMER FESTIVAL, AND THERE'S A CLUB FASHION SHOW AT THE END OF SUMMER BREAK!!
NO MAKEUP
AND THIS AFTERNOON I'M HANGING OUT WITH TAMAKI AND THOSE GUYS!
I WORK PART-TIME ON WEEK-ENDS!!
WHAT ABOUT HOME-WORK?
AARRGH! CRAP!!!
YOU HAD TO REMIND ME, DIDN'T YOU?!
I EVEN MADE A SCHEDULE.
ANYWAY, THIS SUMMER I'M FOCUSING ON HOBBIES AND LOVE!!!
MON.
TUES.
WED.
THURS. LOVE♡
FRI. LOVE♡
SAT. JOB
SUN. JOB SLEEP
FLIP
SURPRISINGLY METICULOUS
O-OKAY.
I'M HUNGRY. GOT ANYTHING TO EAT?
OH, I CAN MAKE SOME BREAKFAST.
HUH?
NO. I'LL JUST HAVE SOME BREAD.

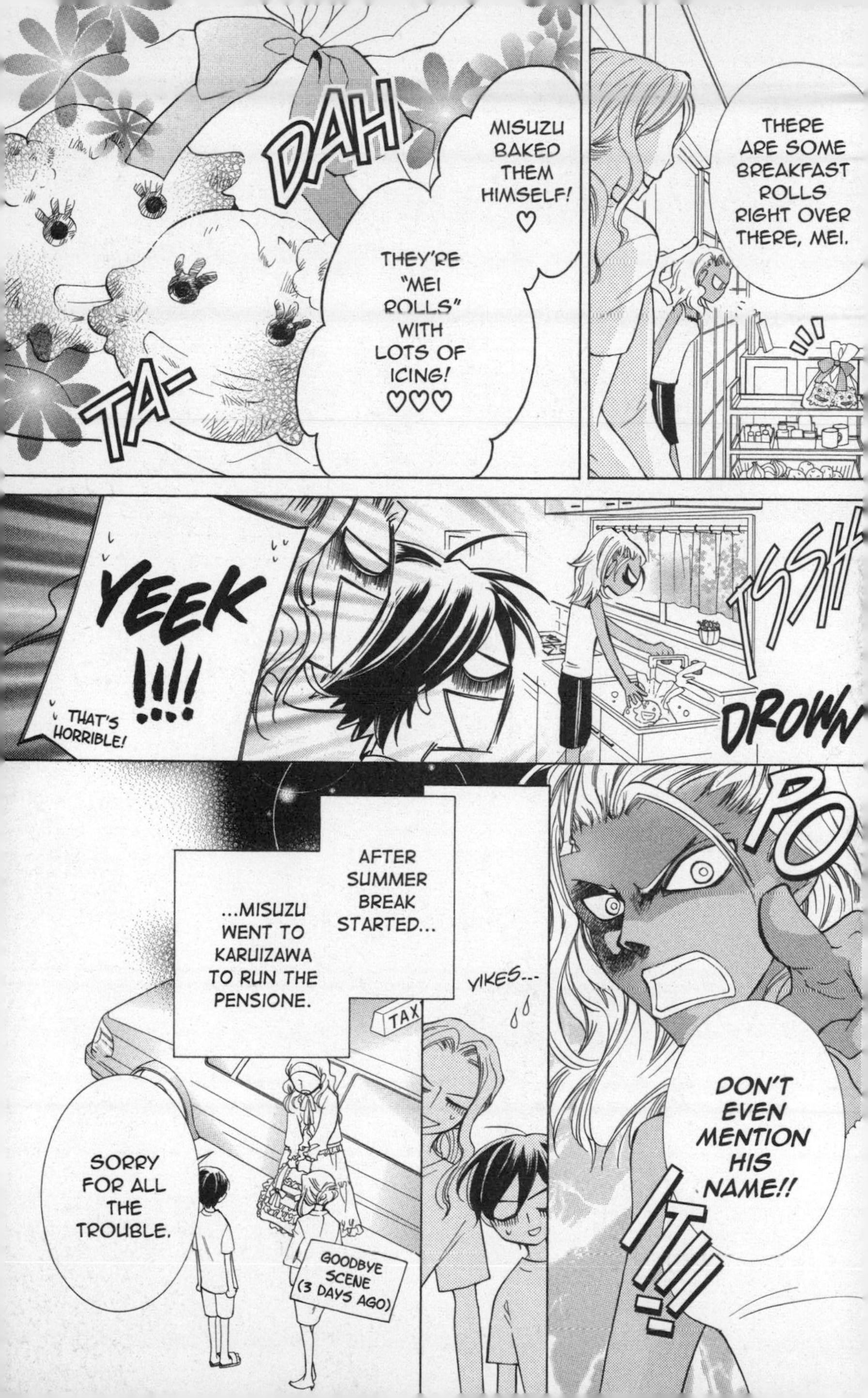
THERE ARE SOME BREAKFAST ROLLS RIGHT OVER THERE, MEI.
MISUZU BAKED THEM HIMSELF! ♡
THEY'RE "MEI ROLLS" WITH LOTS OF ICING! ♡♡♡
TA-
DAH
TSSH
DROWN
YEEK!!!!
THAT'S HORRIBLE!
PO
IT!!
DON'T EVEN MENTION HIS NAME!!
YIKES...
AFTER SUMMER BREAK STARTED...
...MISUZU WENT TO KARUIZAWA TO RUN THE PENSIONE.
TAX
SORRY FOR ALL THE TROUBLE.
GOODBYE SCENE (3 DAYS AGO)

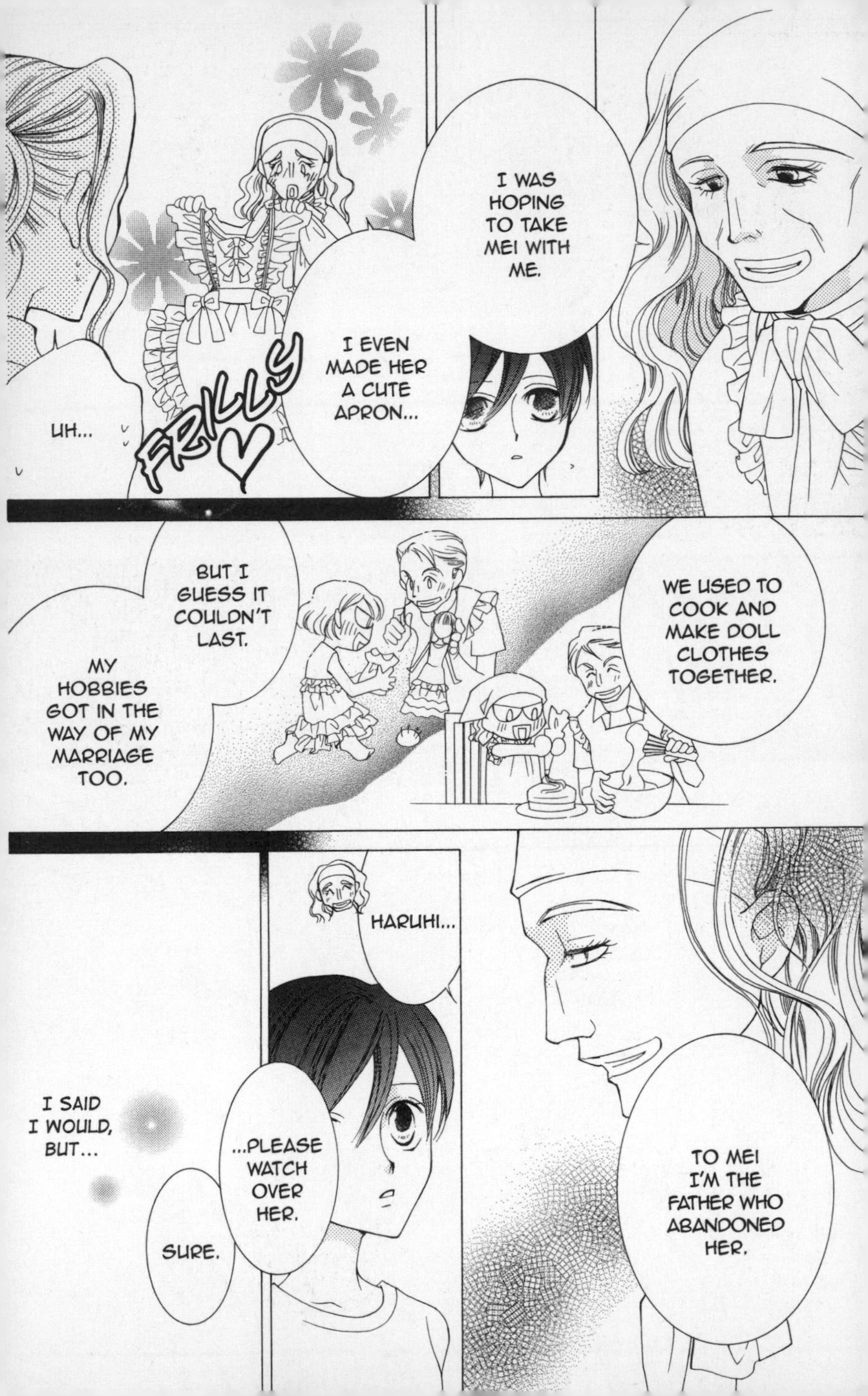
I WAS HOPING TO TAKE MEI WITH ME.
I EVEN MADE HER A CUTE APRON...
FRILLY ♥
UH...
WE USED TO COOK AND MAKE DOLL CLOTHES TOGETHER.
BUT I GUESS IT COULDN'T LAST.
MY HOBBIES GOT IN THE WAY OF MY MARRIAGE TOO.
TO MEI I'M THE FATHER WHO ABANDONED HER.
HARUHI...
...PLEASE WATCH OVER HER.
SURE.
I SAID I WOULD, BUT...

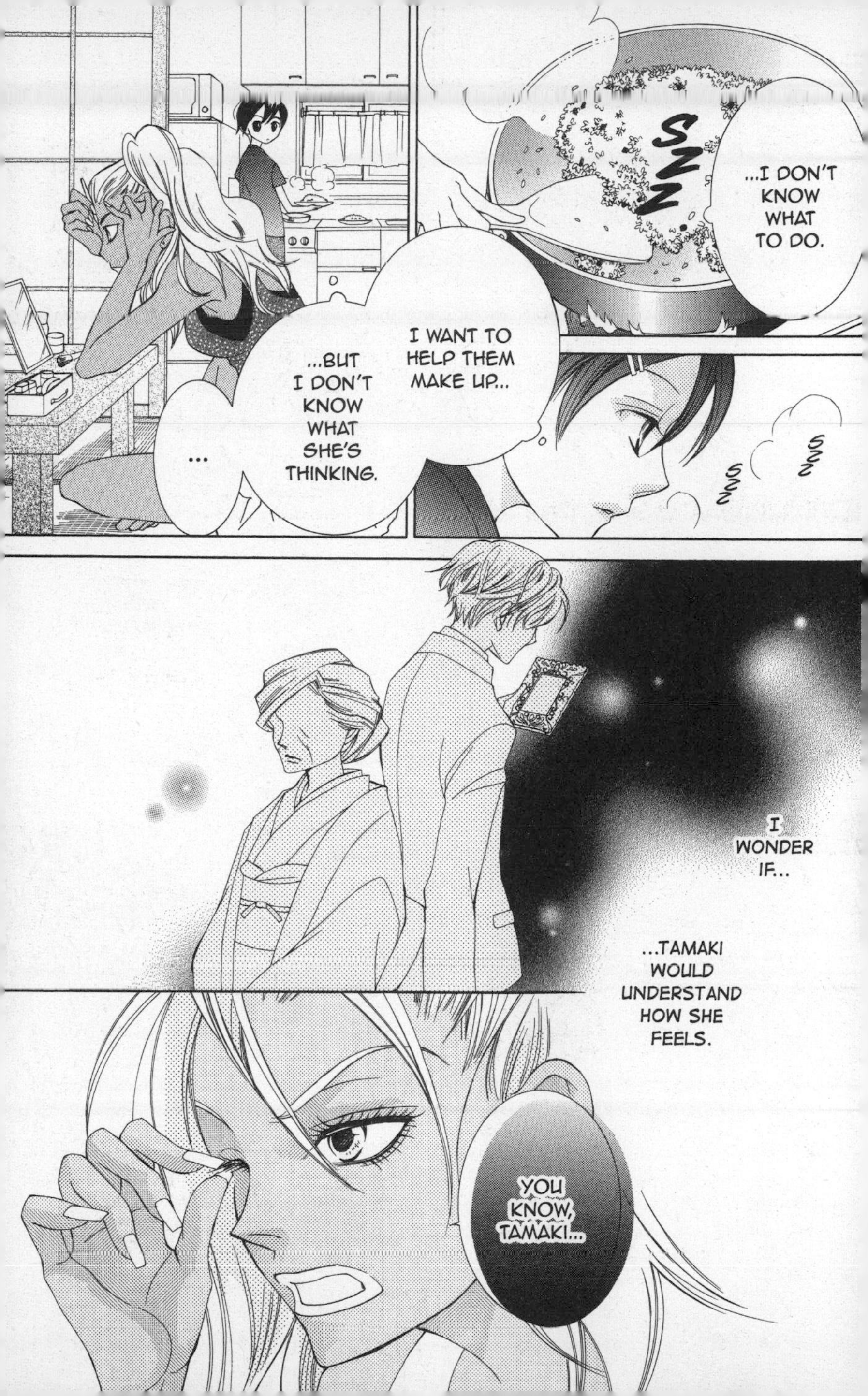
SZZ
...I DON'T KNOW WHAT TO DO.
I WANT TO HELP THEM MAKE UP...
...BUT I DON'T KNOW WHAT SHE'S THINKING.
SZZ
SZZ
...
I WONDER IF...
...TAMAKI WOULD UNDERSTAND HOW SHE FEELS.
YOU KNOW, TAMAKI...

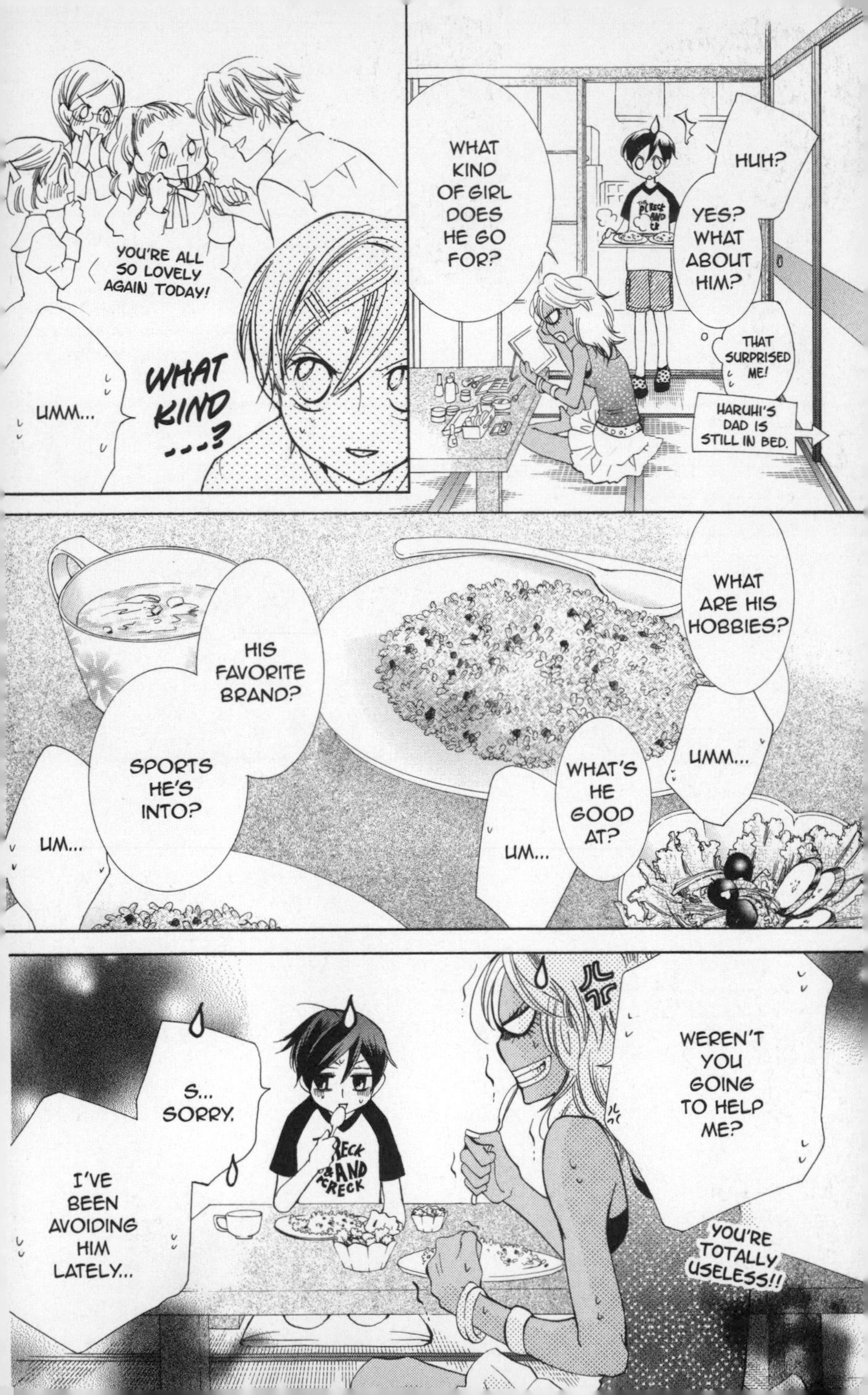
WHAT KIND OF GIRL DOES HE GO FOR?
HUH?
YES? WHAT ABOUT HIM?
THAT SURPRISED ME!
HARUHI'S DAD IS STILL IN BED.
YOU'RE ALL SO LOVELY AGAIN TODAY!
WHAT KIND ...?
UMM...
WHAT ARE HIS HOBBIES?
UMM...
WHAT'S HE GOOD AT?
UM...
HIS FAVORITE BRAND?
SPORTS HE'S INTO?
UM...
WEREN'T YOU GOING TO HELP ME?
YOU'RE TOTALLY USELESS!!
S... SORRY.
I'VE BEEN AVOIDING HIM LATELY...

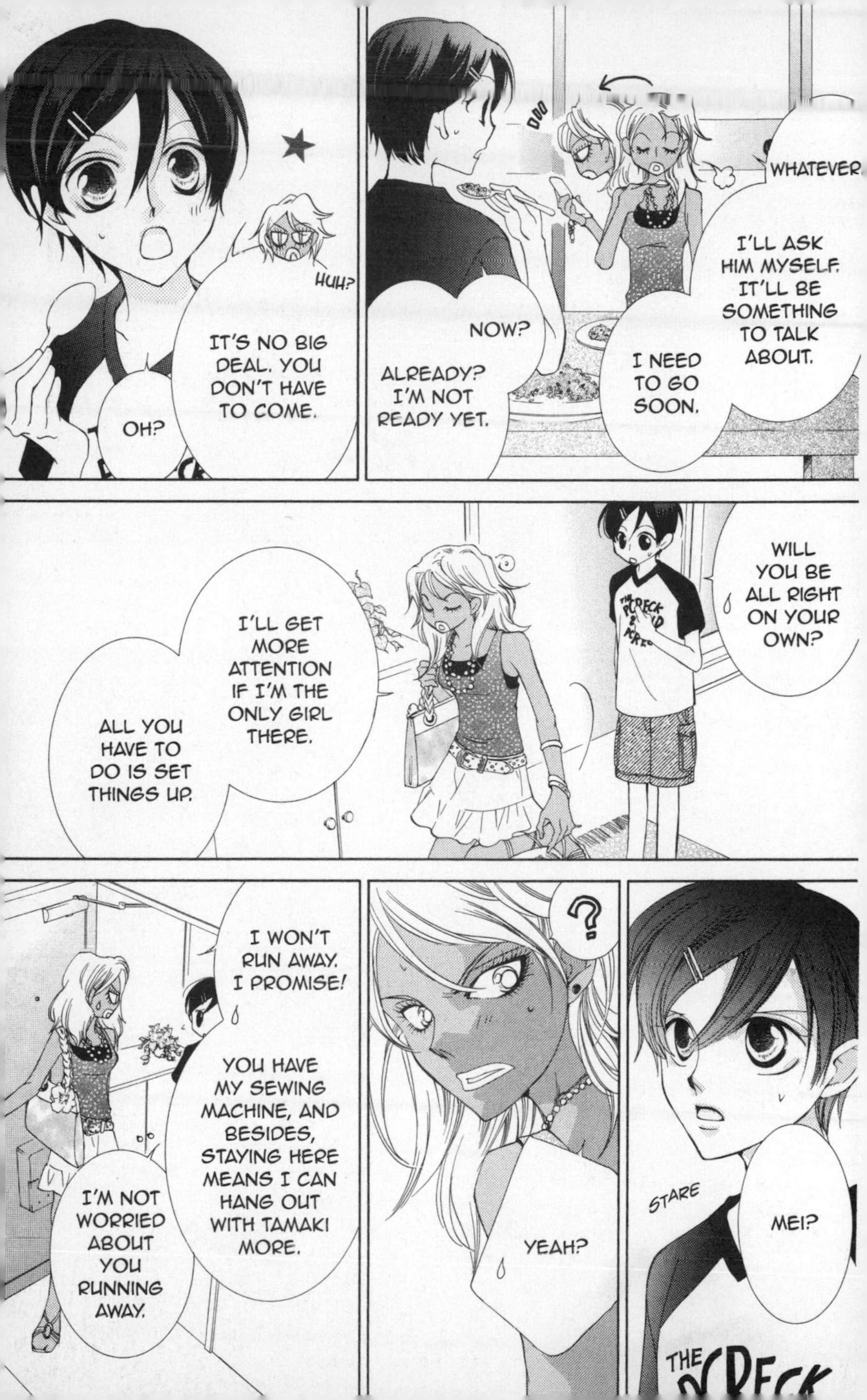
WHATEVER.
I'LL ASK HIM MYSELF. IT'LL BE SOMETHING TO TALK ABOUT.
I NEED TO GO SOON.
NOW?
ALREADY? I'M NOT READY YET.
HUH?
IT'S NO BIG DEAL. YOU DON'T HAVE TO COME.
OH?
WILL YOU BE ALL RIGHT ON YOUR OWN?
I'LL GET MORE ATTENTION IF I'M THE ONLY GIRL THERE.
ALL YOU HAVE TO DO IS SET THINGS UP.
MEI?
STARE
?
YEAH?
I WON'T RUN AWAY. I PROMISE!
YOU HAVE MY SEWING MACHINE, AND BESIDES, STAYING HERE MEANS I CAN HANG OUT WITH TAMAKI MORE.
I'M NOT WORRIED ABOUT YOU RUNNING AWAY.

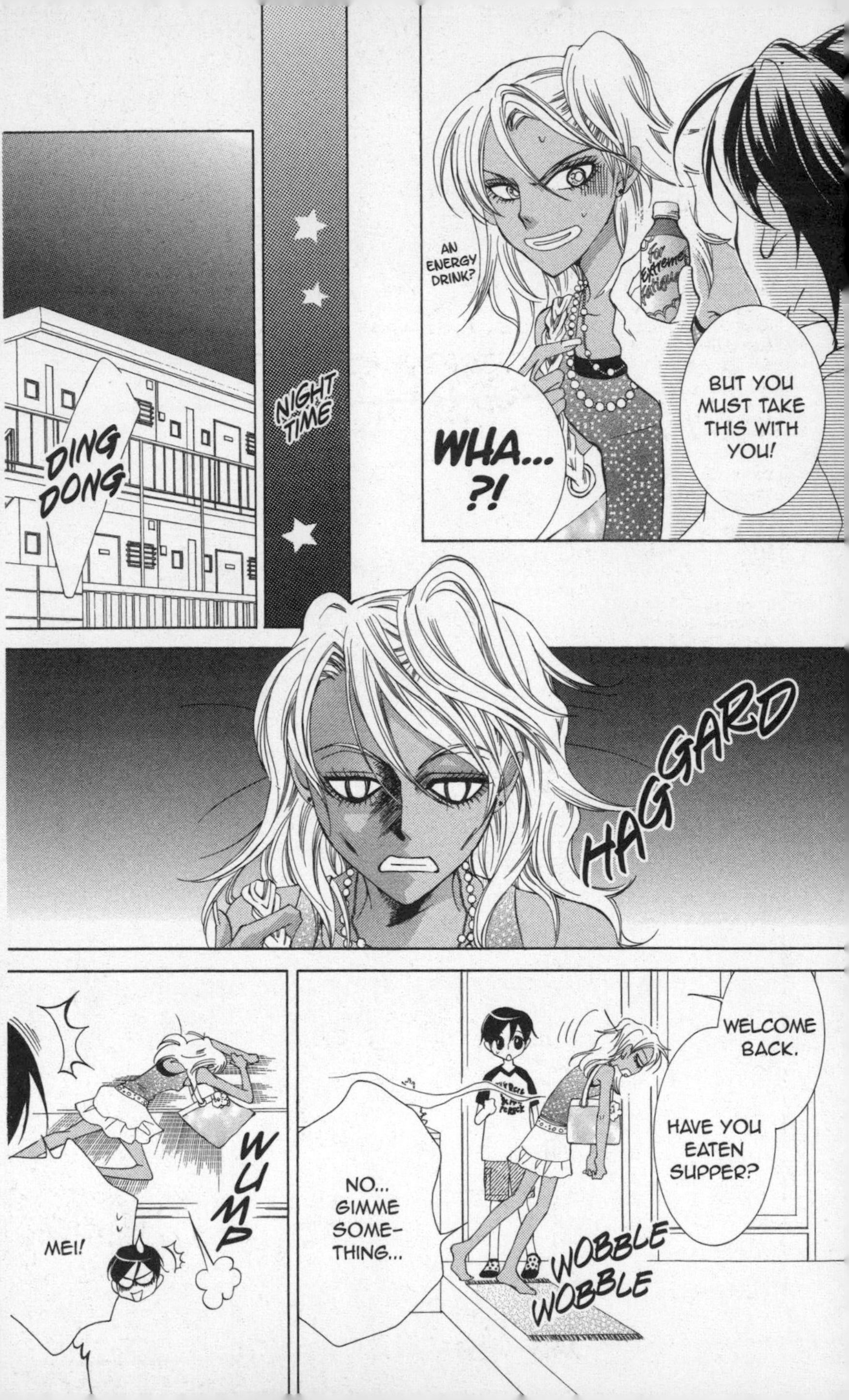
BUT YOU MUST TAKE THIS WITH YOU!
WHA...?!
For Extreme Fatigue
AN ENERGY DRINK?
NIGHT TIME
DING DONG
HAGGARD
WELCOME BACK.
HAVE YOU EATEN SUPPER?
NO... GIMME SOME-THING...
WOBBLE WOBBLE
WUMP
MEI!

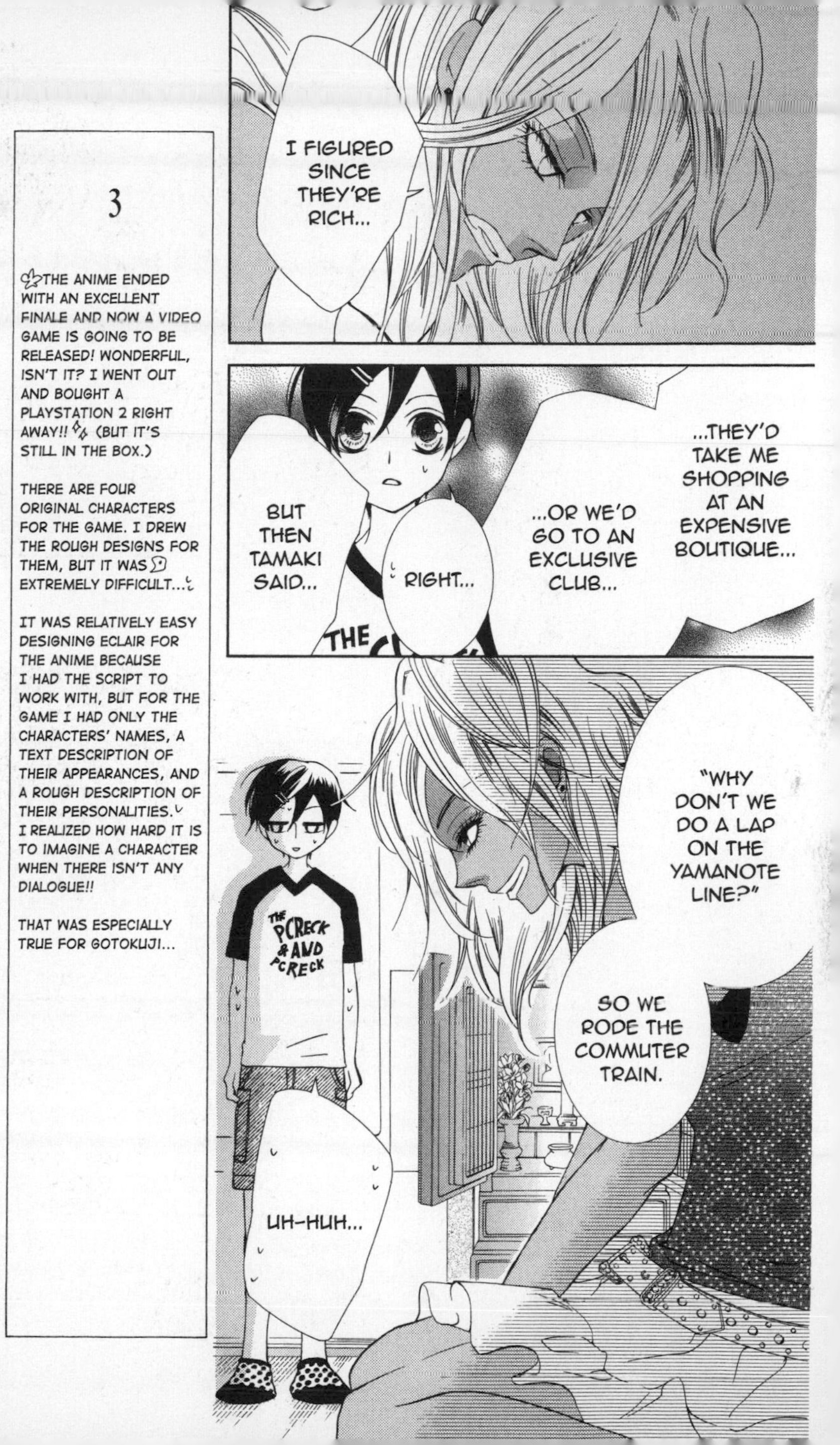
I FIGURED SINCE THEY'RE RICH...
...THEY'D TAKE ME SHOPPING AT AN EXPENSIVE BOUTIQUE...
...OR WE'D GO TO AN EXCLUSIVE CLUB...
RIGHT...
BUT THEN TAMAKI SAID...
"WHY DON'T WE DO A LAP ON THE YAMANOTE LINE?"
SO WE RODE THE COMMUTER TRAIN.
UH-HUH...

3

THE ANIME ENDED WITH AN EXCELLENT FINALE AND NOW A VIDEO GAME IS GOING TO BE RELEASED! WONDERFUL, ISN'T IT? I WENT OUT AND BOUGHT A PLAYSTATION 2 RIGHT AWAY!! (BUT IT'S STILL IN THE BOX.)

THERE ARE FOUR ORIGINAL CHARACTERS FOR THE GAME. I DREW THE ROUGH DESIGNS FOR THEM, BUT IT WAS EXTREMELY DIFFICULT...

IT WAS RELATIVELY EASY DESIGNING ECLAIR FOR THE ANIME BECAUSE I HAD THE SCRIPT TO WORK WITH, BUT FOR THE GAME I HAD ONLY THE CHARACTERS' NAMES, A TEXT DESCRIPTION OF THEIR APPEARANCES, AND A ROUGH DESCRIPTION OF THEIR PERSONALITIES. I REALIZED HOW HARD IT IS TO IMAGINE A CHARACTER WHEN THERE ISN'T ANY DIALOGUE!!

THAT WAS ESPECIALLY TRUE FOR GOTOKUJI...

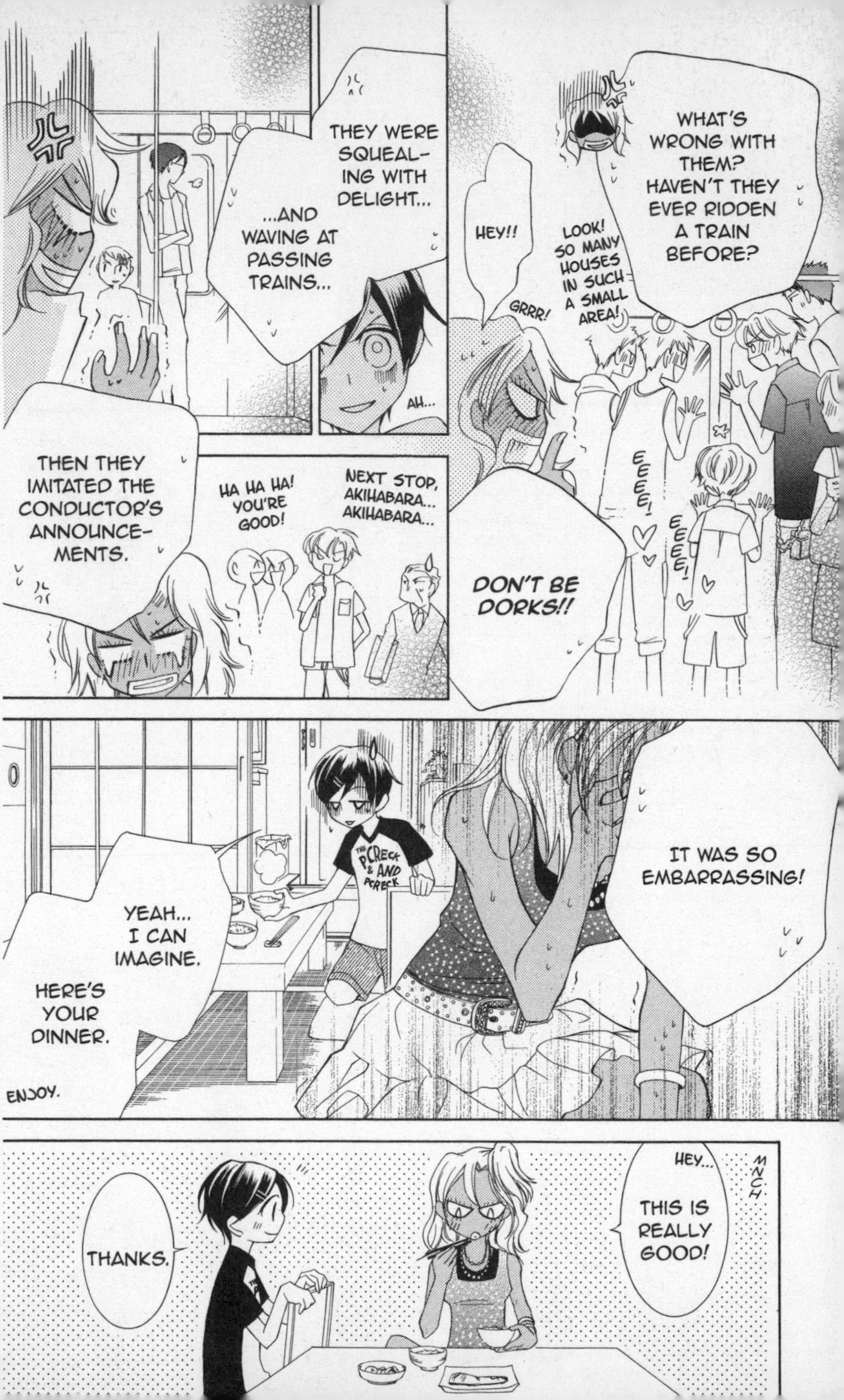
WHAT'S WRONG WITH THEM? HAVEN'T THEY EVER RIDDEN A TRAIN BEFORE?
HEY!!
LOOK! SO MANY HOUSES IN SUCH A SMALL AREA!
GRRR!
EEEE!
EEEE!
DON'T BE DORKS!!
THEY WERE SQUEALING WITH DELIGHT...
...AND WAVING AT PASSING TRAINS...
AH...
NEXT STOP, AKIHABARA... AKIHABARA...
HA HA HA! YOU'RE GOOD!
THEN THEY IMITATED THE CONDUCTOR'S ANNOUNCEMENTS.
IT WAS SO EMBARRASSING!
YEAH... I CAN IMAGINE.
HERE'S YOUR DINNER.
ENJOY.
MNCH
HEY...
THIS IS REALLY GOOD!
THANKS.

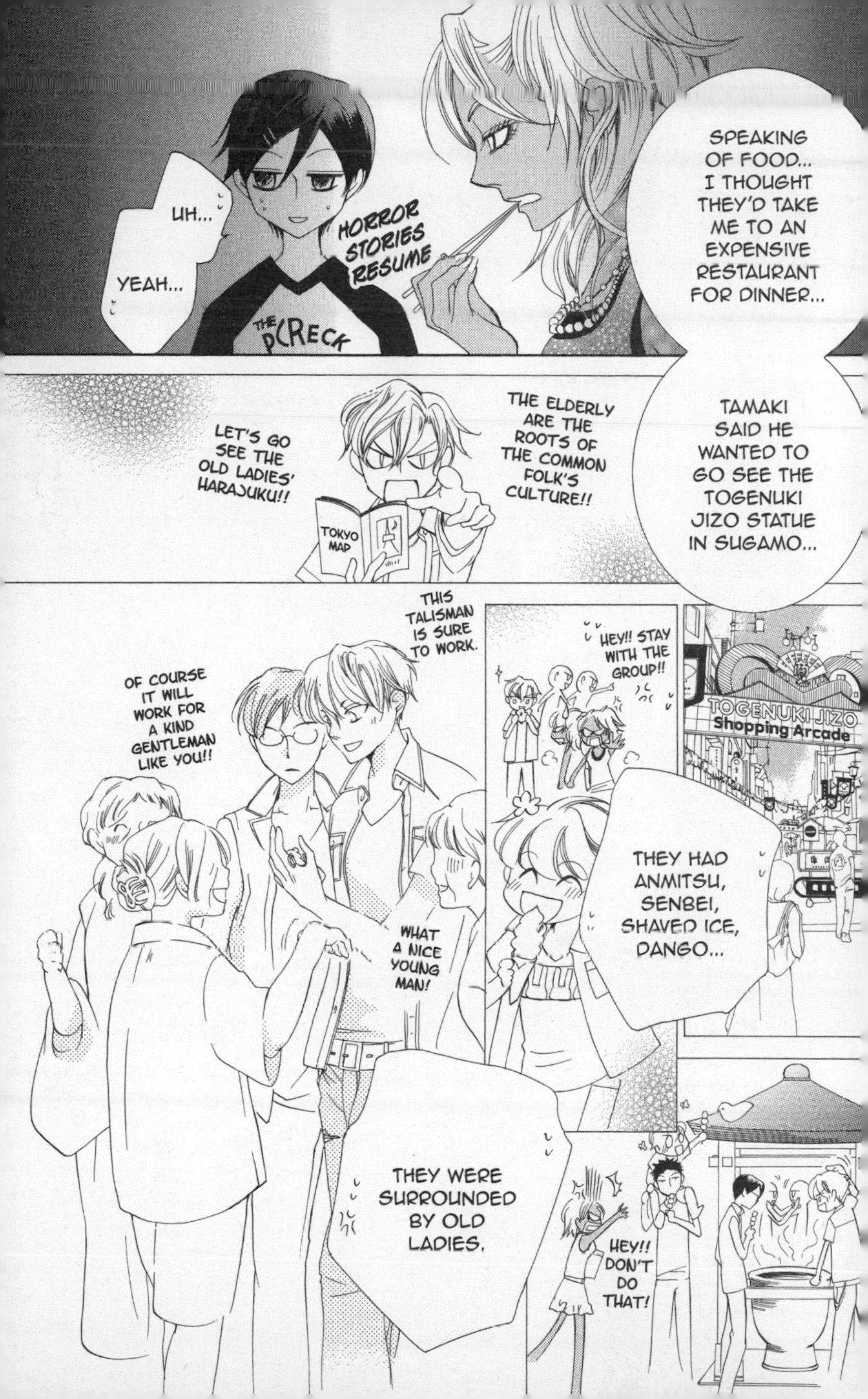
SPEAKING OF FOOD... I THOUGHT THEY'D TAKE ME TO AN EXPENSIVE RESTAURANT FOR DINNER...
HORROR STORIES RESUME
UH...
YEAH...
TAMAKI SAID HE WANTED TO GO SEE THE TOGENUKI JIZO STATUE IN SUGAMO...
THE ELDERLY ARE THE ROOTS OF THE COMMON FOLK'S CULTURE!!
LET'S GO SEE THE OLD LADIES' HARAJUKU!!
TOKYO MAP
TOGENUKI JIZO Shopping Arcade
HEY!! STAY WITH THE GROUP!!
THEY HAD ANMITSU, SENBEI, SHAVED ICE, DANGO...
HEY!! DON'T DO THAT!
THIS TALISMAN IS SURE TO WORK.
OF COURSE IT WILL WORK FOR A KIND GENTLEMAN LIKE YOU!!
WHAT A NICE YOUNG MAN!
THEY WERE SURROUNDED BY OLD LADIES.

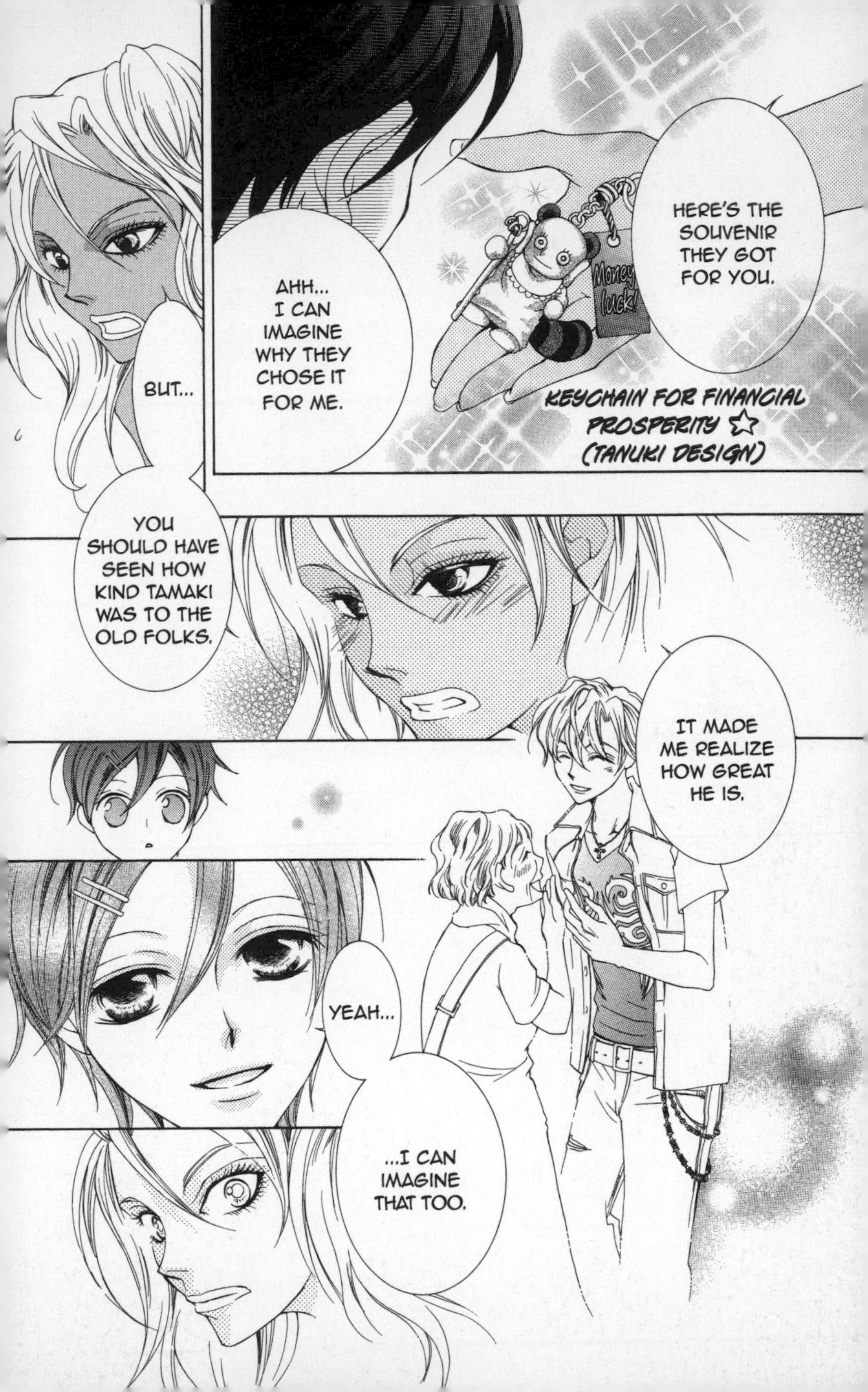
HERE'S THE SOUVENIR THEY GOT FOR YOU.
Money luck!
KEYCHAIN FOR FINANCIAL PROSPERITY ☆ (TANUKI DESIGN)
AHH... I CAN IMAGINE WHY THEY CHOSE IT FOR ME.
BUT...
YOU SHOULD HAVE SEEN HOW KIND TAMAKI WAS TO THE OLD FOLKS.
IT MADE ME REALIZE HOW GREAT HE IS.
YEAH...
...I CAN IMAGINE THAT TOO.

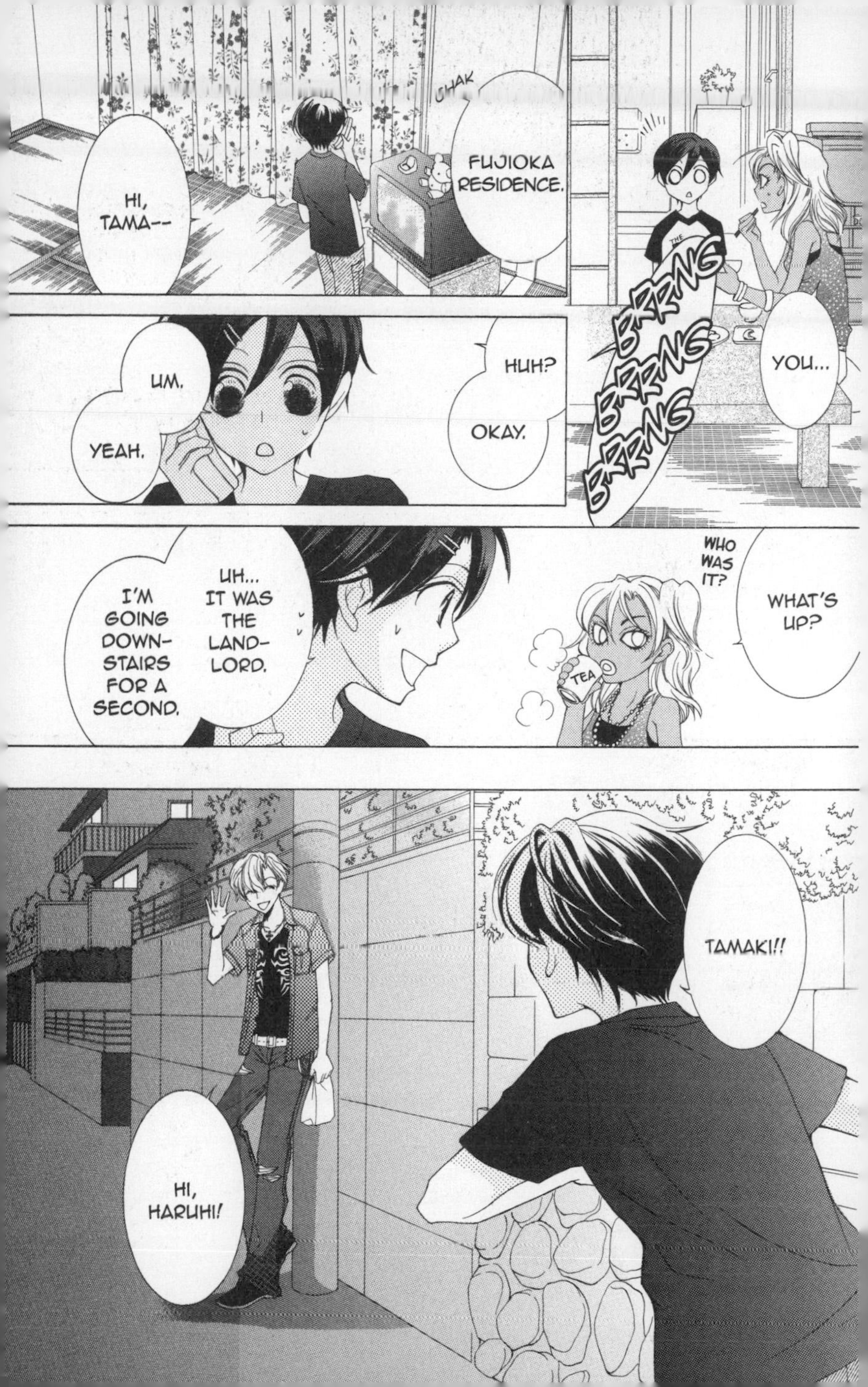
BRRNG BRRNG BRRNG
YOU...
CHAK
FUJIOKA RESIDENCE.
HI, TAMA--
HUH? OKAY.
UM. YEAH.
WHAT'S UP?
WHO WAS IT?
UH... IT WAS THE LANDLORD.
I'M GOING DOWNSTAIRS FOR A SECOND.
TEA
TAMAKI!!
HI, HARUHI!

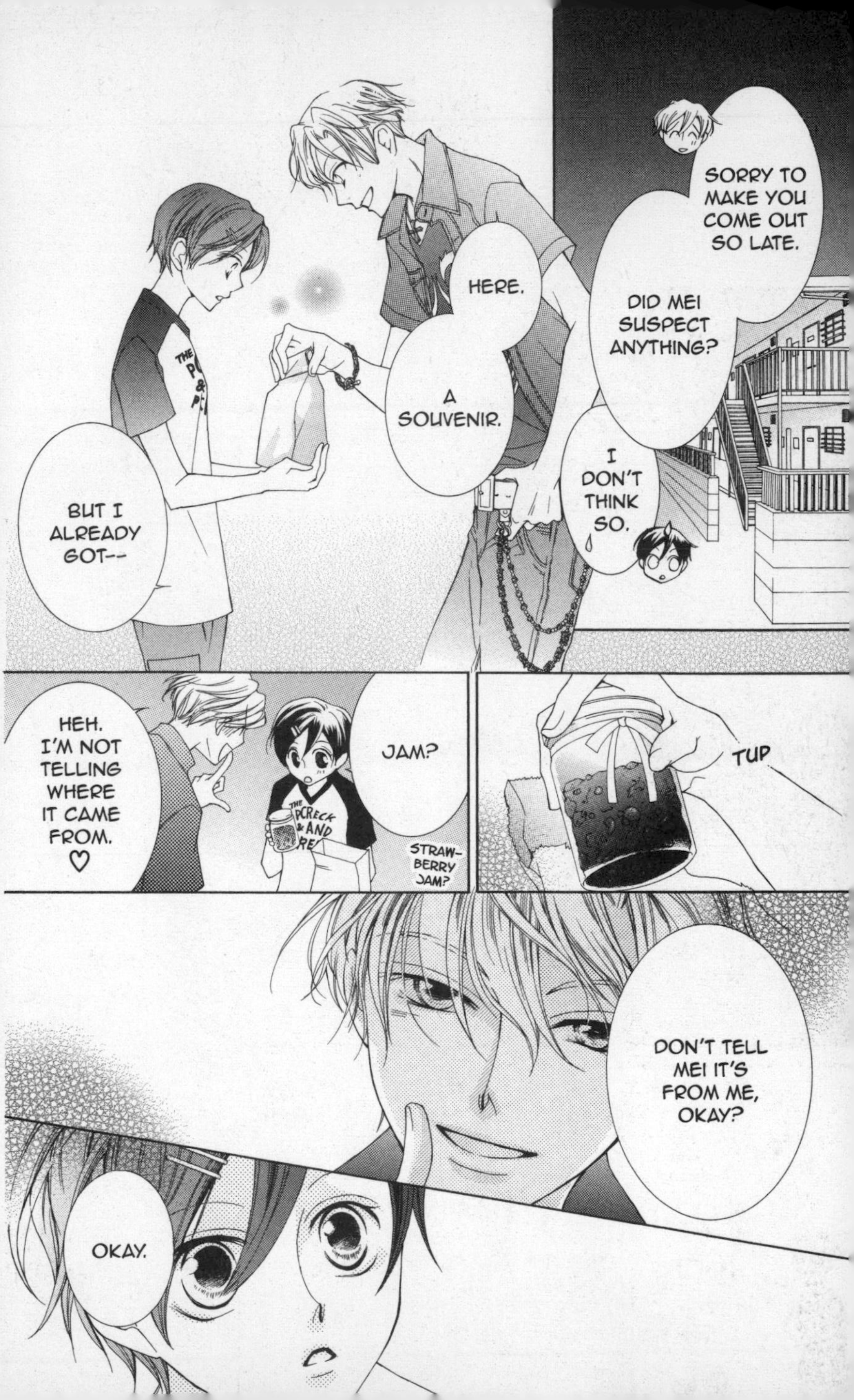
SORRY TO MAKE YOU COME OUT SO LATE.
DID MEI SUSPECT ANYTHING?
I DON'T THINK SO.
HERE.
A SOUVENIR.
BUT I ALREADY GOT--
TUP
JAM?
STRAWBERRY JAM?
HEH. I'M NOT TELLING WHERE IT CAME FROM. ♡
DON'T TELL MEI IT'S FROM ME, OKAY?
OKAY.

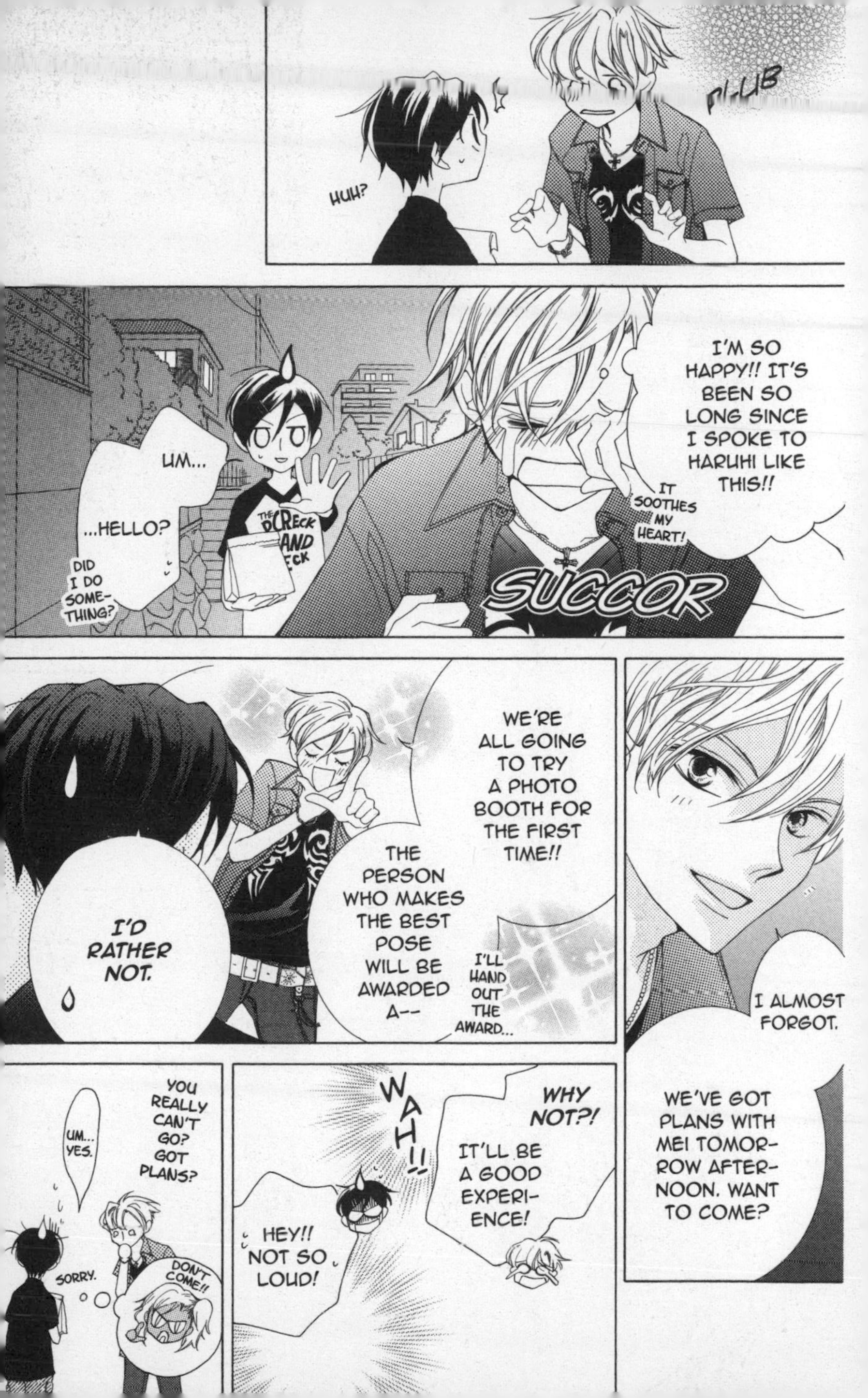
PI-LUB
HUH?
I'M SO HAPPY!! IT'S BEEN SO LONG SINCE I SPOKE TO HARUHI LIKE THIS!!
IT SOOTHES MY HEART!
SUCCOR
UM... ...HELLO?
DID I DO SOME-THING?
I ALMOST FORGOT.
WE'VE GOT PLANS WITH MEI TOMOR-ROW AFTER-NOON. WANT TO COME?
WE'RE ALL GOING TO TRY A PHOTO BOOTH FOR THE FIRST TIME!!
THE PERSON WHO MAKES THE BEST POSE WILL BE AWARDED A--
I'LL HAND OUT THE AWARD...
I'D RATHER NOT.
WAH!!
WHY NOT?!
IT'LL BE A GOOD EXPERI-ENCE!
HEY!! NOT SO LOUD!
YOU REALLY CAN'T GO? GOT PLANS?
UM... YES.
DON'T COME!!
SORRY.

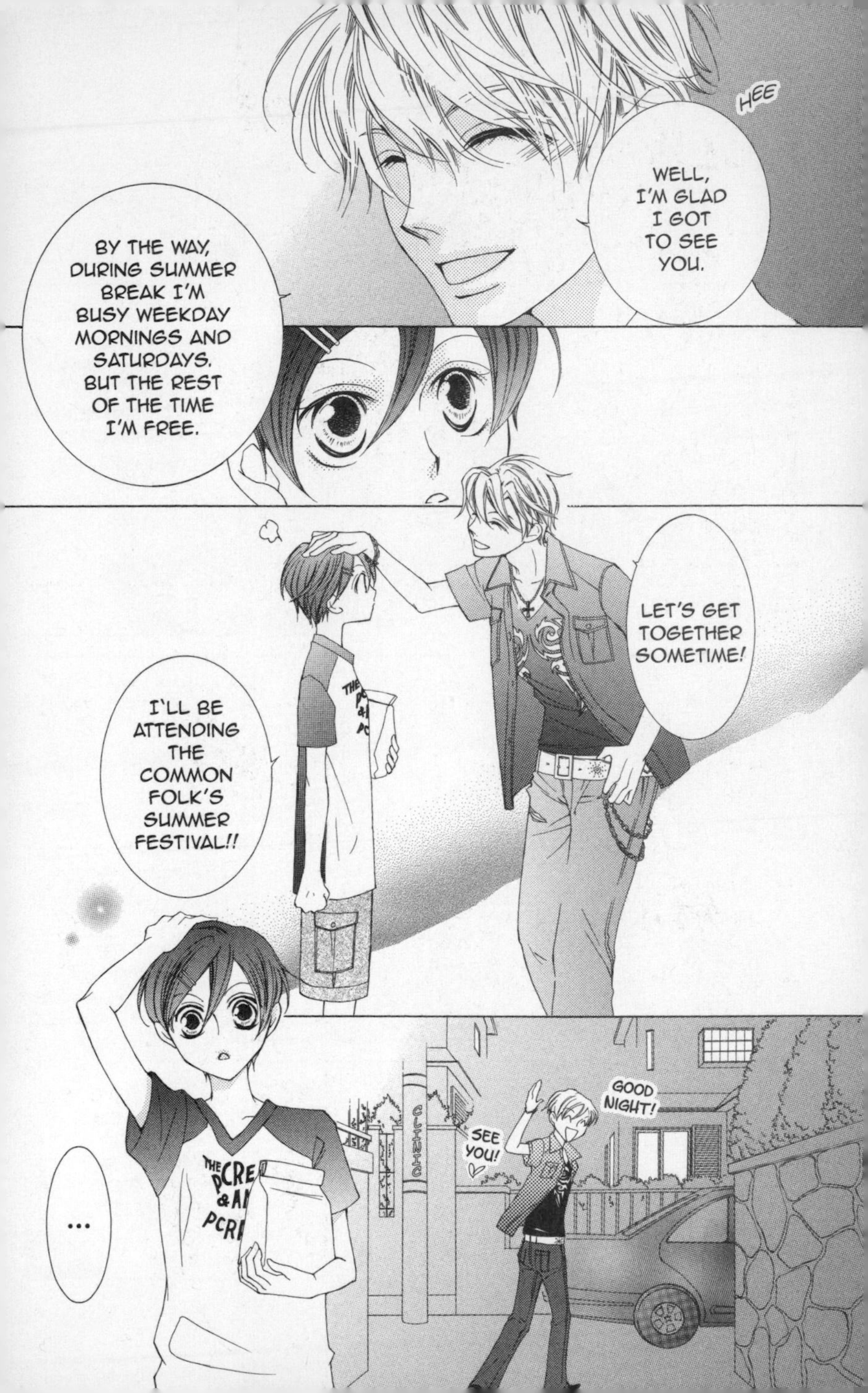
HEE
WELL, I'M GLAD I GOT TO SEE YOU.
BY THE WAY, DURING SUMMER BREAK I'M BUSY WEEKDAY MORNINGS AND SATURDAYS. BUT THE REST OF THE TIME I'M FREE.
LET'S GET TOGETHER SOMETIME!
I'LL BE ATTENDING THE COMMON FOLK'S SUMMER FESTIVAL!!
GOOD NIGHT!
SEE YOU!
CLINIC
...

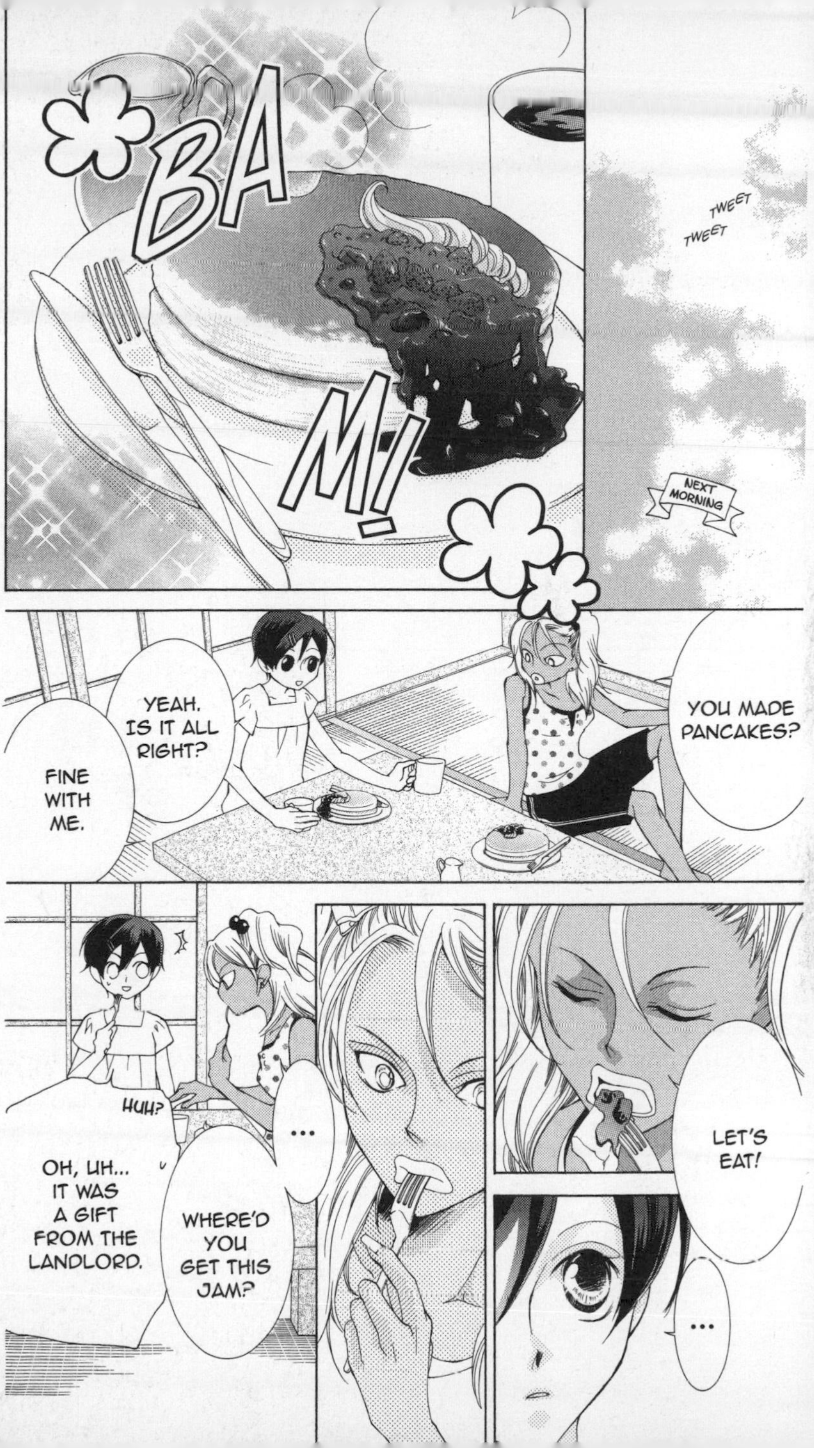
TWEET
TWEET
NEXT MORNING
BAM!
YOU MADE PANCAKES?
YEAH. IS IT ALL RIGHT?
FINE WITH ME.
LET'S EAT!
...
...
WHERE'D YOU GET THIS JAM?
HUH?
OH, UH... IT WAS A GIFT FROM THE LANDLORD.

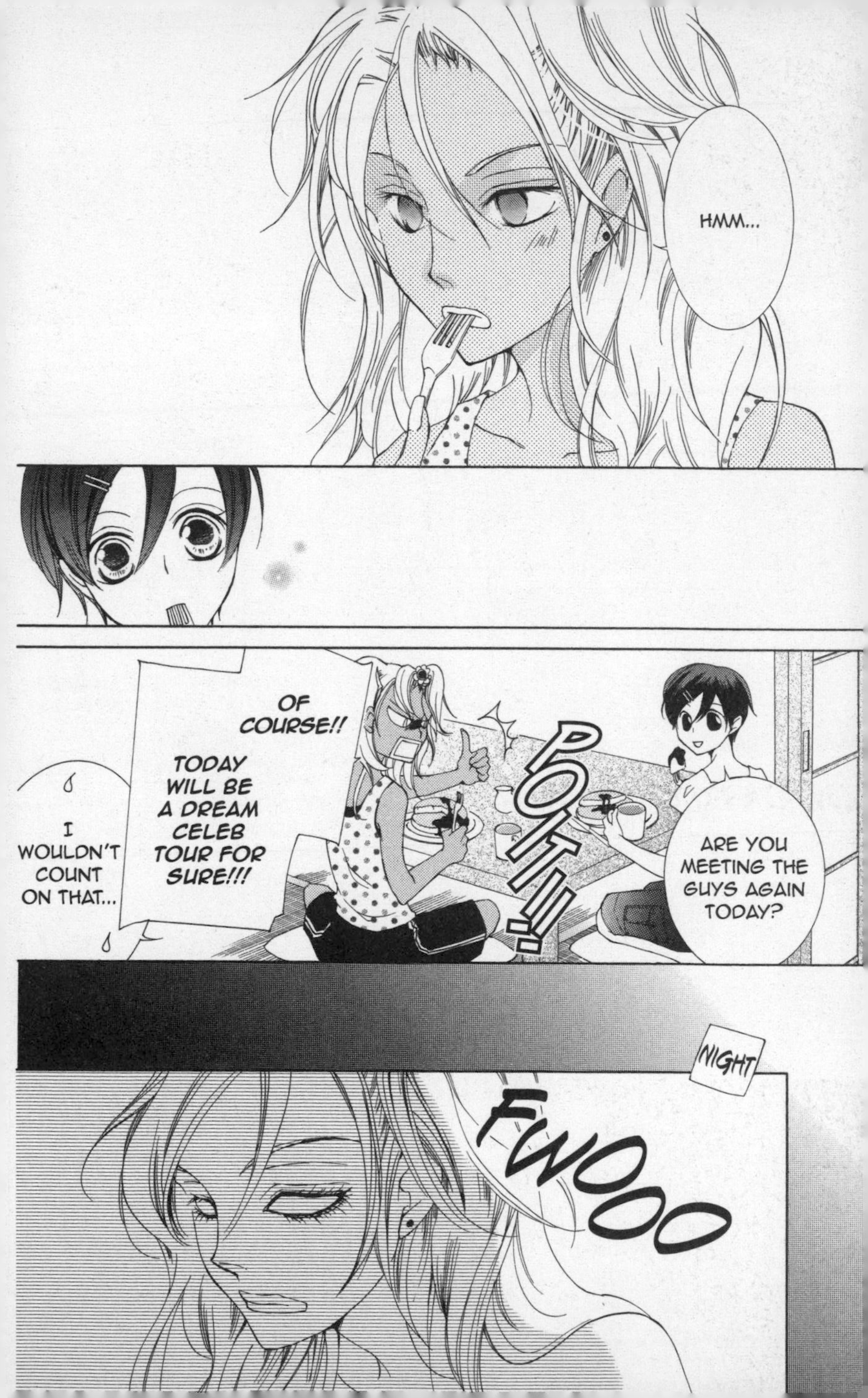
HMM...
ARE YOU MEETING THE GUYS AGAIN TODAY?
POIT!!!
OF COURSE!!
TODAY WILL BE A DREAM CELEB TOUR FOR SURE!!!
I WOULDN'T COUNT ON THAT...
NIGHT
FWOOO

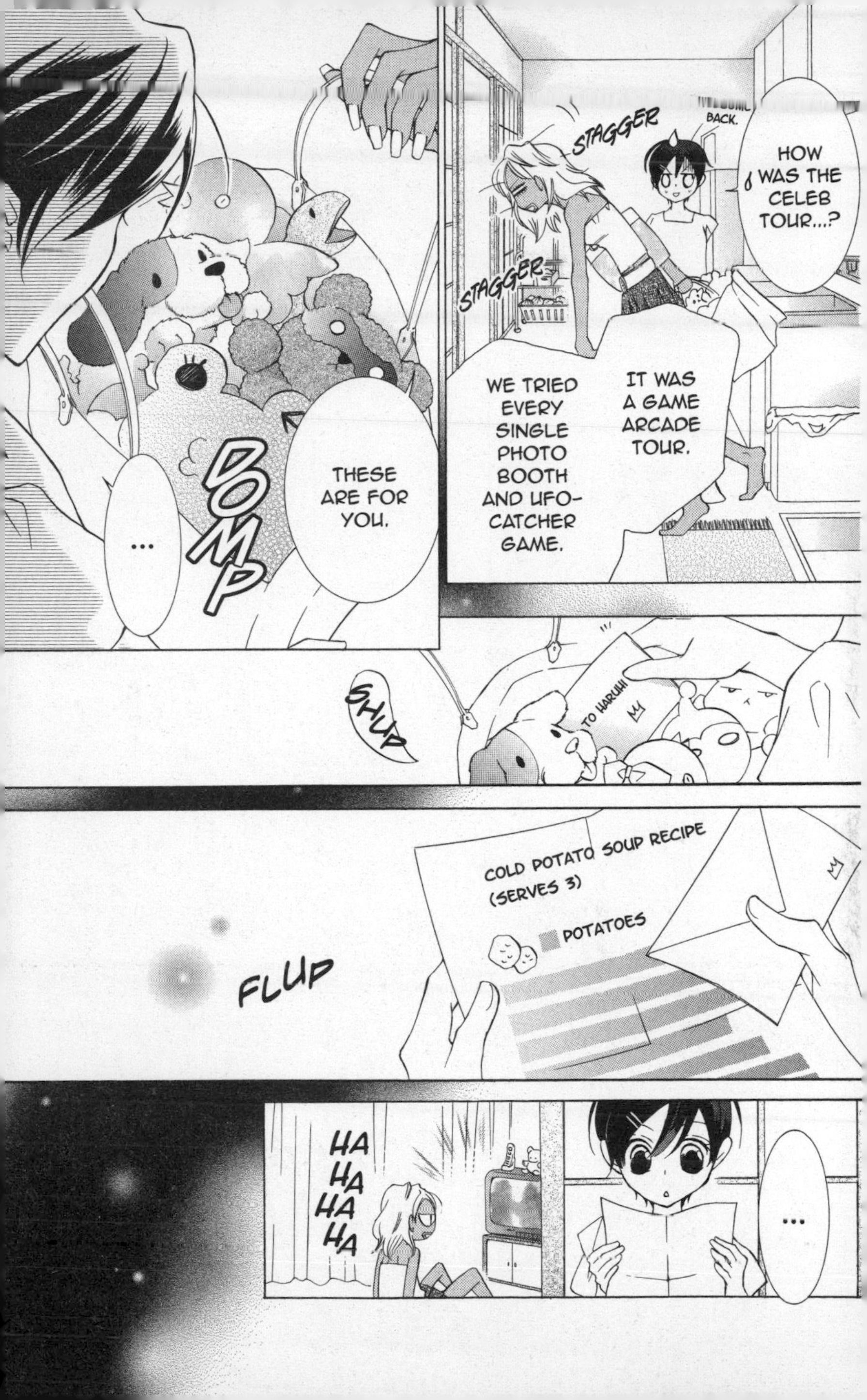
BACK.
HOW WAS THE CELEB TOUR...?
STAGGER
STAGGER
IT WAS A GAME ARCADE TOUR.
WE TRIED EVERY SINGLE PHOTO BOOTH AND UFO-CATCHER GAME.
THESE ARE FOR YOU.
DOMP
...
SHUP
TO HARUHI
COLD POTATO SOUP RECIPE
(SERVES 3)
POTATOES
FLUP
...
HA HA HA HA

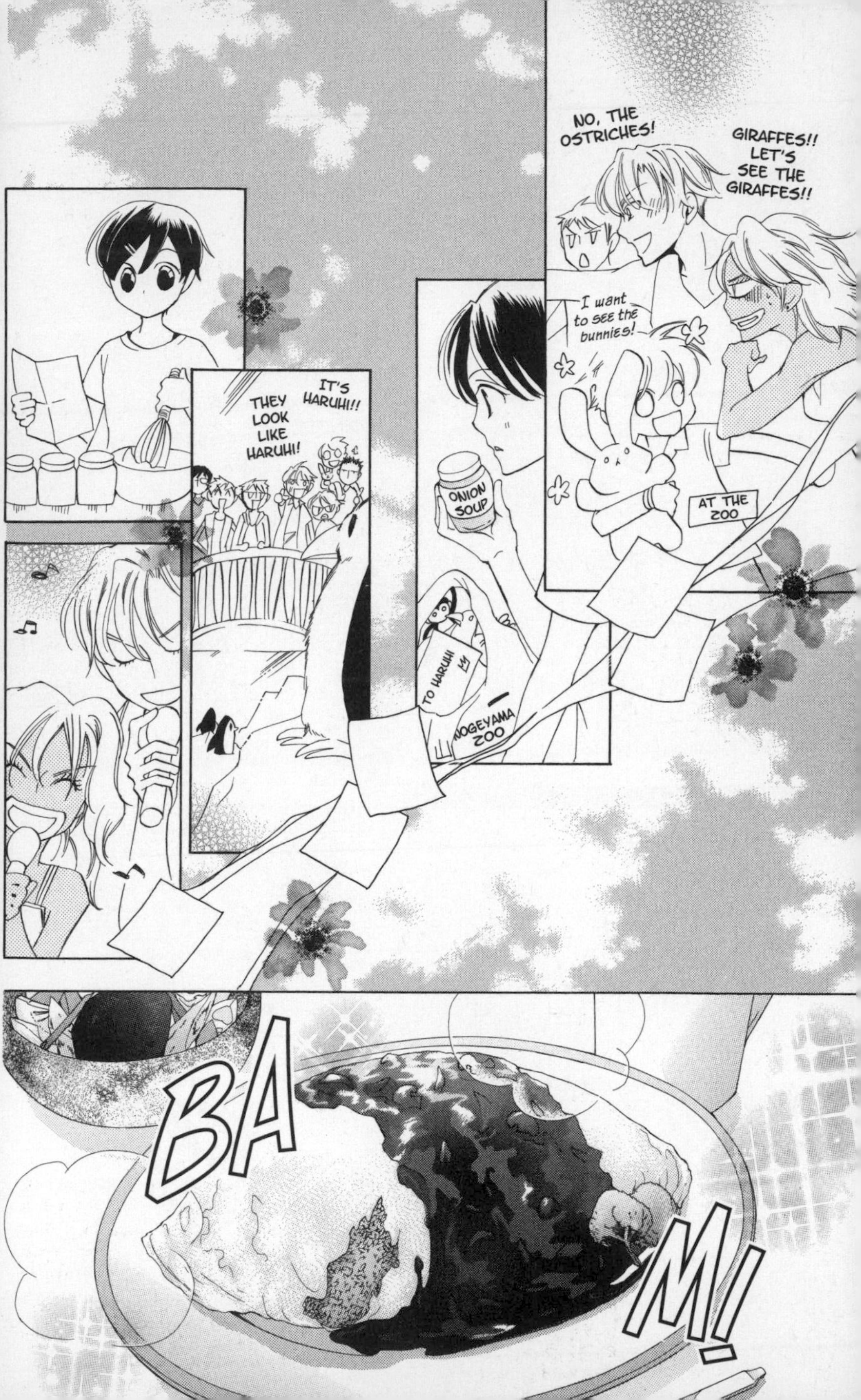
GIRAFFES!! LET'S SEE THE GIRAFFES!!
NO, THE OSTRICHES!
I want to see the bunnies!
AT THE ZOO
ONION SOUP
TO HARUHI
NOGEYAMA ZOO
IT'S HARUHI!!
THEY LOOK LIKE HARUHI!
BAM!

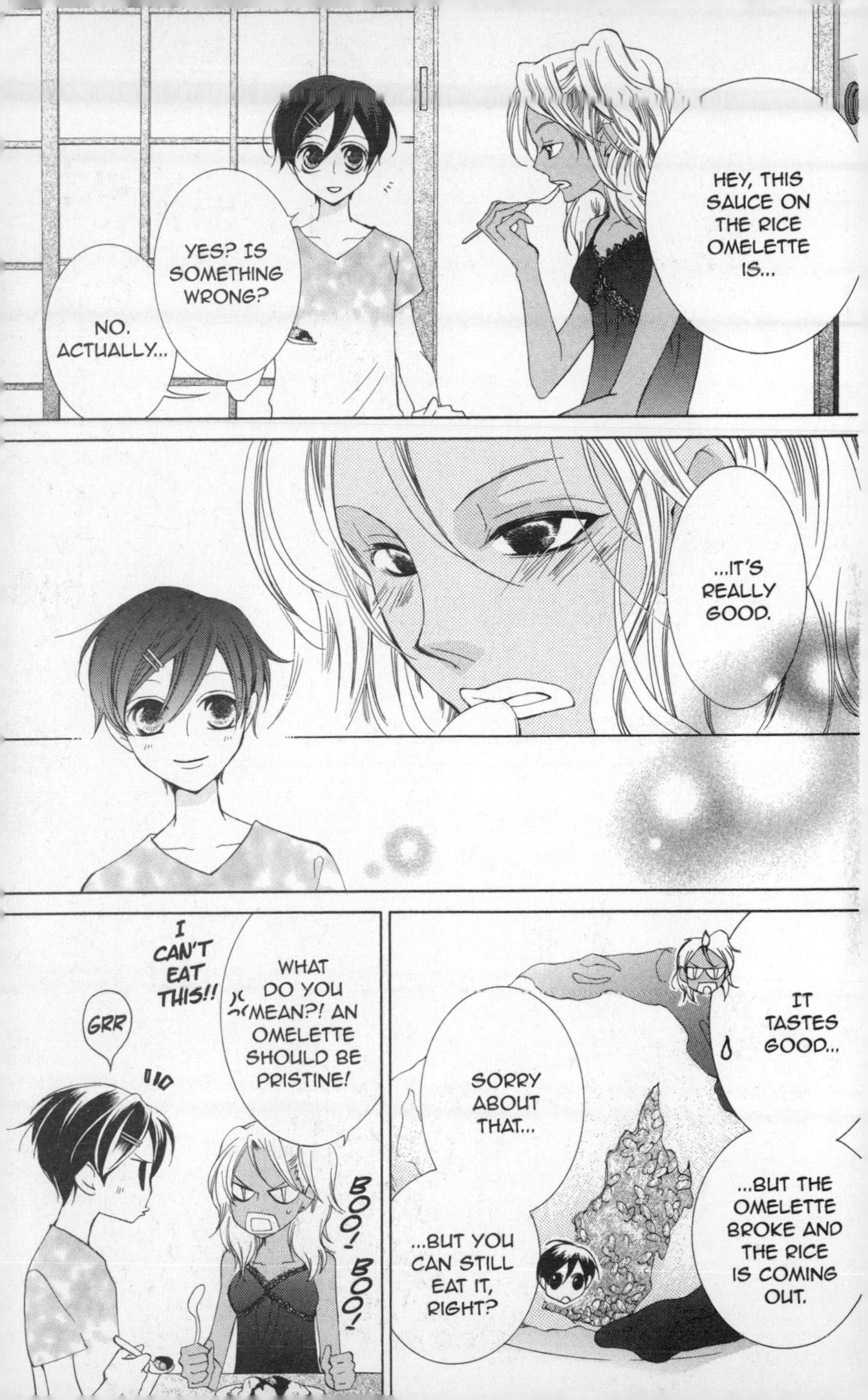
HEY, THIS SAUCE ON THE RICE OMELETTE IS...
YES? IS SOMETHING WRONG?
NO. ACTUALLY...
...IT'S REALLY GOOD.
IT TASTES GOOD...
...BUT THE OMELETTE BROKE AND THE RICE IS COMING OUT.
SORRY ABOUT THAT...
...BUT YOU CAN STILL EAT IT, RIGHT?
WHAT DO YOU MEAN?! AN OMELETTE SHOULD BE PRISTINE!
I CAN'T EAT THIS!!
GRR
BOO! BOO!

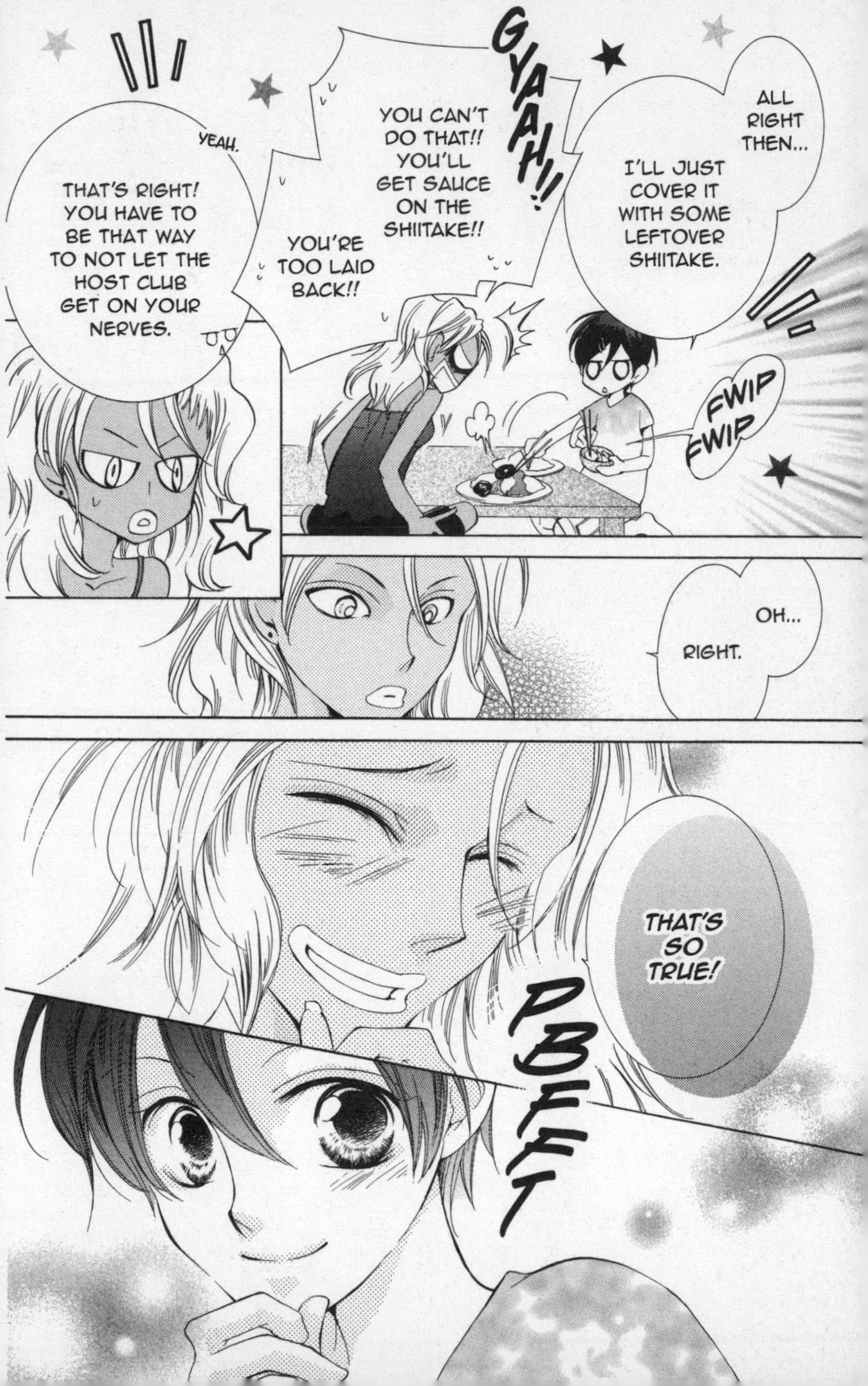

ALL RIGHT THEN...
I'LL JUST COVER IT WITH SOME LEFTOVER SHIITAKE.
FWIP FWIP
GYAAH!!
YOU CAN'T DO THAT!! YOU'LL GET SAUCE ON THE SHIITAKE!!
YOU'RE TOO LAID BACK!!
YEAH.
THAT'S RIGHT! YOU HAVE TO BE THAT WAY TO NOT LET THE HOST CLUB GET ON YOUR NERVES.
OH...
RIGHT.
THAT'S SO TRUE!
PBFFT

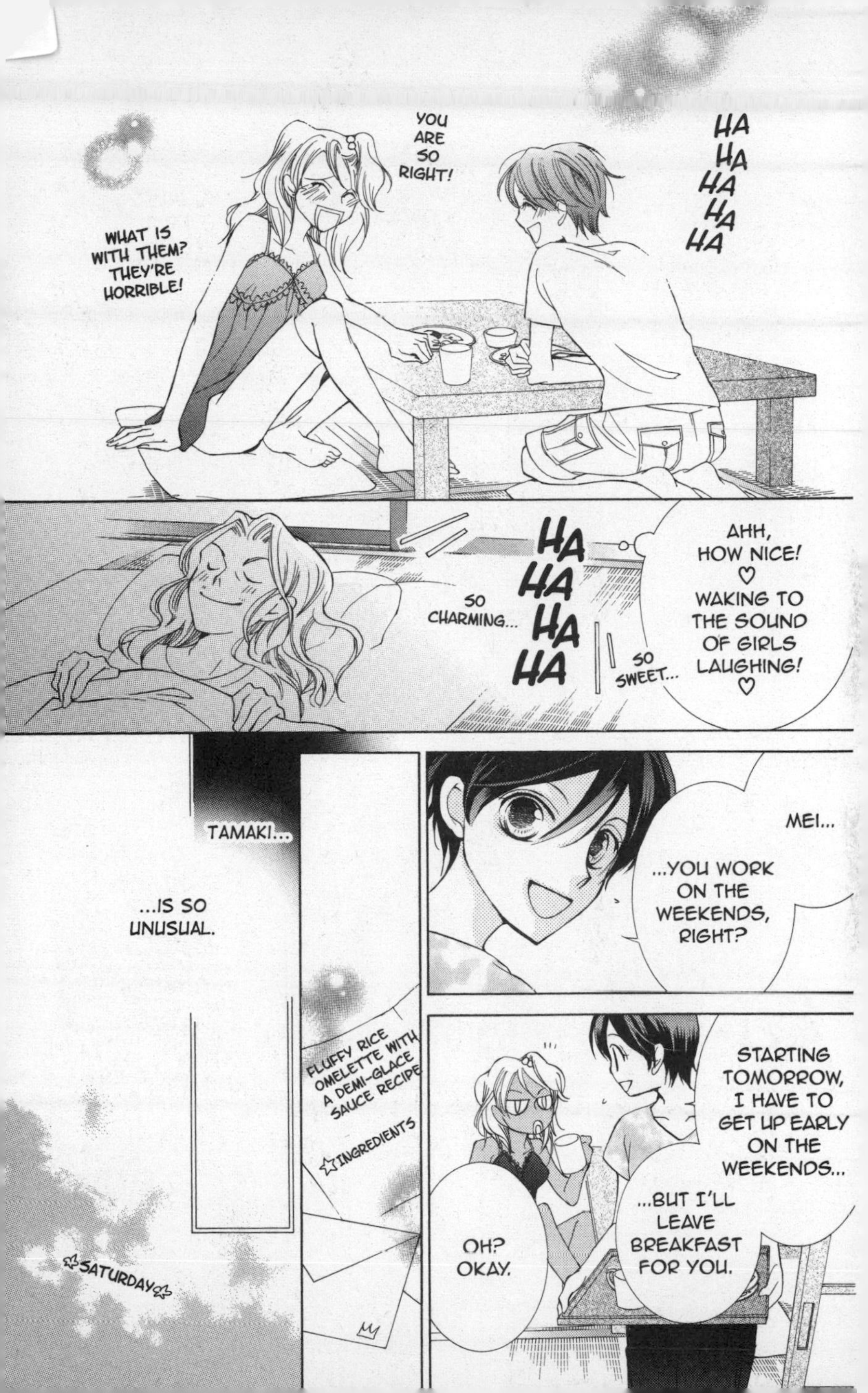
HA HA HA HA HA
YOU ARE SO RIGHT!
WHAT IS WITH THEM? THEY'RE HORRIBLE!
AHH, HOW NICE! ♡ WAKING TO THE SOUND OF GIRLS LAUGHING! ♡
SO SWEET...
HA HA HA HA
SO CHARMING...
MEI...
...YOU WORK ON THE WEEKENDS, RIGHT?
STARTING TOMORROW, I HAVE TO GET UP EARLY ON THE WEEKENDS...
...BUT I'LL LEAVE BREAKFAST FOR YOU.
OH? OKAY.
FLUFFY RICE OMELETTE WITH A DEMI-GLACE SAUCE RECIPE
☆INGREDIENTS
TAMAKI...
...IS SO UNUSUAL.
SATURDAY

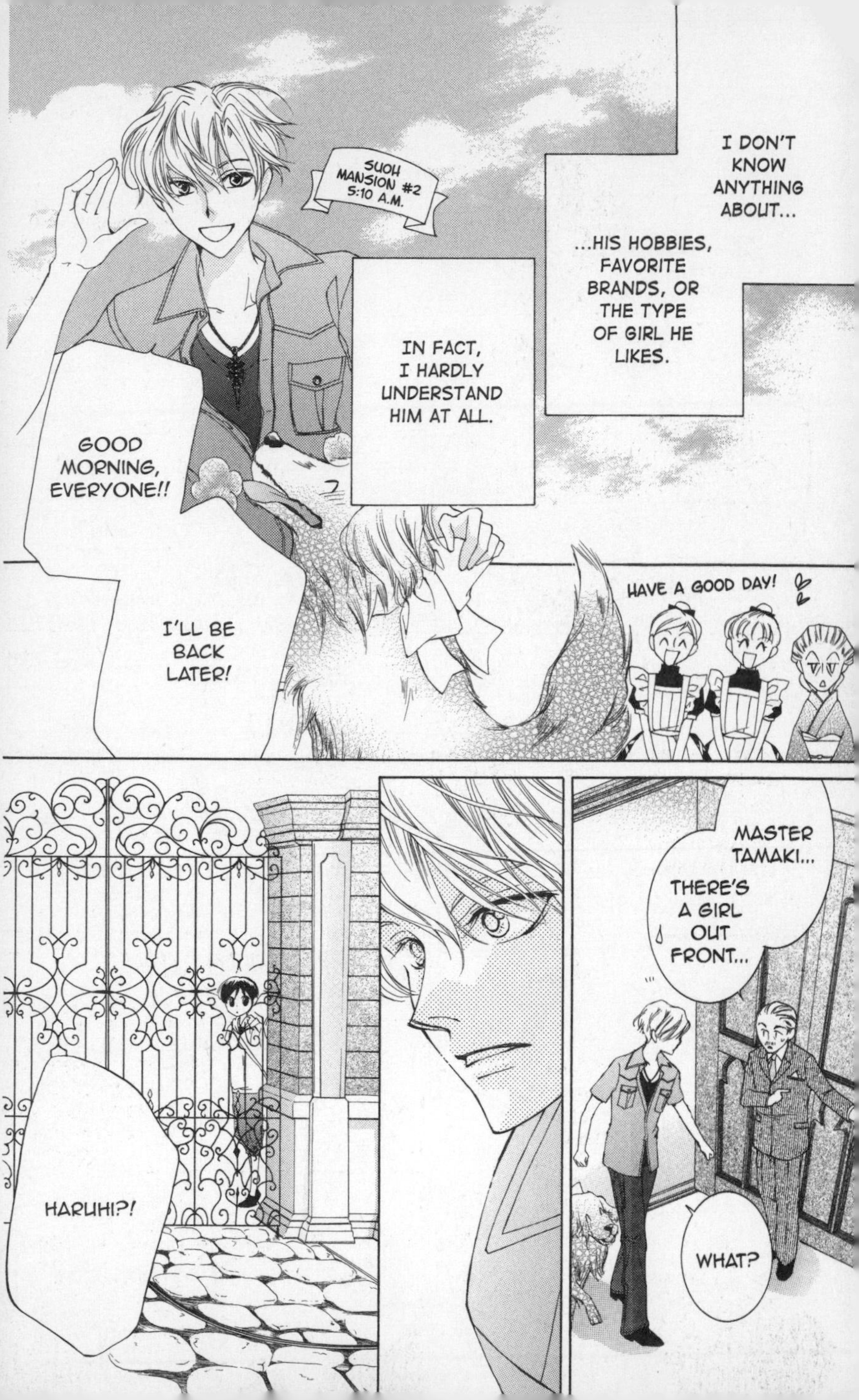
I DON'T KNOW ANYTHING ABOUT...
...HIS HOBBIES, FAVORITE BRANDS, OR THE TYPE OF GIRL HE LIKES.
SUOH MANSION #2 5:10 A.M.
IN FACT, I HARDLY UNDERSTAND HIM AT ALL.
GOOD MORNING, EVERYONE!!
HAVE A GOOD DAY!
I'LL BE BACK LATER!
MASTER TAMAKI... THERE'S A GIRL OUT FRONT...
WHAT?
HARUHI?!

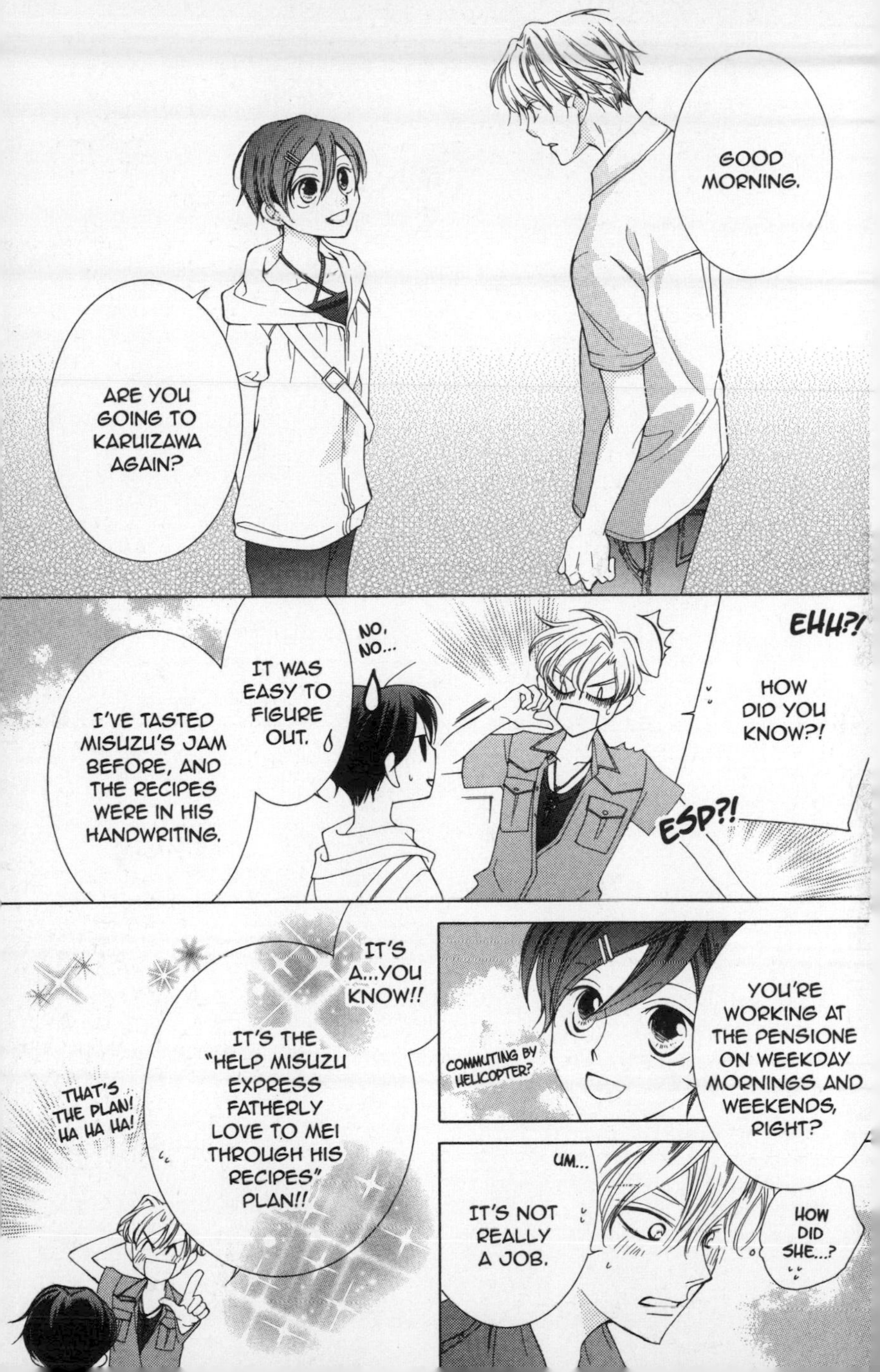
GOOD MORNING.
ARE YOU GOING TO KARUIZAWA AGAIN?
EHH?!
HOW DID YOU KNOW?!
ESP?!
NO, NO...
IT WAS EASY TO FIGURE OUT.
I'VE TASTED MISUZU'S JAM BEFORE, AND THE RECIPES WERE IN HIS HANDWRITING.
YOU'RE WORKING AT THE PENSIONE ON WEEKDAY MORNINGS AND WEEKENDS, RIGHT?
COMMUTING BY HELICOPTER?
HOW DID SHE...?
UM...
IT'S NOT REALLY A JOB.
IT'S A...YOU KNOW!!
IT'S THE "HELP MISUZU EXPRESS FATHERLY LOVE TO MEI THROUGH HIS RECIPES" PLAN!!
THAT'S THE PLAN! HA HA HA!

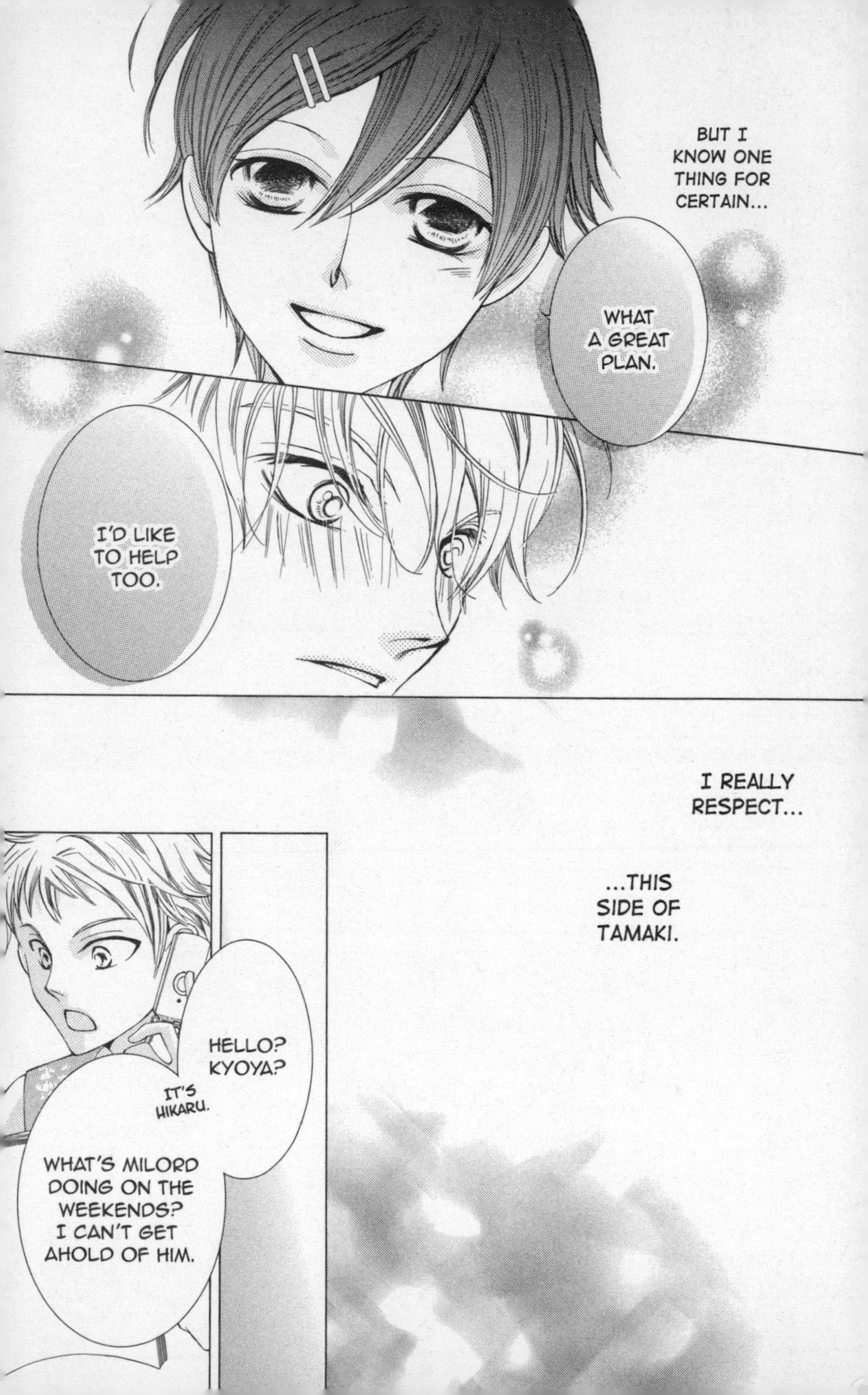
BUT I KNOW ONE THING FOR CERTAIN...
WHAT A GREAT PLAN.
I'D LIKE TO HELP TOO.
I REALLY RESPECT...
...THIS SIDE OF TAMAKI.
HELLO? KYOYA?
IT'S HIKARU.
WHAT'S MILORD DOING ON THE WEEKENDS? I CAN'T GET AHOLD OF HIM.

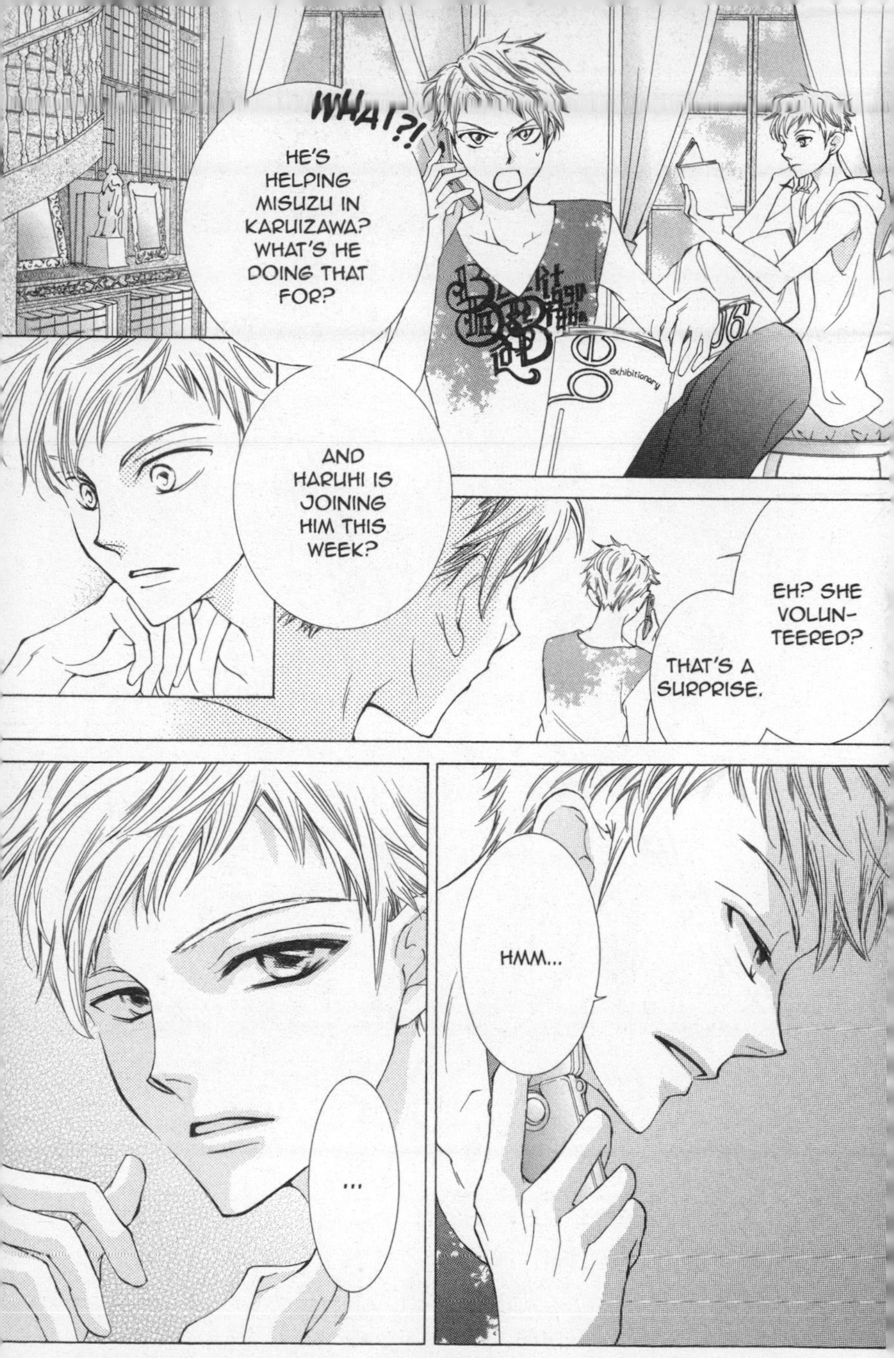
WHAT?!
HE'S HELPING MISUZU IN KARUIZAWA? WHAT'S HE DOING THAT FOR?
exhibitionary
AND HARUHI IS JOINING HIM THIS WEEK?
EH? SHE VOLUNTEERED?
THAT'S A SURPRISE.
HMM...
...

GUEST ROOM: FAXES ③

SPECIAL THANKS TO
TACHIBANA HIGUCHI!!

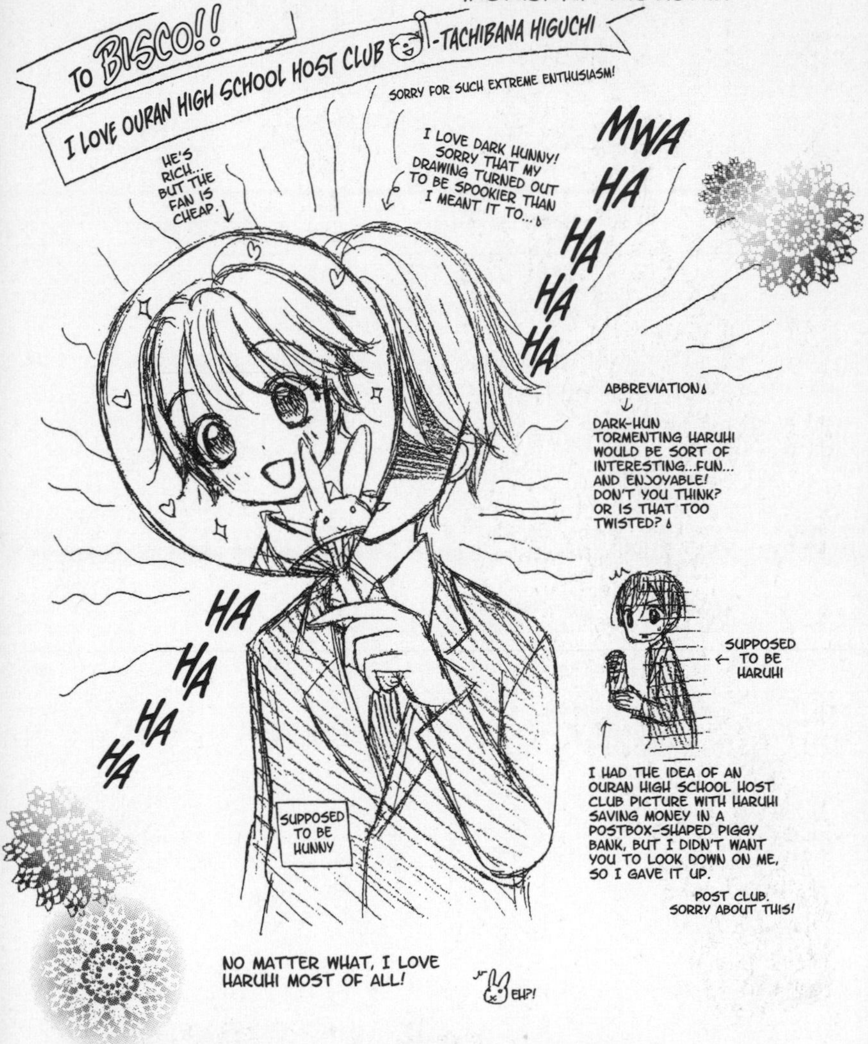
TO BISCO!!
I LOVE OURAN HIGH SCHOOL HOST CLUB -TACHIBANA HIGUCHI
SORRY FOR SUCH EXTREME ENTHUSIASM!
MWA HA HA HA HA
I LOVE DARK HUNNY! SORRY THAT MY DRAWING TURNED OUT TO BE SPOOKIER THAN I MEANT IT TO...
HE'S RICH... BUT THE FAN IS CHEAP.
ABBREVIATION
DARK-HUN TORMENTING HARUHI WOULD BE SORT OF INTERESTING...FUN... AND ENJOYABLE! DON'T YOU THINK? OR IS THAT TOO TWISTED?
HA HA HA HA
SUPPOSED TO BE HARUHI
I HAD THE IDEA OF AN OURAN HIGH SCHOOL HOST CLUB PICTURE WITH HARUHI SAVING MONEY IN A POSTBOX-SHAPED PIGGY BANK, BUT I DIDN'T WANT YOU TO LOOK DOWN ON ME, SO I GAVE IT UP.
POST CLUB. SORRY ABOUT THIS!
SUPPOSED TO BE HUNNY
NO MATTER WHAT, I LOVE HARUHI MOST OF ALL!
EH?!

I RECEIVED THIS FAX FROM TACHIBANA HIGUCHI, WHOM I LOVE SO MUCH!!!! I'LL KEEP IT AS A TREASURE!! SHE GAVE ME A LOT OF GOOD ADVICE FOR THE ANIME. THANK YOU VERY MUCH!

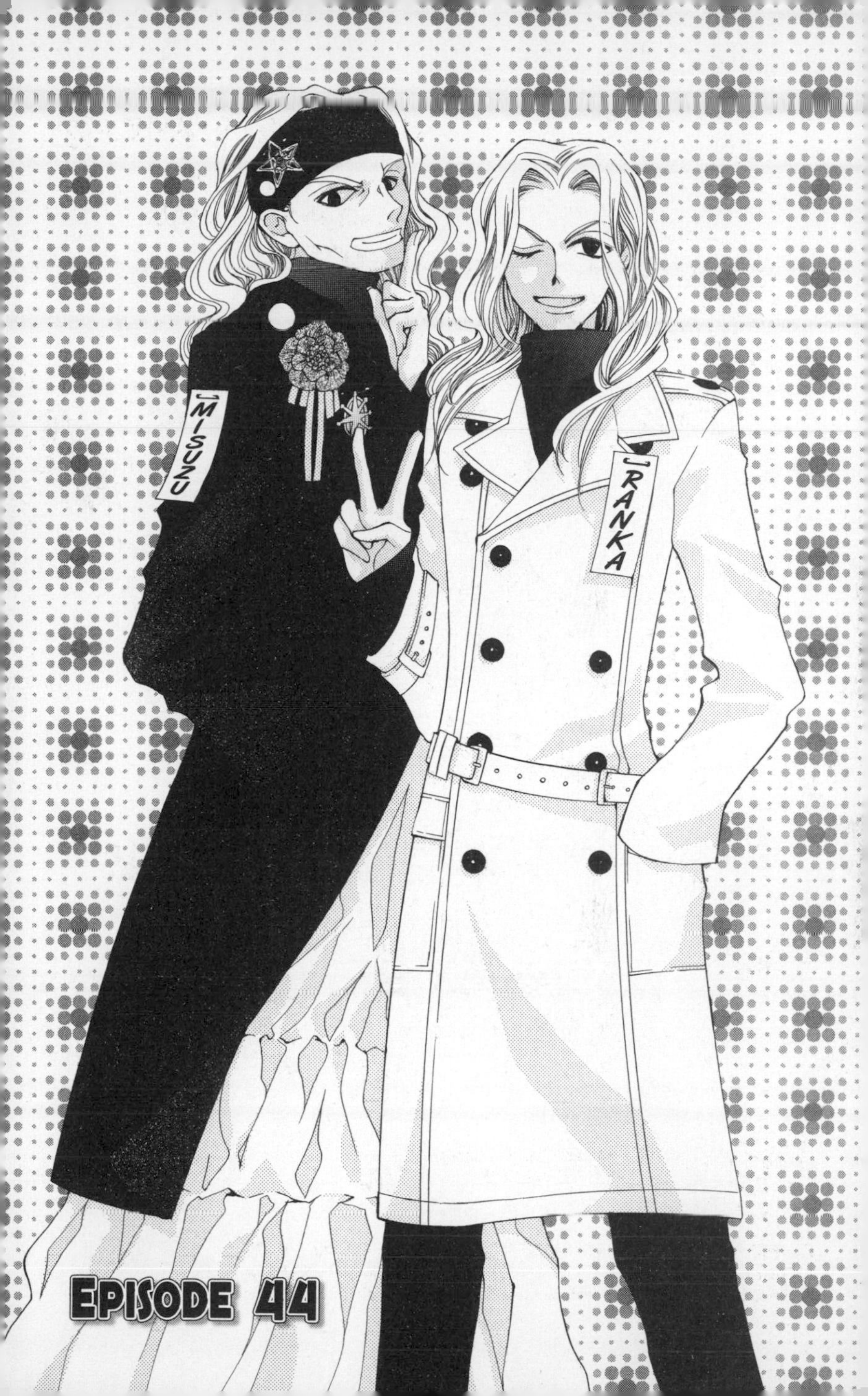
MISUZU
RANKA
EPISODE 44

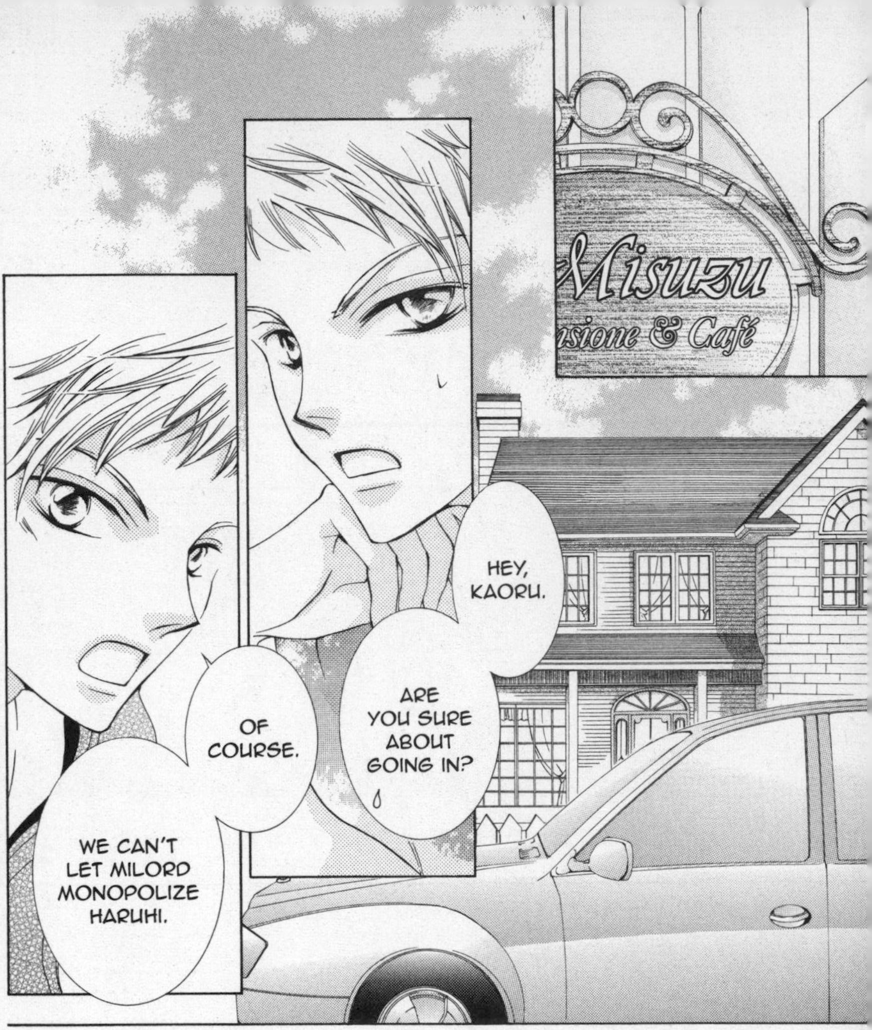
Misuzu
& Café
HEY, KAORU.
ARE YOU SURE ABOUT GOING IN?
OF COURSE.
WE CAN'T LET MILORD MONOPOLIZE HARUHI.

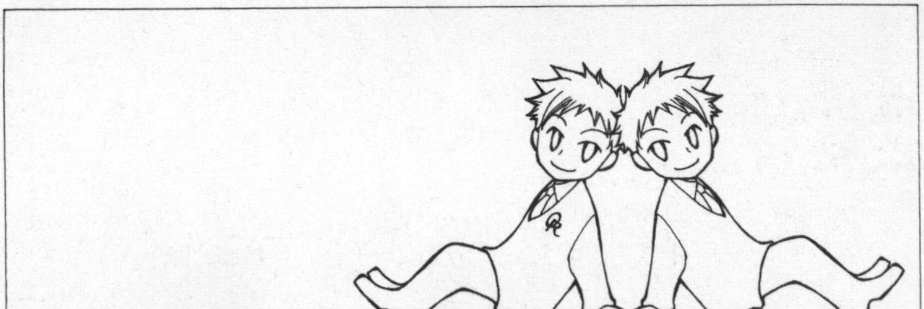

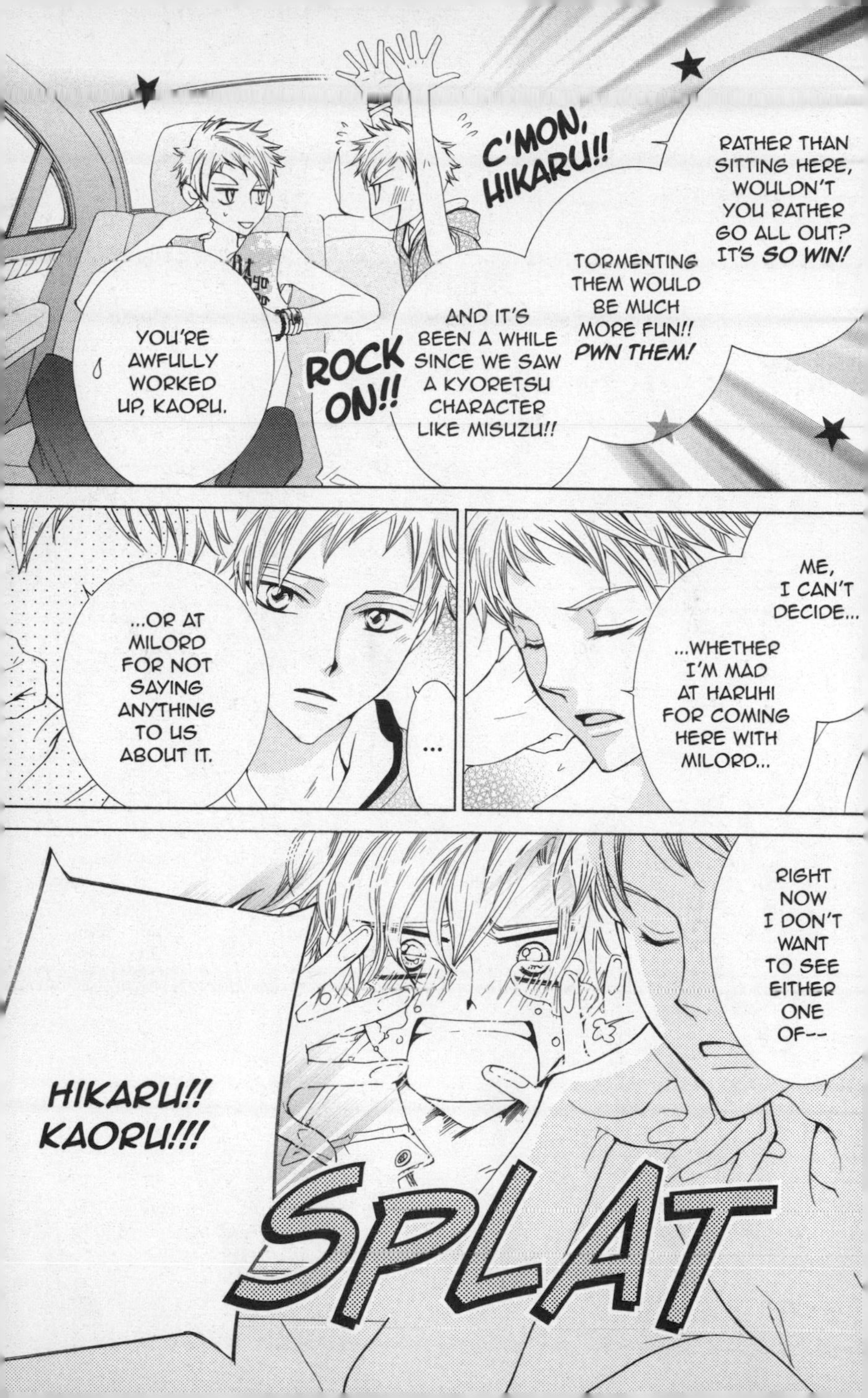
RATHER THAN SITTING HERE, WOULDN'T YOU RATHER GO ALL OUT? IT'S SO WIN!
TORMENTING THEM WOULD BE MUCH MORE FUN!! PWN THEM!
C'MON, HIKARU!!
AND IT'S BEEN A WHILE SINCE WE SAW A KYORETSU CHARACTER LIKE MISUZU!!
ROCK ON!!
YOU'RE AWFULLY WORKED UP, KAORU.
ME, I CAN'T DECIDE...
...WHETHER I'M MAD AT HARUHI FOR COMING HERE WITH MILORD...
...OR AT MILORD FOR NOT SAYING ANYTHING TO US ABOUT IT.
...
RIGHT NOW I DON'T WANT TO SEE EITHER ONE OF--
HIKARU!! KAORU!!!
SPLAT

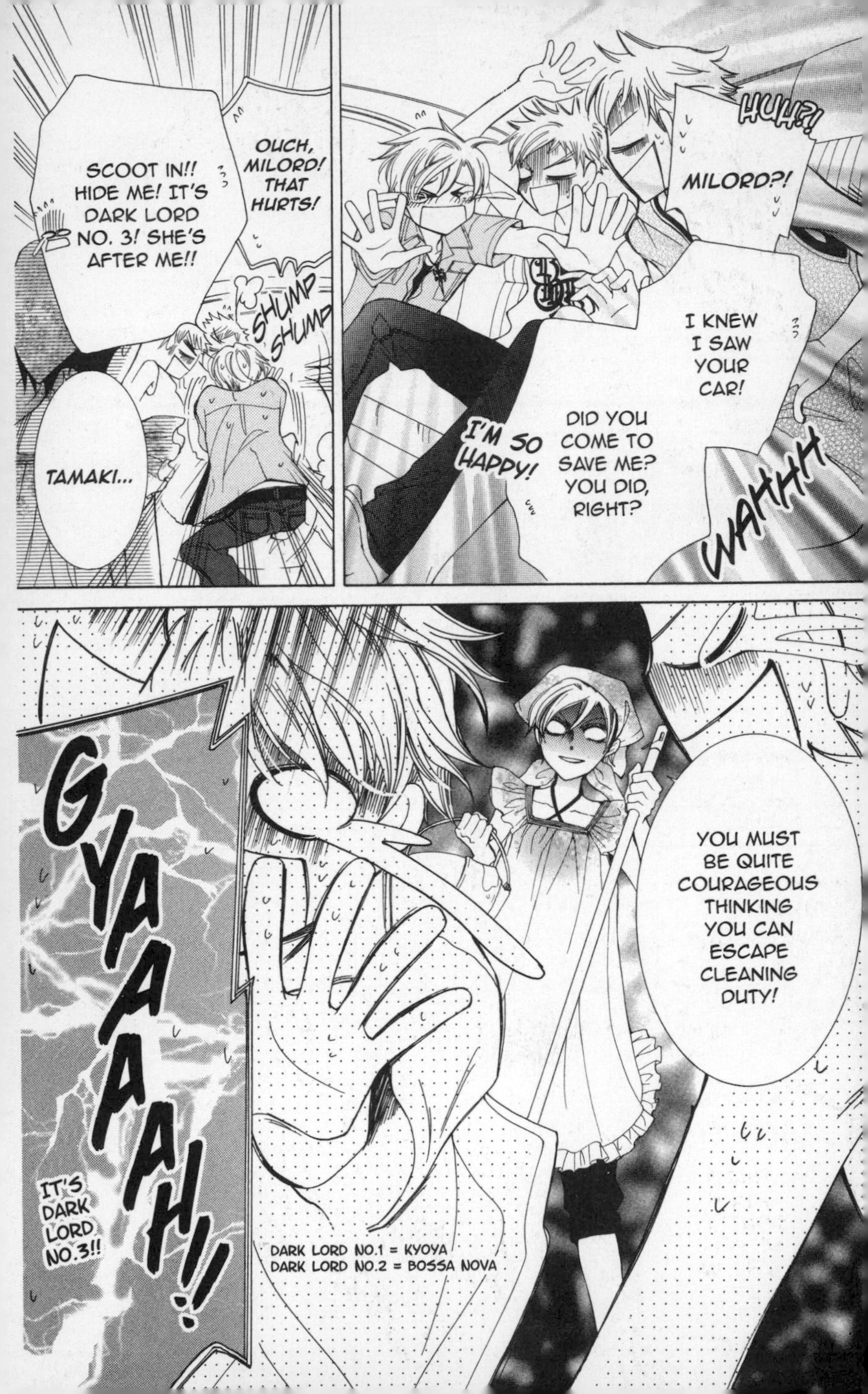
HUH?!
MILORD?!
I KNEW I SAW YOUR CAR!
WAHHH
DID YOU COME TO SAVE ME? YOU DID, RIGHT?
I'M SO HAPPY!
OUCH, MILORD! THAT HURTS!
SCOOT IN!! HIDE ME! IT'S DARK LORD NO. 3! SHE'S AFTER ME!!
SHUMP SHUMP
TAMAKI...
YOU MUST BE QUITE COURAGEOUS THINKING YOU CAN ESCAPE CLEANING DUTY!
GYAAAAH!!
IT'S DARK LORD NO.3!!
DARK LORD NO.1 = KYOYA
DARK LORD NO.2 = BOSSA NOVA

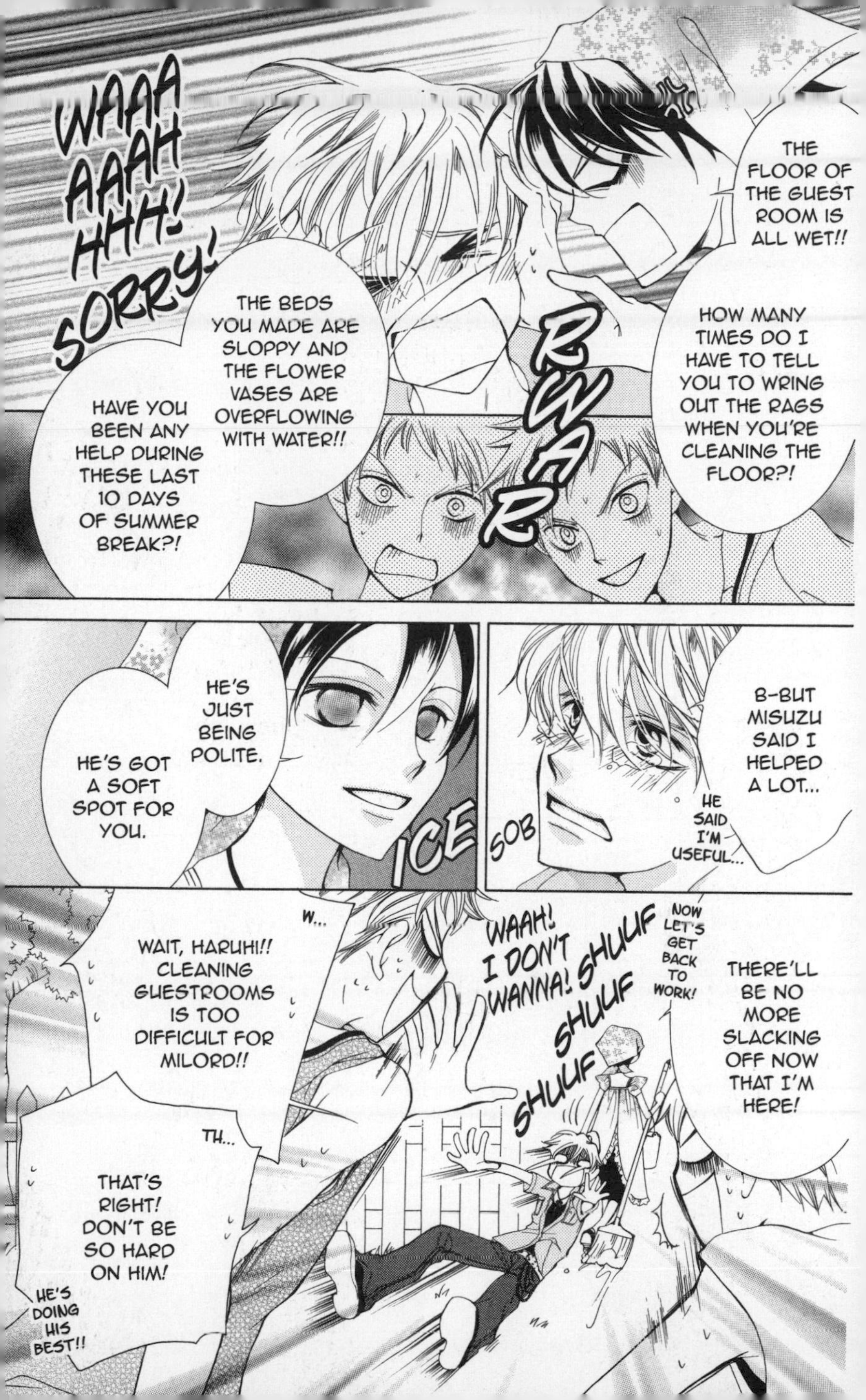
THE FLOOR OF THE GUEST ROOM IS ALL WET!!
HOW MANY TIMES DO I HAVE TO TELL YOU TO WRING OUT THE RAGS WHEN YOU'RE CLEANING THE FLOOR?!
RWAR
THE BEDS YOU MADE ARE SLOPPY AND THE FLOWER VASES ARE OVERFLOWING WITH WATER!!
WAAA AAAH HHH! SORRY!
HAVE YOU BEEN ANY HELP DURING THESE LAST 10 DAYS OF SUMMER BREAK?!
B-BUT MISUZU SAID I HELPED A LOT...
HE SAID I'M USEFUL...
SOB
ICE
HE'S JUST BEING POLITE.
HE'S GOT A SOFT SPOT FOR YOU.
THERE'LL BE NO MORE SLACKING OFF NOW THAT I'M HERE!
NOW LET'S GET BACK TO WORK!
SHUUF SHUUF SHUUF
WAAH! I DON'T WANNA!
W...
WAIT, HARUHI!! CLEANING GUESTROOMS IS TOO DIFFICULT FOR MILORD!!
TH...
THAT'S RIGHT! DON'T BE SO HARD ON HIM!
HE'S DOING HIS BEST!!

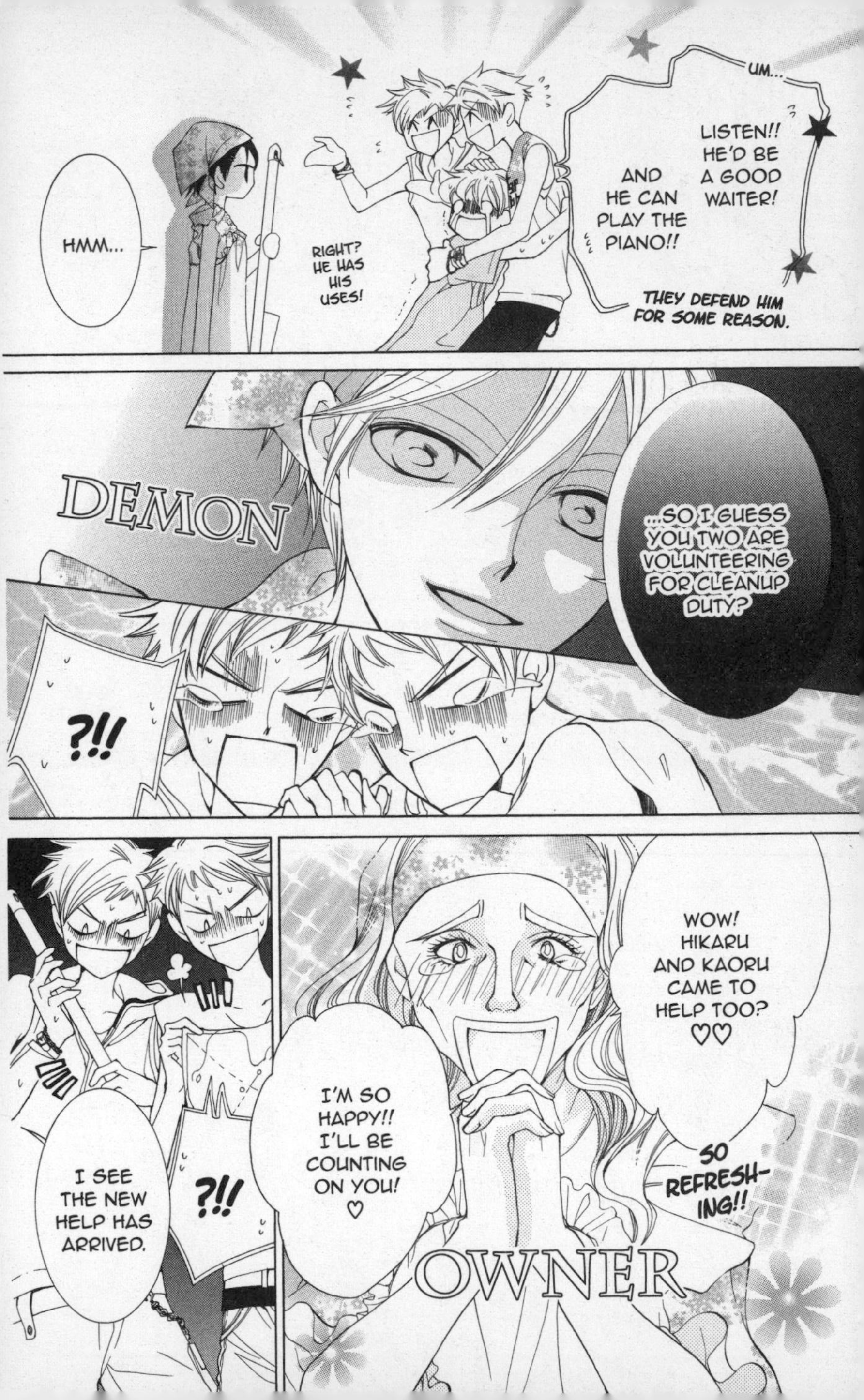
UM...
LISTEN!! HE'D BE A GOOD WAITER!
AND HE CAN PLAY THE PIANO!!
THEY DEFEND HIM FOR SOME REASON.
RIGHT? HE HAS HIS USES!
HMM...
...SO I GUESS YOU TWO ARE VOLUNTEERING FOR CLEANUP DUTY?
DEMON
?!!
WOW! HIKARU AND KAORU CAME TO HELP TOO? ♡♡
SO REFRESH-ING!!
I'M SO HAPPY!! I'LL BE COUNTING ON YOU! ♡
OWNER
?!!
I SEE THE NEW HELP HAS ARRIVED.

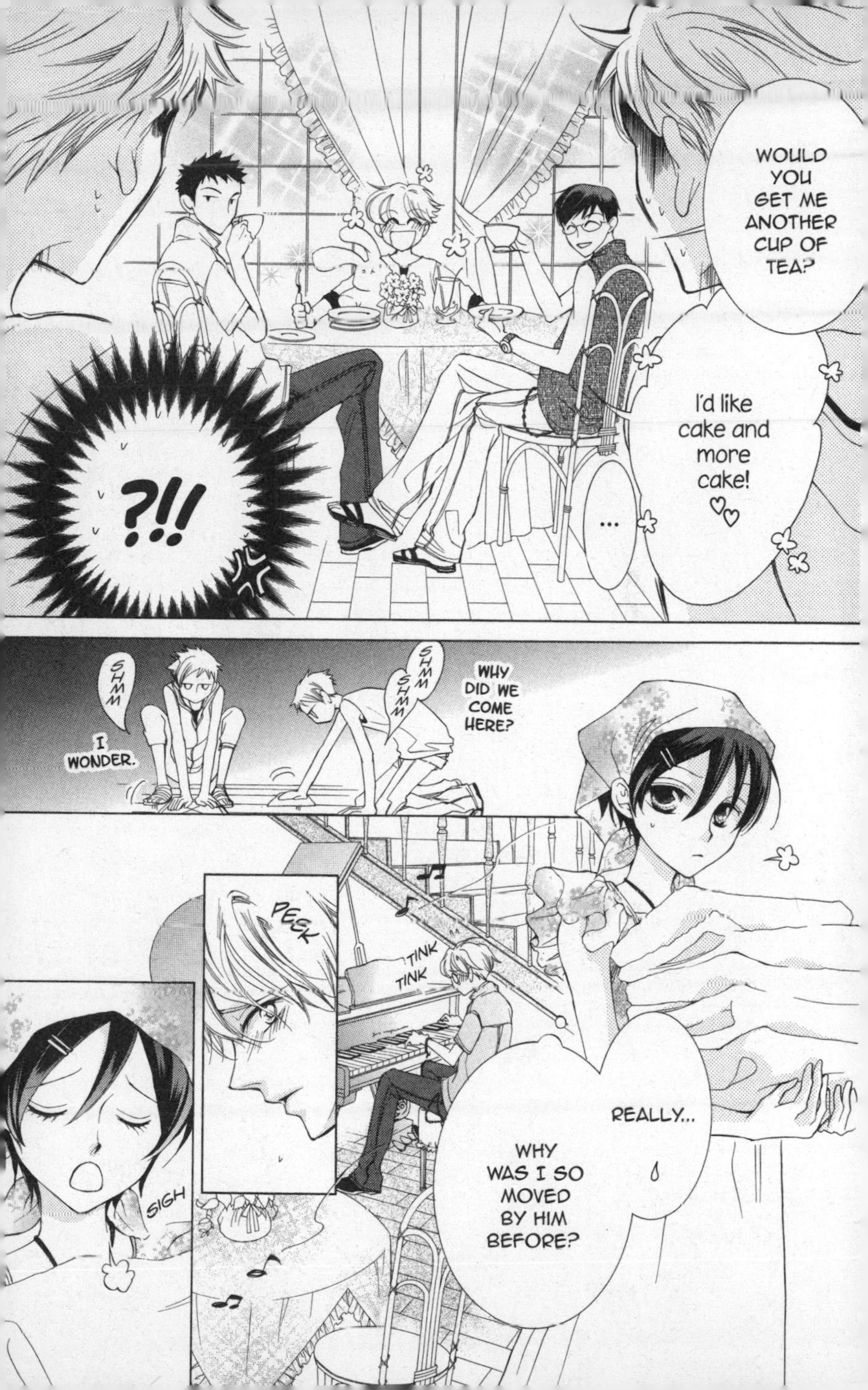
WOULD YOU GET ME ANOTHER CUP OF TEA?
I'd like cake and more cake! ♡♡
...
?!!
WHY DID WE COME HERE?
SHMM SHMM
SHMM
I WONDER.
REALLY...
WHY WAS I SO MOVED BY HIM BEFORE?
TINK TINK
PECK
SIGH

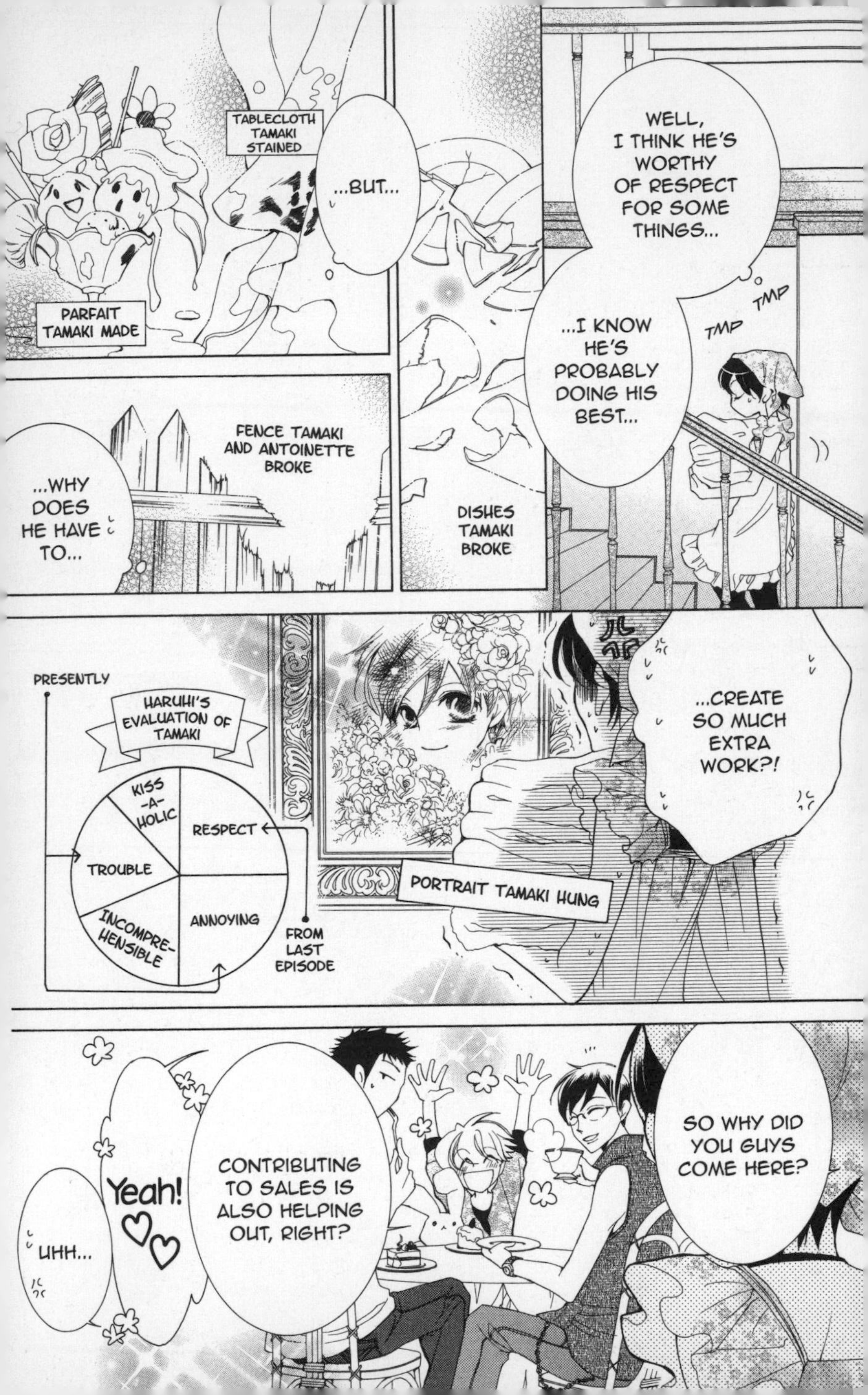
WELL, I THINK HE'S WORTHY OF RESPECT FOR SOME THINGS...
TMP TMP
...I KNOW HE'S PROBABLY DOING HIS BEST...
TABLECLOTH TAMAKI STAINED
...BUT...
PARFAIT TAMAKI MADE
DISHES TAMAKI BROKE
FENCE TAMAKI AND ANTOINETTE BROKE
...WHY DOES HE HAVE TO...
...CREATE SO MUCH EXTRA WORK?!
PORTRAIT TAMAKI HUNG
PRESENTLY
HARUHI'S EVALUATION OF TAMAKI
KISS-A-HOLIC
RESPECT
TROUBLE
INCOMPRE-HENSIBLE
ANNOYING
FROM LAST EPISODE
SO WHY DID YOU GUYS COME HERE?
CONTRIBUTING TO SALES IS ALSO HELPING OUT, RIGHT?
Yeah! ♡♡
UHH...

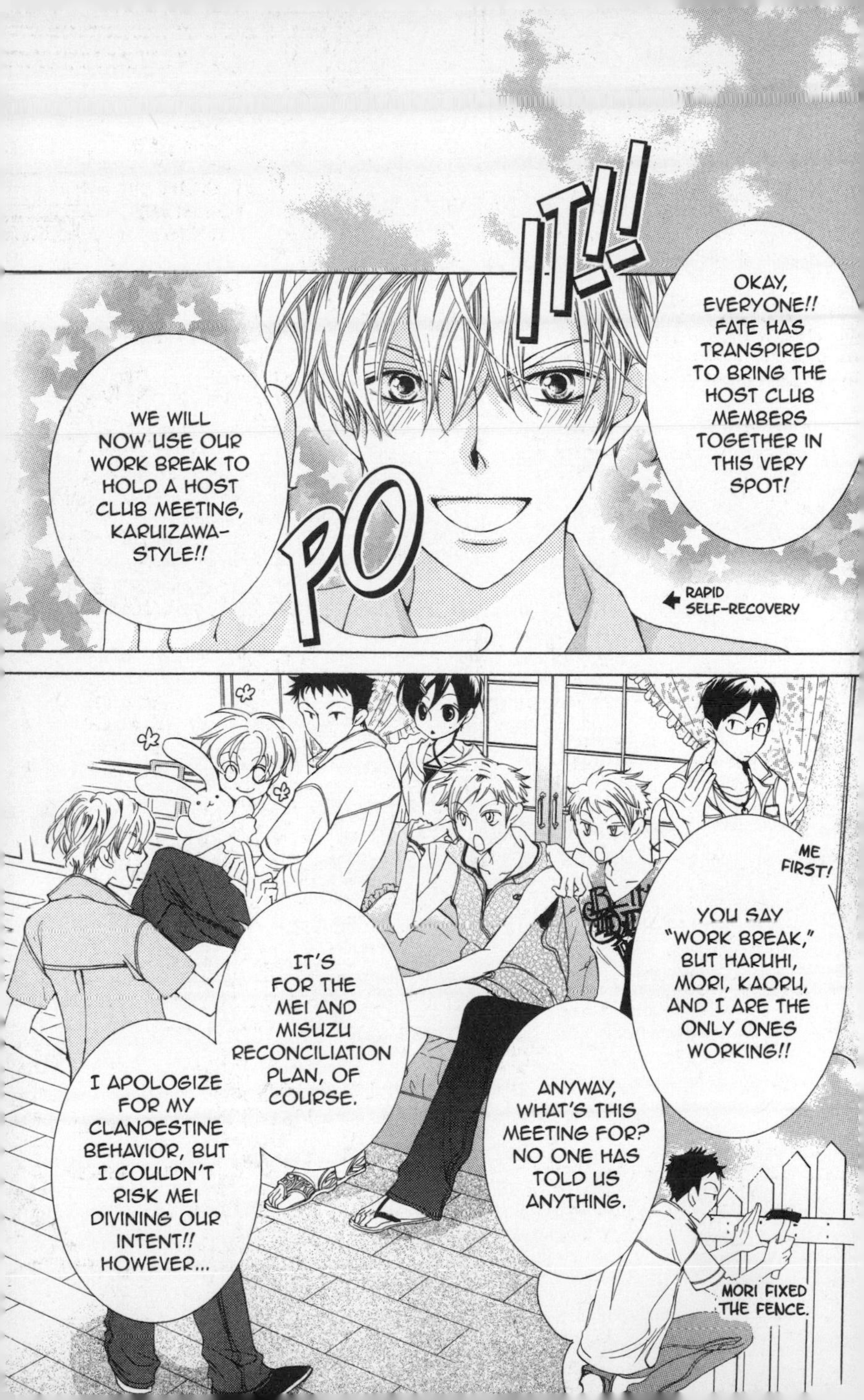
IT!!
OKAY, EVERYONE!! FATE HAS TRANSPIRED TO BRING THE HOST CLUB MEMBERS TOGETHER IN THIS VERY SPOT!
WE WILL NOW USE OUR WORK BREAK TO HOLD A HOST CLUB MEETING, KARUIZAWA-STYLE!!
PO
RAPID SELF-RECOVERY
ME FIRST!
YOU SAY "WORK BREAK," BUT HARUHI, MORI, KAORU, AND I ARE THE ONLY ONES WORKING!!
ANYWAY, WHAT'S THIS MEETING FOR? NO ONE HAS TOLD US ANYTHING.
IT'S FOR THE MEI AND MISUZU RECONCILIATION PLAN, OF COURSE.
I APOLOGIZE FOR MY CLANDESTINE BEHAVIOR, BUT I COULDN'T RISK MEI DIVINING OUR INTENT!! HOWEVER...
MORI FIXED THE FENCE.

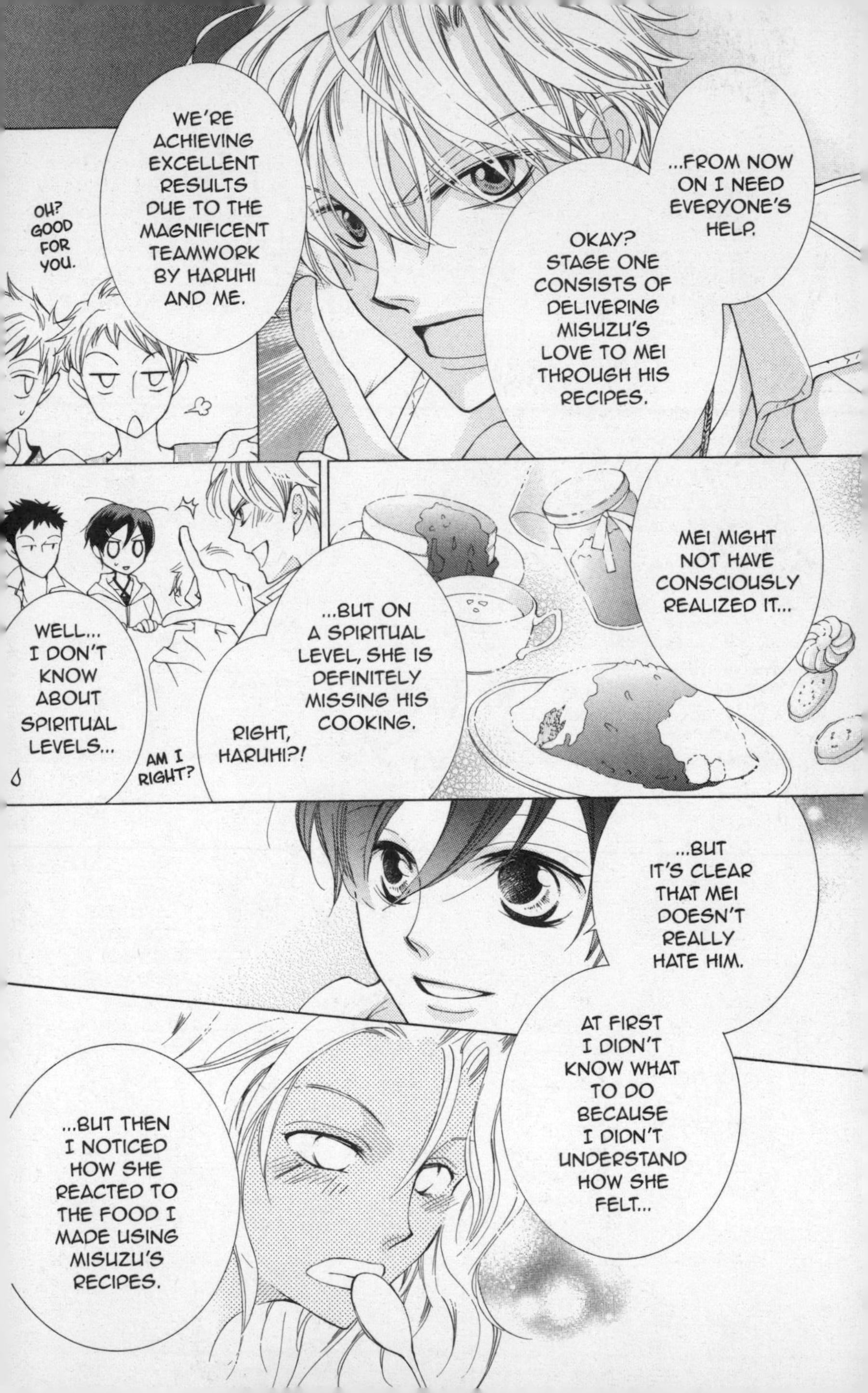
...FROM NOW ON I NEED EVERYONE'S HELP.
OKAY? STAGE ONE CONSISTS OF DELIVERING MISUZU'S LOVE TO MEI THROUGH HIS RECIPES.
WE'RE ACHIEVING EXCELLENT RESULTS DUE TO THE MAGNIFICENT TEAMWORK BY HARUHI AND ME.
OH? GOOD FOR YOU.
MEI MIGHT NOT HAVE CONSCIOUSLY REALIZED IT...
...BUT ON A SPIRITUAL LEVEL, SHE IS DEFINITELY MISSING HIS COOKING.
RIGHT, HARUHI?!
AM I RIGHT?
WELL... I DON'T KNOW ABOUT SPIRITUAL LEVELS...
...BUT IT'S CLEAR THAT MEI DOESN'T REALLY HATE HIM.
AT FIRST I DIDN'T KNOW WHAT TO DO BECAUSE I DIDN'T UNDERSTAND HOW SHE FELT...
...BUT THEN I NOTICED HOW SHE REACTED TO THE FOOD I MADE USING MISUZU'S RECIPES.

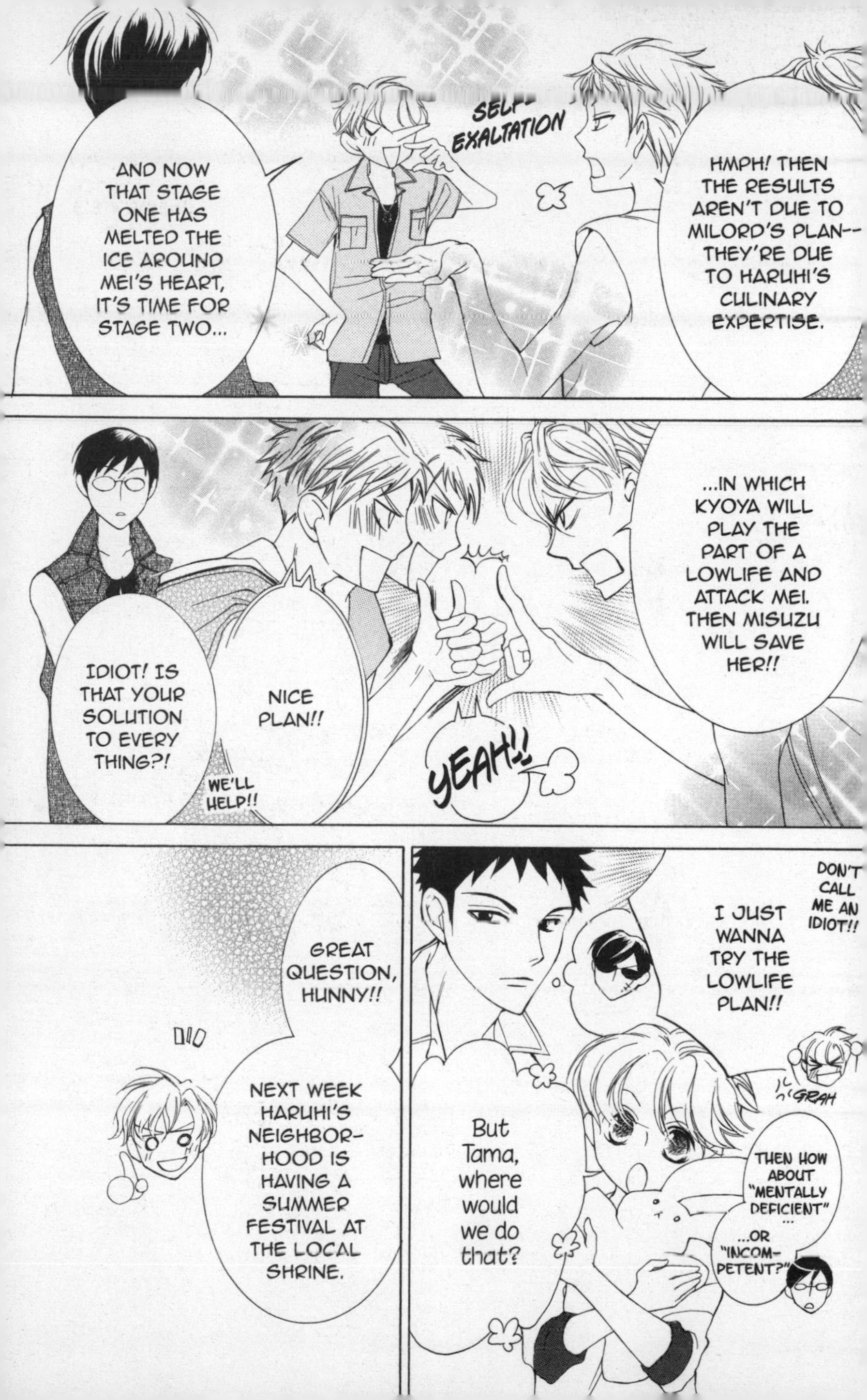
HMPH! THEN THE RESULTS AREN'T DUE TO MILORD'S PLAN-- THEY'RE DUE TO HARUHI'S CULINARY EXPERTISE.
SELF-EXALTATION
AND NOW THAT STAGE ONE HAS MELTED THE ICE AROUND MEI'S HEART, IT'S TIME FOR STAGE TWO...
...IN WHICH KYOYA WILL PLAY THE PART OF A LOWLIFE AND ATTACK MEI. THEN MISUZU WILL SAVE HER!!
YEAH!!
NICE PLAN!!
WE'LL HELP!!
IDIOT! IS THAT YOUR SOLUTION TO EVERY THING?!
DON'T CALL ME AN IDIOT!!
I JUST WANNA TRY THE LOWLIFE PLAN!!
GRAH
THEN HOW ABOUT "MENTALLY DEFICIENT" ... ...OR "INCOMPETENT?"
But Tama, where would we do that?
GREAT QUESTION, HUNNY!!
NEXT WEEK HARUHI'S NEIGHBORHOOD IS HAVING A SUMMER FESTIVAL AT THE LOCAL SHRINE.

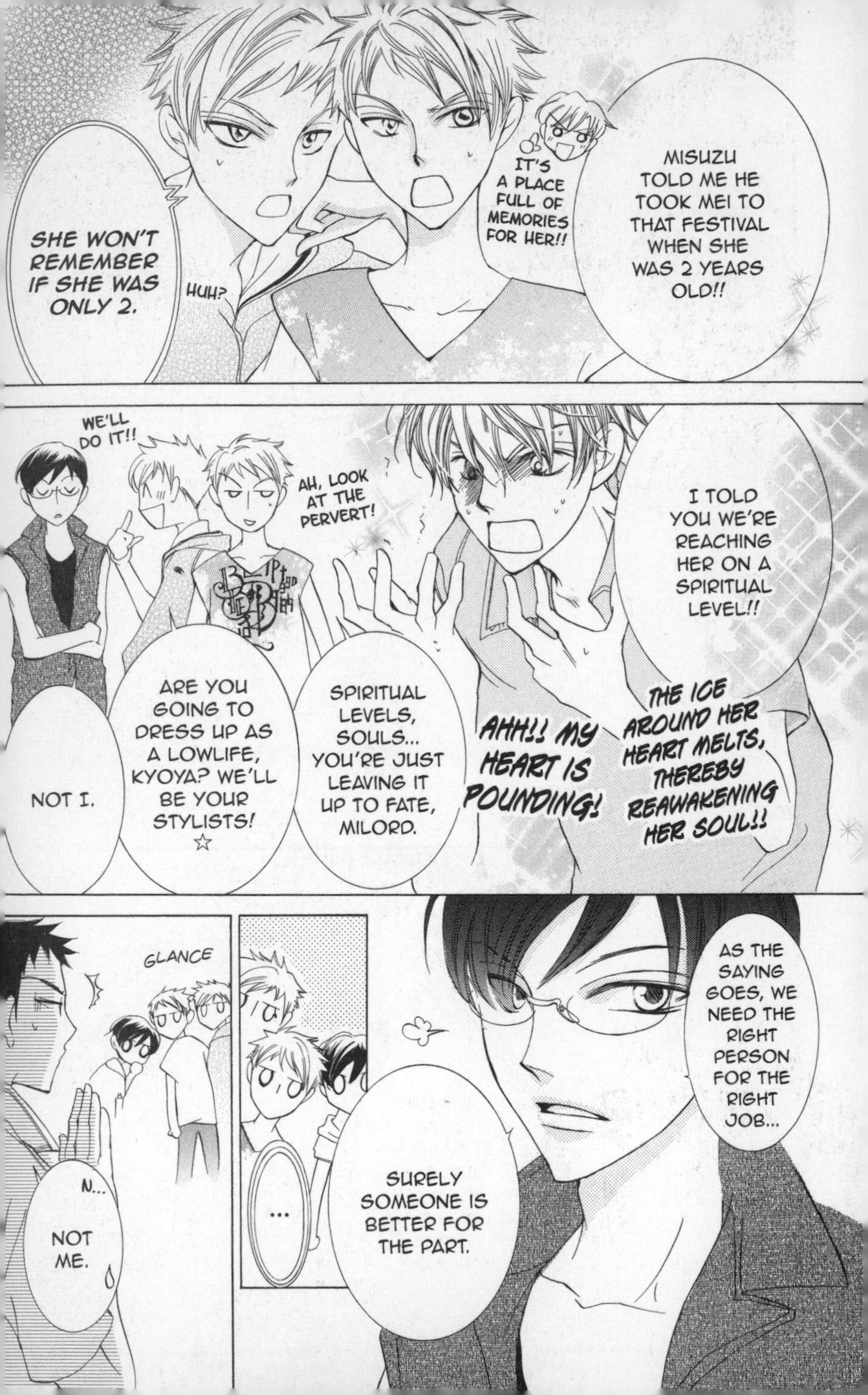
MISUZU TOLD ME HE TOOK MEI TO THAT FESTIVAL WHEN SHE WAS 2 YEARS OLD!!
IT'S A PLACE FULL OF MEMORIES FOR HER!!
HUH?
SHE WON'T REMEMBER IF SHE WAS ONLY 2.
I TOLD YOU WE'RE REACHING HER ON A SPIRITUAL LEVEL!!
THE ICE AROUND HER HEART MELTS, THEREBY REAWAKENING HER SOUL!!
AHH!! MY HEART IS POUNDING!
AH, LOOK AT THE PERVERT!
SPIRITUAL LEVELS, SOULS... YOU'RE JUST LEAVING IT UP TO FATE, MILORD.
WE'LL DO IT!!
ARE YOU GOING TO DRESS UP AS A LOWLIFE, KYOYA? WE'LL BE YOUR STYLISTS! ☆
NOT I.
AS THE SAYING GOES, WE NEED THE RIGHT PERSON FOR THE RIGHT JOB...
SURELY SOMEONE IS BETTER FOR THE PART.
...
GLANCE
N... NOT ME.

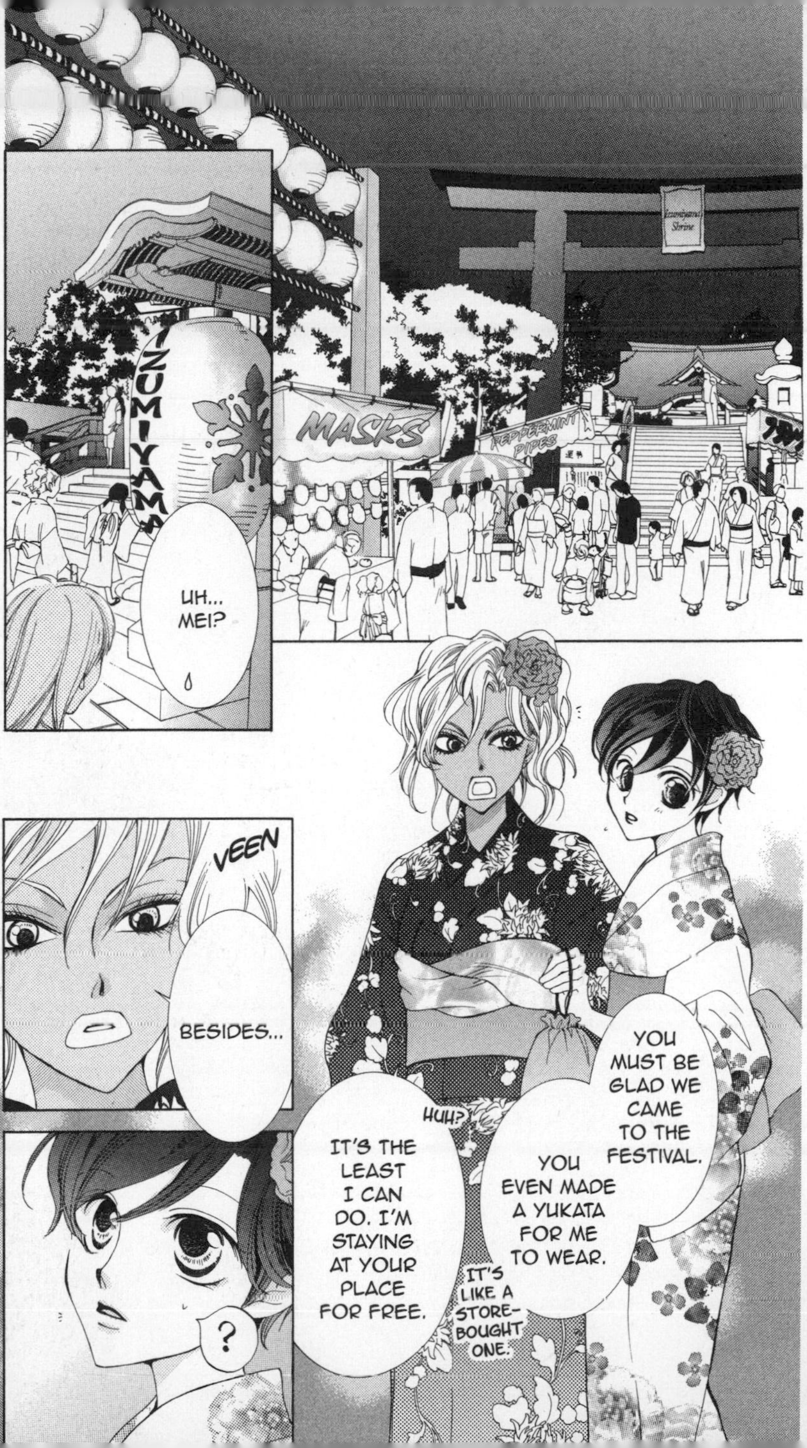

Izumiyama Shrine
IZUMIYAMA
MASKS
PEPPERMINT PIPES
UH... MEI?
YOU MUST BE GLAD WE CAME TO THE FESTIVAL.
YOU EVEN MADE A YUKATA FOR ME TO WEAR.
HUH?
IT'S THE LEAST I CAN DO. I'M STAYING AT YOUR PLACE FOR FREE.
IT'S LIKE A STORE-BOUGHT ONE.
VEEN
BESIDES...
?

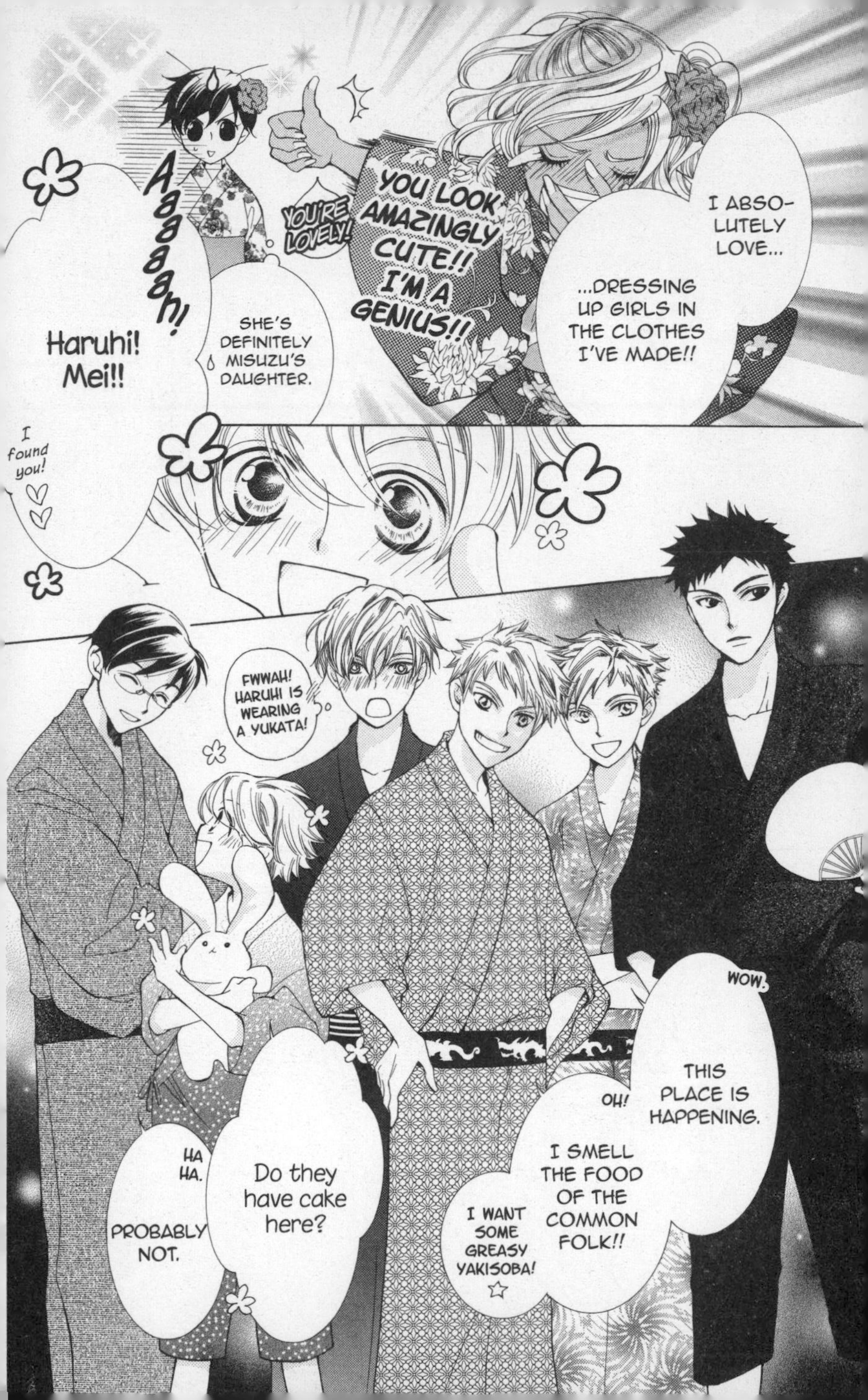
I ABSO-LUTELY LOVE...
...DRESSING UP GIRLS IN THE CLOTHES I'VE MADE!!
YOU LOOK AMAZINGLY CUTE!! I'M A GENIUS!!
YOU'RE LOVELY!
SHE'S DEFINITELY MISUZU'S DAUGHTER.
Aaaaan!
Haruhi! Mei!!
I found you! ♡♡
WOW.
THIS PLACE IS HAPPENING.
OH!
I SMELL THE FOOD OF THE COMMON FOLK!!
I WANT SOME GREASY YAKISOBA! ☆
FWWAH! HARUHI IS WEARING A YUKATA!
Do they have cake here?
HA HA.
PROBABLY NOT.

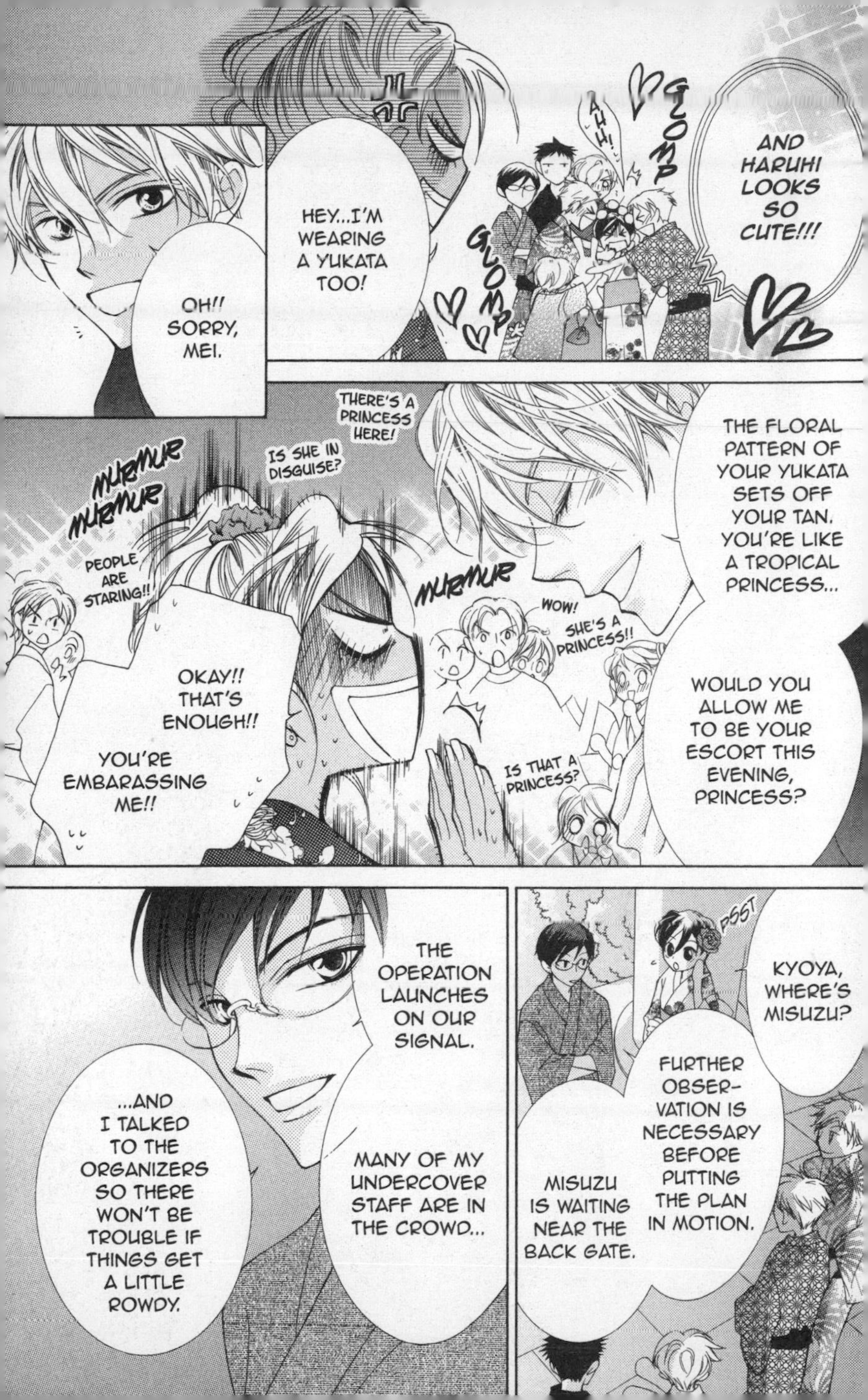
AND HARUHI LOOKS SO CUTE!!!
GLOMP
AHHH!
GLOMP
GLOMP
HEY...I'M WEARING A YUKATA TOO!
OH!! SORRY, MEI.
THE FLORAL PATTERN OF YOUR YUKATA SETS OFF YOUR TAN. YOU'RE LIKE A TROPICAL PRINCESS...
WOULD YOU ALLOW ME TO BE YOUR ESCORT THIS EVENING, PRINCESS?
THERE'S A PRINCESS HERE!
IS SHE IN DISGUISE?
MURMUR
WOW!
SHE'S A PRINCESS!!
IS THAT A PRINCESS?
MURMUR
MURMUR
OKAY!! THAT'S ENOUGH!!
YOU'RE EMBARASSING ME!!
PEOPLE ARE STARING!!
PSST
KYOYA, WHERE'S MISUZU?
FURTHER OBSERVATION IS NECESSARY BEFORE PUTTING THE PLAN IN MOTION.
MISUZU IS WAITING NEAR THE BACK GATE.
THE OPERATION LAUNCHES ON OUR SIGNAL.
MANY OF MY UNDERCOVER STAFF ARE IN THE CROWD...
...AND I TALKED TO THE ORGANIZERS SO THERE WON'T BE TROUBLE IF THINGS GET A LITTLE ROWDY.

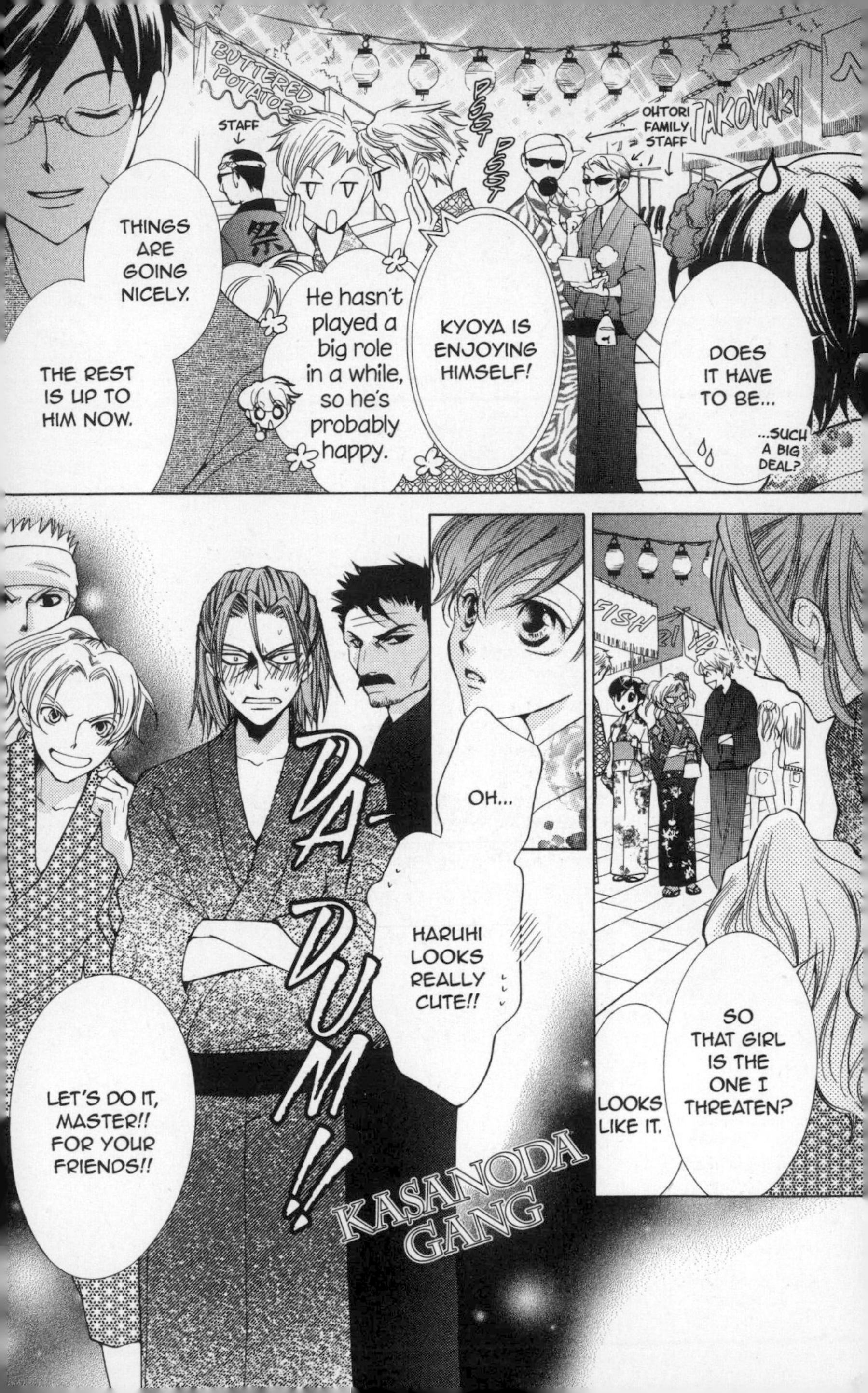
TAKOYAKI
DOES IT HAVE TO BE...
...SUCH A BIG DEAL?
OHTORI FAMILY STAFF
POST POST
KYOYA IS ENJOYING HIMSELF!
He hasn't played a big role in a while, so he's probably happy.
STAFF
BUTTERED POTATOES
THINGS ARE GOING NICELY.
THE REST IS UP TO HIM NOW.
FISH
SO THAT GIRL IS THE ONE I THREATEN?
LOOKS LIKE IT.
OH...
HARUHI LOOKS REALLY CUTE!!
DA-DUM!!
KASANODA GANG
LET'S DO IT, MASTER!! FOR YOUR FRIENDS!!

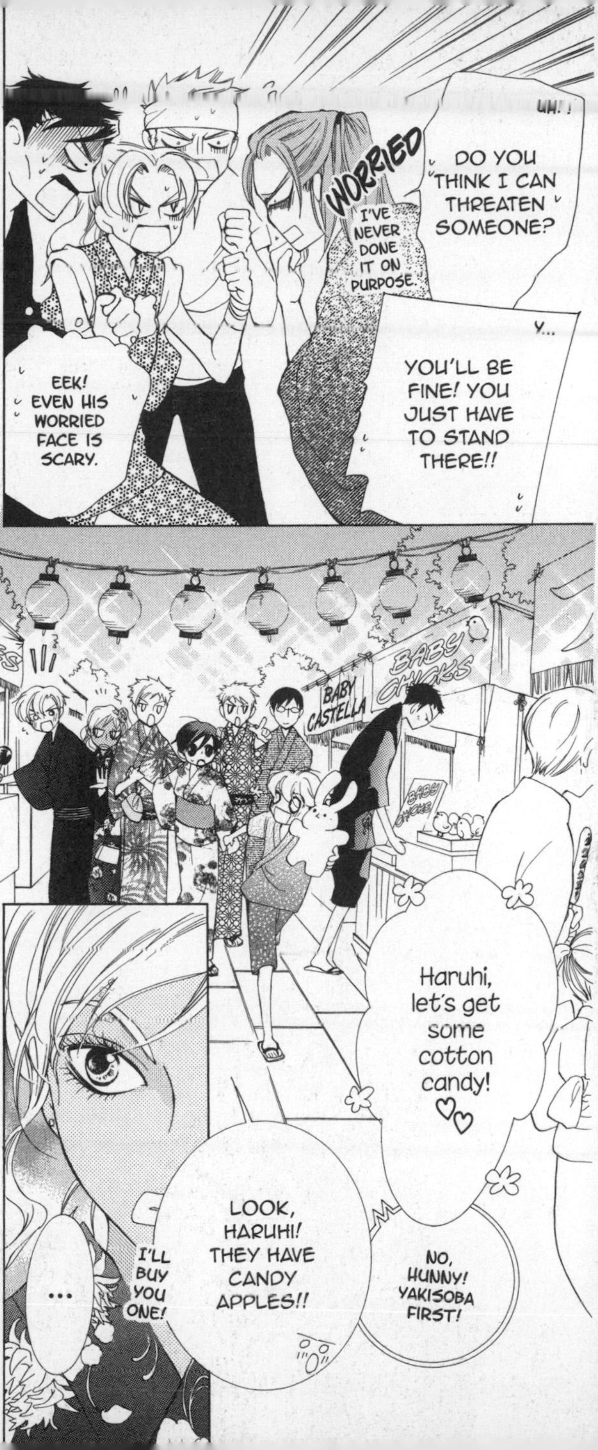
UH!
DO YOU THINK I CAN THREATEN SOMEONE?
WORRIED
I'VE NEVER DONE IT ON PURPOSE.
Y...
YOU'LL BE FINE! YOU JUST HAVE TO STAND THERE!!
EEK! EVEN HIS WORRIED FACE IS SCARY.
BABY CHICKS
BABY CASTELLA
BABY CHICKS
Haruhi, let's get some cotton candy! ♡♡
NO, HUNNY! YAKISOBA FIRST!
LOOK, HARUHI! THEY HAVE CANDY APPLES!!
I'LL BUY YOU ONE!
...

4

✿ WHEN I SAW SOME OF THE DESCRIPTIONS OF THE ORIGINAL CHARACTERS FOR THE VIDEO GAME, I WAS LIKE, "WHAT? TAMAKI'S BEST FRIEND?!" AND "HARUHI'S BEST FRIEND?!" I DIDN'T KNOW WHAT TO DO, BUT KUMIKO TAKAHASHI, WHO DID CHARACTER DESIGN FOR THE ANIME, HELPED ME OUT A LOT, AND THAT HELPED ME GET THROUGH.

THANK YOU VERY MUCH!!

I ONLY KNOW BITS AND PIECES ABOUT THE VIDEO GAME SO FAR, BUT THE ART I'VE SEEN LOOKS GREAT!!!!! BE SURE TO CHECK IT OUT!

AND DON'T WORRY, MORI HAS LOTS OF LINES (LAUGH)!!

EVERY TIME WE DO AUDIO, EVERYONE WORRIES ABOUT THIS GUY. ➜

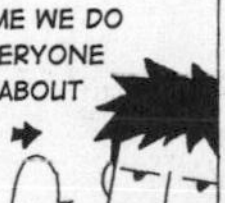
...

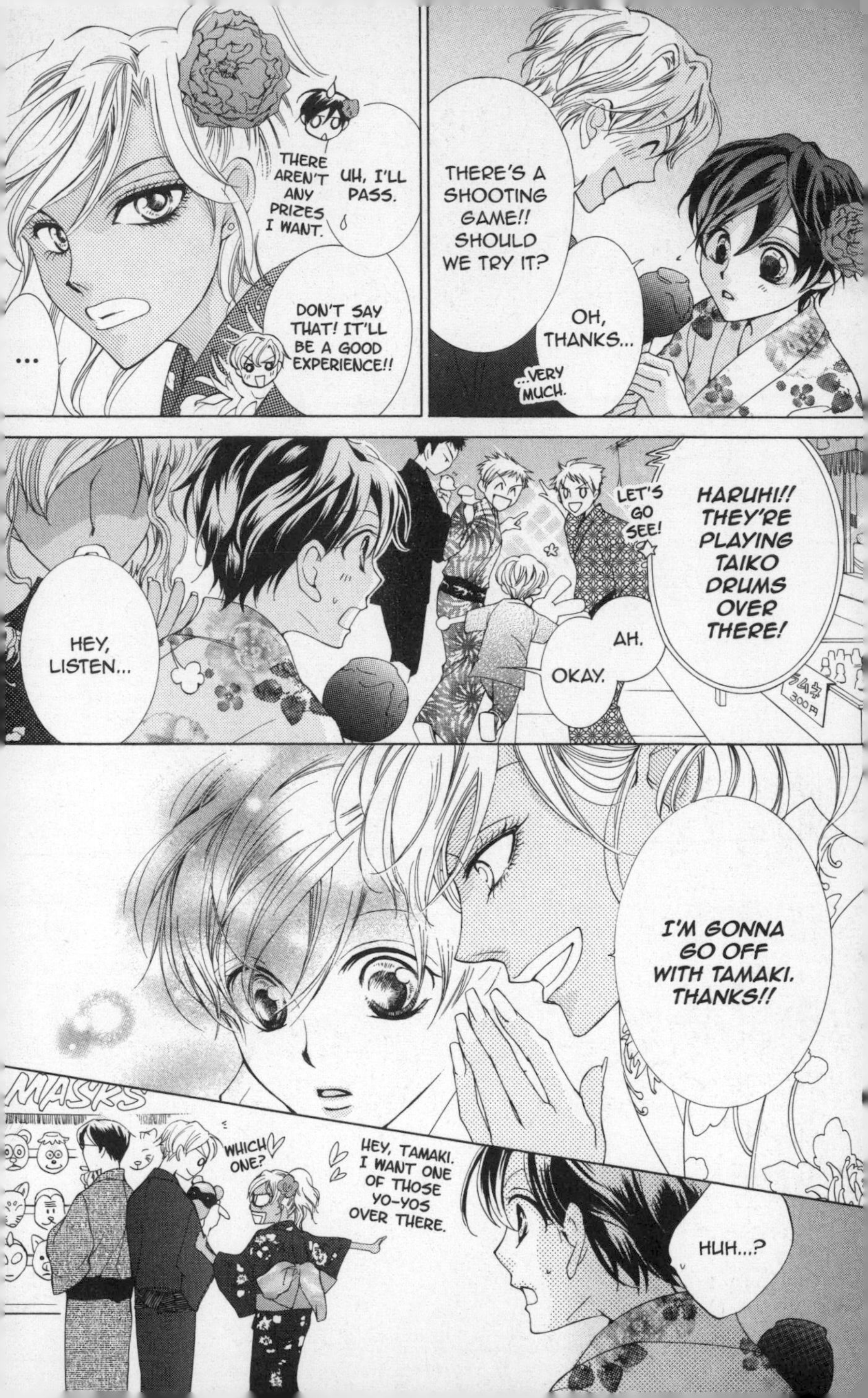
THERE'S A SHOOTING GAME!! SHOULD WE TRY IT?
OH, THANKS...
...VERY MUCH.
UH, I'LL PASS.
THERE AREN'T ANY PRIZES I WANT.
DON'T SAY THAT! IT'LL BE A GOOD EXPERIENCE!!
...
HARUHI!! THEY'RE PLAYING TAIKO DRUMS OVER THERE!
LET'S GO SEE!
ラムネ 300円
AH.
OKAY.
HEY, LISTEN...
I'M GONNA GO OFF WITH TAMAKI. THANKS!!
HUH...?
HEY, TAMAKI. I WANT ONE OF THOSE YO-YOS OVER THERE.
WHICH ONE?
MASKS

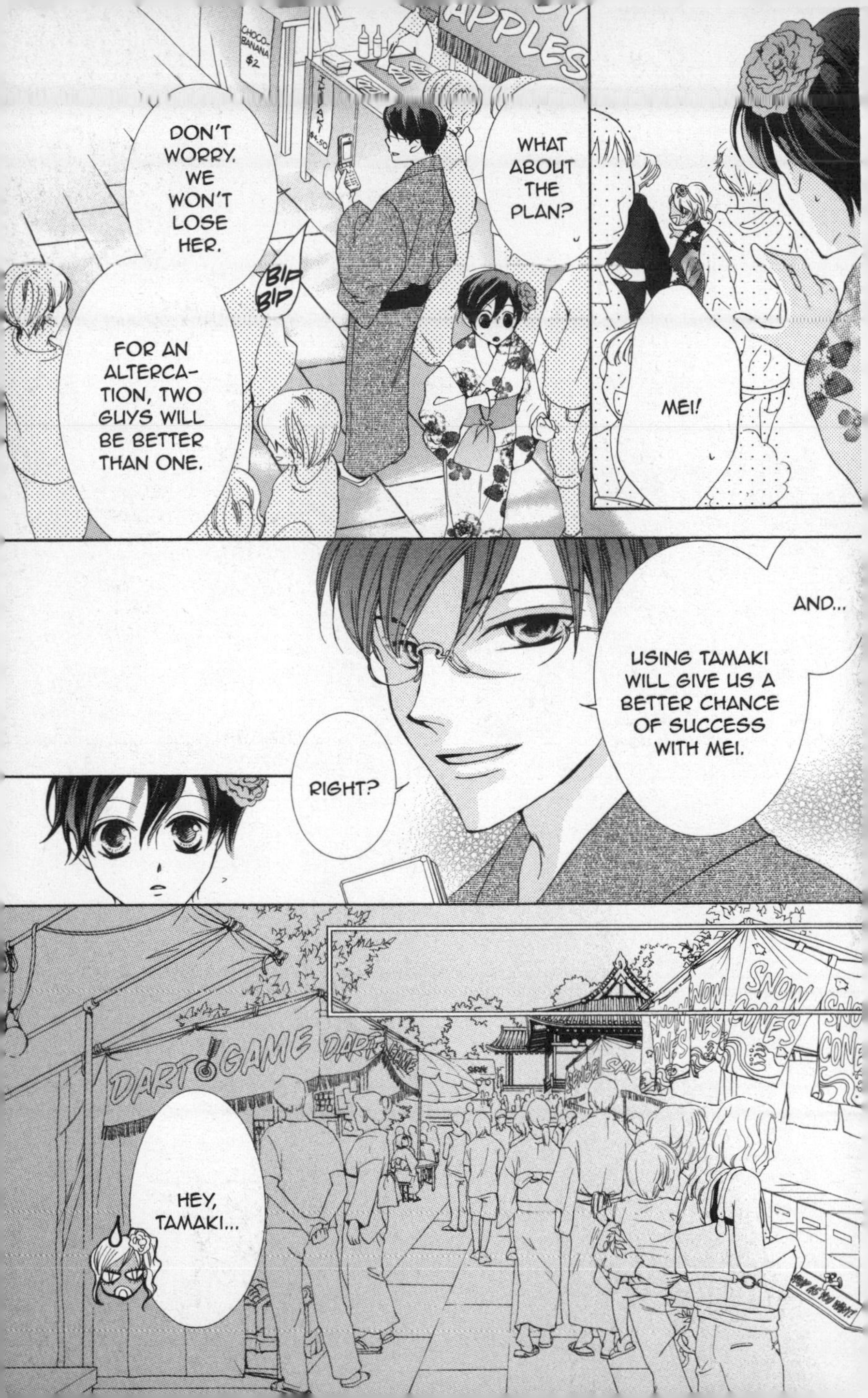
MEI!
APPLES
CHOCO-BANANA $2
WHAT ABOUT THE PLAN?
DON'T WORRY. WE WON'T LOSE HER.
BIP BIP
FOR AN ALTERCATION, TWO GUYS WILL BE BETTER THAN ONE.
AND...
USING TAMAKI WILL GIVE US A BETTER CHANCE OF SUCCESS WITH MEI.
RIGHT?
SNOW CONES
SNOW CONES
SNOW CONES
DART GAME
HEY, TAMAKI...

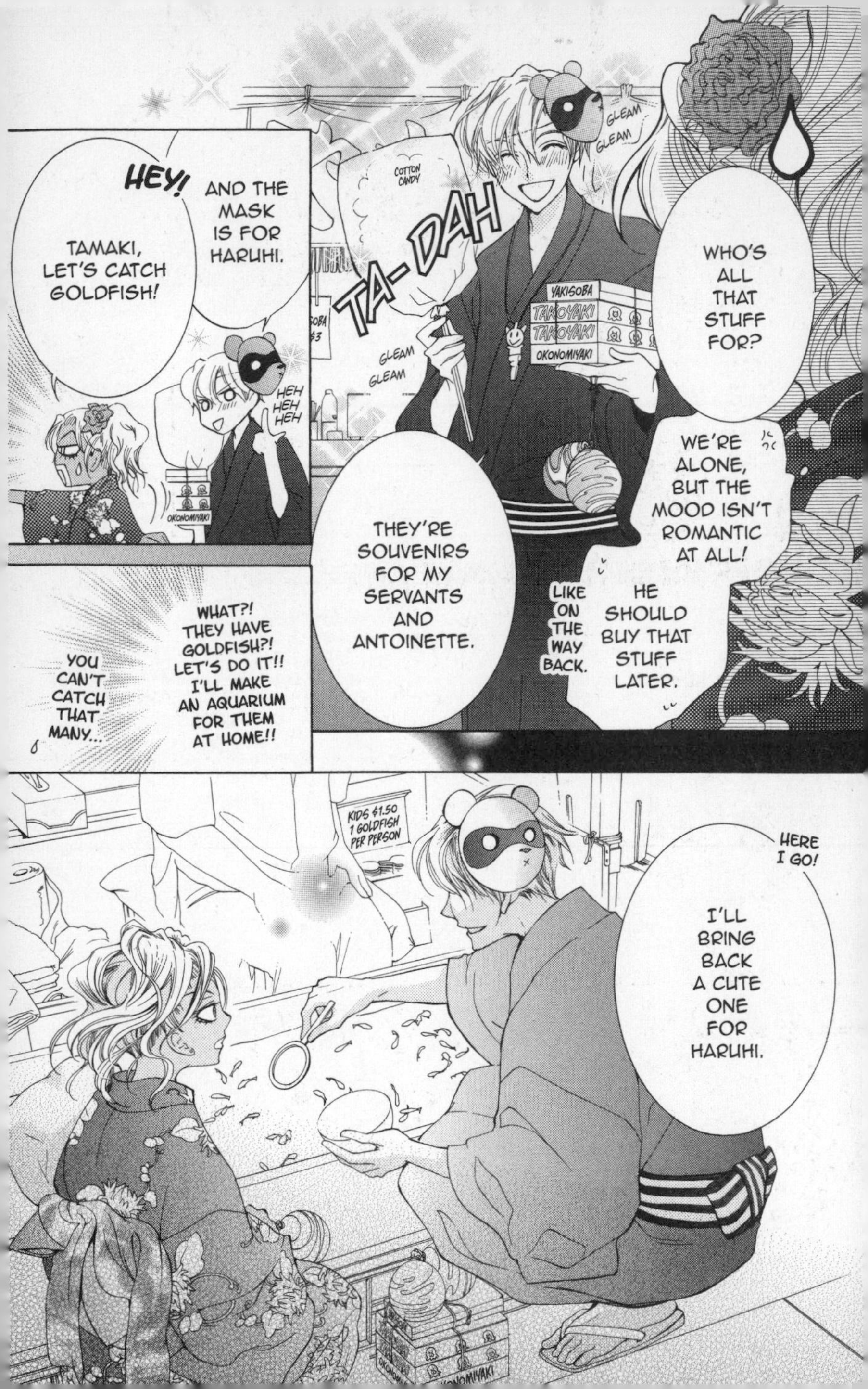
GLEAM GLEAM
COTTON CANDY
TA-DAH
YAKISOBA
TAKOYAKI
TAKOYAKI
OKONOMIYAKI
GLEAM GLEAM
WHO'S ALL THAT STUFF FOR?
THEY'RE SOUVENIRS FOR MY SERVANTS AND ANTOINETTE.
WE'RE ALONE, BUT THE MOOD ISN'T ROMANTIC AT ALL!
HE SHOULD BUY THAT STUFF LATER.
LIKE ON THE WAY BACK.
AND THE MASK IS FOR HARUHI.
HEH HEH HEH
HEY!
TAMAKI, LET'S CATCH GOLDFISH!
OKONOMIYAKI
WHAT?! THEY HAVE GOLDFISH?! LET'S DO IT!! I'LL MAKE AN AQUARIUM FOR THEM AT HOME!!
YOU CAN'T CATCH THAT MANY...
HERE I GO!
I'LL BRING BACK A CUTE ONE FOR HARUHI.
KIDS $1.50 1 GOLDFISH PER PERSON
OKONOMIYAKI

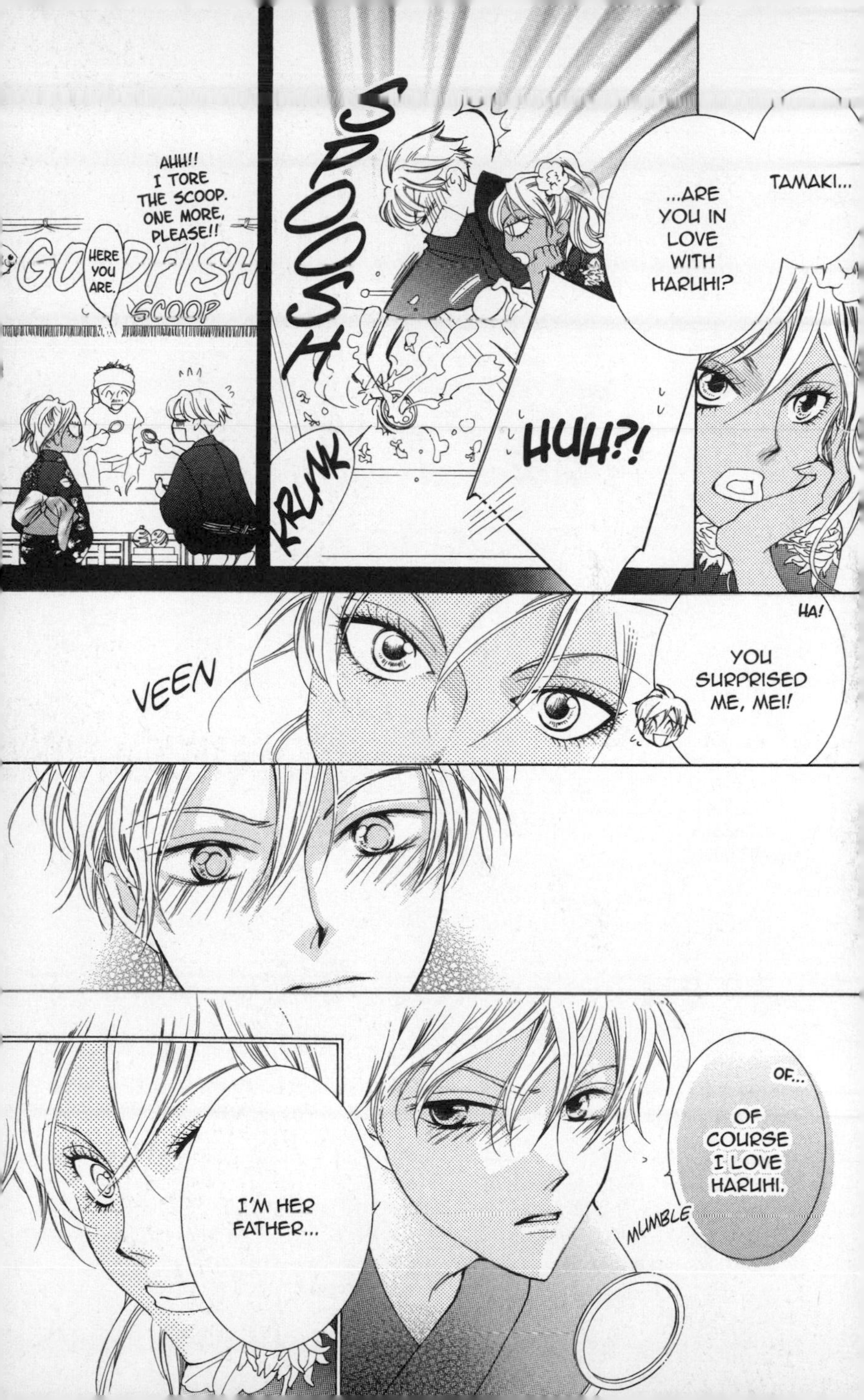
TAMAKI...
...ARE YOU IN LOVE WITH HARUHI?
HUH?!
SPOOSH
KRUNK
AHH!! I TORE THE SCOOP. ONE MORE, PLEASE!!
HERE YOU ARE.
GO DFISH
SCOOP
HA! YOU SURPRISED ME, MEI!
VEEN
OF... OF COURSE I LOVE HARUHI.
MUMBLE
I'M HER FATHER...

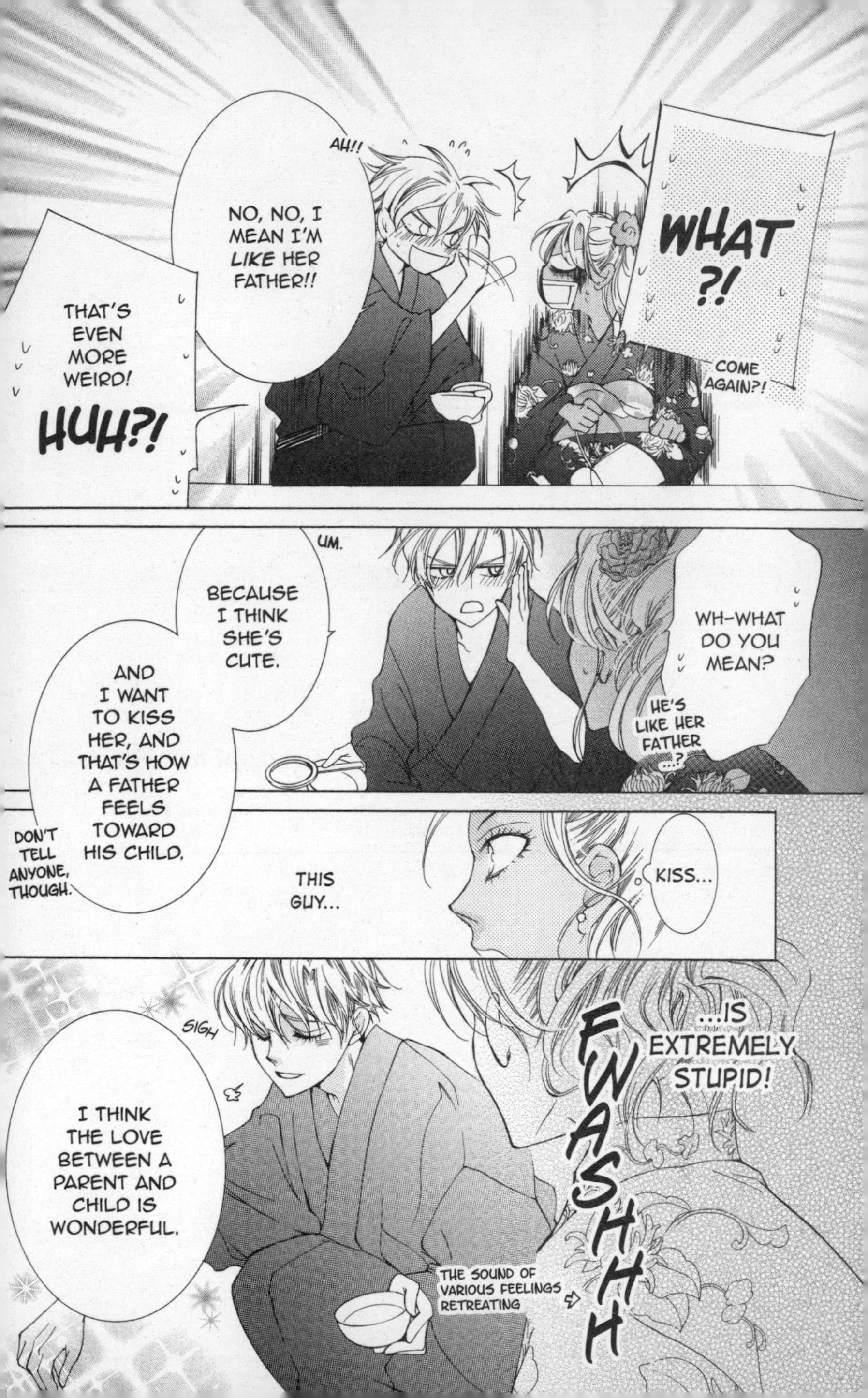
WHAT ?!
COME AGAIN?!
AH!!
NO, NO, I MEAN I'M *LIKE* HER FATHER!!
THAT'S EVEN MORE WEIRD!
HUH?!
WH-WHAT DO YOU MEAN?
HE'S LIKE HER FATHER ...?
UM.
BECAUSE I THINK SHE'S CUTE.
AND I WANT TO KISS HER, AND THAT'S HOW A FATHER FEELS TOWARD HIS CHILD.
DON'T TELL ANYONE, THOUGH.
KISS...
THIS GUY...
...IS EXTREMELY STUPID!
FWASHHH
THE SOUND OF VARIOUS FEELINGS RETREATING
SIGH
I THINK THE LOVE BETWEEN A PARENT AND CHILD IS WONDERFUL.

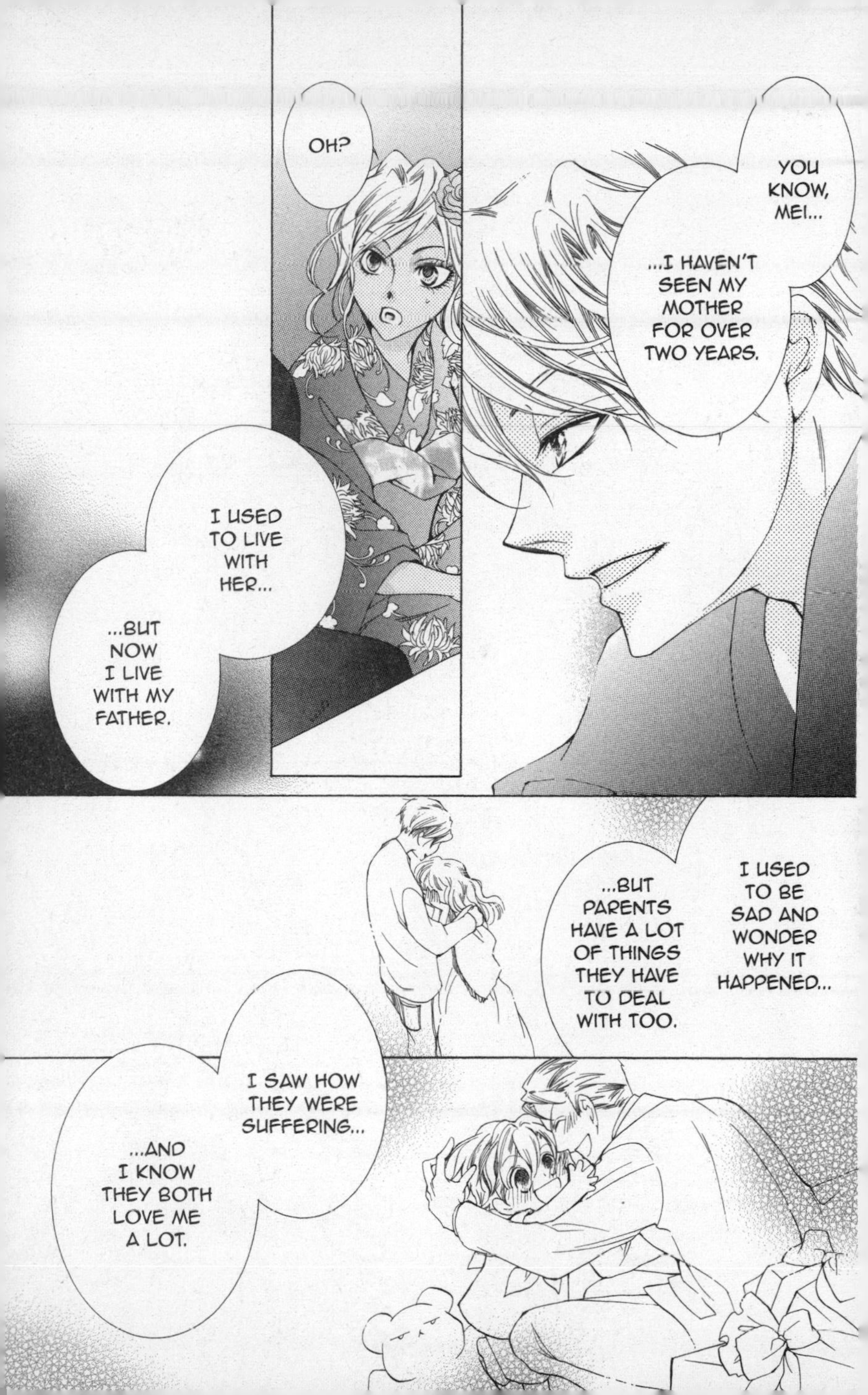
YOU KNOW, MEI...
...I HAVEN'T SEEN MY MOTHER FOR OVER TWO YEARS.
OH?
I USED TO LIVE WITH HER...
...BUT NOW I LIVE WITH MY FATHER.
I USED TO BE SAD AND WONDER WHY IT HAPPENED...
...BUT PARENTS HAVE A LOT OF THINGS THEY HAVE TO DEAL WITH TOO.
I SAW HOW THEY WERE SUFFERING...
...AND I KNOW THEY BOTH LOVE ME A LOT.

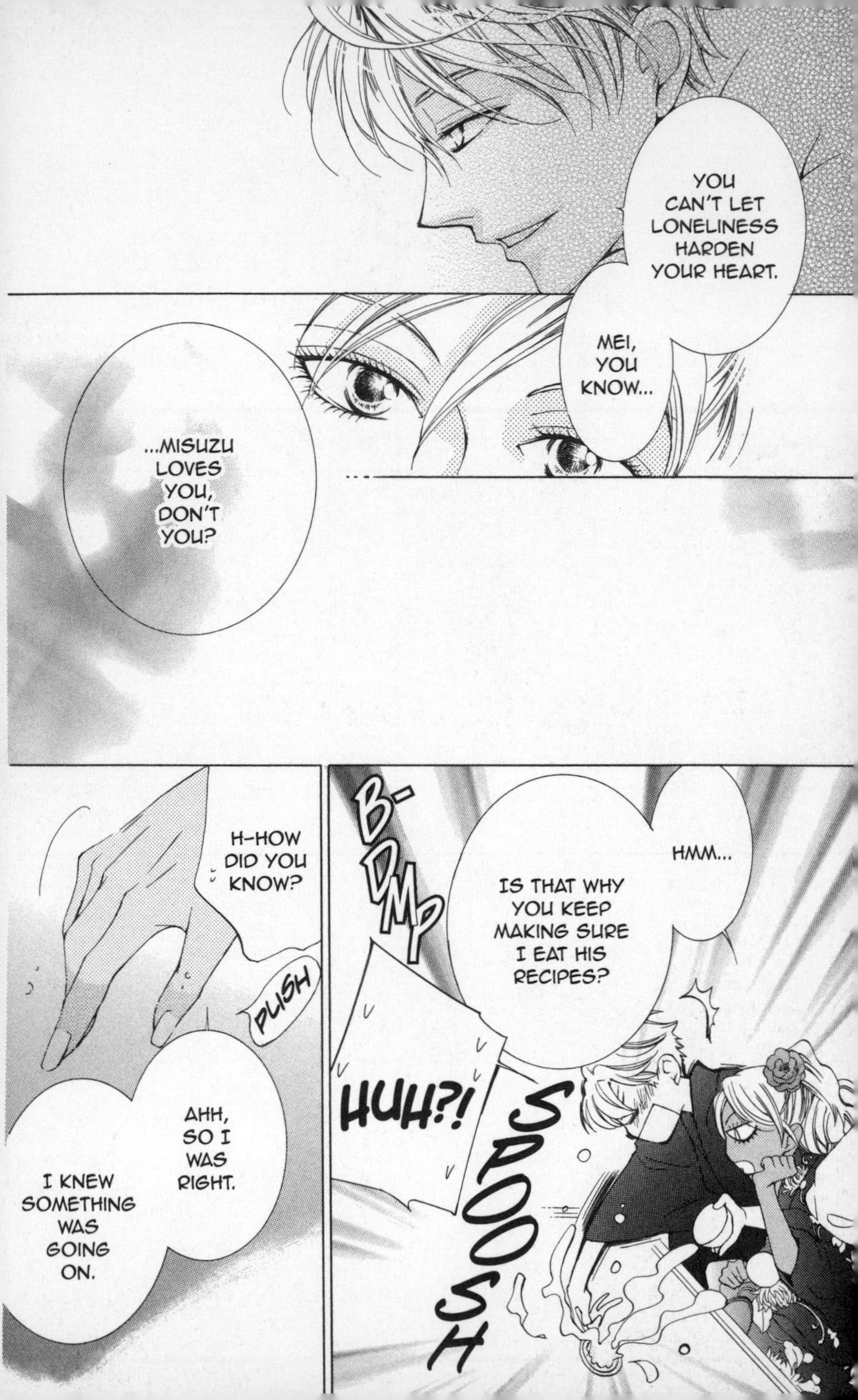
YOU CAN'T LET LONELINESS HARDEN YOUR HEART.
MEI, YOU KNOW...
...MISUZU LOVES YOU, DON'T YOU?
B-DMP
HMM...
IS THAT WHY YOU KEEP MAKING SURE I EAT HIS RECIPES?
HUH?!
SPOOSH
H-HOW DID YOU KNOW?
PUSH
AHH, SO I WAS RIGHT.
I KNEW SOMETHING WAS GOING ON.

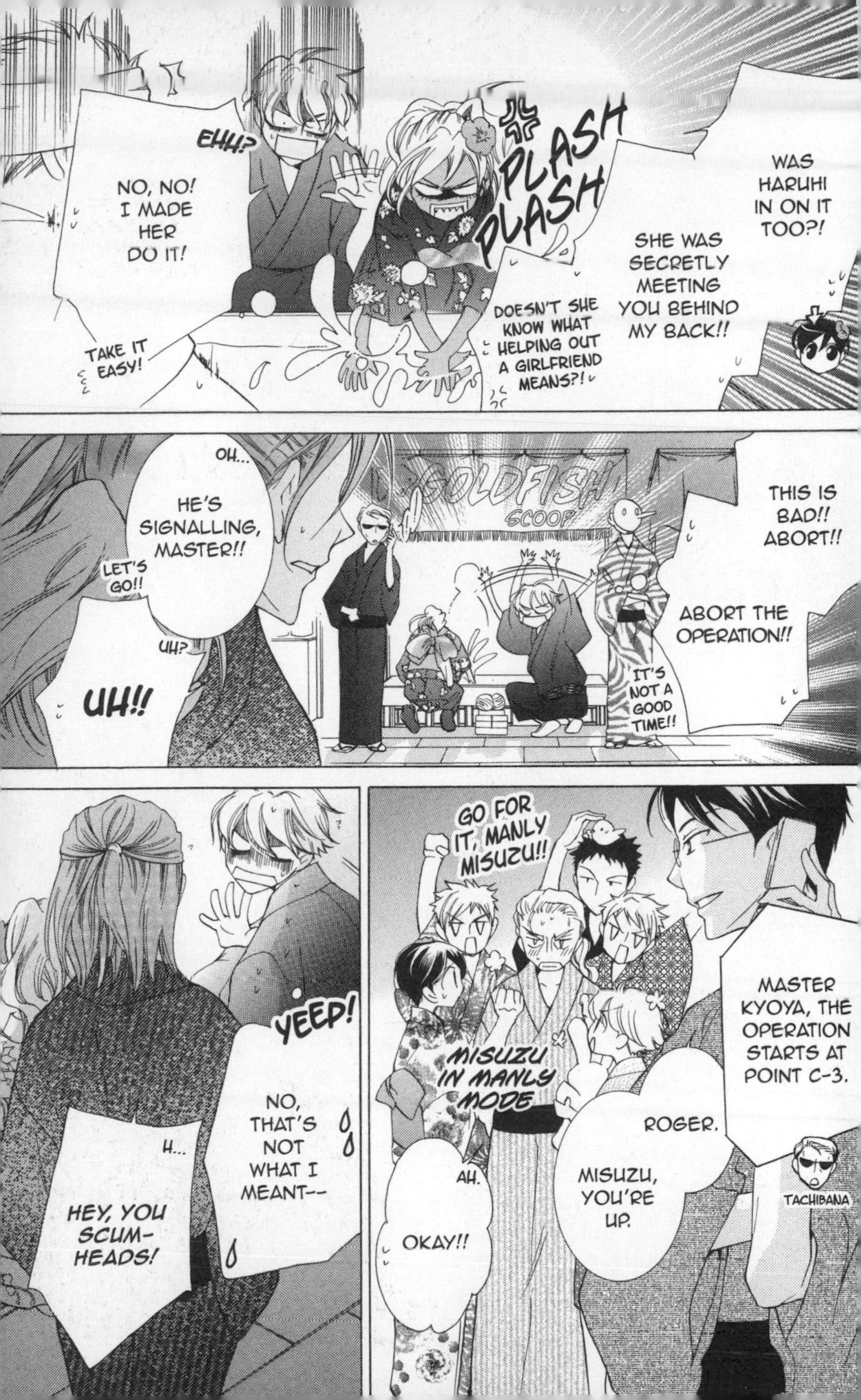
WAS HARUHI IN ON IT TOO?!
SHE WAS SECRETLY MEETING YOU BEHIND MY BACK!!
PLASH PLASH
DOESN'T SHE KNOW WHAT HELPING OUT A GIRLFRIEND MEANS?!
EHH?
NO, NO! I MADE HER DO IT!
TAKE IT EASY!
THIS IS BAD!! ABORT!!
ABORT THE OPERATION!!
IT'S NOT A GOOD TIME!!
GOLDFISH SCOOP
OH...
HE'S SIGNALLING, MASTER!!
LET'S GO!!
UH?
UH!!
GO FOR IT, MANLY MISUZU!!
MASTER KYOYA, THE OPERATION STARTS AT POINT C-3.
MISUZU IN MANLY MODE
ROGER.
MISUZU, YOU'RE UP.
TACHIBANA
AH.
OKAY!!
YEEP!
NO, THAT'S NOT WHAT I MEANT--
H...
HEY, YOU SCUM-HEADS!

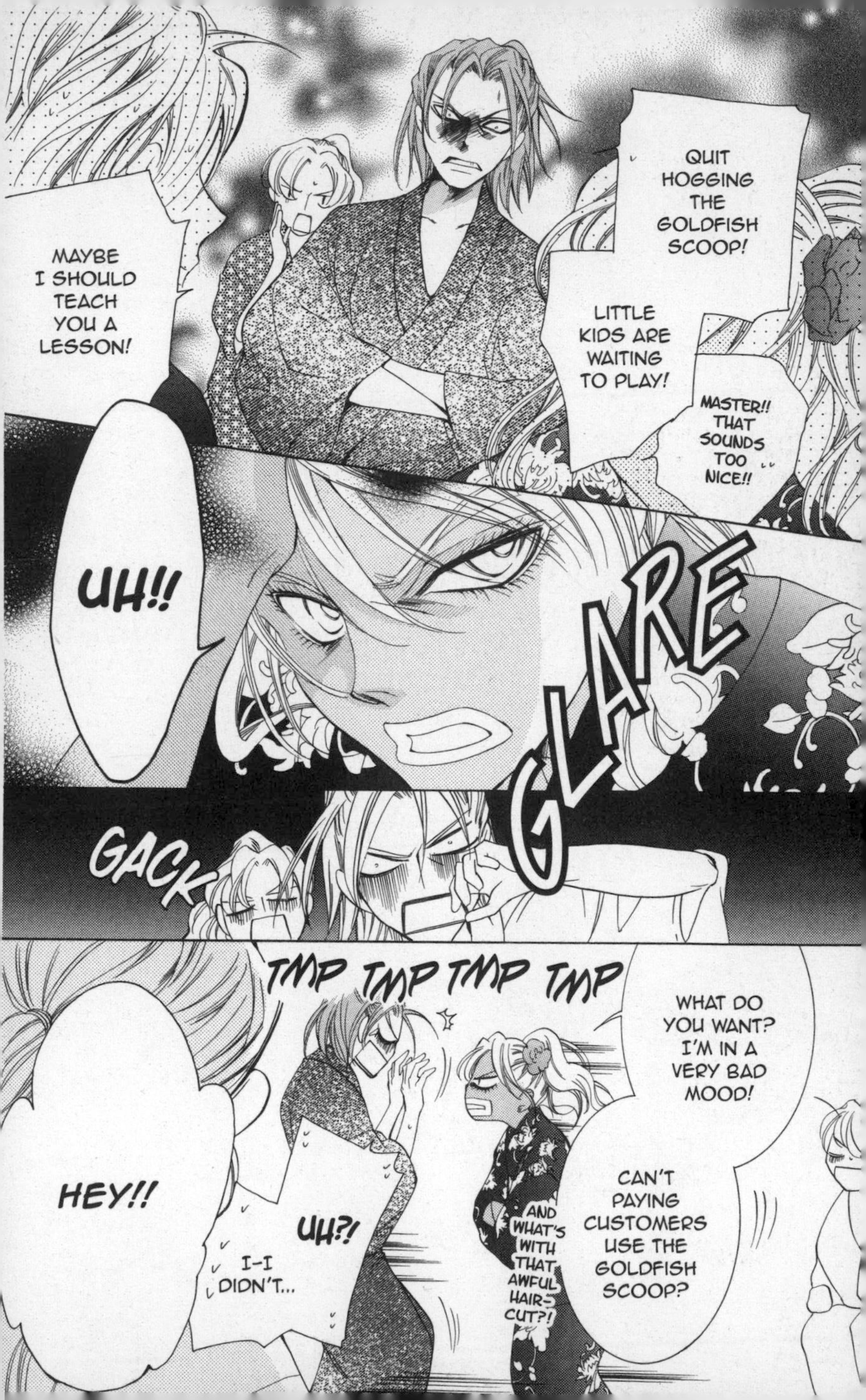
QUIT HOGGING THE GOLDFISH SCOOP!
LITTLE KIDS ARE WAITING TO PLAY!
MASTER!! THAT SOUNDS TOO NICE!!
MAYBE I SHOULD TEACH YOU A LESSON!
GLARE
UH!!
GACK
TMP TMP TMP TMP
WHAT DO YOU WANT? I'M IN A VERY BAD MOOD!
CAN'T PAYING CUSTOMERS USE THE GOLDFISH SCOOP?
AND WHAT'S WITH THAT AWFUL HAIR-CUT?!
UH?!
I-I DIDN'T...
HEY!!

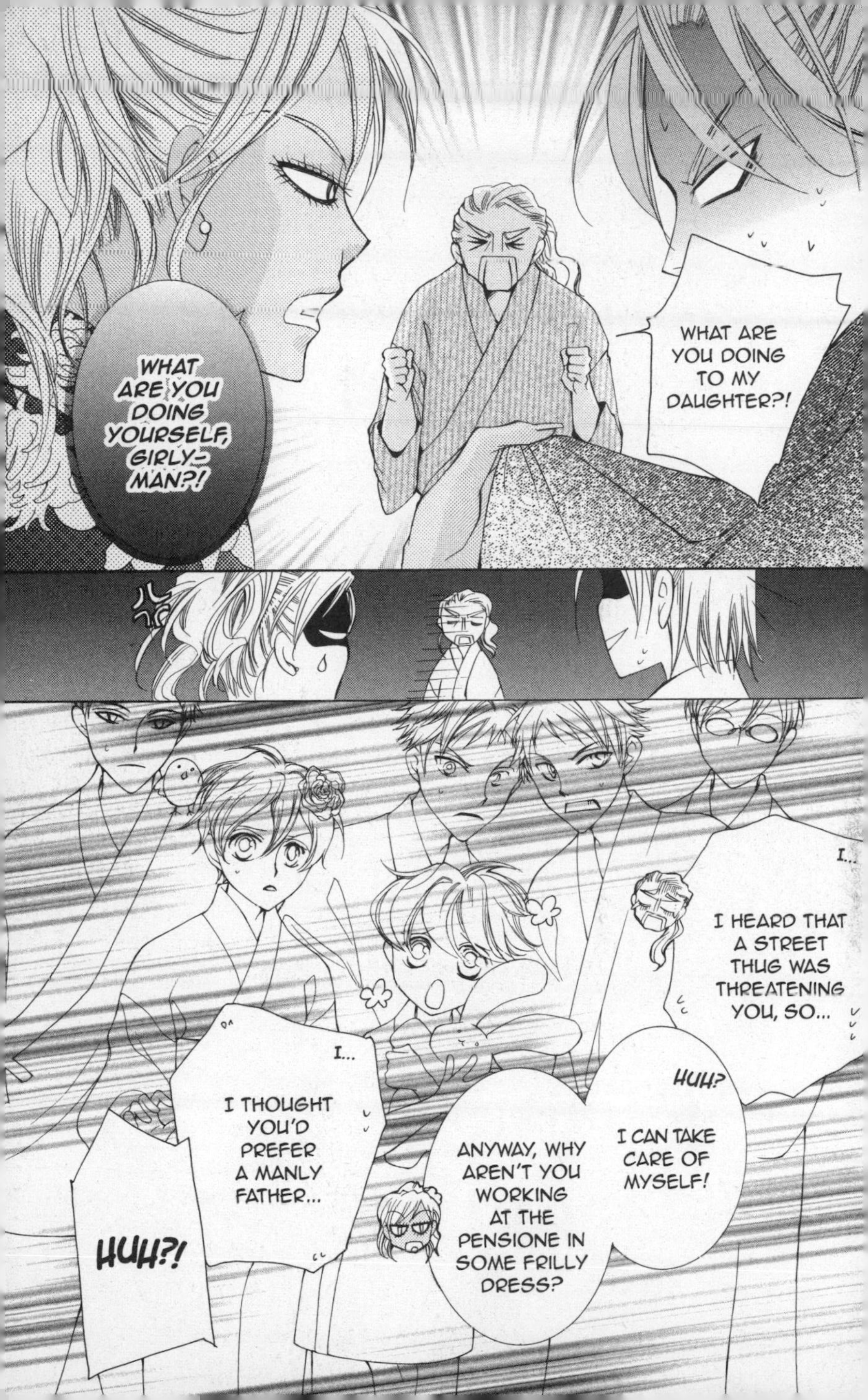
WHAT ARE YOU DOING TO MY DAUGHTER?!
WHAT ARE YOU DOING YOURSELF, GIRLY-MAN?!
I...
I HEARD THAT A STREET THUG WAS THREATENING YOU, SO...
HUH?
I CAN TAKE CARE OF MYSELF!
ANYWAY, WHY AREN'T YOU WORKING AT THE PENSIONE IN SOME FRILLY DRESS?
I...
I THOUGHT YOU'D PREFER A MANLY FATHER...
HUH?!

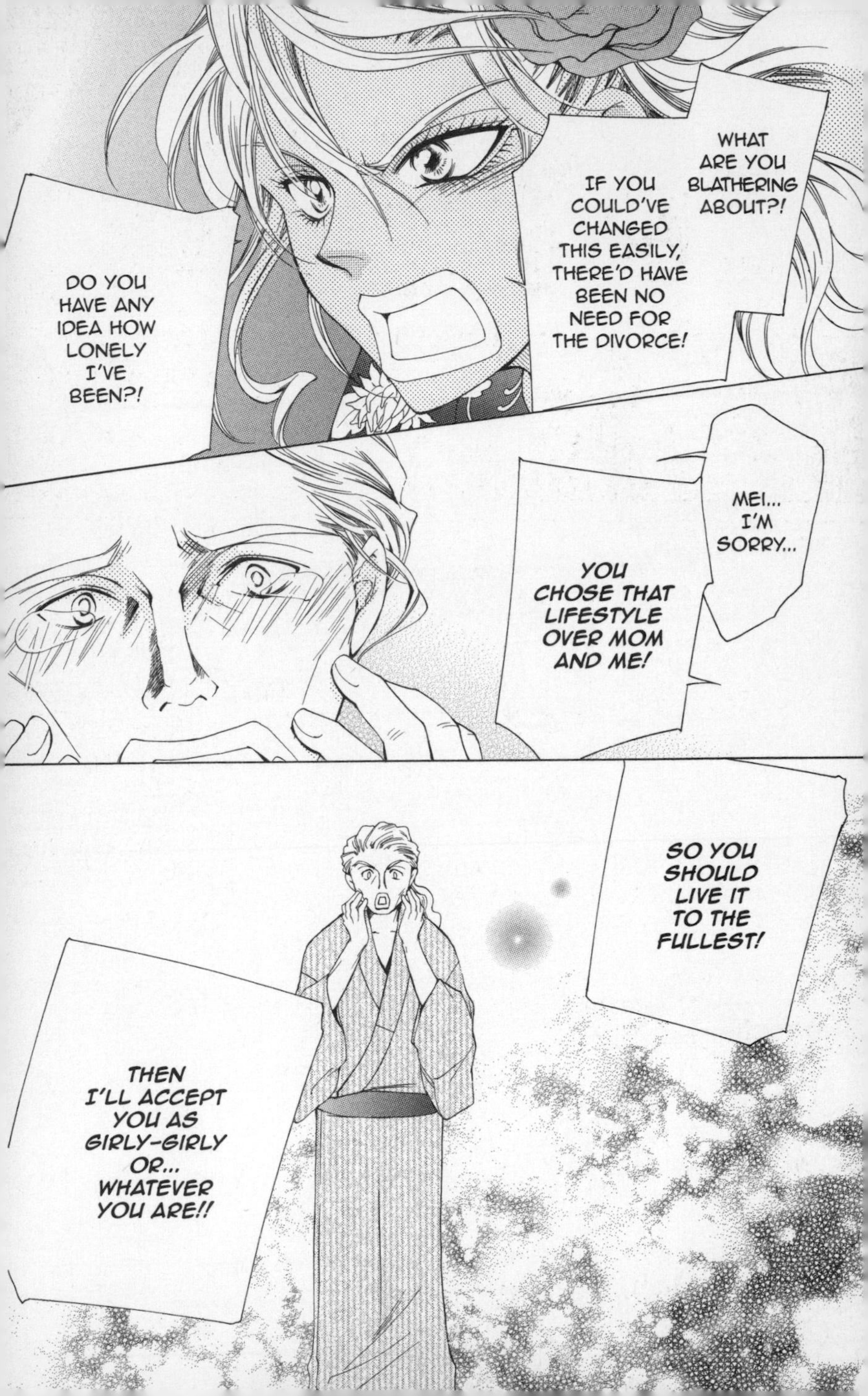
WHAT ARE YOU BLATHERING ABOUT?!
IF YOU COULD'VE CHANGED THIS EASILY, THERE'D HAVE BEEN NO NEED FOR THE DIVORCE!
DO YOU HAVE ANY IDEA HOW LONELY I'VE BEEN?!
MEI... I'M SORRY...
YOU CHOSE THAT LIFESTYLE OVER MOM AND ME!
SO YOU SHOULD LIVE IT TO THE FULLEST!
THEN I'LL ACCEPT YOU AS GIRLY-GIRLY OR... WHATEVER YOU ARE!!

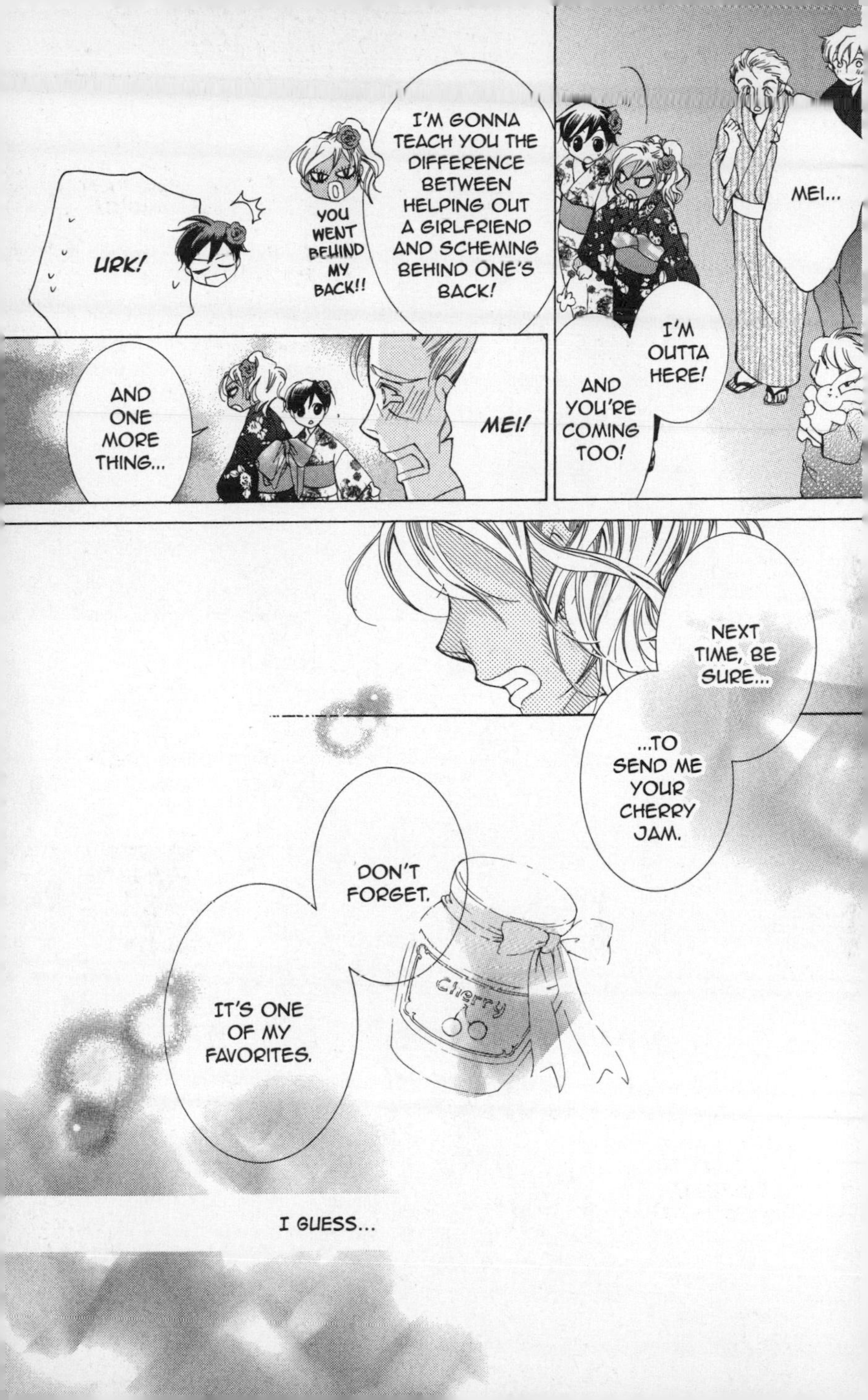
MEI...
I'M OUTTA HERE!
AND YOU'RE COMING TOO!
I'M GONNA TEACH YOU THE DIFFERENCE BETWEEN HELPING OUT A GIRLFRIEND AND SCHEMING BEHIND ONE'S BACK!
YOU WENT BEHIND MY BACK!!
URK!
MEI!
AND ONE MORE THING...
NEXT TIME, BE SURE...
...TO SEND ME YOUR CHERRY JAM.
DON'T FORGET.
Cherry
IT'S ONE OF MY FAVORITES.
I GUESS...

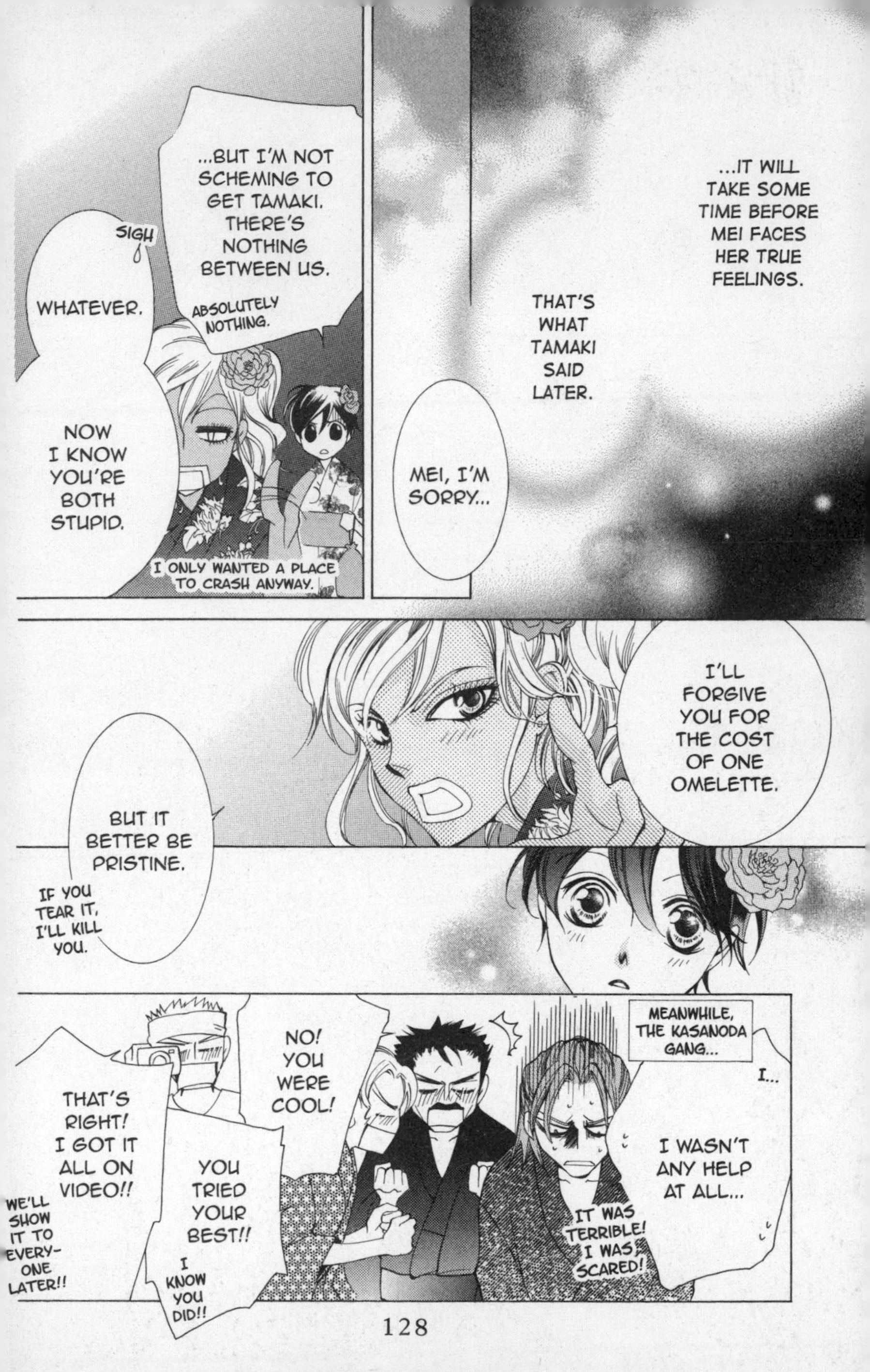
...IT WILL TAKE SOME TIME BEFORE MEI FACES HER TRUE FEELINGS.
THAT'S WHAT TAMAKI SAID LATER.
MEI, I'M SORRY...
...BUT I'M NOT SCHEMING TO GET TAMAKI. THERE'S NOTHING BETWEEN US.
ABSOLUTELY NOTHING.
SIGH
WHATEVER.
NOW I KNOW YOU'RE BOTH STUPID.
I ONLY WANTED A PLACE TO CRASH ANYWAY.
I'LL FORGIVE YOU FOR THE COST OF ONE OMELETTE.
BUT IT BETTER BE PRISTINE.
IF YOU TEAR IT, I'LL KILL YOU.
MEANWHILE, THE KASANODA GANG...
I...
I WASN'T ANY HELP AT ALL...
IT WAS TERRIBLE! I WAS SCARED!
NO! YOU WERE COOL!
YOU TRIED YOUR BEST!!
I KNOW YOU DID!!
THAT'S RIGHT! I GOT IT ALL ON VIDEO!!
WE'LL SHOW IT TO EVERY-ONE LATER!!

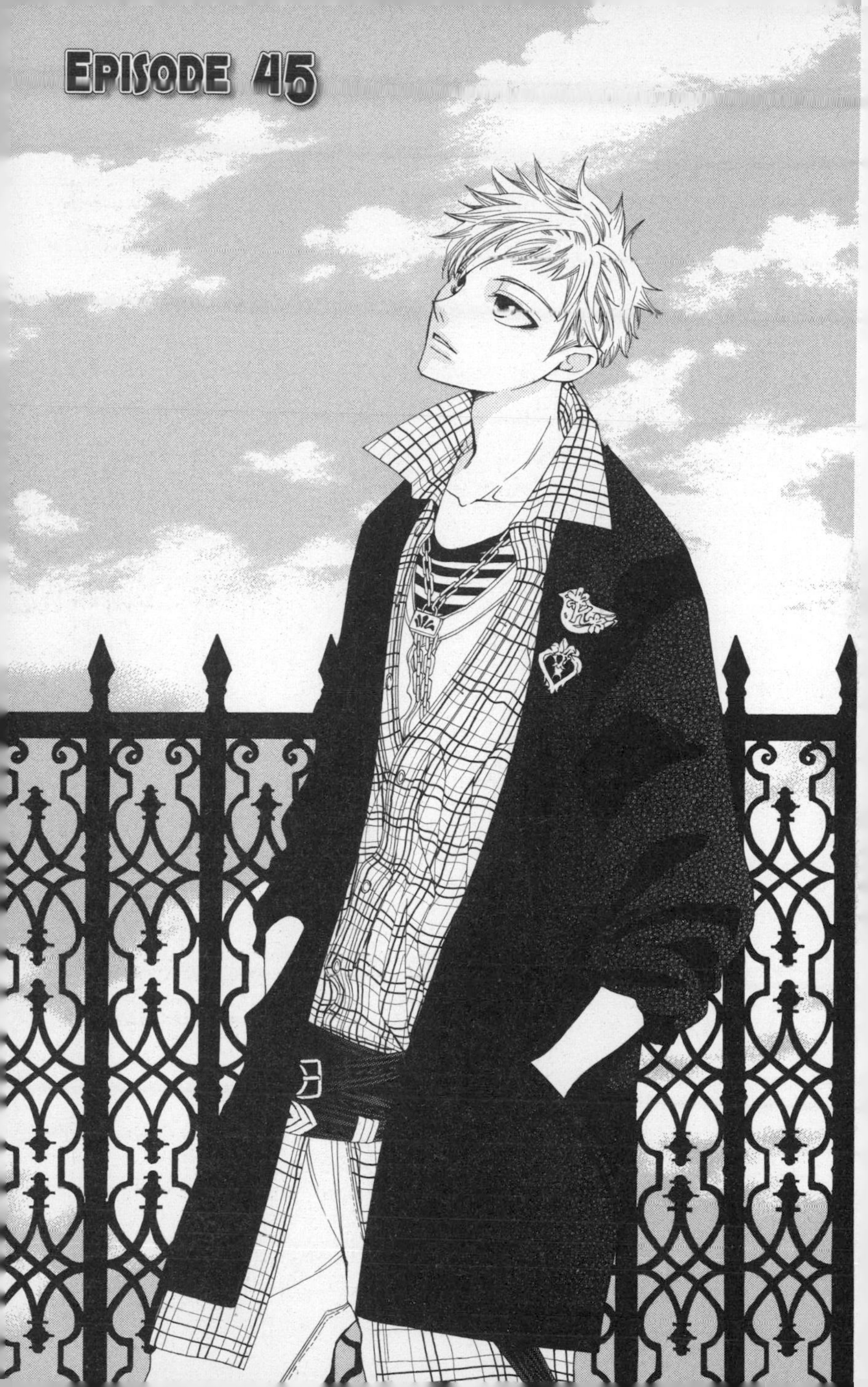
Episode 45

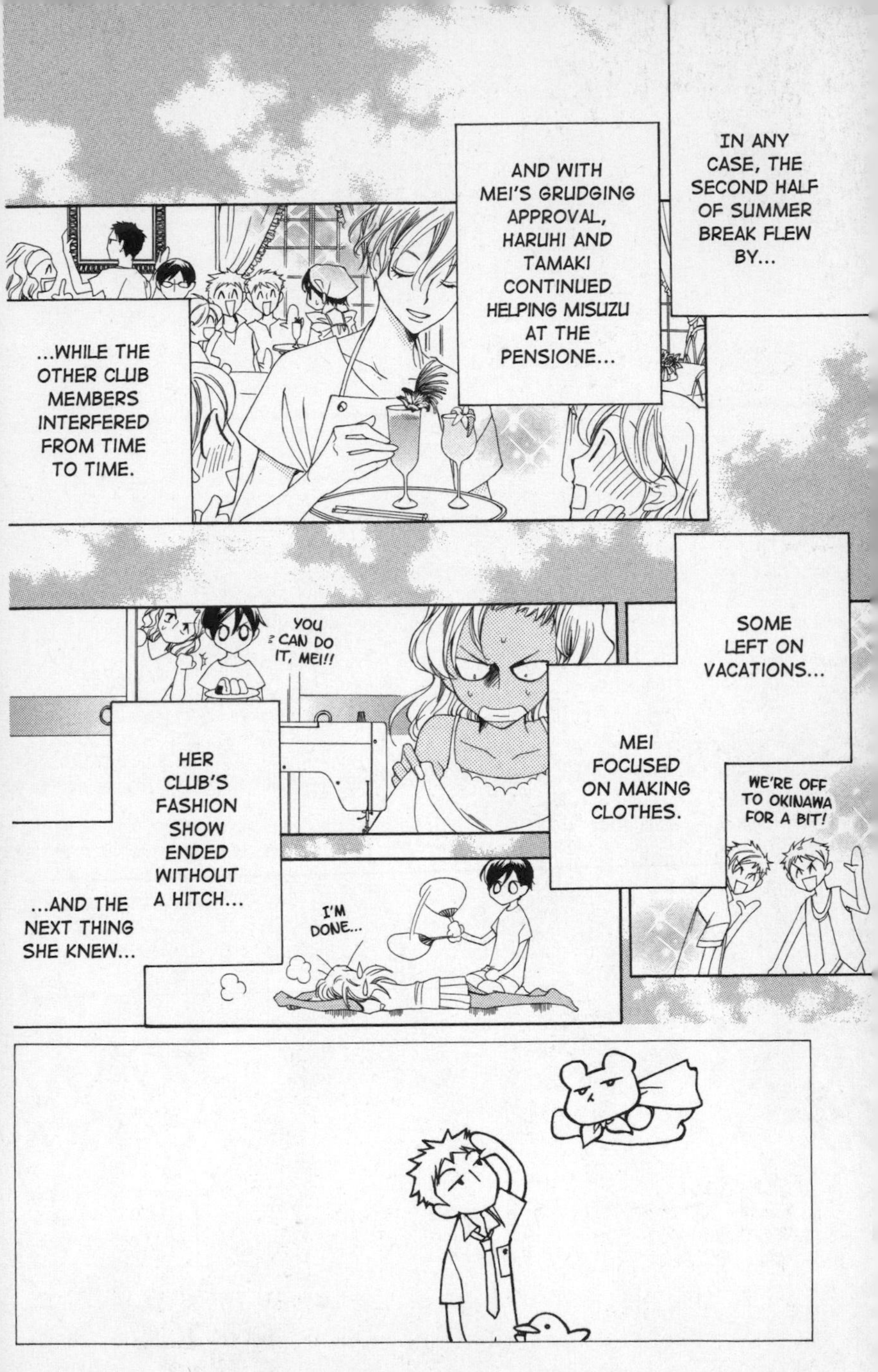
IN ANY CASE, THE SECOND HALF OF SUMMER BREAK FLEW BY...
AND WITH MEI'S GRUDGING APPROVAL, HARUHI AND TAMAKI CONTINUED HELPING MISUZU AT THE PENSIONE...
...WHILE THE OTHER CLUB MEMBERS INTERFERED FROM TIME TO TIME.
SOME LEFT ON VACATIONS...
WE'RE OFF TO OKINAWA FOR A BIT!
MEI FOCUSED ON MAKING CLOTHES.
YOU CAN DO IT, MEI!!
HER CLUB'S FASHION SHOW ENDED WITHOUT A HITCH...
I'M DONE...
...AND THE NEXT THING SHE KNEW...

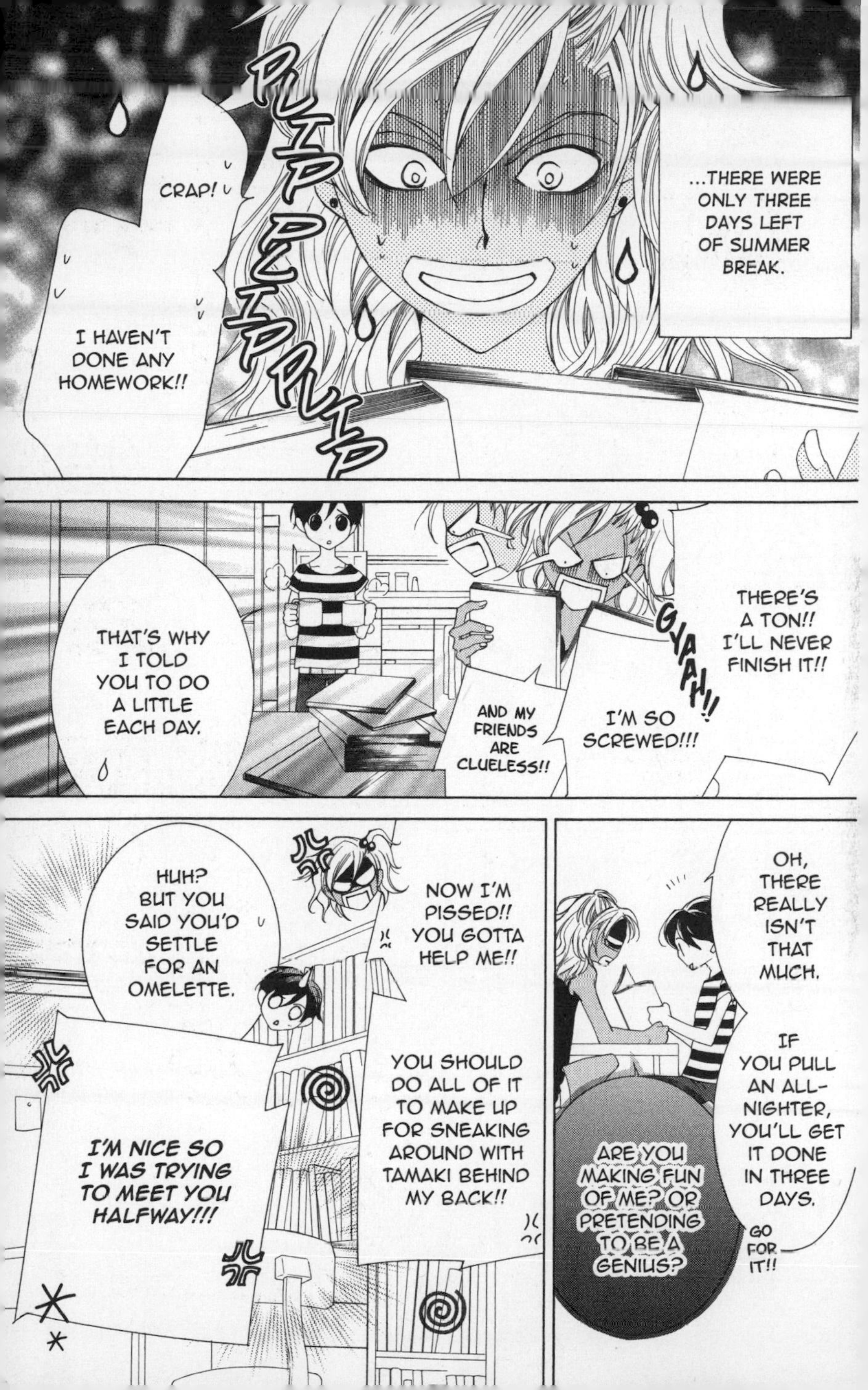
...THERE WERE ONLY THREE DAYS LEFT OF SUMMER BREAK.
PUIP PUIP PUIP
CRAP!
I HAVEN'T DONE ANY HOMEWORK!!
THERE'S A TON!! I'LL NEVER FINISH IT!!
GYAAH!!
I'M SO SCREWED!!!
AND MY FRIENDS ARE CLUELESS!!
THAT'S WHY I TOLD YOU TO DO A LITTLE EACH DAY.
OH, THERE REALLY ISN'T THAT MUCH.
IF YOU PULL AN ALL-NIGHTER, YOU'LL GET IT DONE IN THREE DAYS.
GO FOR IT!!
ARE YOU MAKING FUN OF ME? OR PRETENDING TO BE A GENIUS?
NOW I'M PISSED!! YOU GOTTA HELP ME!!
YOU SHOULD DO ALL OF IT TO MAKE UP FOR SNEAKING AROUND WITH TAMAKI BEHIND MY BACK!!
HUH? BUT YOU SAID YOU'D SETTLE FOR AN OMELETTE.
I'M NICE SO I WAS TRYING TO MEET YOU HALFWAY!!!

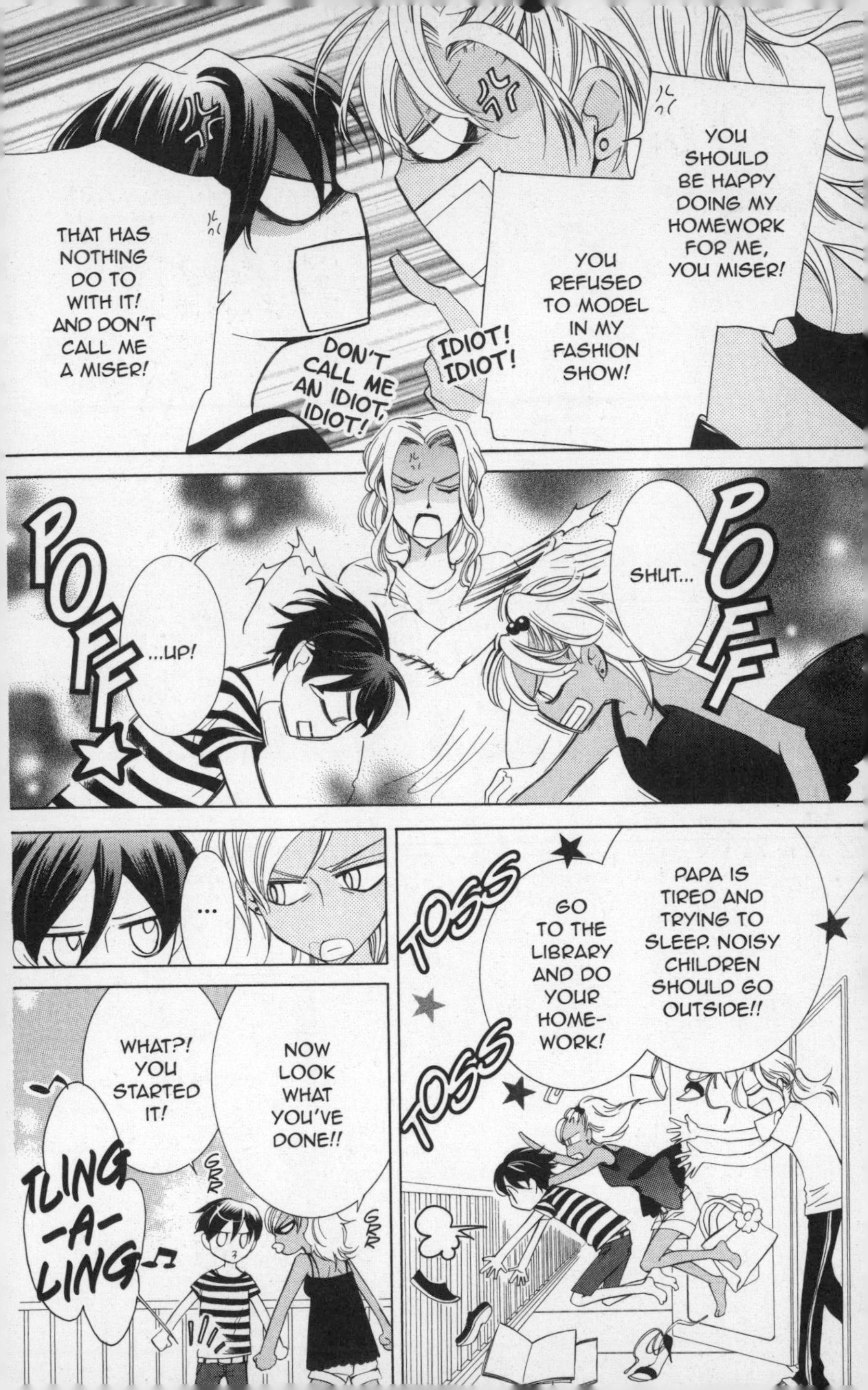
YOU SHOULD BE HAPPY DOING MY HOMEWORK FOR ME, YOU MISER!
YOU REFUSED TO MODEL IN MY FASHION SHOW!
IDIOT! IDIOT!
DON'T CALL ME AN IDIOT, IDIOT!
THAT HAS NOTHING DO TO WITH IT! AND DON'T CALL ME A MISER!
POFF
SHUT...
...UP!
POFF
TOSS
PAPA IS TIRED AND TRYING TO SLEEP. NOISY CHILDREN SHOULD GO OUTSIDE!!
GO TO THE LIBRARY AND DO YOUR HOME-WORK!
TOSS
...
NOW LOOK WHAT YOU'VE DONE!!
GRR
WHAT?! YOU STARTED IT!
GRR
TLING-A-LING

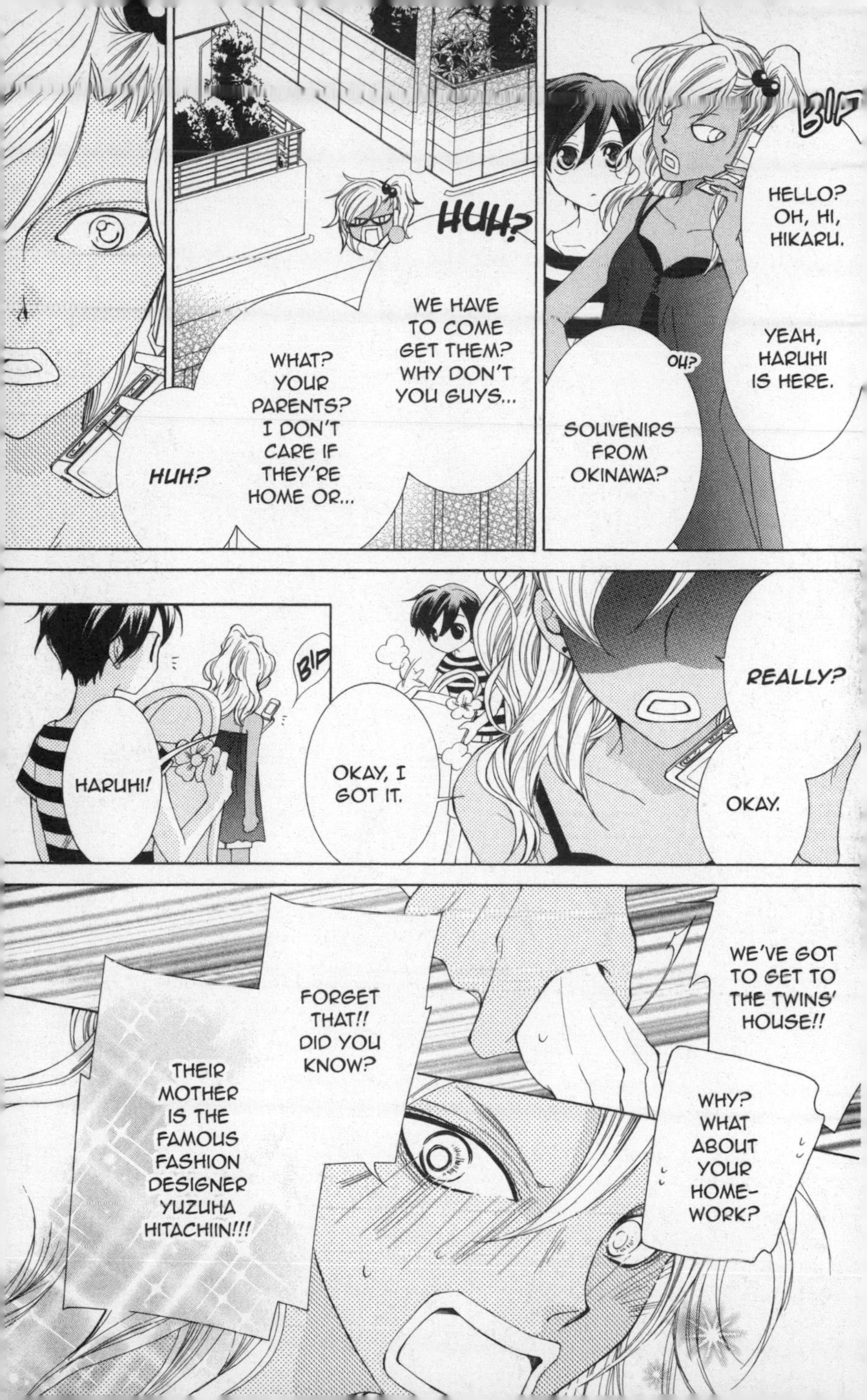
BIP
HELLO? OH, HI, HIKARU.
YEAH, HARUHI IS HERE.
OH?
SOUVENIRS FROM OKINAWA?
HUH?
WE HAVE TO COME GET THEM? WHY DON'T YOU GUYS...
WHAT? YOUR PARENTS? I DON'T CARE IF THEY'RE HOME OR...
HUH?
REALLY?
OKAY.
OKAY, I GOT IT.
BIP
HARUHI!
WE'VE GOT TO GET TO THE TWINS' HOUSE!!
WHY? WHAT ABOUT YOUR HOME-WORK?
FORGET THAT!! DID YOU KNOW?
THEIR MOTHER IS THE FAMOUS FASHION DESIGNER YUZUHA HITACHIIN!!!

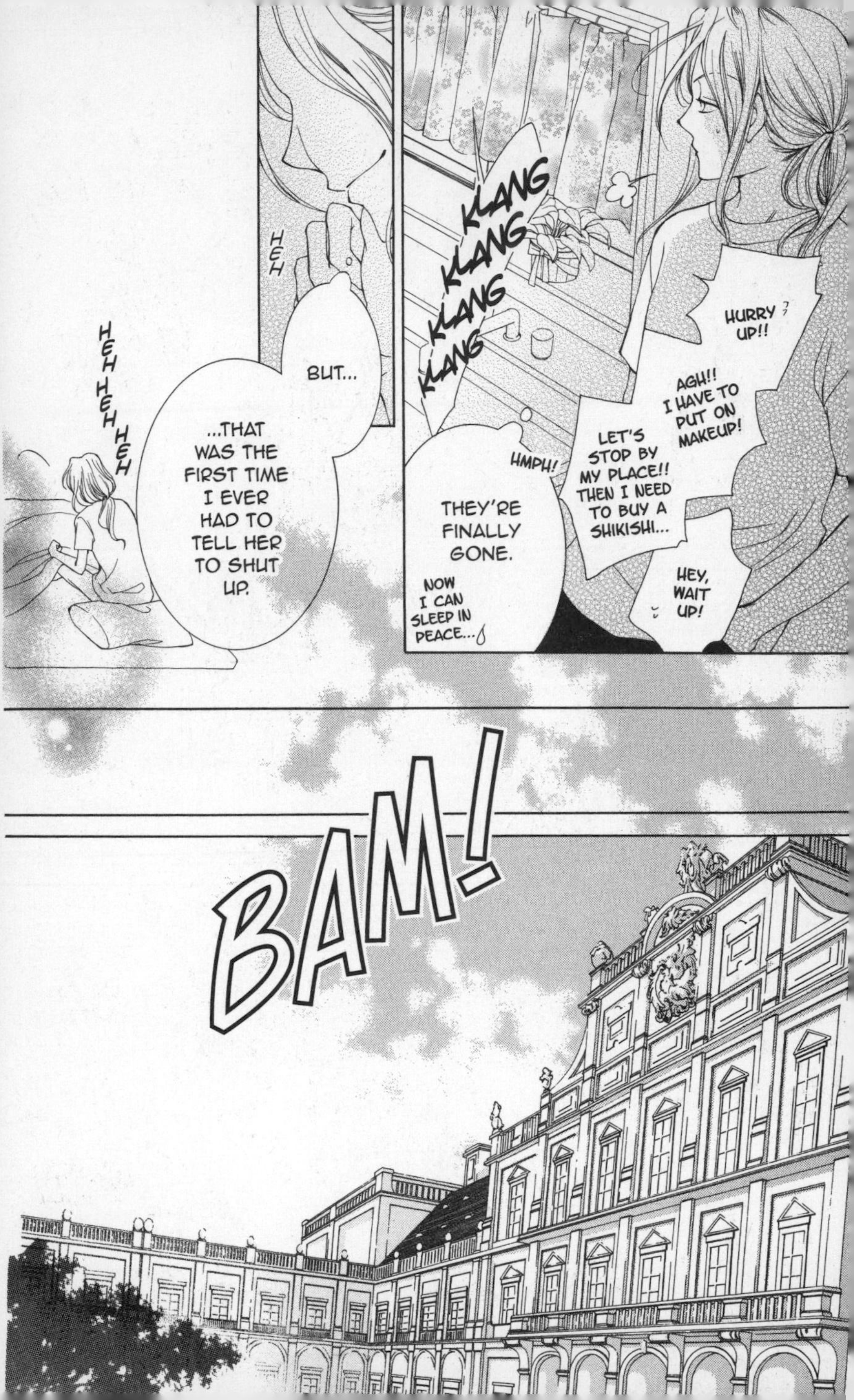
HURRY UP!!
AGH!! I HAVE TO PUT ON MAKEUP!
LET'S STOP BY MY PLACE!! THEN I NEED TO BUY A SHIKISHI...
HEY, WAIT UP!
KLANG KLANG KLANG KLANG
HMPH!
THEY'RE FINALLY GONE.
NOW I CAN SLEEP IN PEACE...
HEH
BUT...
...THAT WAS THE FIRST TIME I EVER HAD TO TELL HER TO SHUT UP.
HEH HEH HEH HEH
BAM!

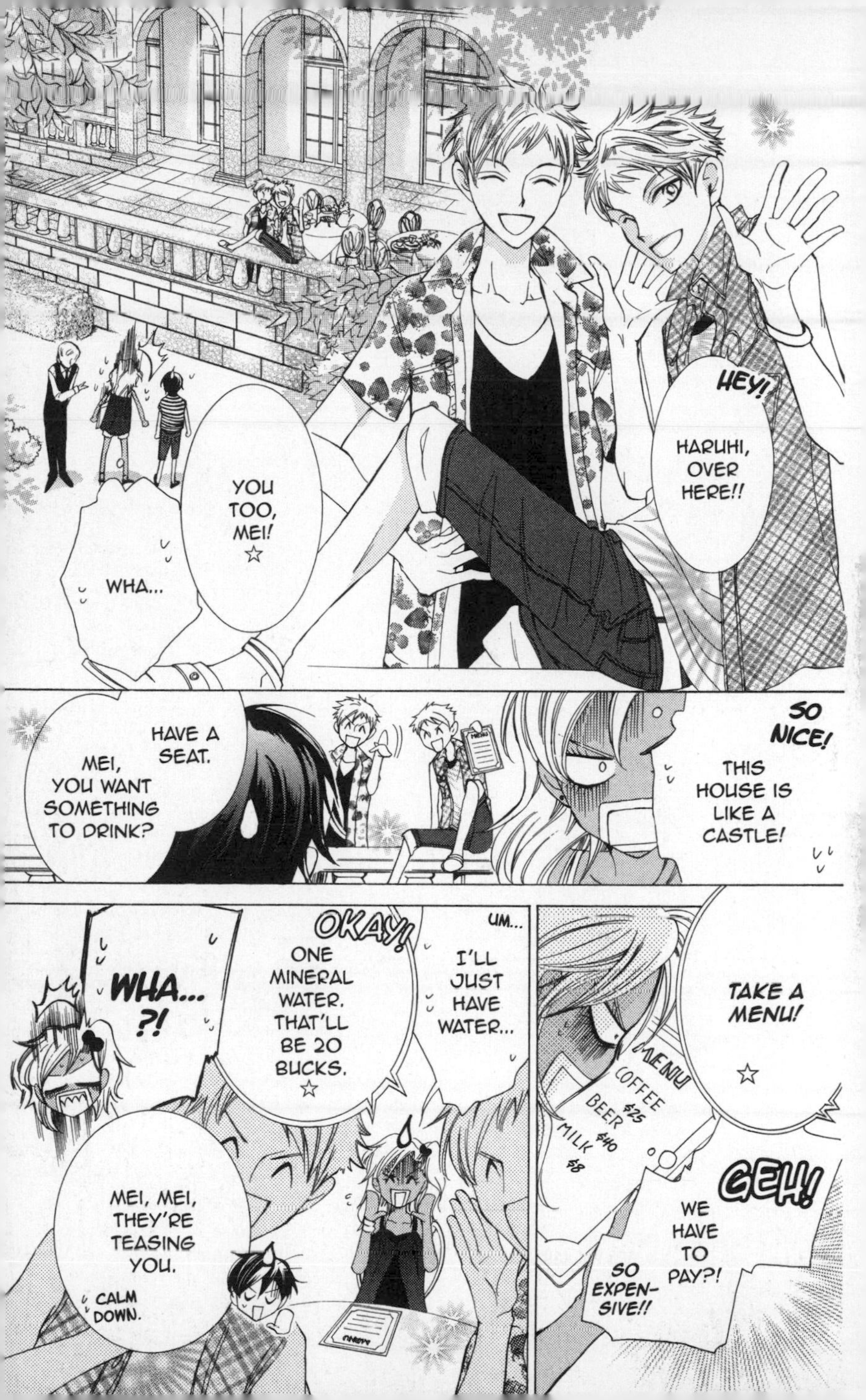
HEY!
HARUHI, OVER HERE!!
YOU TOO, MEI! ☆
WHA...
SO NICE!
THIS HOUSE IS LIKE A CASTLE!
HAVE A SEAT.
MEI, YOU WANT SOMETHING TO DRINK?
TAKE A MENU! ☆
MENU COFFEE $25 BEER $40 MILK $8
GEH!
WE HAVE TO PAY?!
SO EXPEN-SIVE!!
UM...
I'LL JUST HAVE WATER...
OKAY!
ONE MINERAL WATER. THAT'LL BE 20 BUCKS. ☆
WHA...?!
MEI, MEI, THEY'RE TEASING YOU.
CALM DOWN.

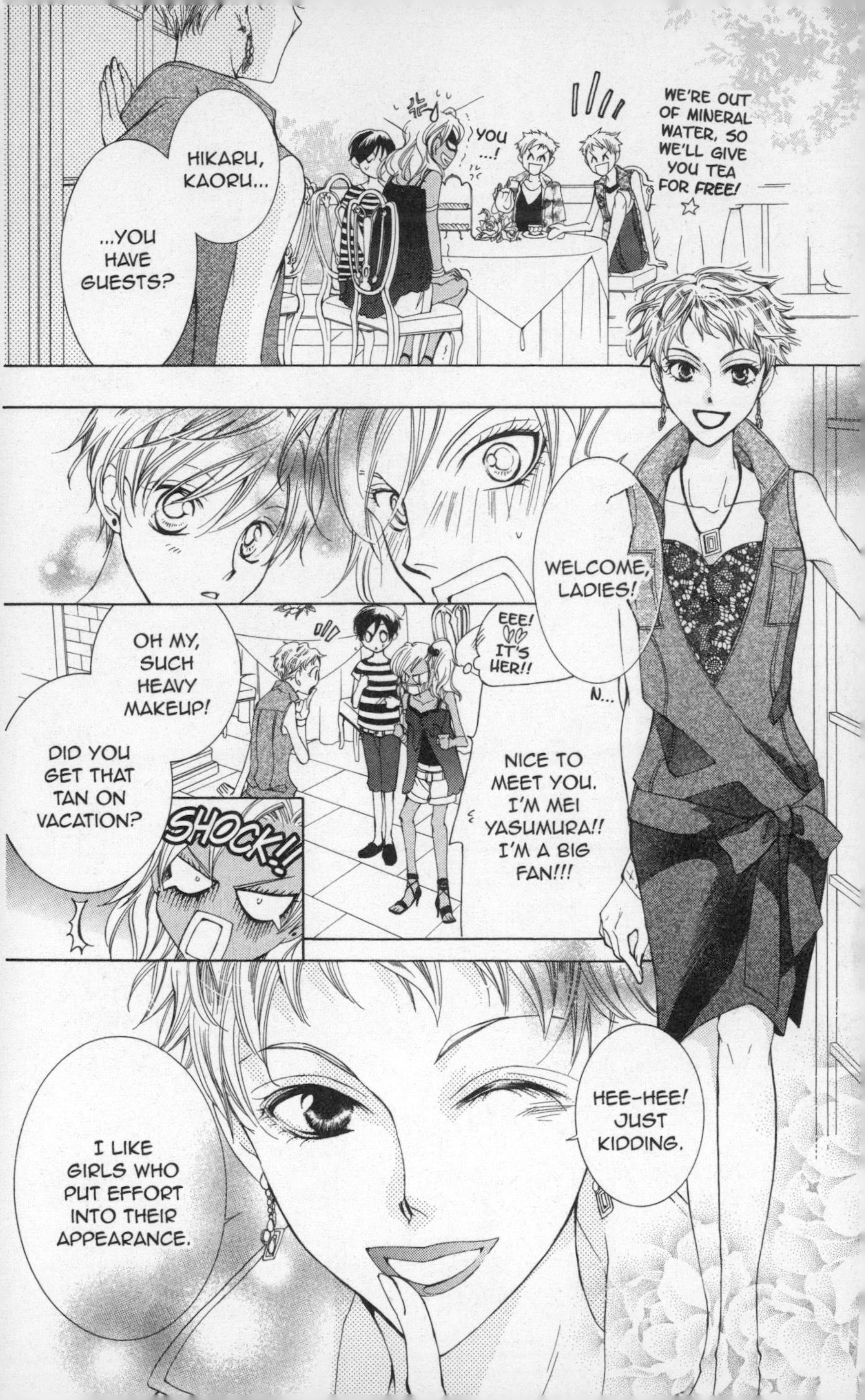
WE'RE OUT OF MINERAL WATER, SO WE'LL GIVE YOU TEA FOR FREE!
YOU ...!
HIKARU, KAORU...
...YOU HAVE GUESTS?
WELCOME, LADIES!
N...
EEE! IT'S HER!!
NICE TO MEET YOU. I'M MEI YASUMURA!! I'M A BIG FAN!!!
OH MY, SUCH HEAVY MAKEUP!
DID YOU GET THAT TAN ON VACATION?
SHOCK!!
HEE-HEE! JUST KIDDING.
I LIKE GIRLS WHO PUT EFFORT INTO THEIR APPEARANCE.

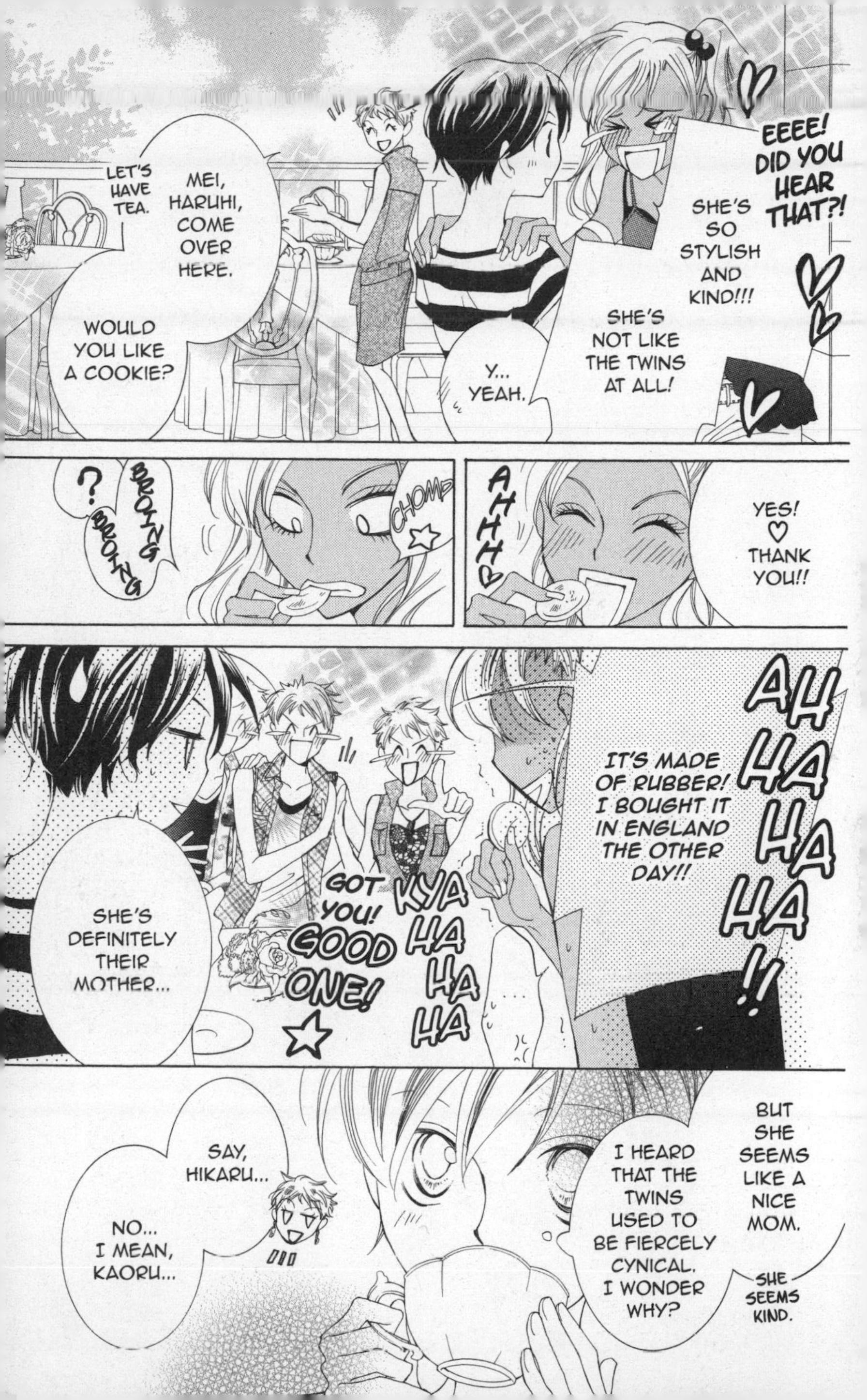
EEEE! DID YOU HEAR THAT?!
SHE'S SO STYLISH AND KIND!!!
SHE'S NOT LIKE THE TWINS AT ALL!
Y... YEAH.
MEI, HARUHI, COME OVER HERE.
LET'S HAVE TEA.
WOULD YOU LIKE A COOKIE?
YES! ♡ THANK YOU!!
AHHHH♡
CHOMP
BROING BROING
?
AH HA HA HA HA!!
IT'S MADE OF RUBBER! I BOUGHT IT IN ENGLAND THE OTHER DAY!!
KYA HA HA HA
GOT YOU! GOOD ONE!
SHE'S DEFINITELY THEIR MOTHER...
BUT SHE SEEMS LIKE A NICE MOM.
SHE SEEMS KIND.
I HEARD THAT THE TWINS USED TO BE FIERCELY CYNICAL. I WONDER WHY?
SAY, HIKARU...
NO... I MEAN, KAORU...

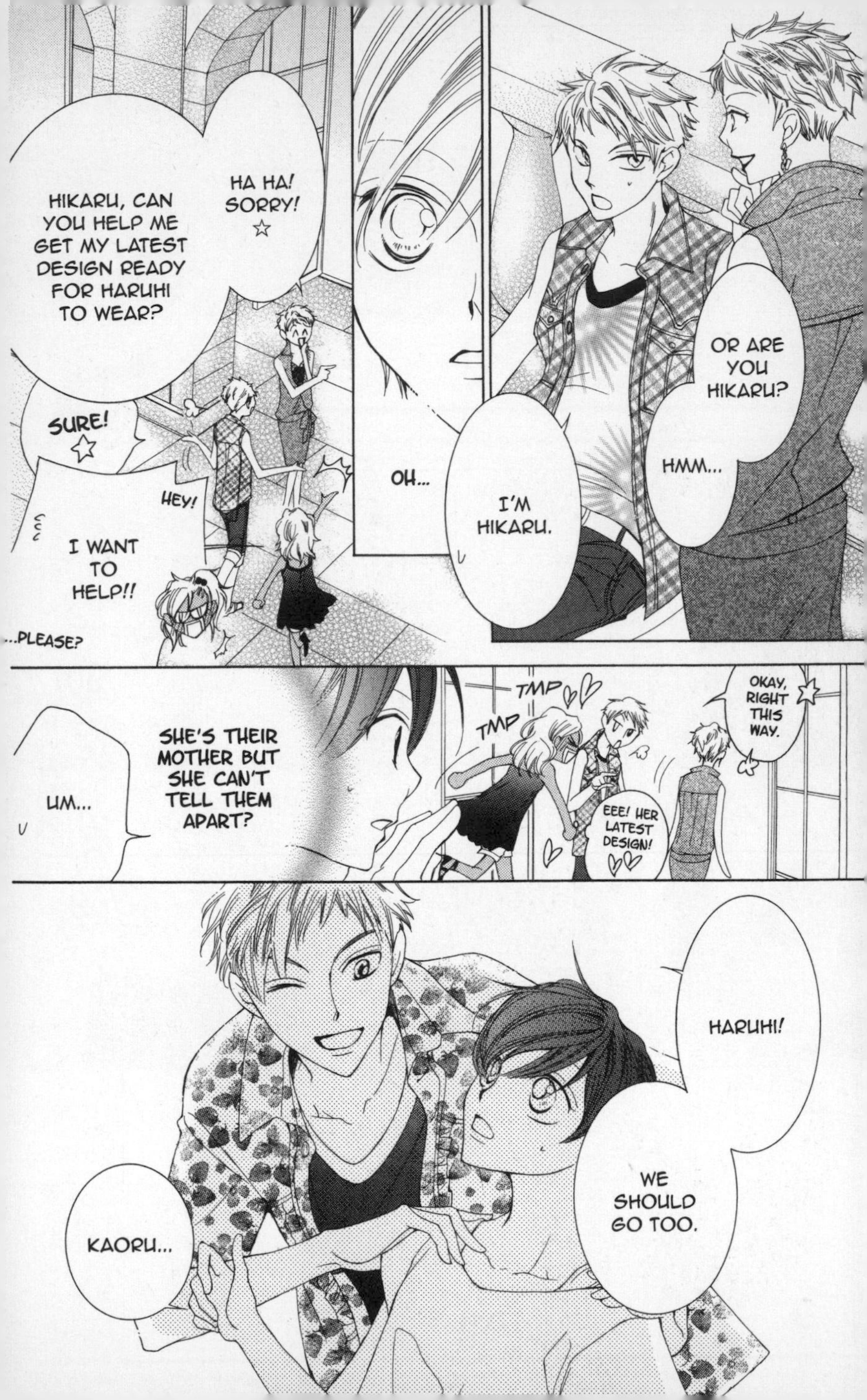
OR ARE YOU HIKARU?
HMM...
I'M HIKARU.
OH...
HA HA! SORRY! ☆
HIKARU, CAN YOU HELP ME GET MY LATEST DESIGN READY FOR HARUHI TO WEAR?
SURE! ☆
HEY!
I WANT TO HELP!!
...PLEASE?
OKAY, RIGHT THIS WAY.
TMP
TMP
EEE! HER LATEST DESIGN!
SHE'S THEIR MOTHER BUT SHE CAN'T TELL THEM APART?
UM...
HARUHI!
WE SHOULD GO TOO.
KAORU...

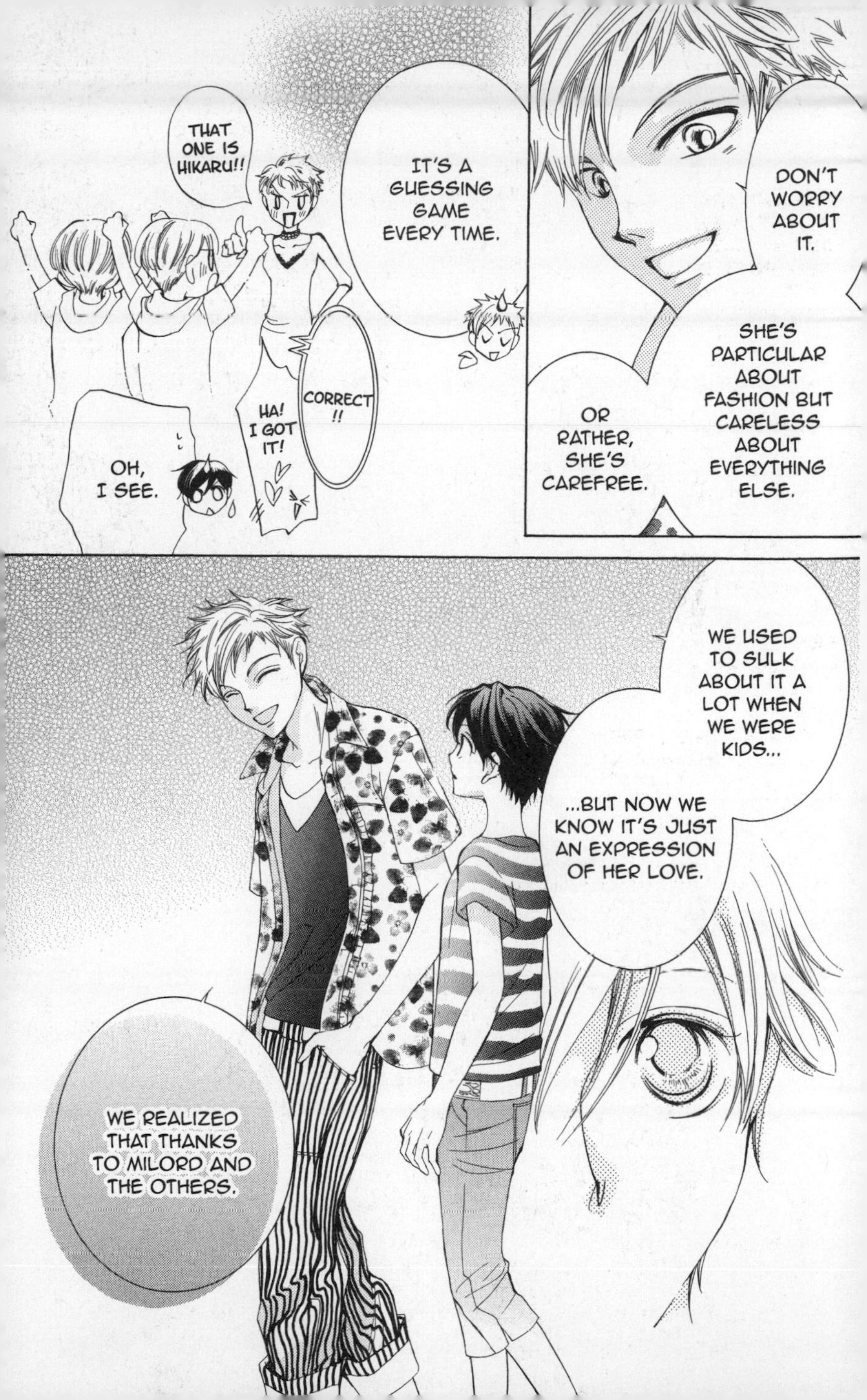
DON'T WORRY ABOUT IT.
SHE'S PARTICULAR ABOUT FASHION BUT CARELESS ABOUT EVERYTHING ELSE.
OR RATHER, SHE'S CAREFREE.
IT'S A GUESSING GAME EVERY TIME.
THAT ONE IS HIKARU!!
CORRECT!!
HA! I GOT IT!
OH, I SEE.
WE USED TO SULK ABOUT IT A LOT WHEN WE WERE KIDS...
...BUT NOW WE KNOW IT'S JUST AN EXPRESSION OF HER LOVE.
WE REALIZED THAT THANKS TO MILORD AND THE OTHERS.

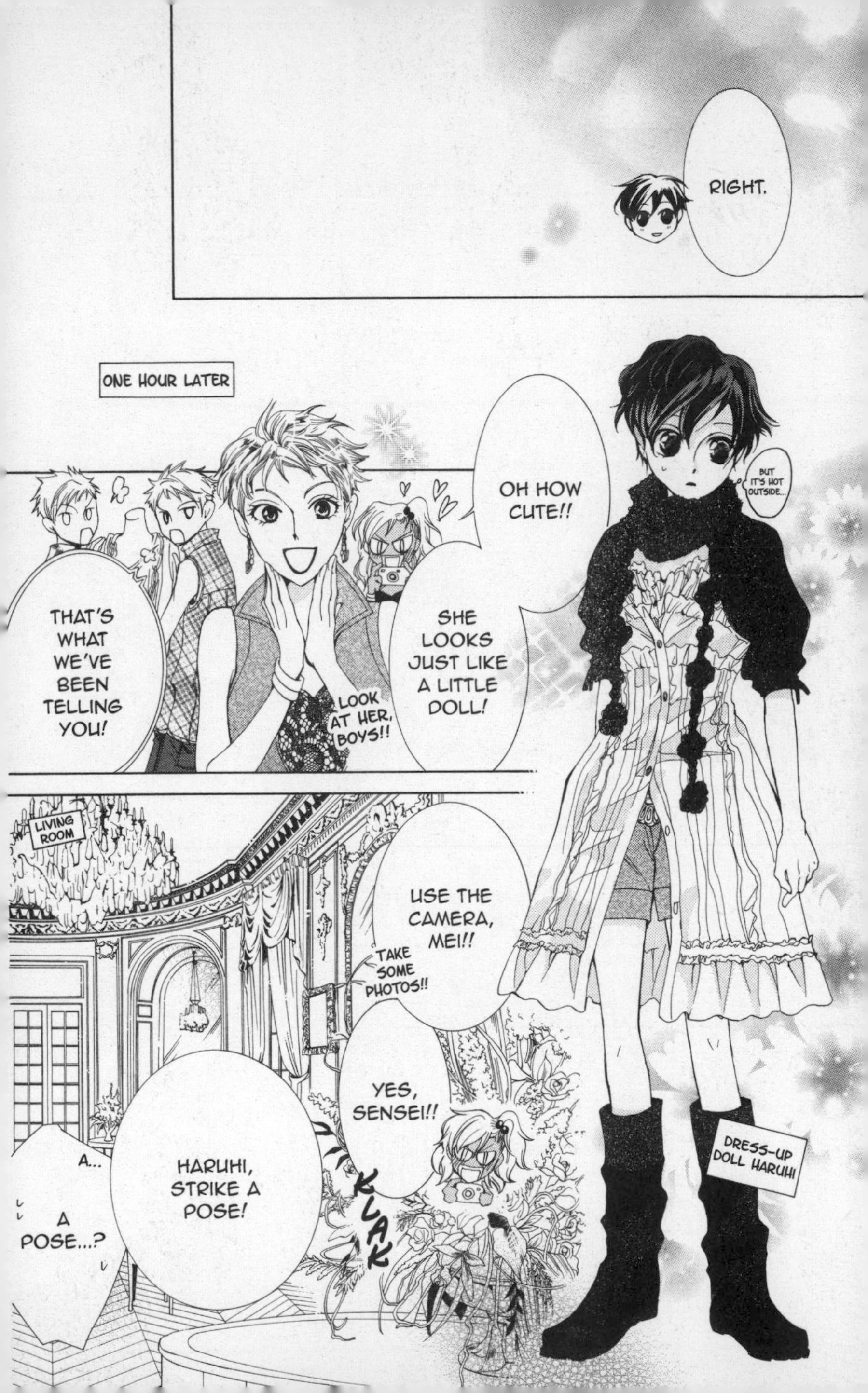
RIGHT.
BUT IT'S HOT OUTSIDE...
DRESS-UP DOLL HARUHI
ONE HOUR LATER
OH HOW CUTE!!
SHE LOOKS JUST LIKE A LITTLE DOLL!
LOOK AT HER, BOYS!!
THAT'S WHAT WE'VE BEEN TELLING YOU!
LIVING ROOM
USE THE CAMERA, MEI!!
TAKE SOME PHOTOS!!
YES, SENSEI!!
KLAK
HARUHI, STRIKE A POSE!
A...
A POSE...?

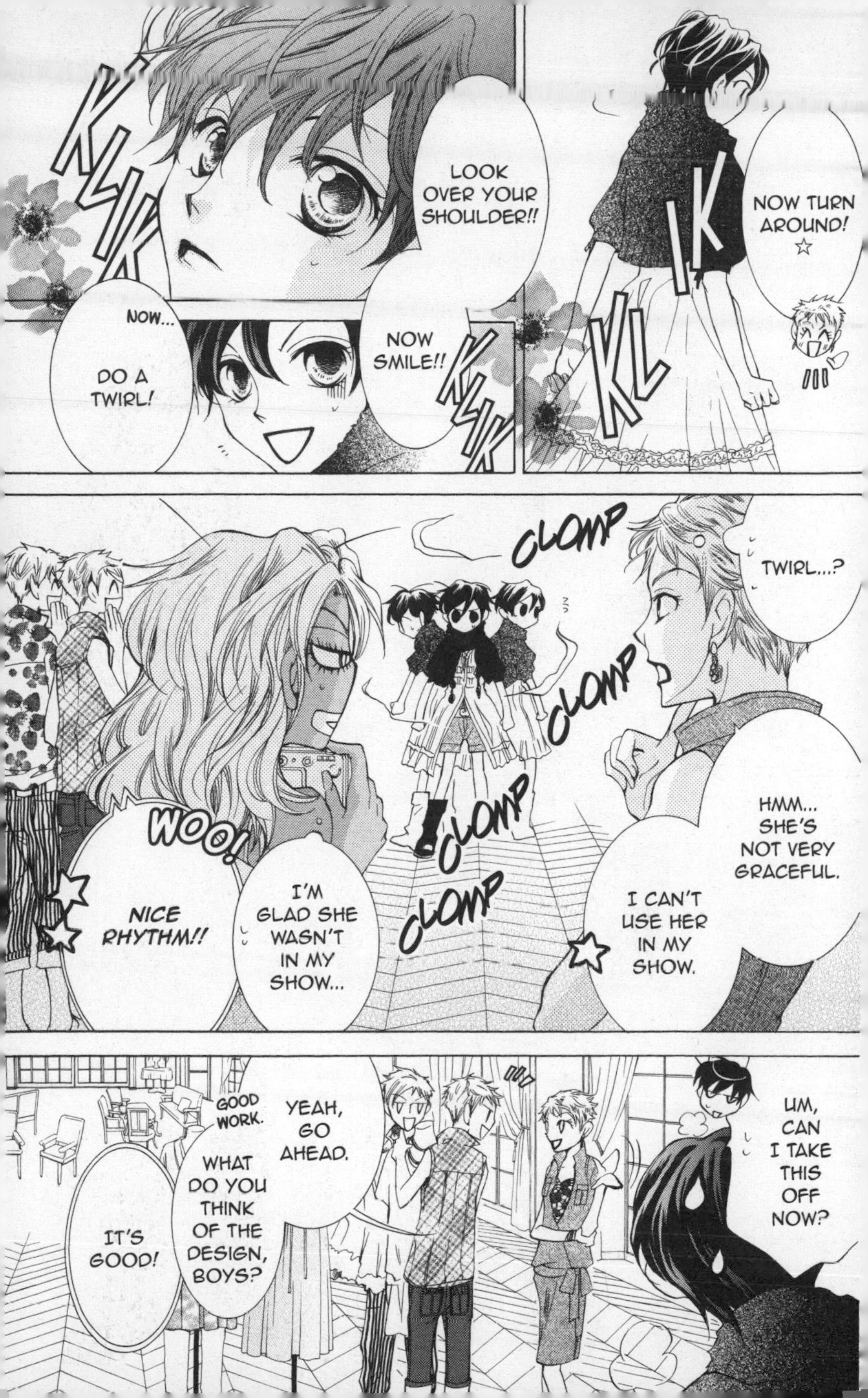
NOW TURN AROUND! ☆
KLIK
LOOK OVER YOUR SHOULDER!!
KLIK
NOW SMILE!!
KLIK
NOW... DO A TWIRL!
TWIRL...?
HMM... SHE'S NOT VERY GRACEFUL.
I CAN'T USE HER IN MY SHOW.
CLOMP
CLOMP
CLOMP
CLOMP
I'M GLAD SHE WASN'T IN MY SHOW...
WOO!
NICE RHYTHM!!
UM, CAN I TAKE THIS OFF NOW?
YEAH, GO AHEAD.
GOOD WORK. WHAT DO YOU THINK OF THE DESIGN, BOYS?
IT'S GOOD!

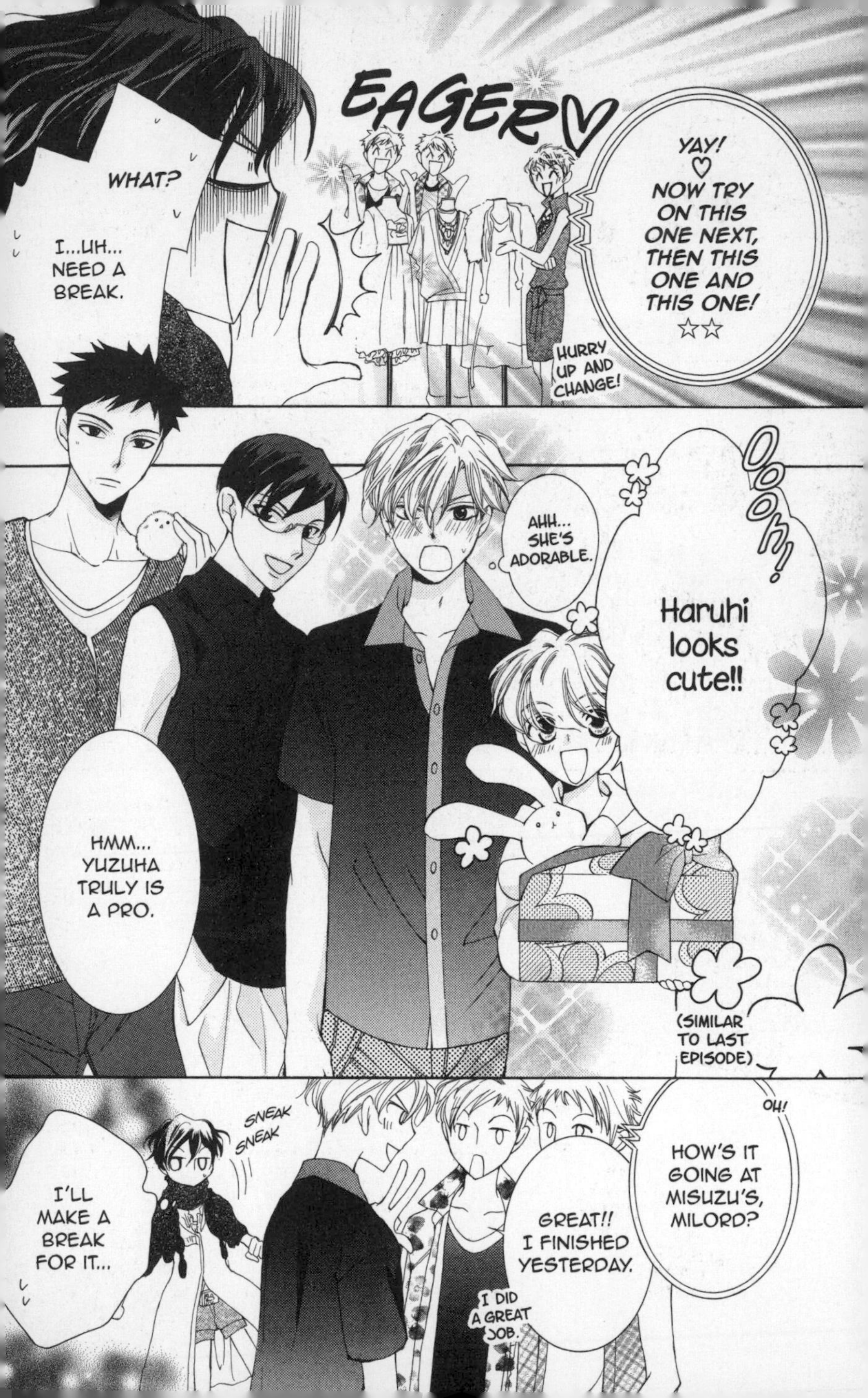
EAGER♥
YAY! ♡ NOW TRY ON THIS ONE NEXT, THEN THIS ONE AND THIS ONE! ☆☆
HURRY UP AND CHANGE!
WHAT?
I...UH... NEED A BREAK.
OOOH!
Haruhi looks cute!!
AHH... SHE'S ADORABLE.
HMM... YUZUHA TRULY IS A PRO.
(SIMILAR TO LAST EPISODE)
OH!
HOW'S IT GOING AT MISUZU'S, MILORD?
GREAT!! I FINISHED YESTERDAY.
I DID A GREAT JOB.
SNEAK SNEAK
I'LL MAKE A BREAK FOR IT...

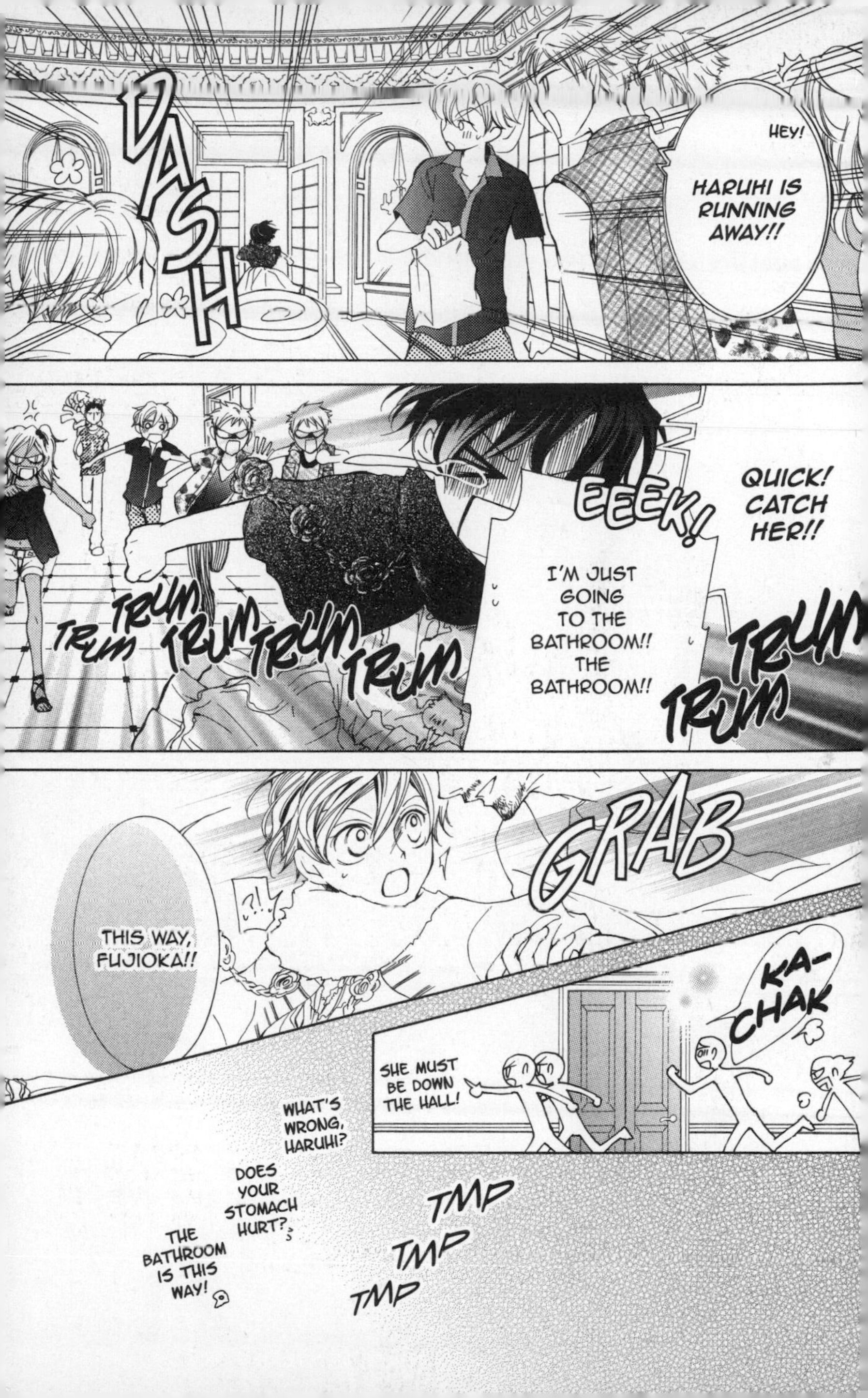
HEY!
HARUHI IS RUNNING AWAY!!
DASH
QUICK! CATCH HER!!
EEEK!
I'M JUST GOING TO THE BATHROOM!! THE BATHROOM!!
TRUM TRUM
TRUM TRUM TRUM TRUM TRUM
GRAB
?!
THIS WAY, FUJIOKA!!
KA-CHAK
SHE MUST BE DOWN THE HALL!
WHAT'S WRONG, HARUHI?
DOES YOUR STOMACH HURT?
THE BATHROOM IS THIS WAY!
TMP TMP TMP

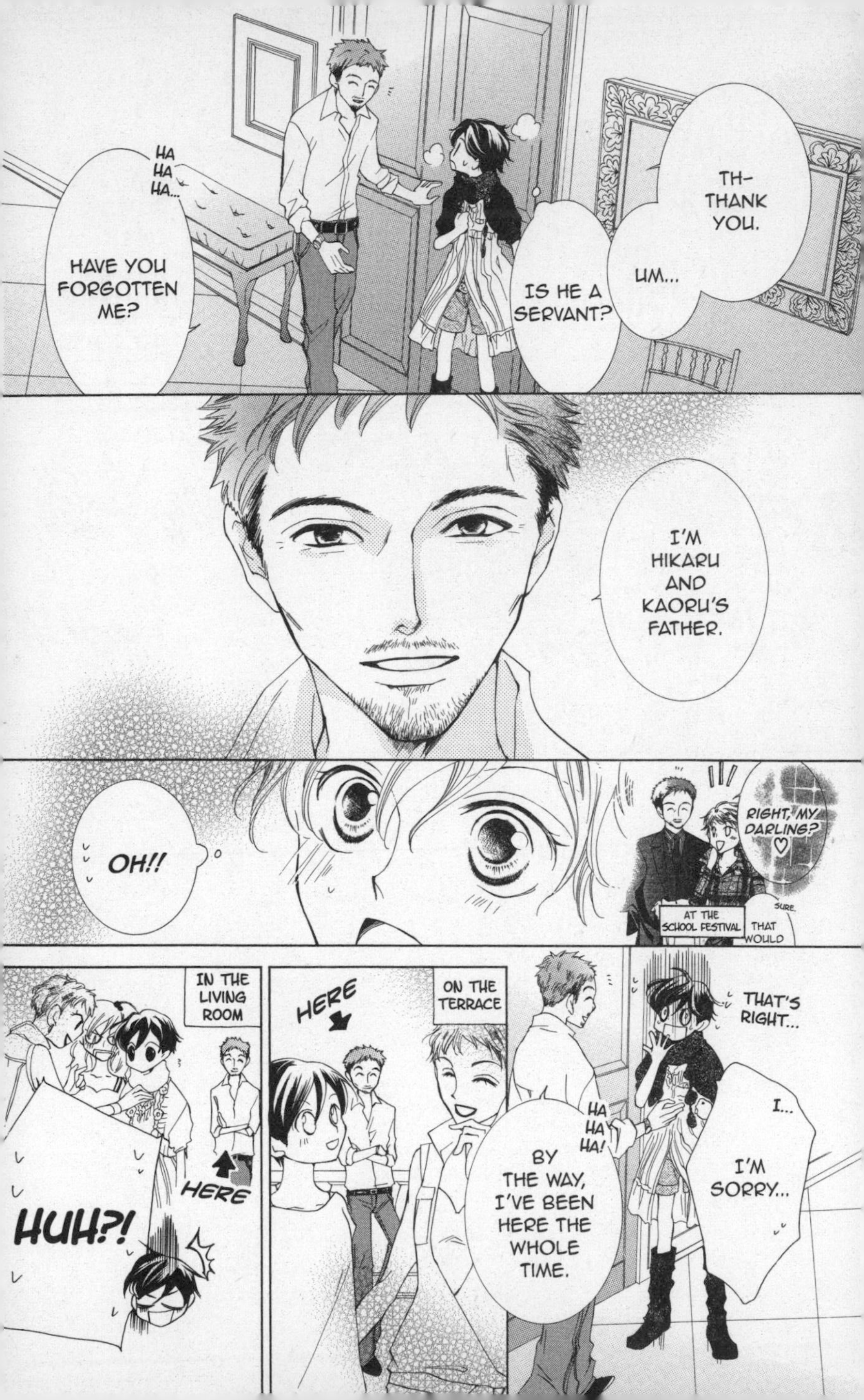
TH-THANK YOU.
UM...
IS HE A SERVANT?
HA HA HA...
HAVE YOU FORGOTTEN ME?
I'M HIKARU AND KAORU'S FATHER.
AT THE SCHOOL FESTIVAL
RIGHT, MY DARLING? ♡
SURE. THAT WOULD
OH!!
THAT'S RIGHT...
I... I'M SORRY...
HA HA HA!
BY THE WAY, I'VE BEEN HERE THE WHOLE TIME.
ON THE TERRACE
HERE
IN THE LIVING ROOM
HERE
HUH?!

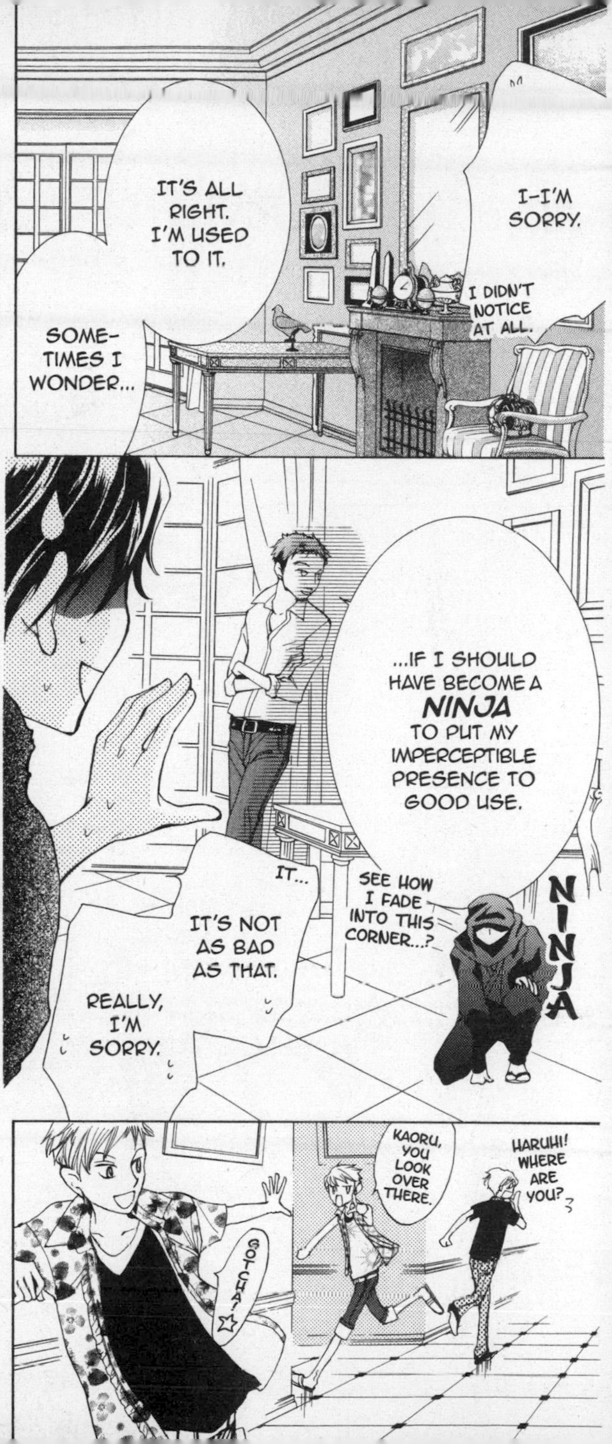
I-I'M SORRY.
I DIDN'T NOTICE AT ALL.
IT'S ALL RIGHT. I'M USED TO IT.
SOME-TIMES I WONDER...
...IF I SHOULD HAVE BECOME A NINJA TO PUT MY IMPERCEPTIBLE PRESENCE TO GOOD USE.
NINJA
SEE HOW I FADE INTO THIS CORNER...?
IT...
IT'S NOT AS BAD AS THAT.
REALLY, I'M SORRY.
HARUHI! WHERE ARE YOU?
KAORU, YOU LOOK OVER THERE.
GOTCHA!

5

SPEAKING OF THE ANIME, I WASN'T ABLE TO ATTEND THE OFFICIAL POST-PRODUCTION PARTY BECAUSE OF MY WORK. I WAS REALLY DISAPPOINTED, BUT LATER THERE WAS A SMALLER GET-TOGETHER FOR ME SO I COULD MEET IGARASHI-SAN (THE DIRECTOR), ENOKIDO-SAN, OHYABU-SAN, AND KUMIKO TAKAHASHI AND TELL THEM IN PERSON WHAT I THOUGHT ABOUT THE ANIME...!!

I WAS TOLD ONLY SOME OF THE CAST WHO PLAYED HOST CLUB MEMBERS WOULD BE ABLE TO MAKE IT, BUT EVERYONE BESIDES MIYANO-KUN AND AYAKA SAITO--WHO WERE BUSY WORKING--MADE IT. I WAS OVERJOYED!!

MAYA-SAN GAVE ME HER BOOK OF ESSAYS AND A CARD WITH A LOT OF NICE COMMENTS IN IT, ALONG WITH A PICTURE FROM THE LAST DAY OF RECORDING.

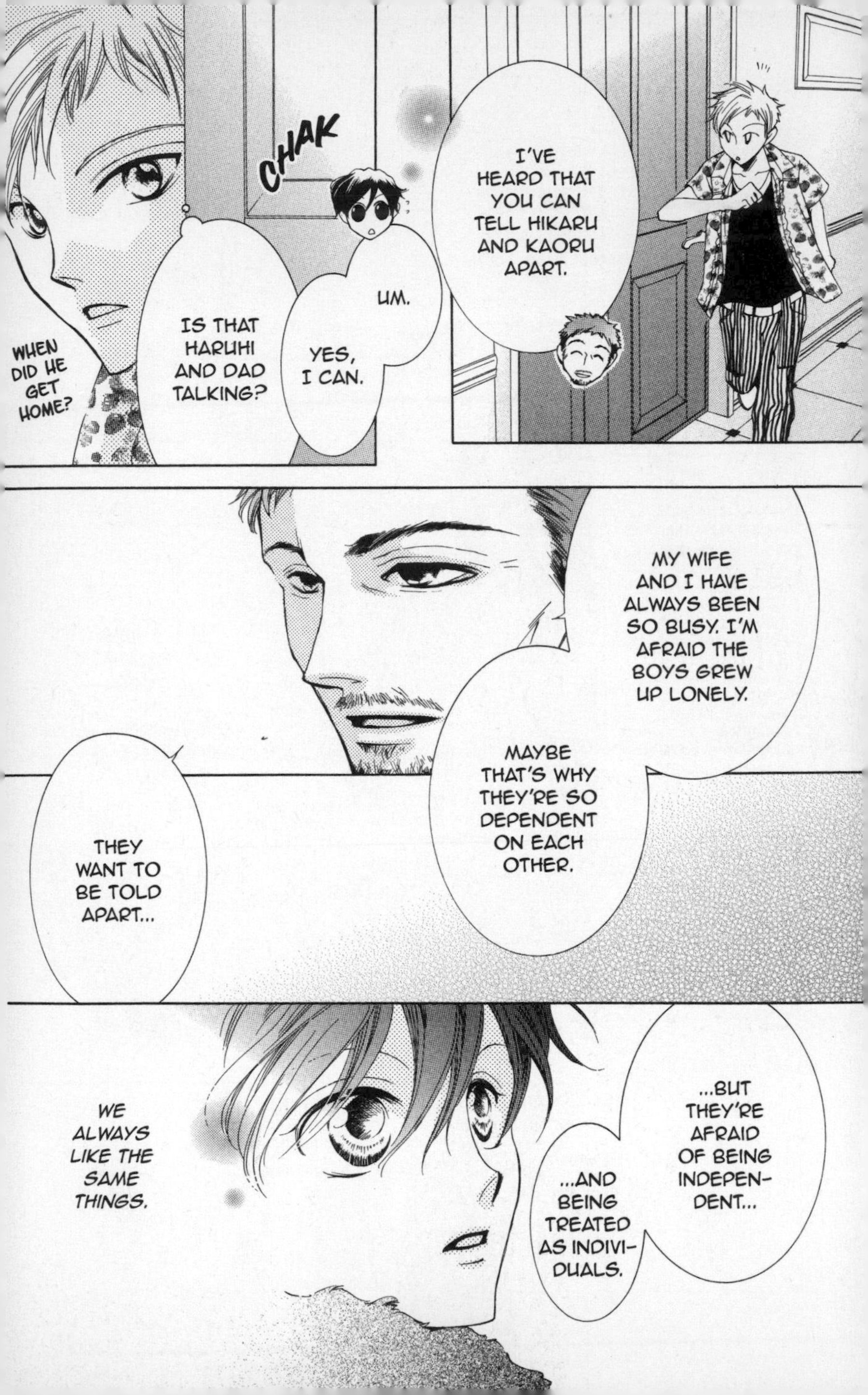
I'VE HEARD THAT YOU CAN TELL HIKARU AND KAORU APART.
UM.
YES, I CAN.
CHAK
IS THAT HARUHI AND DAD TALKING?
WHEN DID HE GET HOME?
MY WIFE AND I HAVE ALWAYS BEEN SO BUSY. I'M AFRAID THE BOYS GREW UP LONELY.
MAYBE THAT'S WHY THEY'RE SO DEPENDENT ON EACH OTHER.
THEY WANT TO BE TOLD APART...
...BUT THEY'RE AFRAID OF BEING INDEPEN-DENT...
...AND BEING TREATED AS INDIVI-DUALS.
WE ALWAYS LIKE THE SAME THINGS.

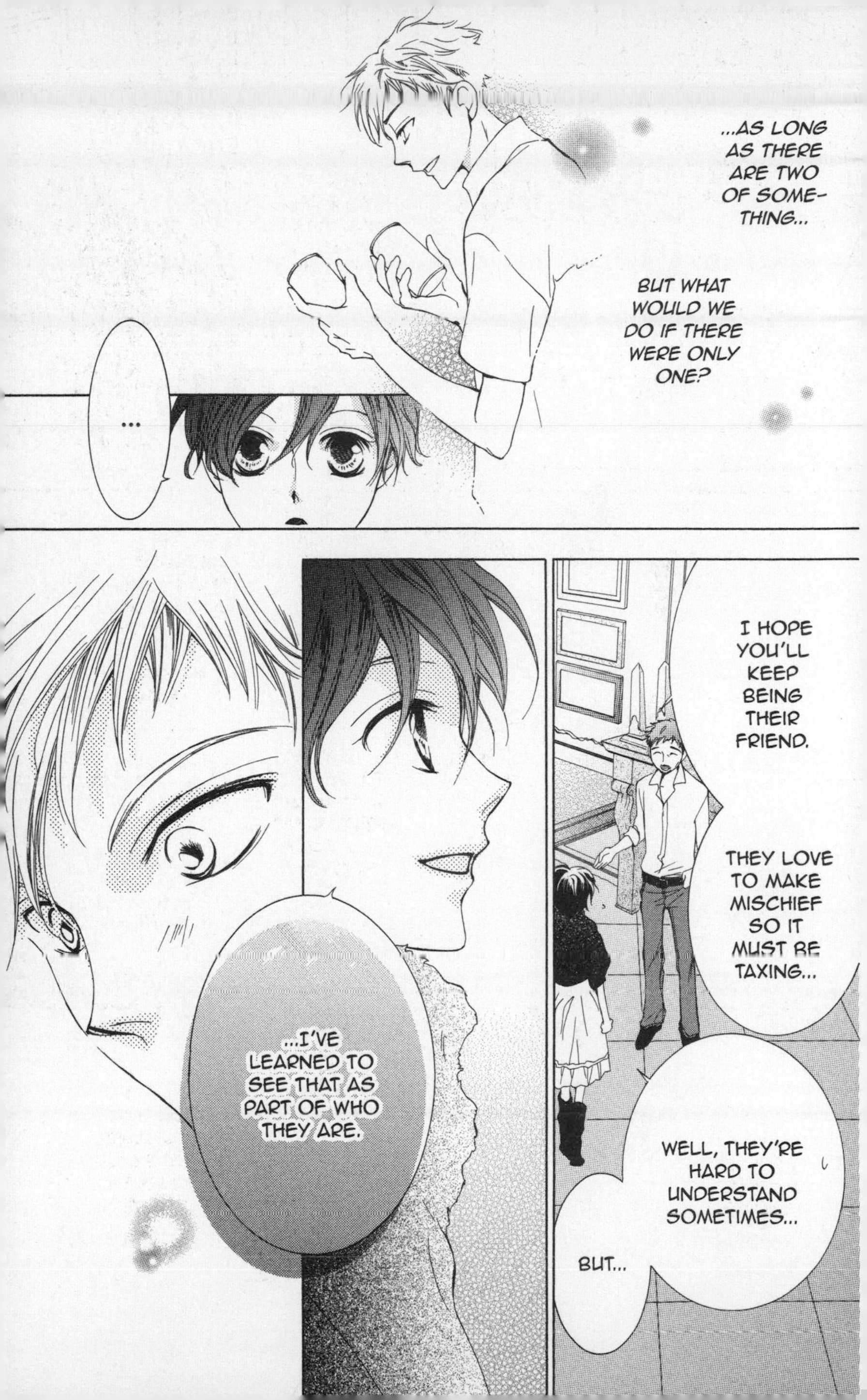
...AS LONG AS THERE ARE TWO OF SOMETHING...
BUT WHAT WOULD WE DO IF THERE WERE ONLY ONE?
...
I HOPE YOU'LL KEEP BEING THEIR FRIEND.
THEY LOVE TO MAKE MISCHIEF SO IT MUST BE TAXING...
WELL, THEY'RE HARD TO UNDERSTAND SOMETIMES...
BUT...
...I'VE LEARNED TO SEE THAT AS PART OF WHO THEY ARE.

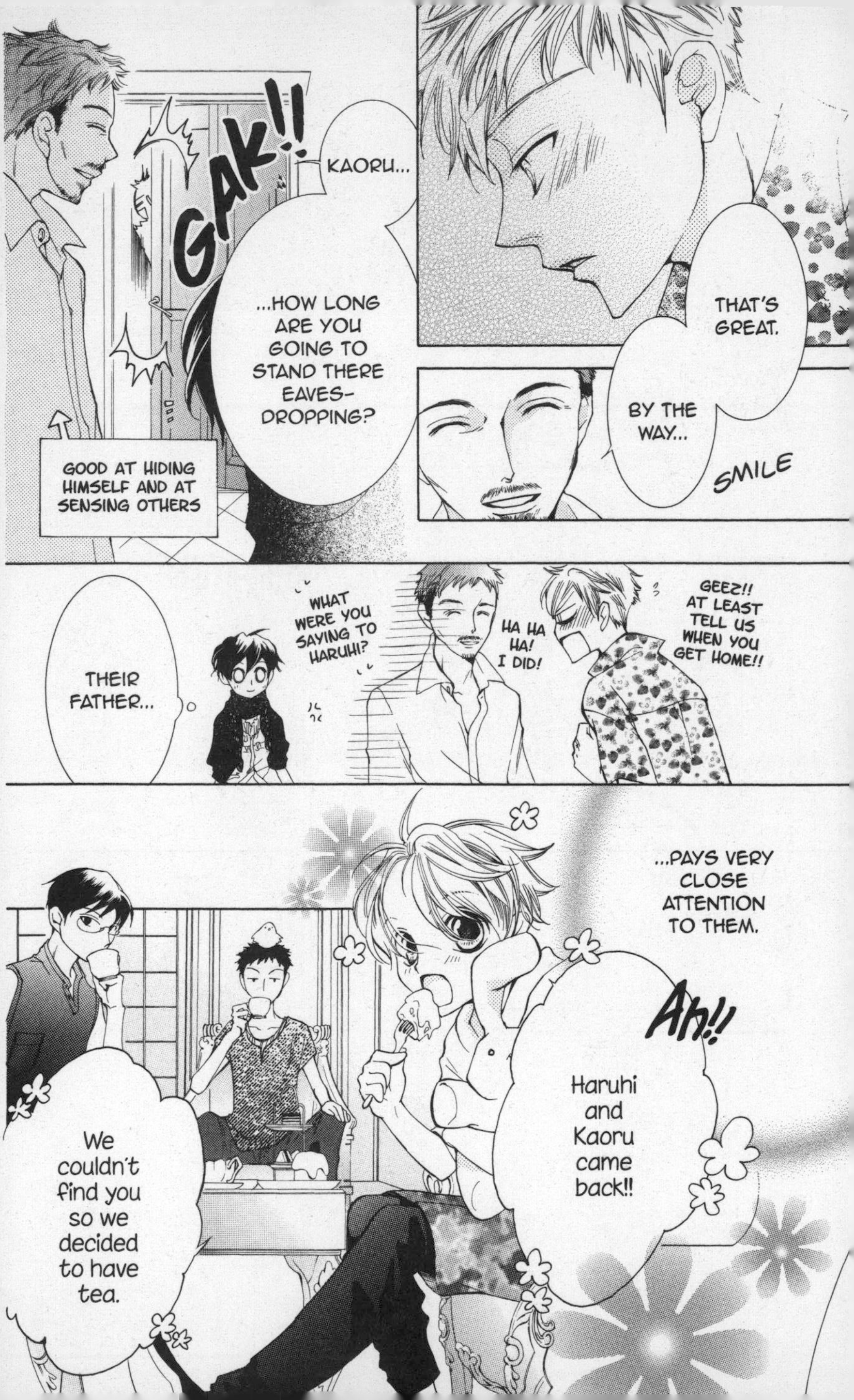
THAT'S GREAT.
BY THE WAY...
SMILE
KAORU...
...HOW LONG ARE YOU GOING TO STAND THERE EAVES-DROPPING?
GAK!!
GOOD AT HIDING HIMSELF AND AT SENSING OTHERS
GEEZ!! AT LEAST TELL US WHEN YOU GET HOME!!
HA HA HA! I DID!
WHAT WERE YOU SAYING TO HARUHI?
THEIR FATHER...
...PAYS VERY CLOSE ATTENTION TO THEM.
Ah!!
Haruhi and Kaoru came back!!
We couldn't find you so we decided to have tea.

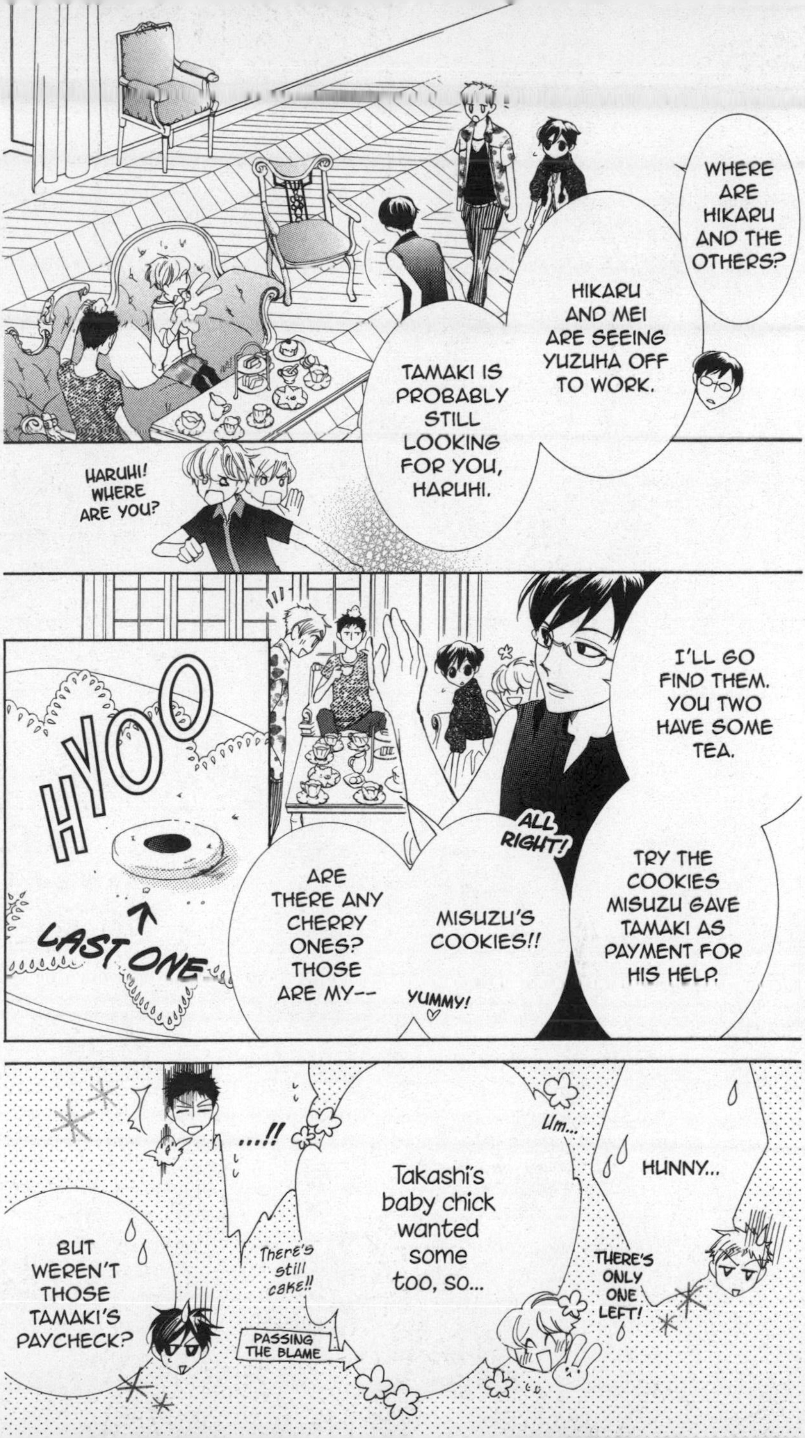

WHERE ARE HIKARU AND THE OTHERS?
HIKARU AND MEI ARE SEEING YUZUHA OFF TO WORK.
TAMAKI IS PROBABLY STILL LOOKING FOR YOU, HARUHI.
HARUHI! WHERE ARE YOU?
I'LL GO FIND THEM. YOU TWO HAVE SOME TEA.
TRY THE COOKIES MISUZU GAVE TAMAKI AS PAYMENT FOR HIS HELP.
ALL RIGHT!
MISUZU'S COOKIES!!
YUMMY!
ARE THERE ANY CHERRY ONES? THOSE ARE MY--
HYOO
LAST ONE
HUNNY...
THERE'S ONLY ONE LEFT!
Um...
Takashi's baby chick wanted some too, so...
...!!
There's still cake!!
PASSING THE BLAME
BUT WEREN'T THOSE TAMAKI'S PAYCHECK?

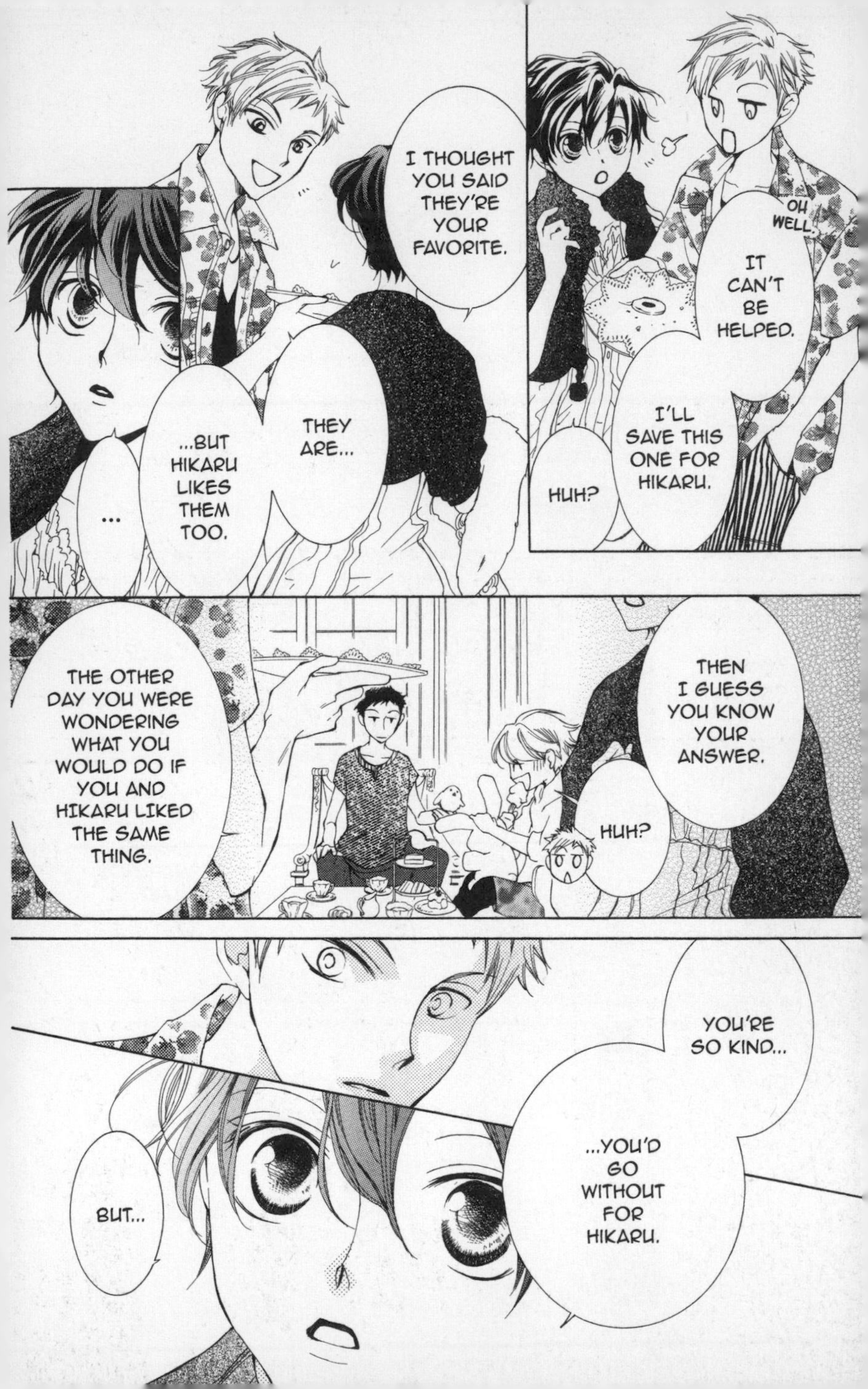
OH WELL.
IT CAN'T BE HELPED.
I'LL SAVE THIS ONE FOR HIKARU.
HUH?
I THOUGHT YOU SAID THEY'RE YOUR FAVORITE.
THEY ARE...
...BUT HIKARU LIKES THEM TOO.
...
THEN I GUESS YOU KNOW YOUR ANSWER.
HUH?
THE OTHER DAY YOU WERE WONDERING WHAT YOU WOULD DO IF YOU AND HIKARU LIKED THE SAME THING.
YOU'RE SO KIND...
...YOU'D GO WITHOUT FOR HIKARU.
BUT...

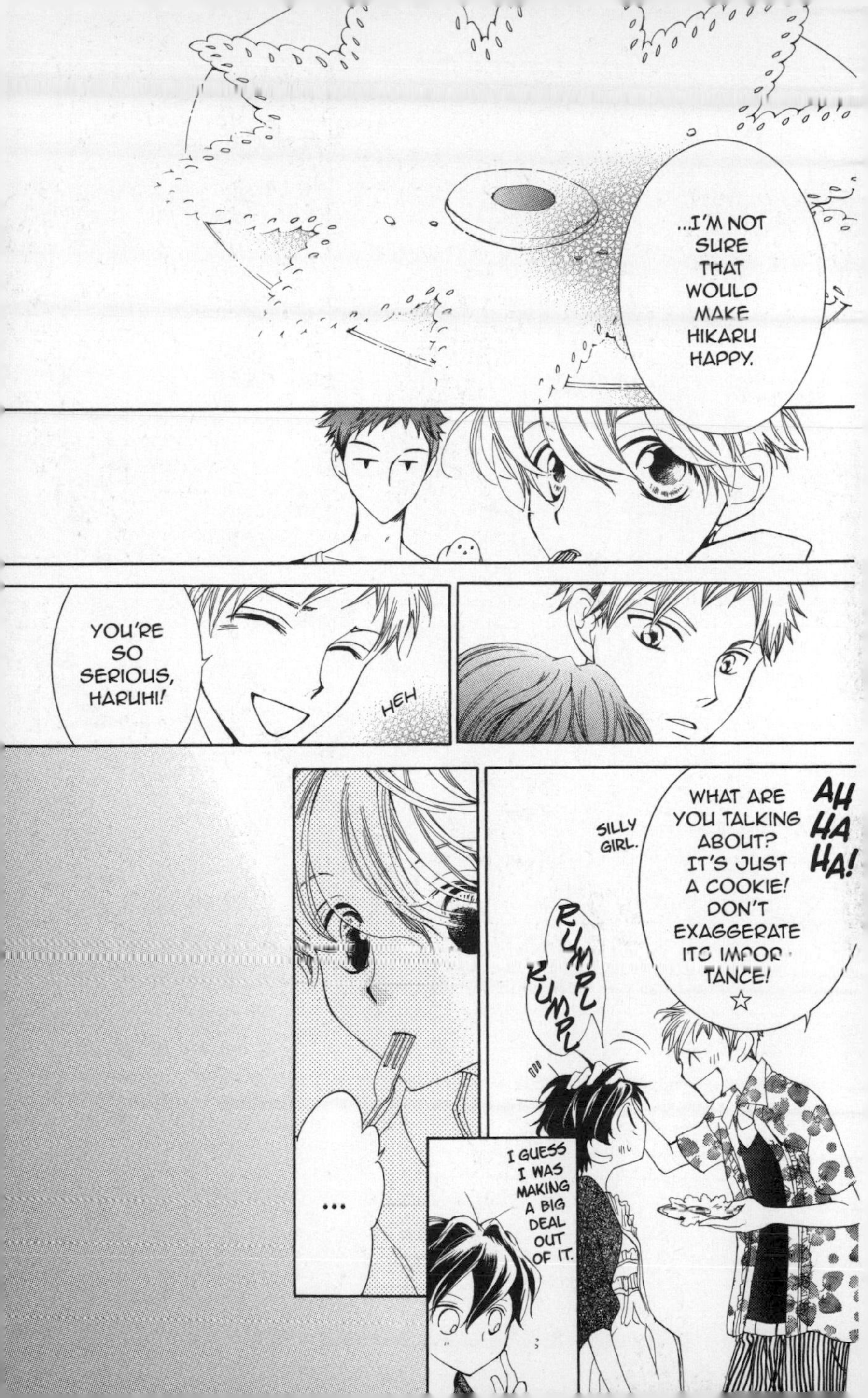
...I'M NOT SURE THAT WOULD MAKE HIKARU HAPPY.
YOU'RE SO SERIOUS, HARUHI!
HEH
AH HA HA!
WHAT ARE YOU TALKING ABOUT? IT'S JUST A COOKIE! DON'T EXAGGERATE ITS IMPORTANCE! ☆
SILLY GIRL.
RUMPL RUMPL
...
I GUESS I WAS MAKING A BIG DEAL OUT OF IT.

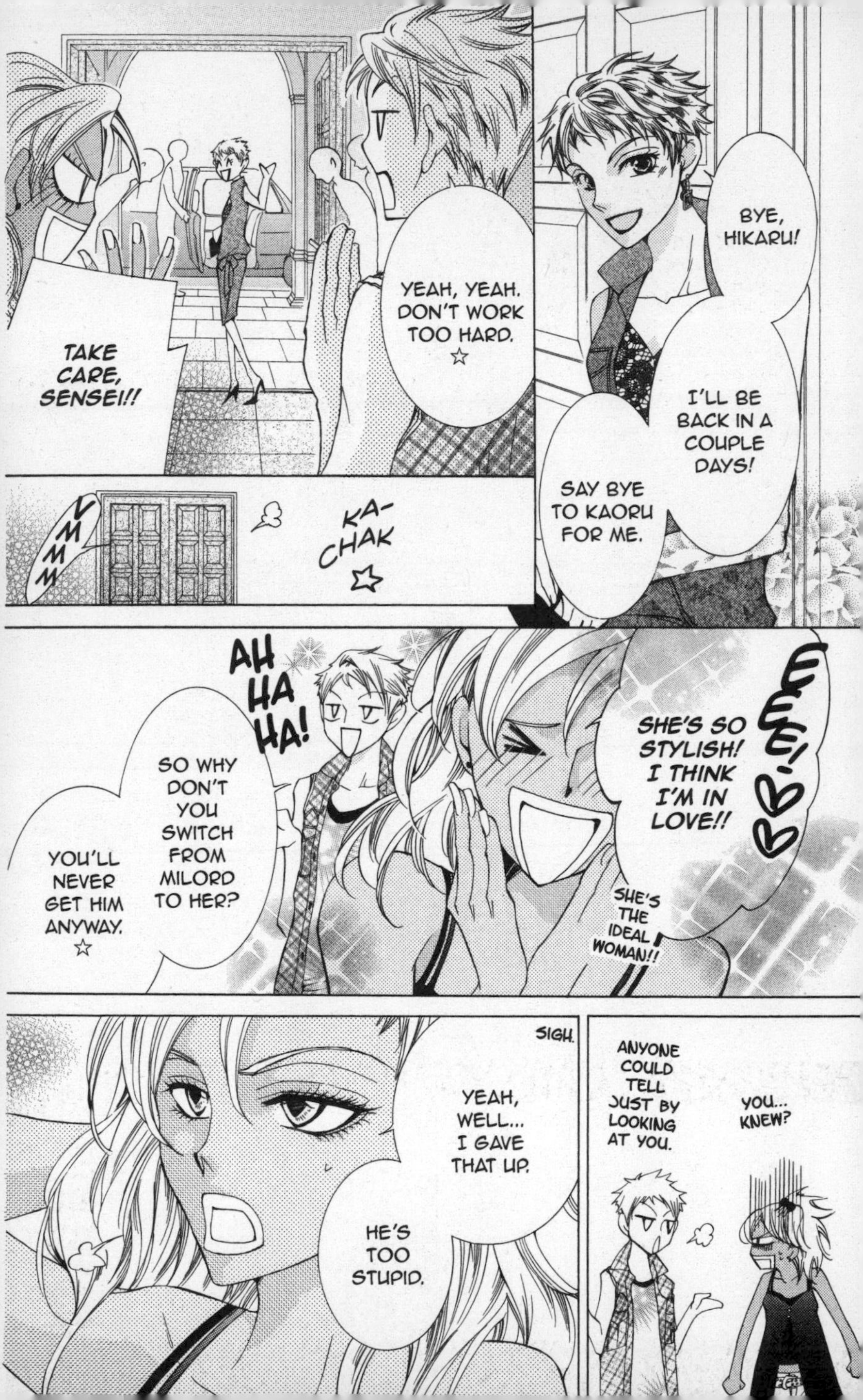
BYE, HIKARU!
I'LL BE BACK IN A COUPLE DAYS!
SAY BYE TO KAORU FOR ME.
YEAH, YEAH. DON'T WORK TOO HARD. ☆
TAKE CARE, SENSEI!!
KA-CHAK ☆
VMMM
EEEE!
SHE'S SO STYLISH! I THINK I'M IN LOVE!!
SHE'S THE IDEAL WOMAN!!
AH HA HA!
SO WHY DON'T YOU SWITCH FROM MILORD TO HER?
YOU'LL NEVER GET HIM ANYWAY. ☆
YOU... KNEW?
ANYONE COULD TELL JUST BY LOOKING AT YOU.
SIGH.
YEAH, WELL... I GAVE THAT UP.
HE'S TOO STUPID.

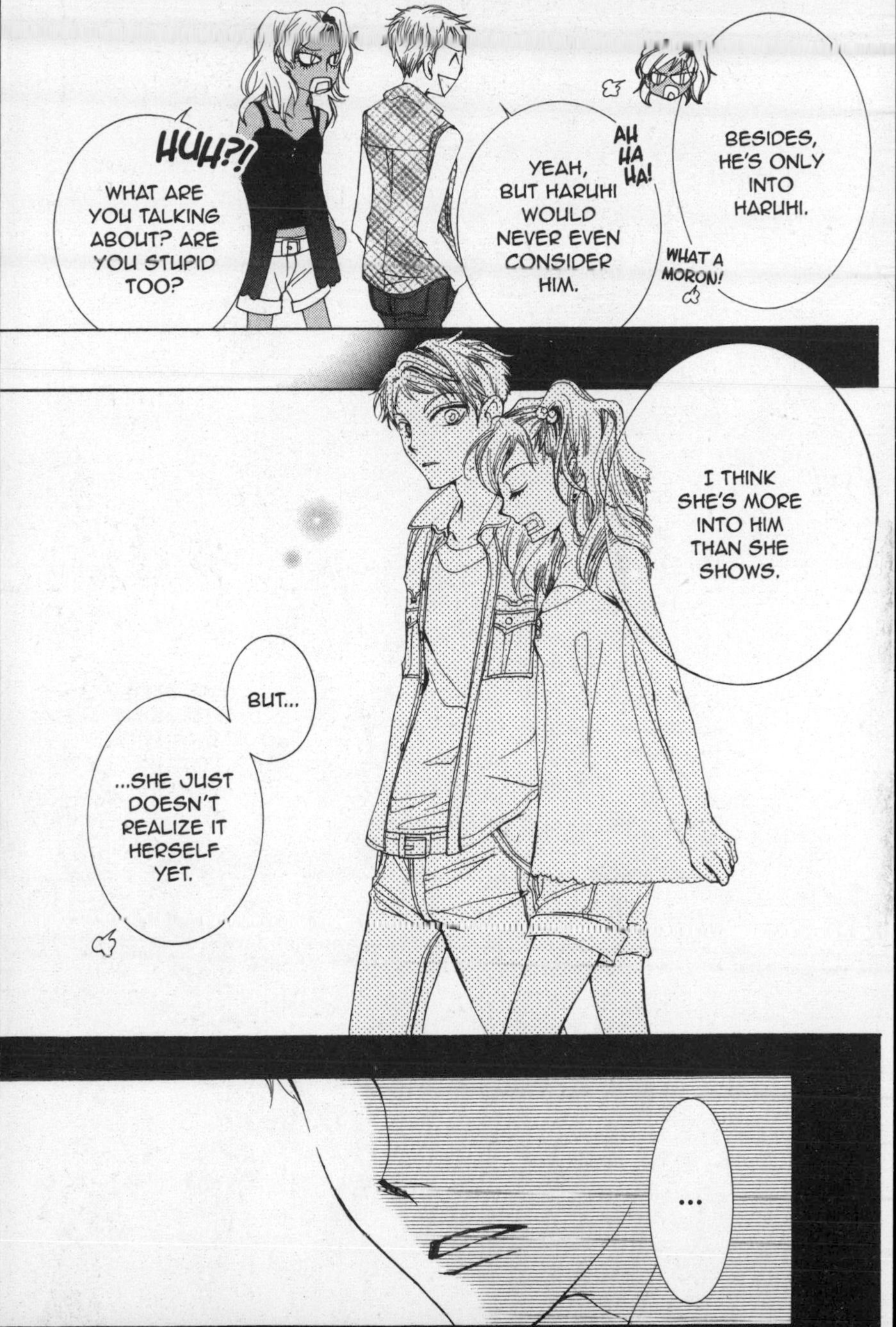
BESIDES, HE'S ONLY INTO HARUHI.
WHAT A MORON!
AH HA HA!
YEAH, BUT HARUHI WOULD NEVER EVEN CONSIDER HIM.
HUH?!
WHAT ARE YOU TALKING ABOUT? ARE YOU STUPID TOO?
I THINK SHE'S MORE INTO HIM THAN SHE SHOWS.
BUT...
...SHE JUST DOESN'T REALIZE IT HERSELF YET.
...

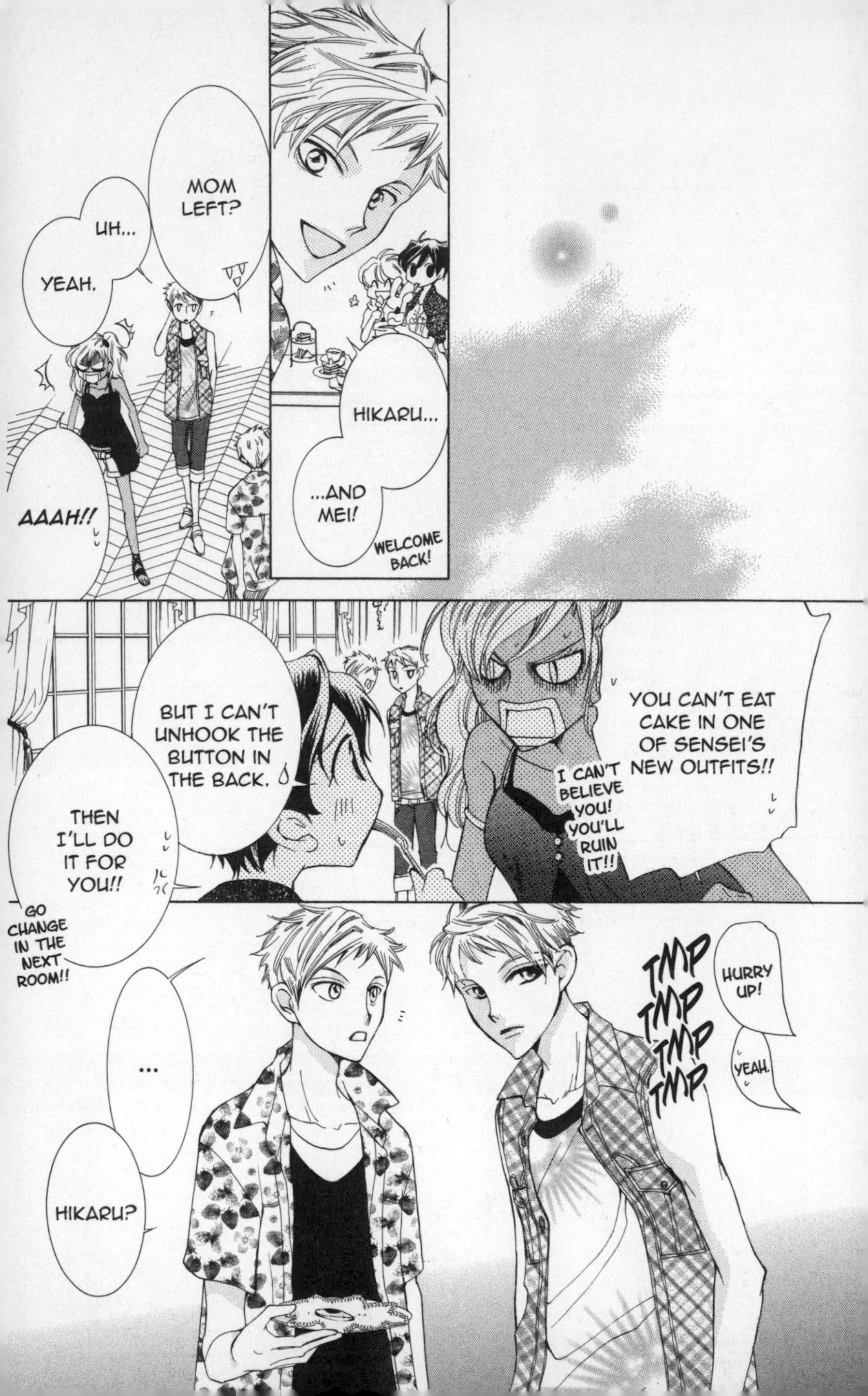
HIKARU...
...AND MEI!
WELCOME BACK!
MOM LEFT?
UH... YEAH.
AAAH!!
YOU CAN'T EAT CAKE IN ONE OF SENSEI'S NEW OUTFITS!!
I CAN'T BELIEVE YOU! YOU'LL RUIN IT!!
BUT I CAN'T UNHOOK THE BUTTON IN THE BACK.
THEN I'LL DO IT FOR YOU!!
GO CHANGE IN THE NEXT ROOM!!
HURRY UP!
YEAH.
TMP TMP TMP TMP
...
HIKARU?

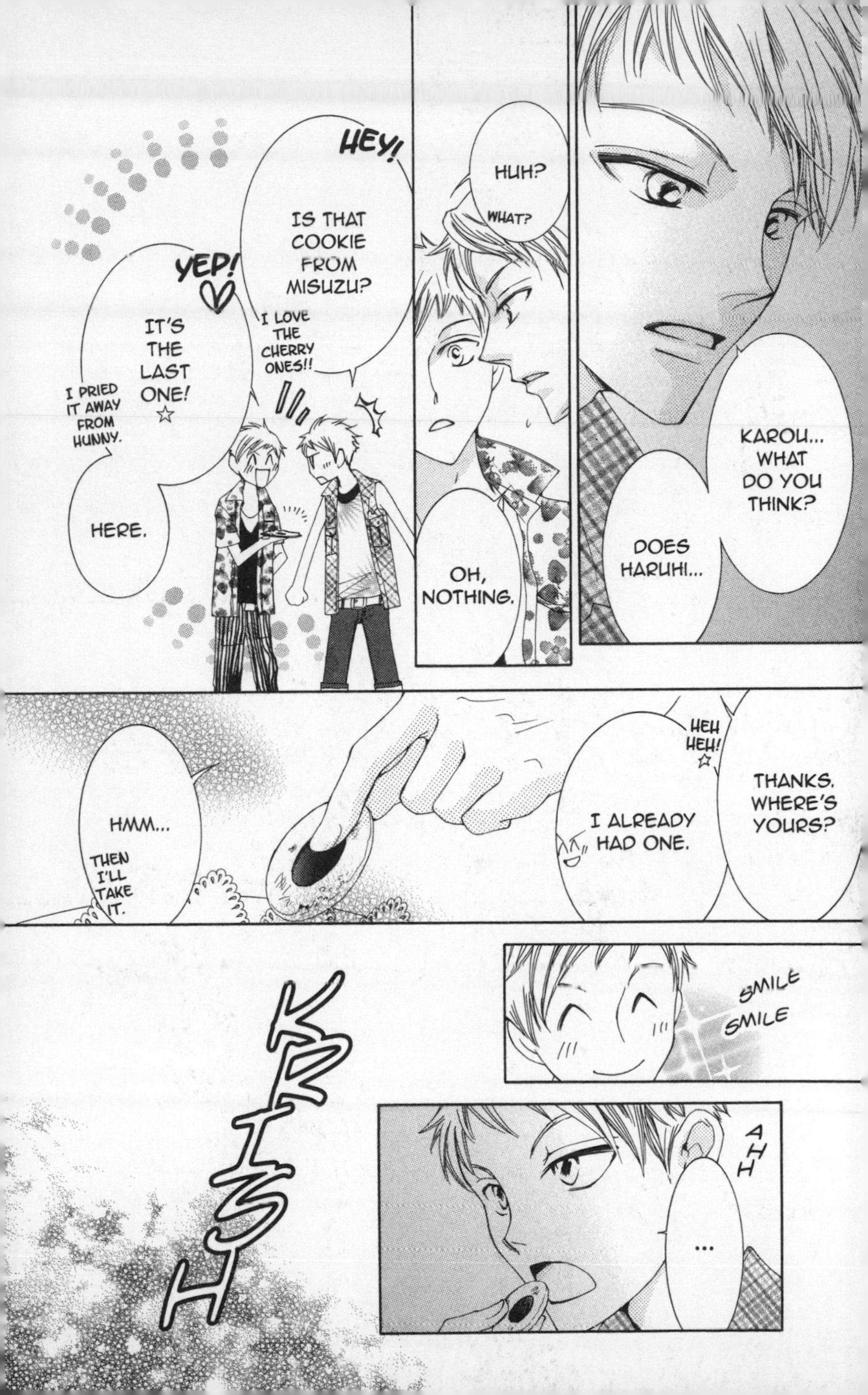
KAROU... WHAT DO YOU THINK?
DOES HARUHI...
HUH?
WHAT?
OH, NOTHING.
HEY!
IS THAT COOKIE FROM MISUZU?
I LOVE THE CHERRY ONES!!
YEP! ♡
IT'S THE LAST ONE! ☆
I PRIED IT AWAY FROM HUNNY.
HERE.
THANKS. WHERE'S YOURS?
HEH HEH! ☆
I ALREADY HAD ONE.
HMM...
THEN I'LL TAKE IT.
SMILE
SMILE
AHH
...
KRISH

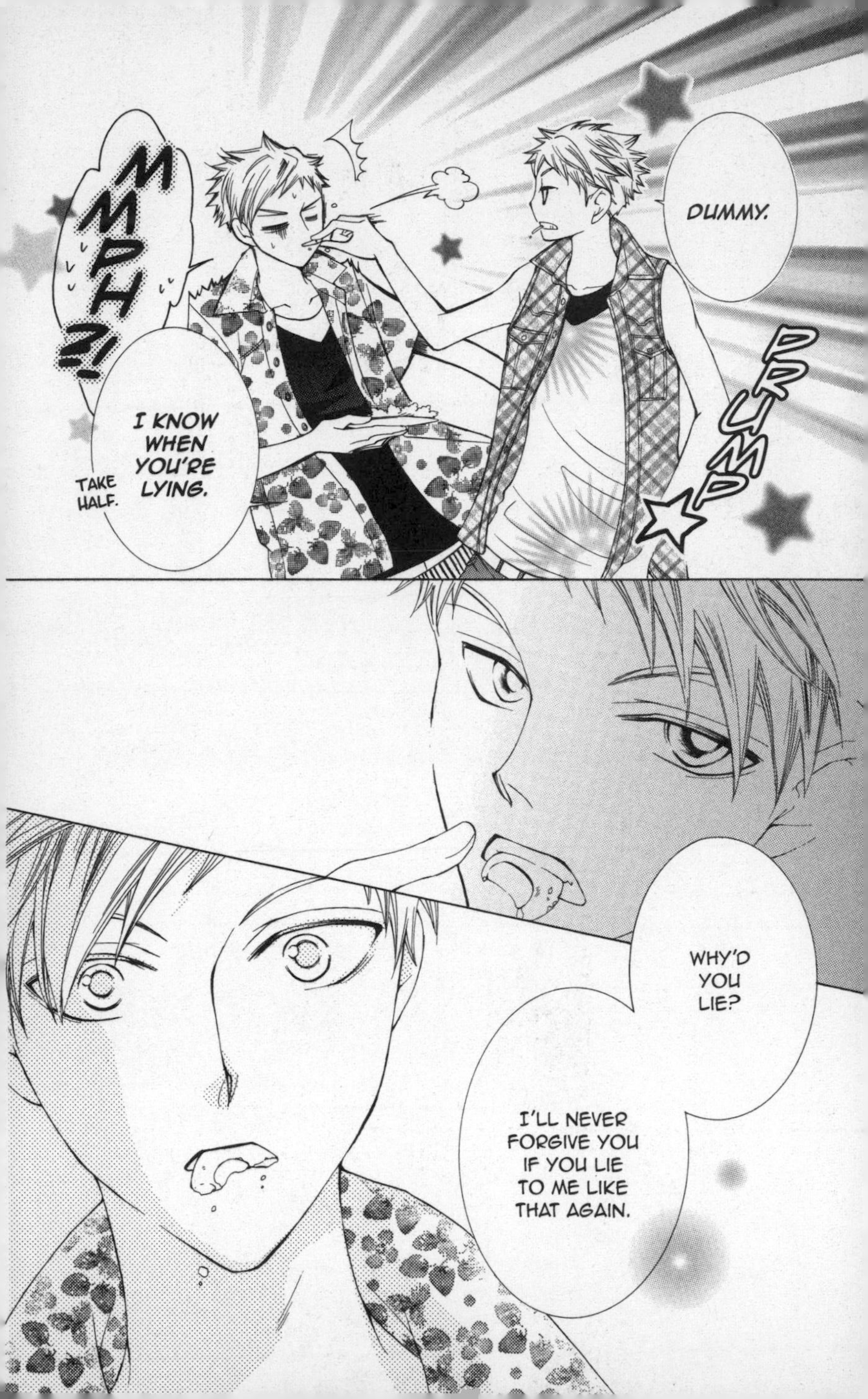
DUMMY.
PRUMP
MMPH?!
I KNOW WHEN YOU'RE LYING.
TAKE HALF.
WHY'D YOU LIE?
I'LL NEVER FORGIVE YOU IF YOU LIE TO ME LIKE THAT AGAIN.

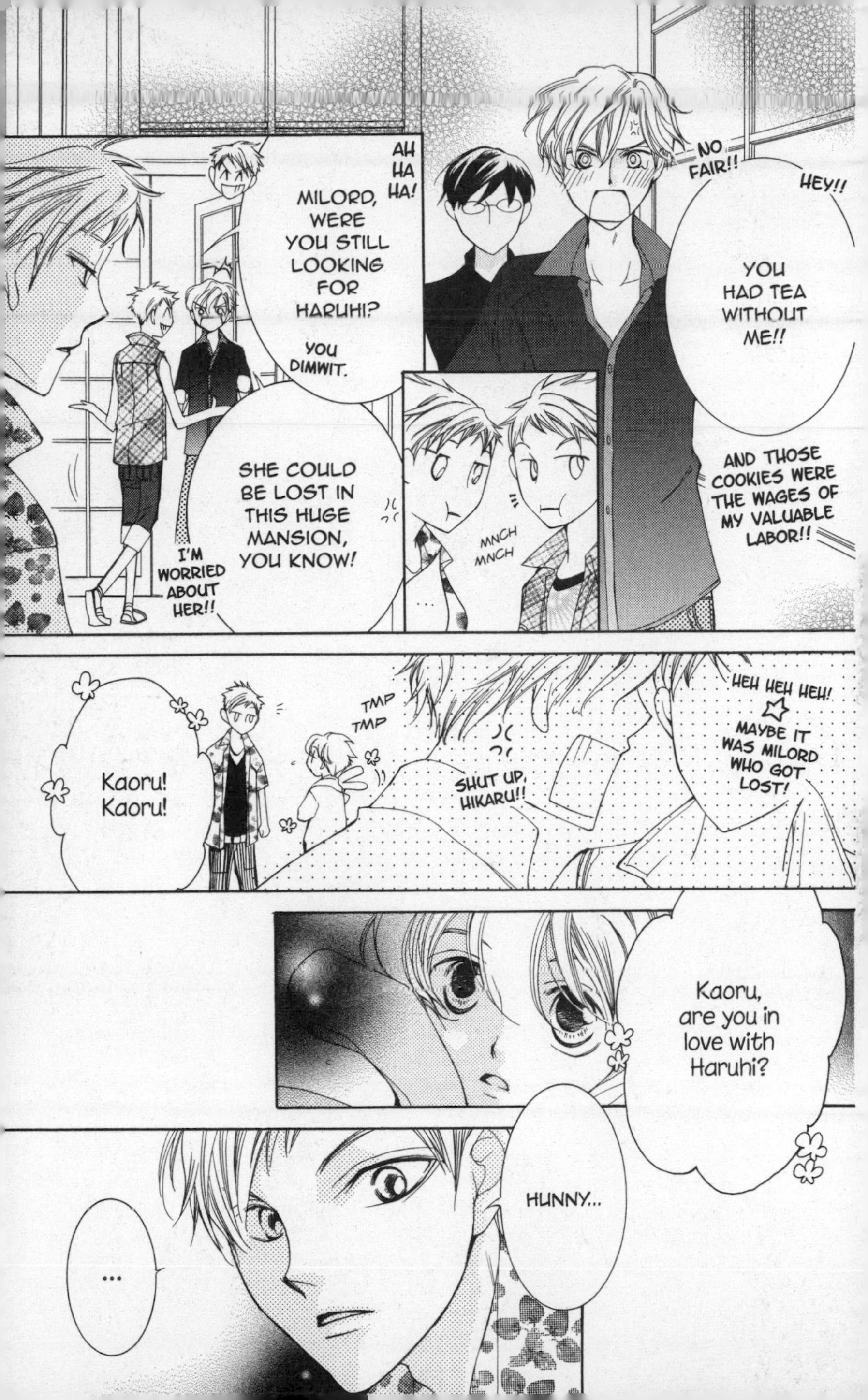
HEY!!
NO FAIR!!
YOU HAD TEA WITHOUT ME!!
AND THOSE COOKIES WERE THE WAGES OF MY VALUABLE LABOR!!
MNCH MNCH
...
AH HA HA!
MILORD, WERE YOU STILL LOOKING FOR HARUHI?
YOU DIMWIT.
SHE COULD BE LOST IN THIS HUGE MANSION, YOU KNOW!
I'M WORRIED ABOUT HER!!
HEH HEH HEH!
MAYBE IT WAS MILORD WHO GOT LOST!
SHUT UP, HIKARU!!
TMP TMP
Kaoru! Kaoru!
Kaoru, are you in love with Haruhi?
HUNNY...
...

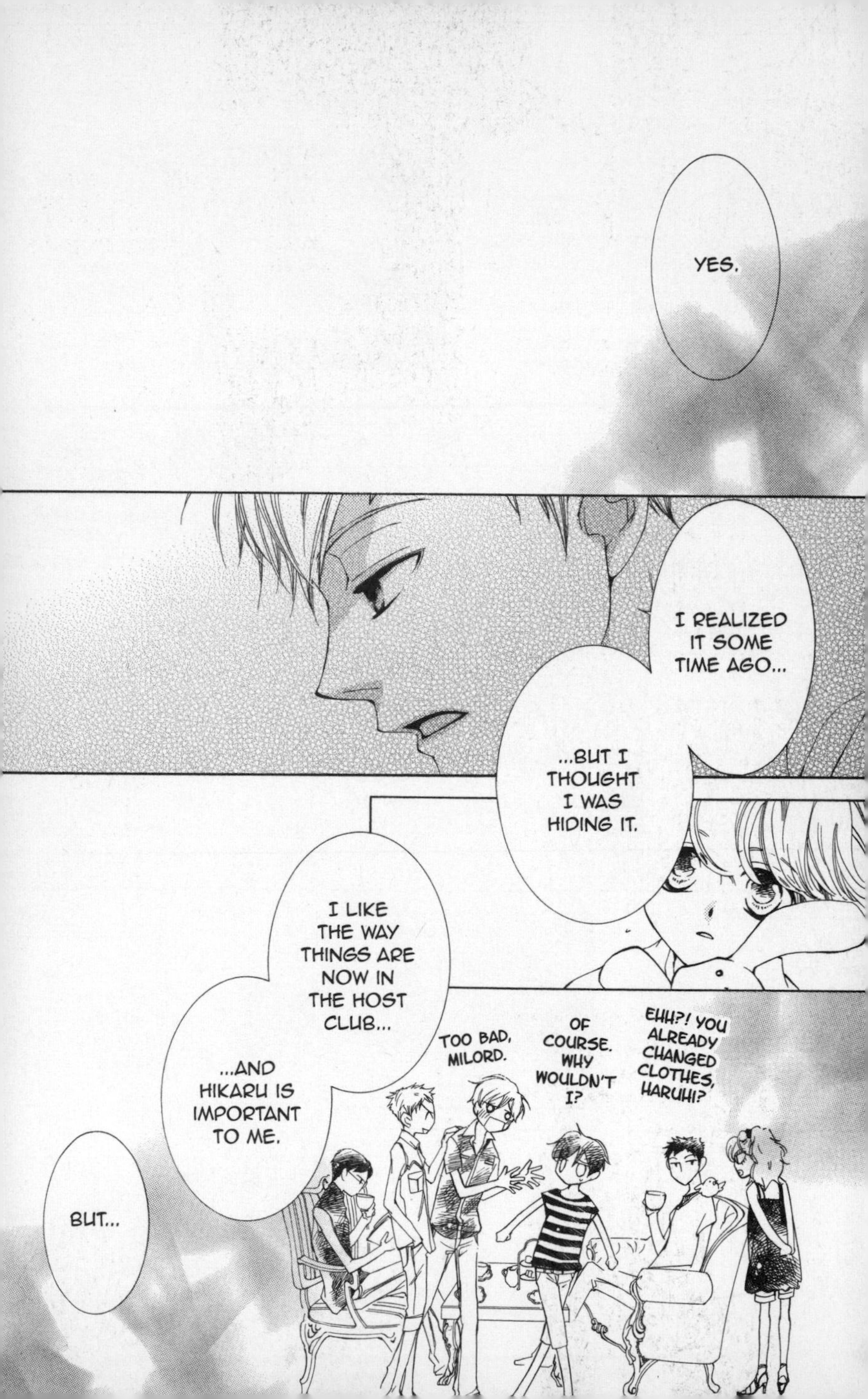
YES.
I REALIZED IT SOME TIME AGO...
...BUT I THOUGHT I WAS HIDING IT.
I LIKE THE WAY THINGS ARE NOW IN THE HOST CLUB...
...AND HIKARU IS IMPORTANT TO ME.
EHH?! YOU ALREADY CHANGED CLOTHES, HARUHI?
OF COURSE. WHY WOULDN'T I?
TOO BAD, MILORD.
BUT...

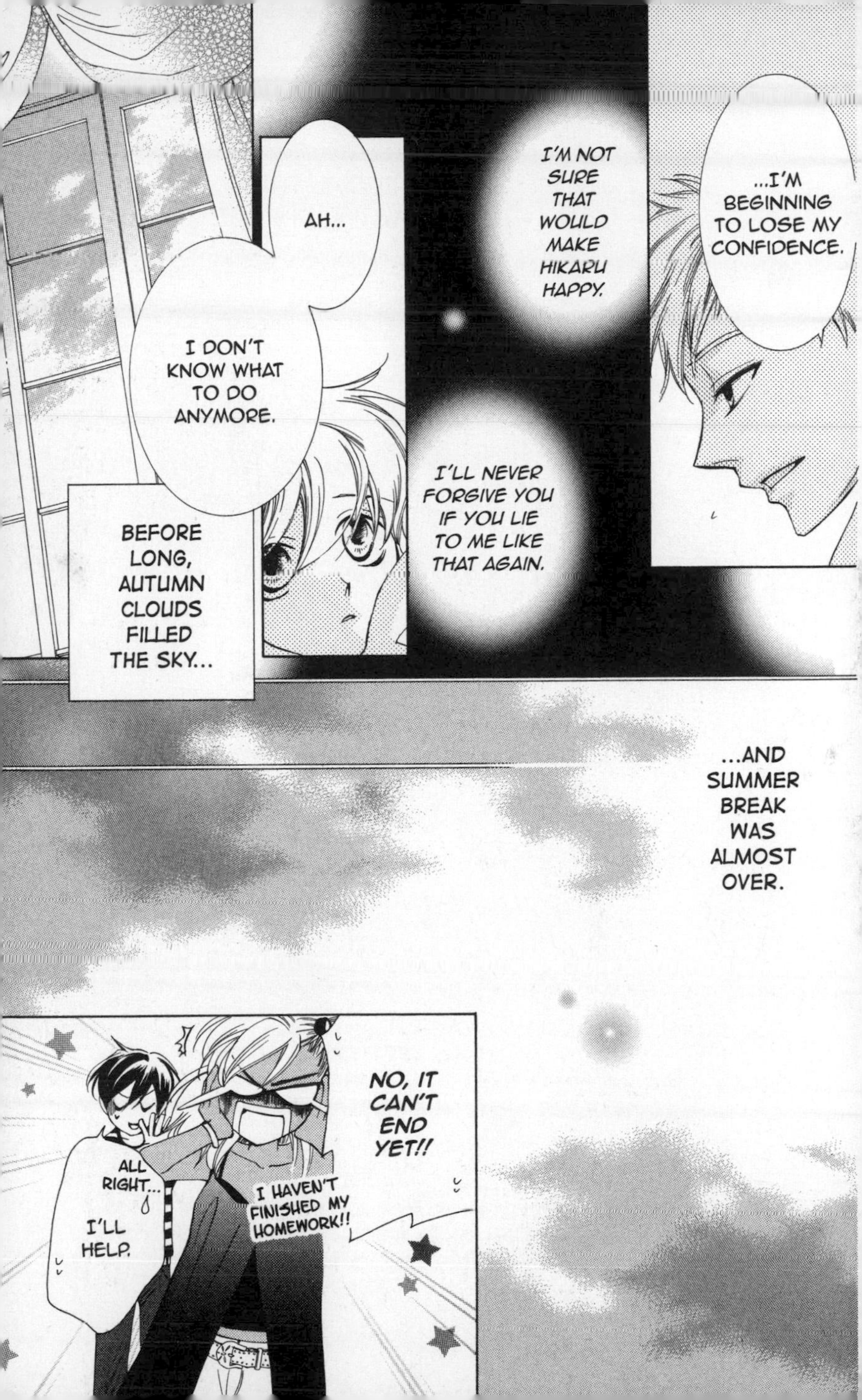
...I'M BEGINNING TO LOSE MY CONFIDENCE.
I'M NOT SURE THAT WOULD MAKE HIKARU HAPPY.
I'LL NEVER FORGIVE YOU IF YOU LIE TO ME LIKE THAT AGAIN.
AH...
I DON'T KNOW WHAT TO DO ANYMORE.
BEFORE LONG, AUTUMN CLOUDS FILLED THE SKY...
...AND SUMMER BREAK WAS ALMOST OVER.
NO, IT CAN'T END YET!!
I HAVEN'T FINISHED MY HOMEWORK!!
ALL RIGHT...
I'LL HELP.

GUEST ROOM: FAXES ④

SPECIAL THANKS TO WATARU HIBIKI!!

HARUHI & TAMAKI KEEP BEING SINFULLY BEAUTIFUL AS ALWAYS...!!

HIBIKI

TAMAKI LOOKS AMAZINGLY COOL, BUT HIS PINKY FINGER IS RAISED. I COULD JUST CRY! YOU COULD HAVE, UH...JUST DRAWN HIM NORMAL.
WATARU IS FAMOUS FOR BEING A BIG EATER (EVEN THOUGH SHE'S SKINNY). THE FIRST TIME I CALLED HER FOR HELP, A LOT OF PEOPLE WHO KNEW HER TOLD ME TO PREPARE A LOT OF FOOD, WHICH SURPRISED ME.
KEEP EATING AND CREATING YOUR POWERFUL AND BEAUTIFUL MANGA AS ALWAYS, WATARU!! AND LET'S GO TO SENDAI TOGETHER SOMETIME FOR OX TONGUE.

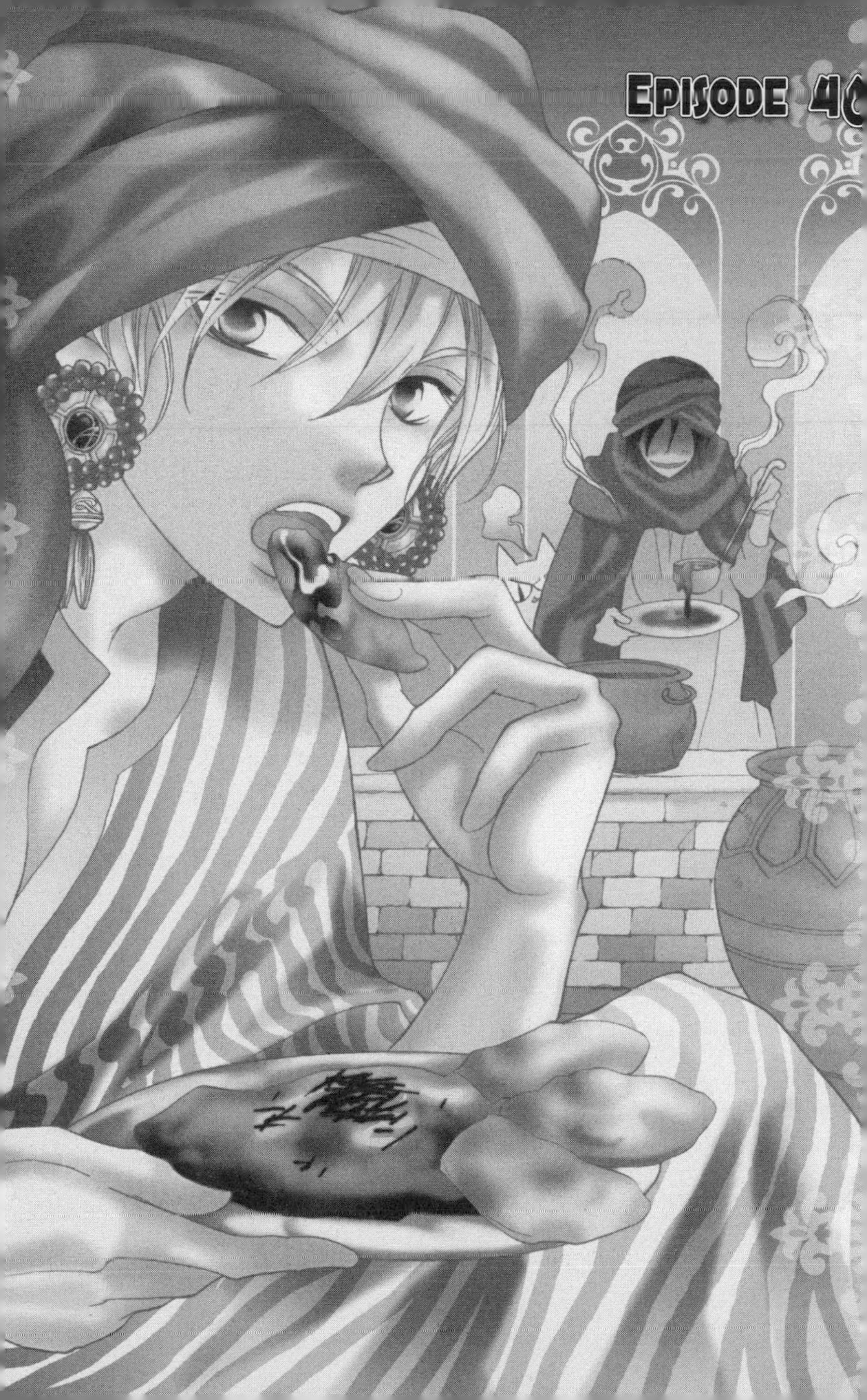
Episode 46

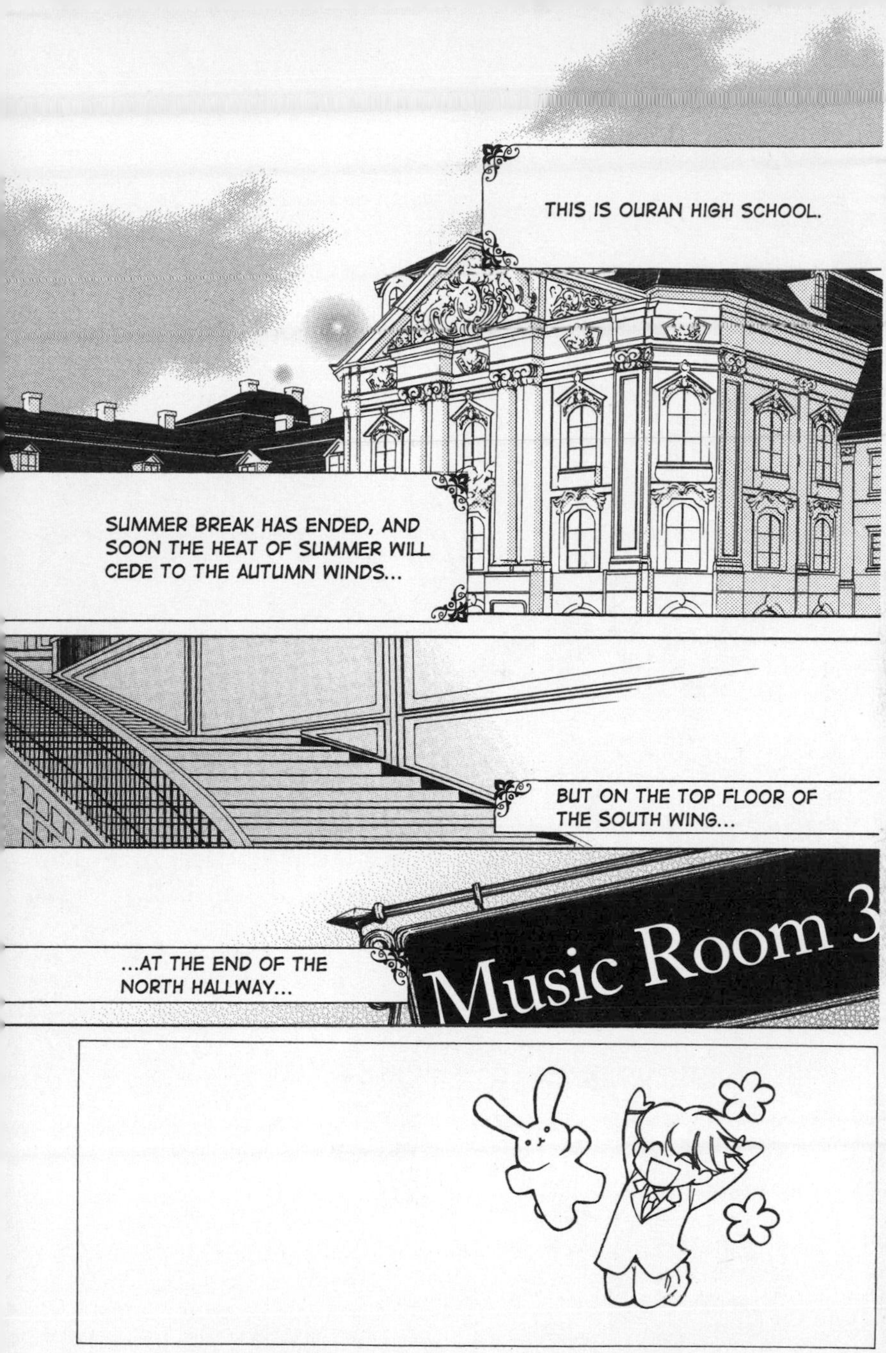
THIS IS OURAN HIGH SCHOOL.
SUMMER BREAK HAS ENDED, AND SOON THE HEAT OF SUMMER WILL CEDE TO THE AUTUMN WINDS...
BUT ON THE TOP FLOOR OF THE SOUTH WING...
...AT THE END OF THE NORTH HALLWAY...
Music Room 3

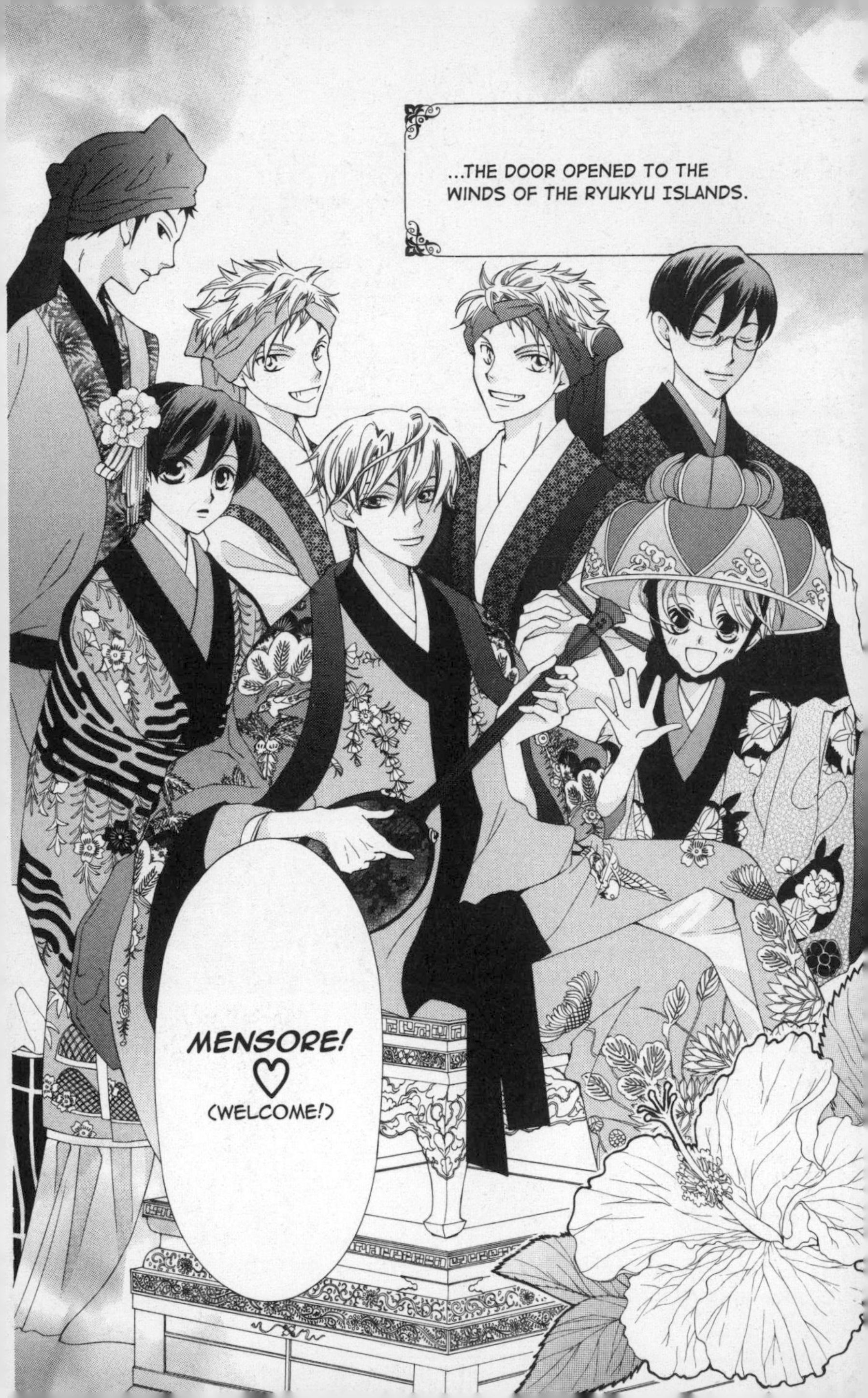
...THE DOOR OPENED TO THE WINDS OF THE RYUKYU ISLANDS.
MENSORE! ♡ (WELCOME!)

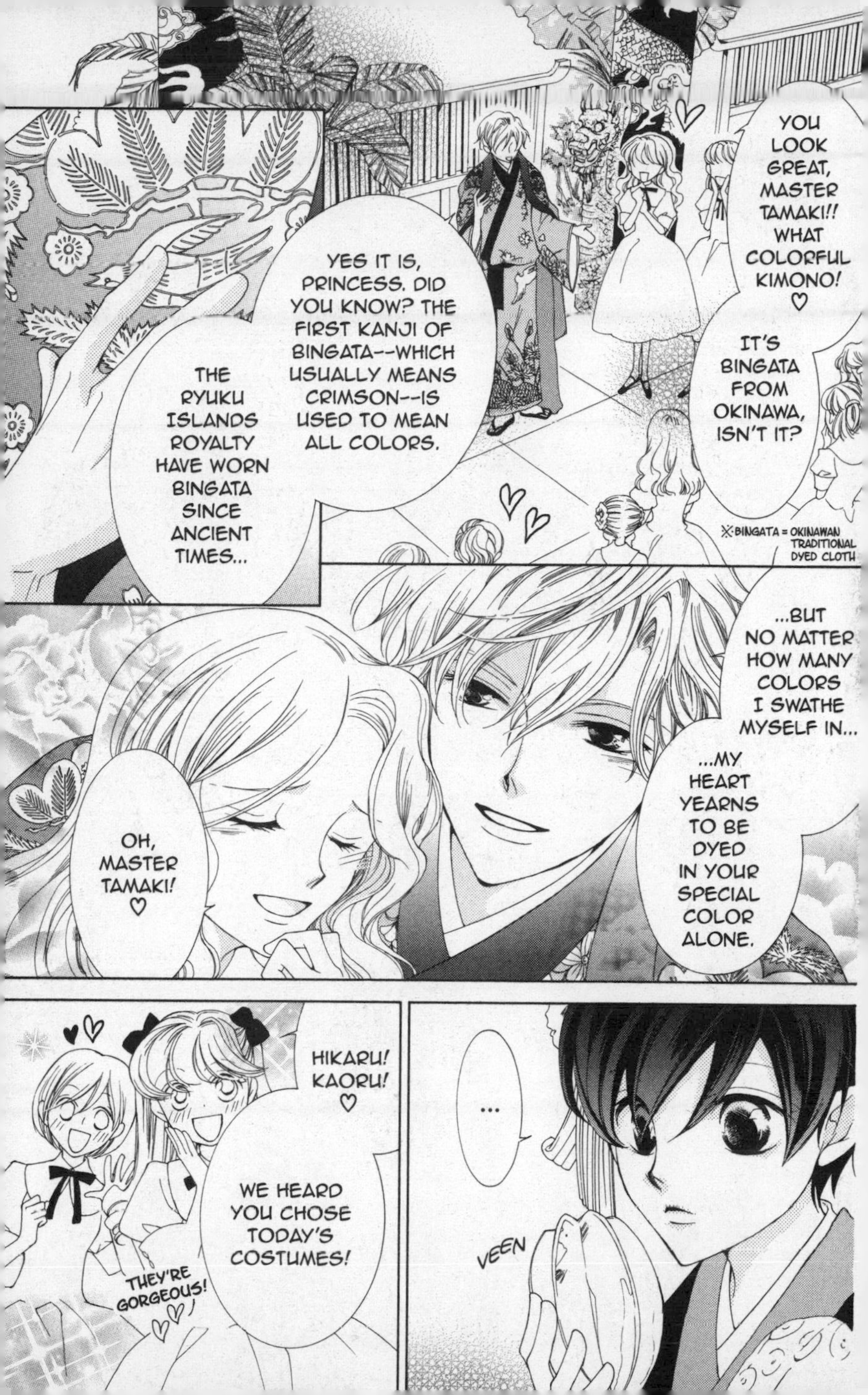
YOU LOOK GREAT, MASTER TAMAKI!! WHAT COLORFUL KIMONO! ♡
IT'S BINGATA FROM OKINAWA, ISN'T IT?
※BINGATA = OKINAWAN TRADITIONAL DYED CLOTH
YES IT IS, PRINCESS. DID YOU KNOW? THE FIRST KANJI OF BINGATA--WHICH USUALLY MEANS CRIMSON--IS USED TO MEAN ALL COLORS.
THE RYUKU ISLANDS ROYALTY HAVE WORN BINGATA SINCE ANCIENT TIMES...
...BUT NO MATTER HOW MANY COLORS I SWATHE MYSELF IN...
...MY HEART YEARNS TO BE DYED IN YOUR SPECIAL COLOR ALONE.
OH, MASTER TAMAKI! ♡
...
VEEN
HIKARU! KAORU! ♡
WE HEARD YOU CHOSE TODAY'S COSTUMES!
THEY'RE GORGEOUS! ♡

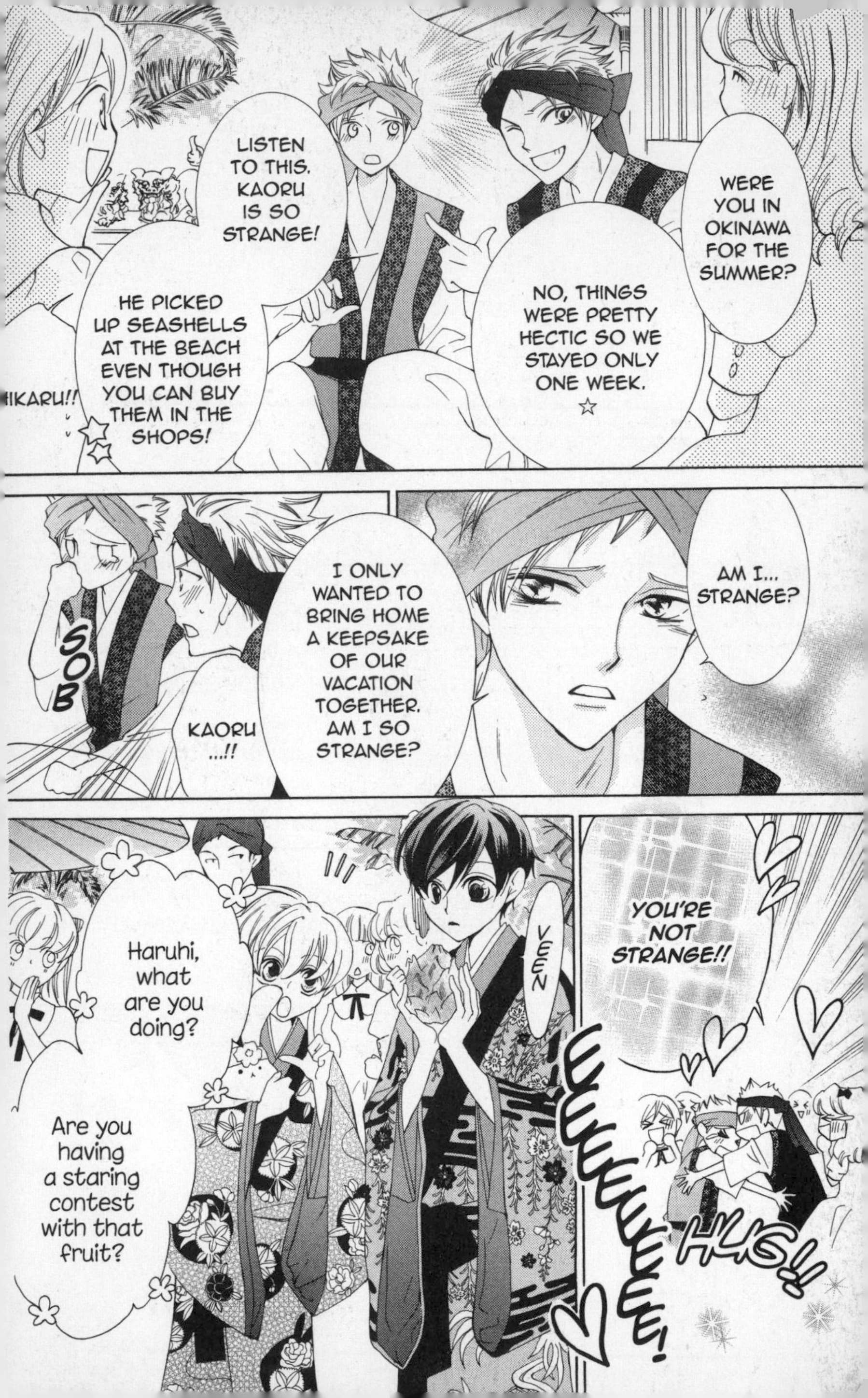
WERE YOU IN OKINAWA FOR THE SUMMER?
NO, THINGS WERE PRETTY HECTIC SO WE STAYED ONLY ONE WEEK. ☆
LISTEN TO THIS. KAORU IS SO STRANGE!
HE PICKED UP SEASHELLS AT THE BEACH EVEN THOUGH YOU CAN BUY THEM IN THE SHOPS!
HIKARU!!
AM I... STRANGE?
I ONLY WANTED TO BRING HOME A KEEPSAKE OF OUR VACATION TOGETHER. AM I SO STRANGE?
KAORU ...!!
SOB
YOU'RE NOT STRANGE!!
EEEEEEEE!
HUG!!
VEEN
Haruhi, what are you doing?
Are you having a staring contest with that fruit?

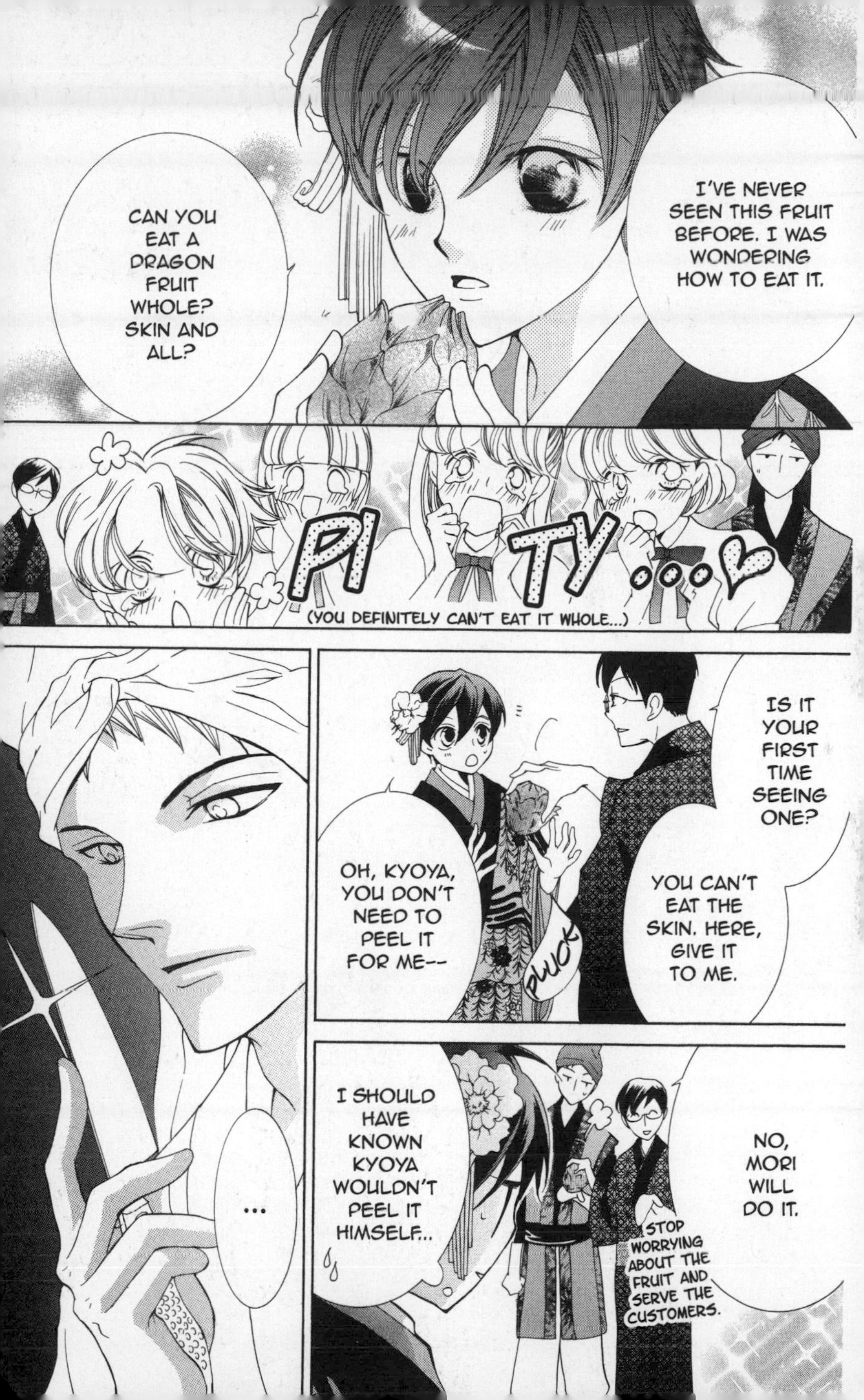
I'VE NEVER SEEN THIS FRUIT BEFORE. I WAS WONDERING HOW TO EAT IT.
CAN YOU EAT A DRAGON FRUIT WHOLE? SKIN AND ALL?
PITY...♥
(YOU DEFINITELY CAN'T EAT IT WHOLE...)
IS IT YOUR FIRST TIME SEEING ONE?
YOU CAN'T EAT THE SKIN. HERE, GIVE IT TO ME.
PLUCK
OH, KYOYA, YOU DON'T NEED TO PEEL IT FOR ME--
NO, MORI WILL DO IT.
STOP WORRYING ABOUT THE FRUIT AND SERVE THE CUSTOMERS.
I SHOULD HAVE KNOWN KYOYA WOULDN'T PEEL IT HIMSELF...
...

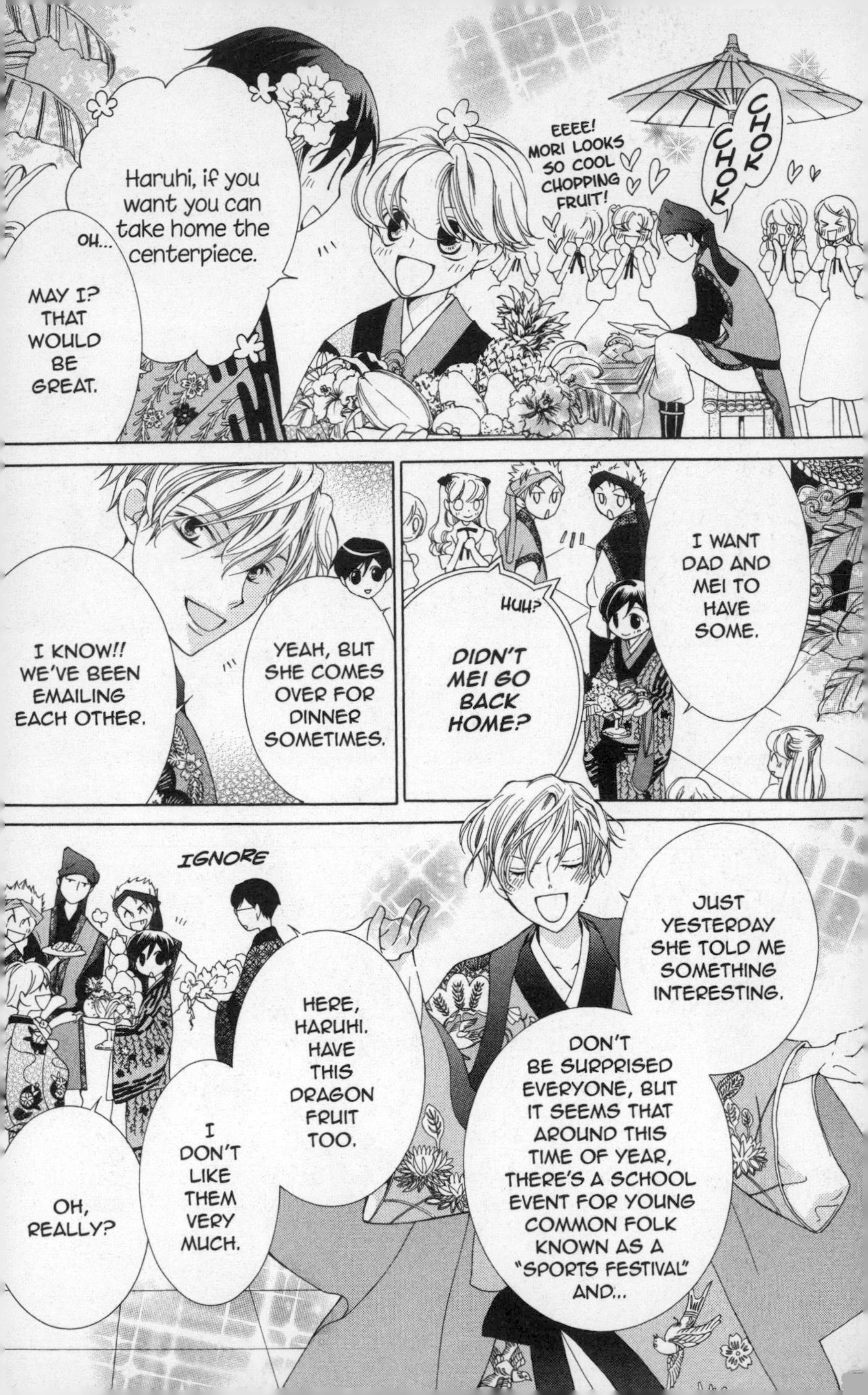
CHOK CHOK
EEEE! MORI LOOKS SO COOL CHOPPING FRUIT!
Haruhi, if you want you can take home the centerpiece.
OH...
MAY I? THAT WOULD BE GREAT.
I WANT DAD AND MEI TO HAVE SOME.
HUH?
DIDN'T MEI GO BACK HOME?
YEAH, BUT SHE COMES OVER FOR DINNER SOMETIMES.
I KNOW!! WE'VE BEEN EMAILING EACH OTHER.
JUST YESTERDAY SHE TOLD ME SOMETHING INTERESTING.
DON'T BE SURPRISED EVERYONE, BUT IT SEEMS THAT AROUND THIS TIME OF YEAR, THERE'S A SCHOOL EVENT FOR YOUNG COMMON FOLK KNOWN AS A "SPORTS FESTIVAL" AND...
IGNORE
HERE, HARUHI. HAVE THIS DRAGON FRUIT TOO.
I DON'T LIKE THEM VERY MUCH.
OH, REALLY?

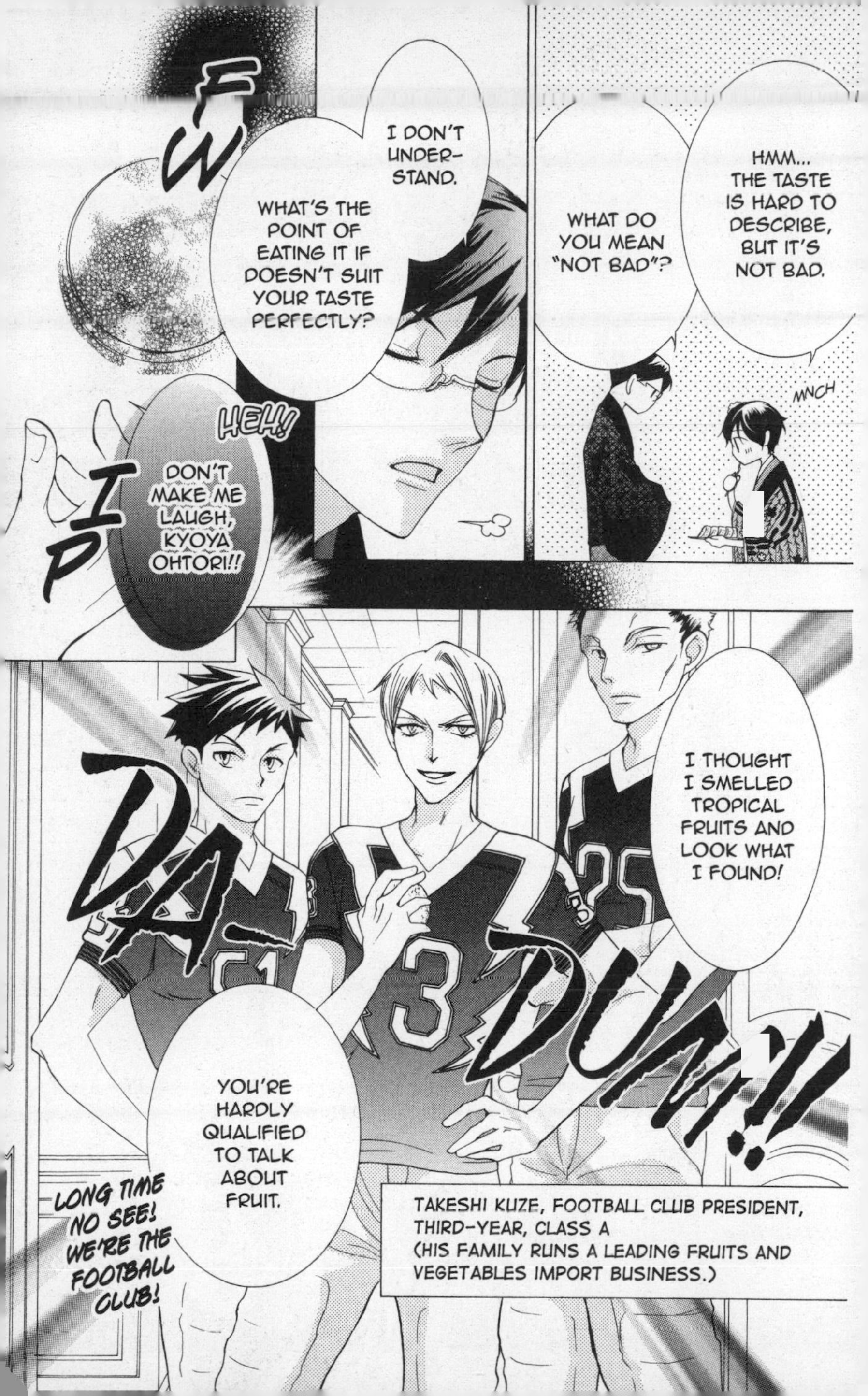
HMM... THE TASTE IS HARD TO DESCRIBE, BUT IT'S NOT BAD.
WHAT DO YOU MEAN "NOT BAD"?
MNCH
I DON'T UNDER-STAND.
WHAT'S THE POINT OF EATING IT IF DOESN'T SUIT YOUR TASTE PERFECTLY?
FWIP
HEH!!
DON'T MAKE ME LAUGH, KYOYA OHTORI!!
I THOUGHT I SMELLED TROPICAL FRUITS AND LOOK WHAT I FOUND!
DA-DUN!!
YOU'RE HARDLY QUALIFIED TO TALK ABOUT FRUIT.
TAKESHI KUZE, FOOTBALL CLUB PRESIDENT, THIRD-YEAR, CLASS A (HIS FAMILY RUNS A LEADING FRUITS AND VEGETABLES IMPORT BUSINESS.)
LONG TIME NO SEE! WE'RE THE FOOTBALL CLUB!

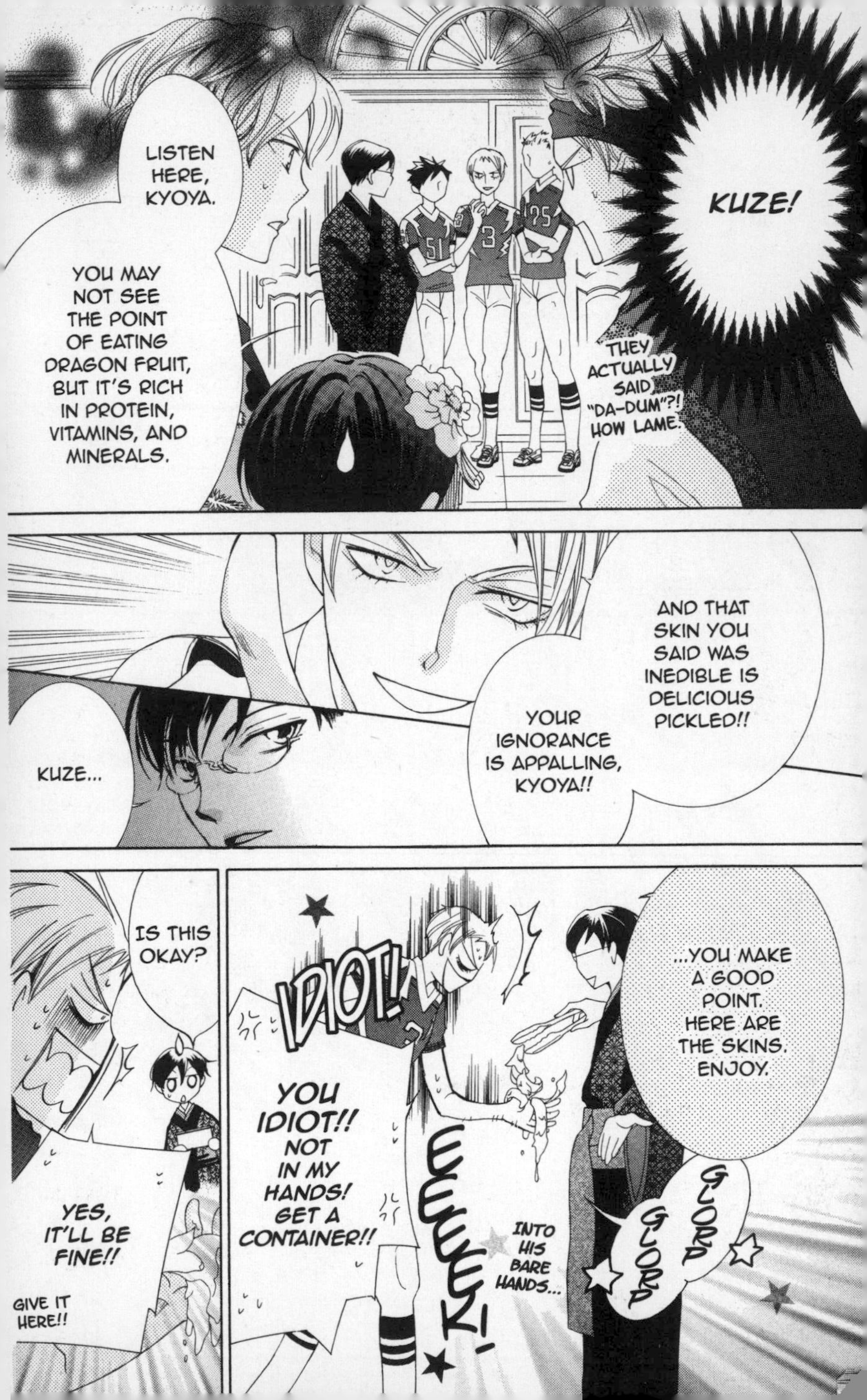
KUZE!
LISTEN HERE, KYOYA.
YOU MAY NOT SEE THE POINT OF EATING DRAGON FRUIT, BUT IT'S RICH IN PROTEIN, VITAMINS, AND MINERALS.
THEY ACTUALLY SAID "DA-DUM"?! HOW LAME.
AND THAT SKIN YOU SAID WAS INEDIBLE IS DELICIOUS PICKLED!!
YOUR IGNORANCE IS APPALLING, KYOYA!!
KUZE...
...YOU MAKE A GOOD POINT. HERE ARE THE SKINS. ENJOY.
GLORP GLORP
INTO HIS BARE HANDS...
EEEEEK!
IDIOT!
YOU IDIOT!! NOT IN MY HANDS! GET A CONTAINER!!
IS THIS OKAY?
YES, IT'LL BE FINE!!
GIVE IT HERE!!

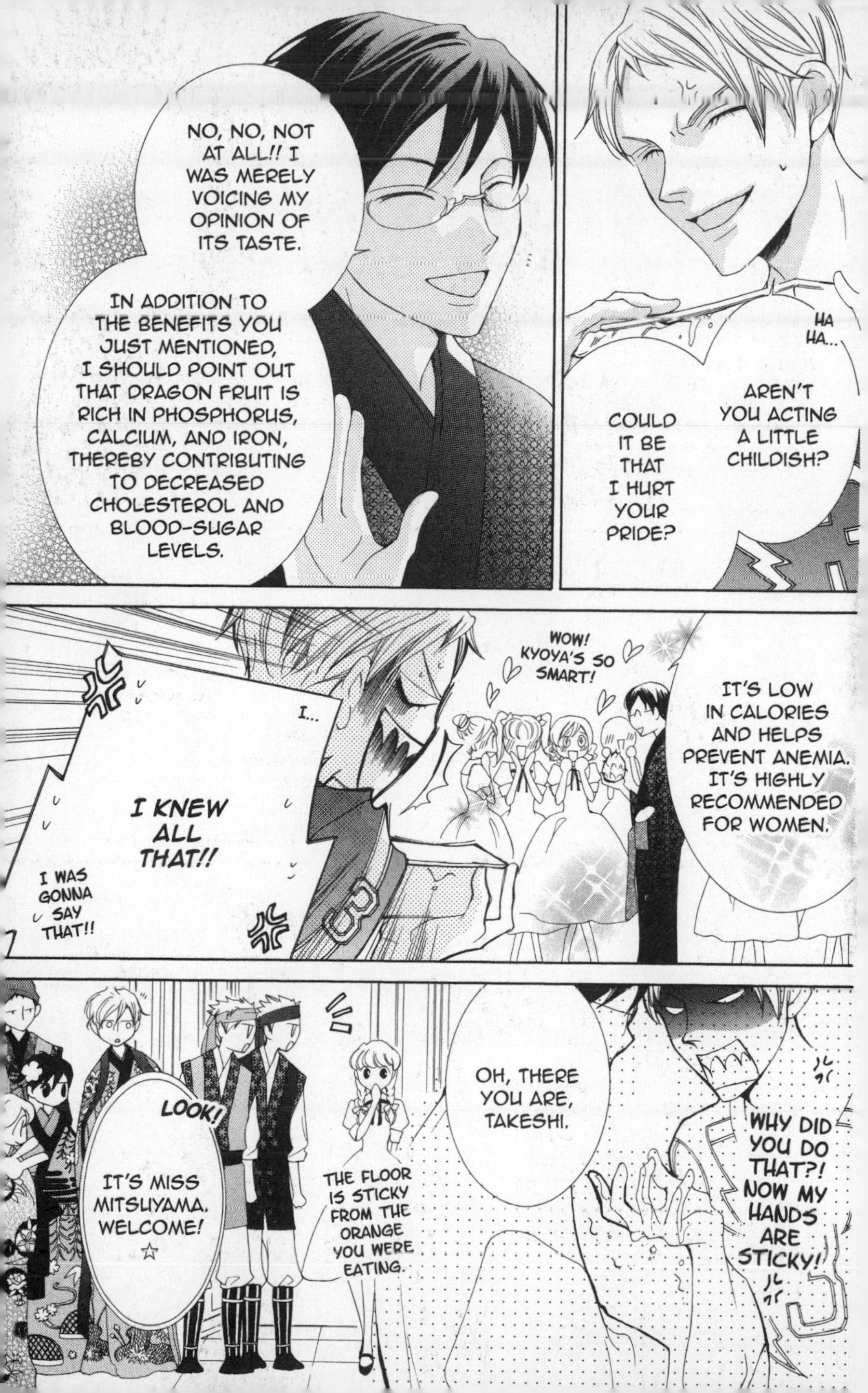
HA HA...
AREN'T YOU ACTING A LITTLE CHILDISH?
COULD IT BE THAT I HURT YOUR PRIDE?
NO, NO, NOT AT ALL!! I WAS MERELY VOICING MY OPINION OF ITS TASTE.
IN ADDITION TO THE BENEFITS YOU JUST MENTIONED, I SHOULD POINT OUT THAT DRAGON FRUIT IS RICH IN PHOSPHORUS, CALCIUM, AND IRON, THEREBY CONTRIBUTING TO DECREASED CHOLESTEROL AND BLOOD-SUGAR LEVELS.
IT'S LOW IN CALORIES AND HELPS PREVENT ANEMIA. IT'S HIGHLY RECOMMENDED FOR WOMEN.
WOW! KYOYA'S SO SMART!
I...
I KNEW ALL THAT!!
I WAS GONNA SAY THAT!!
OH, THERE YOU ARE, TAKESHI.
WHY DID YOU DO THAT?! NOW MY HANDS ARE STICKY!
THE FLOOR IS STICKY FROM THE ORANGE YOU WERE EATING.
LOOK!
IT'S MISS MITSUYAMA. WELCOME! ☆

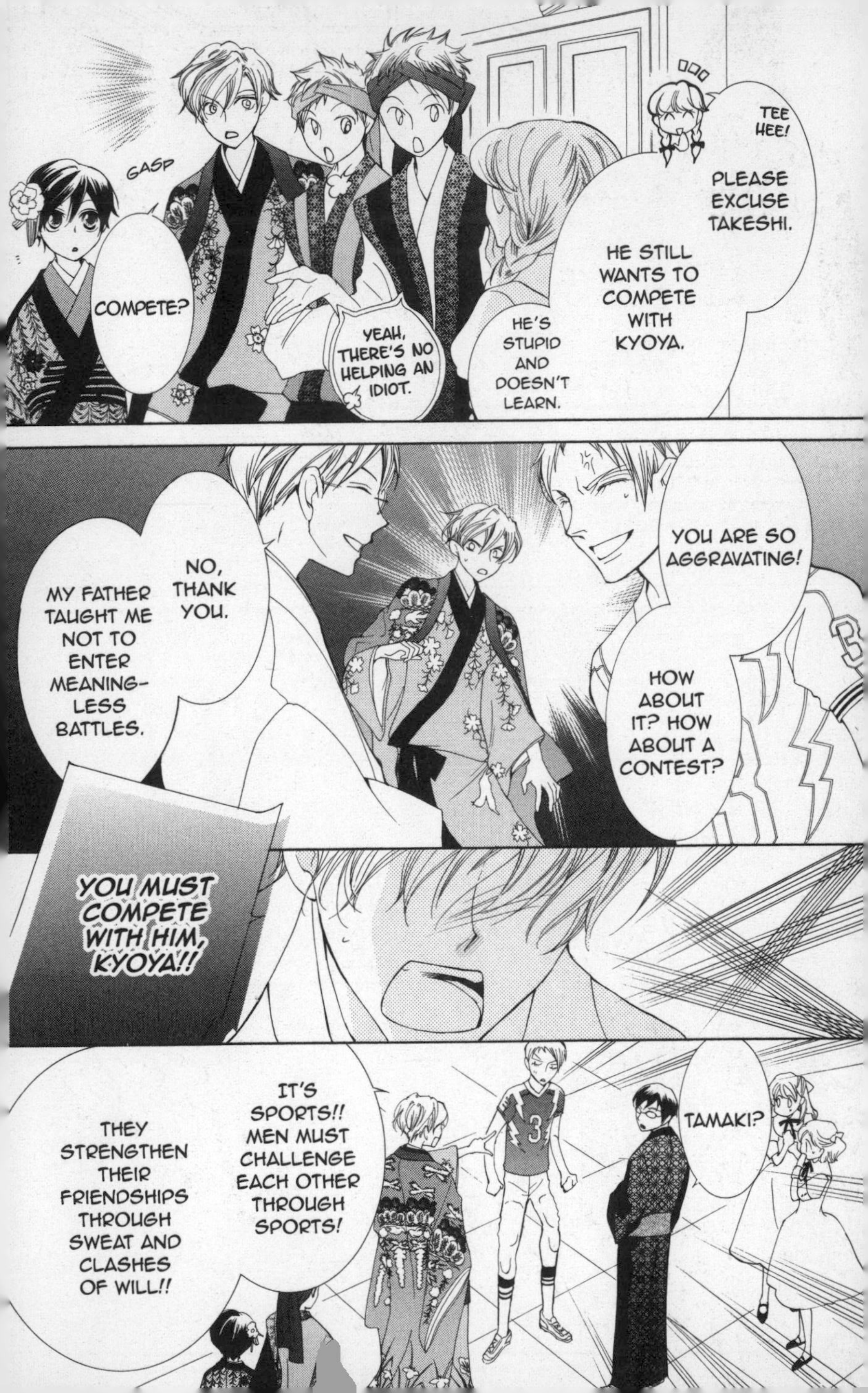
TEE HEE!
PLEASE EXCUSE TAKESHI.
HE STILL WANTS TO COMPETE WITH KYOYA.
HE'S STUPID AND DOESN'T LEARN.
YEAH, THERE'S NO HELPING AN IDIOT.
GASP
COMPETE?
YOU ARE SO AGGRAVATING!
HOW ABOUT IT? HOW ABOUT A CONTEST?
NO, THANK YOU.
MY FATHER TAUGHT ME NOT TO ENTER MEANINGLESS BATTLES.
YOU MUST COMPETE WITH HIM, KYOYA!!
TAMAKI?
IT'S SPORTS!! MEN MUST CHALLENGE EACH OTHER THROUGH SPORTS!
THEY STRENGTHEN THEIR FRIENDSHIPS THROUGH SWEAT AND CLASHES OF WILL!!

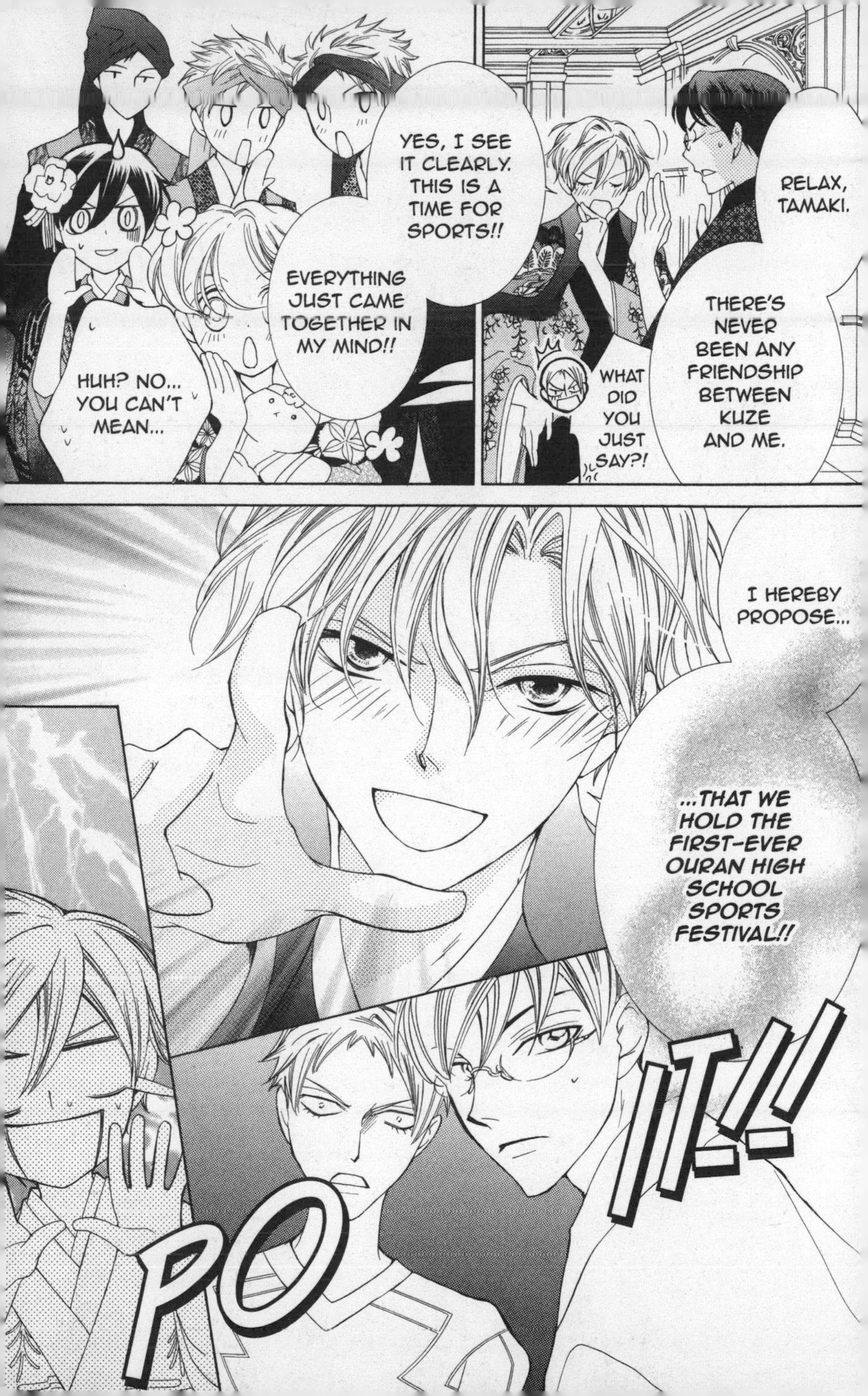
RELAX, TAMAKI.
THERE'S NEVER BEEN ANY FRIENDSHIP BETWEEN KUZE AND ME.
WHAT DID YOU JUST SAY?!
YES, I SEE IT CLEARLY. THIS IS A TIME FOR SPORTS!!
EVERYTHING JUST CAME TOGETHER IN MY MIND!!
HUH? NO... YOU CAN'T MEAN...
I HEREBY PROPOSE...
...THAT WE HOLD THE FIRST-EVER OURAN HIGH SCHOOL SPORTS FESTIVAL!!
POIT!!

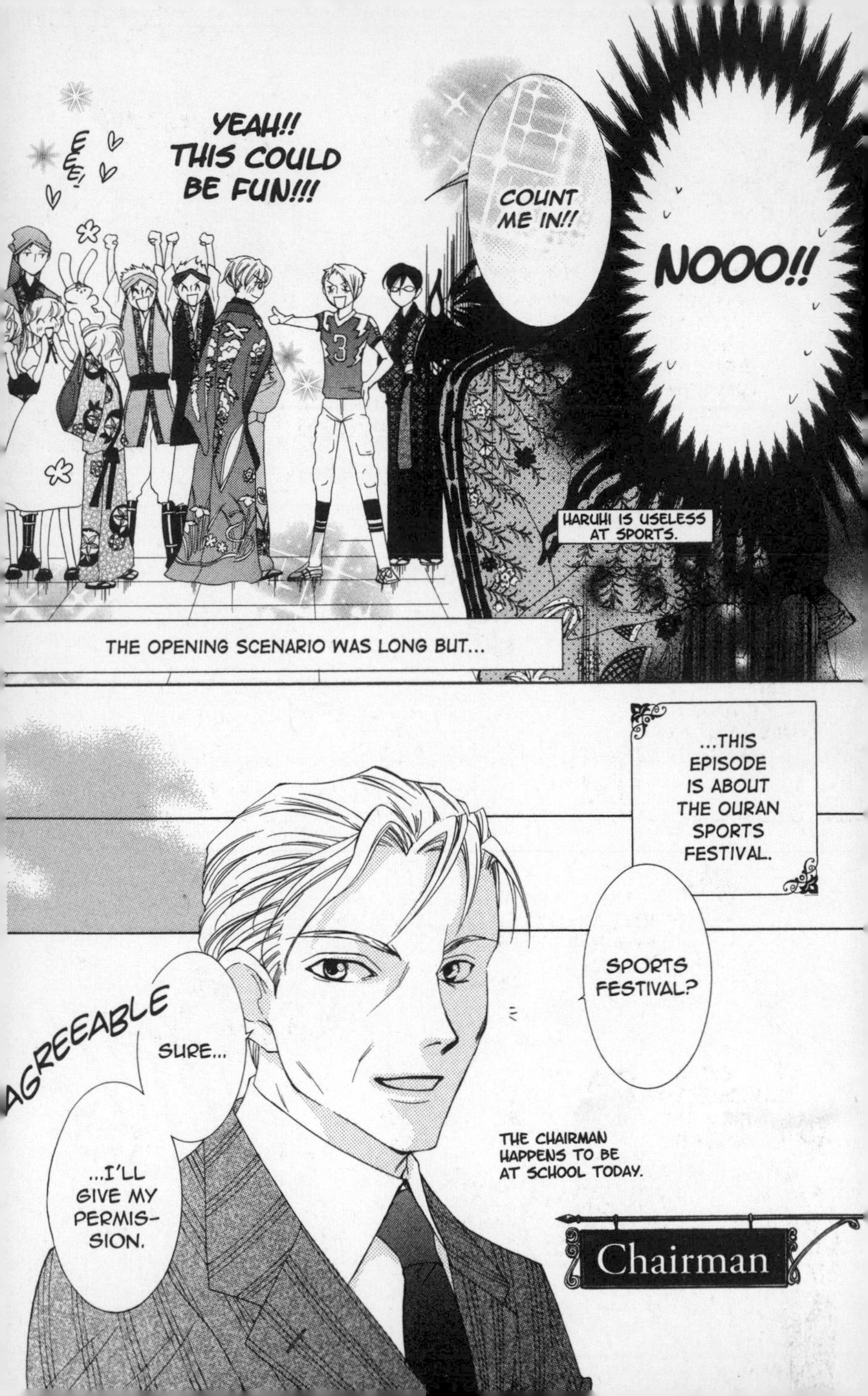
NOOO!!
COUNT ME IN!!
HARUHI IS USELESS AT SPORTS.
YEAH!! THIS COULD BE FUN!!!
EEE!
THE OPENING SCENARIO WAS LONG BUT...
...THIS EPISODE IS ABOUT THE OURAN SPORTS FESTIVAL.
SPORTS FESTIVAL?
THE CHAIRMAN HAPPENS TO BE AT SCHOOL TODAY.
Chairman
AGREEABLE
SURE...
...I'LL GIVE MY PERMIS-SION.

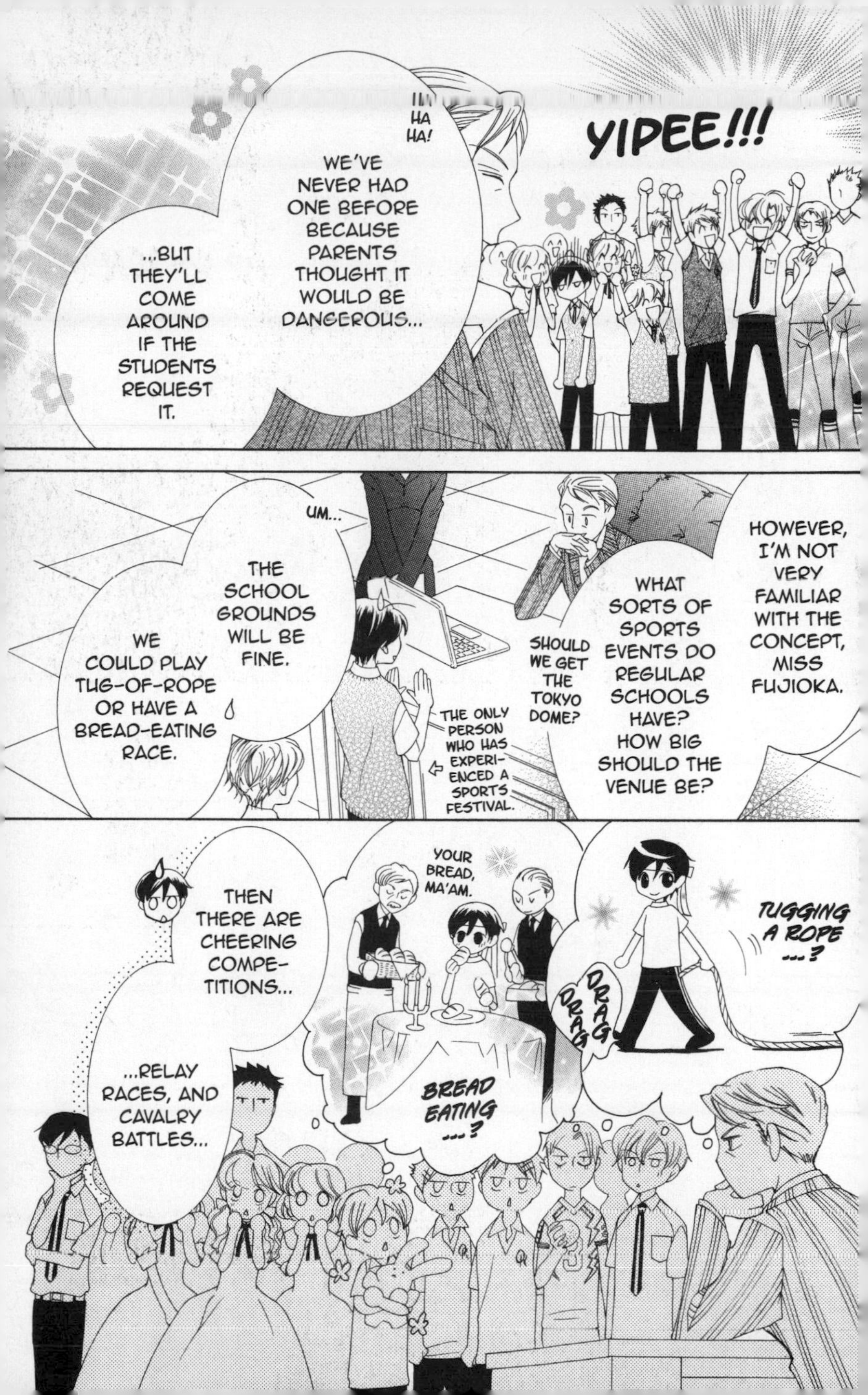
YIPEE!!!
HA HA HA!
WE'VE NEVER HAD ONE BEFORE BECAUSE PARENTS THOUGHT IT WOULD BE DANGEROUS...
...BUT THEY'LL COME AROUND IF THE STUDENTS REQUEST IT.
HOWEVER, I'M NOT VERY FAMILIAR WITH THE CONCEPT, MISS FUJIOKA.
WHAT SORTS OF SPORTS EVENTS DO REGULAR SCHOOLS HAVE? HOW BIG SHOULD THE VENUE BE?
SHOULD WE GET THE TOKYO DOME?
THE ONLY PERSON WHO HAS EXPERIENCED A SPORTS FESTIVAL.
UM...
THE SCHOOL GROUNDS WILL BE FINE.
WE COULD PLAY TUG-OF-ROPE OR HAVE A BREAD-EATING RACE.
TUGGING A ROPE ...?
DRAG DRAG
YOUR BREAD, MA'AM.
BREAD EATING ...?
THEN THERE ARE CHEERING COMPETITIONS...
...RELAY RACES, AND CAVALRY BATTLES...

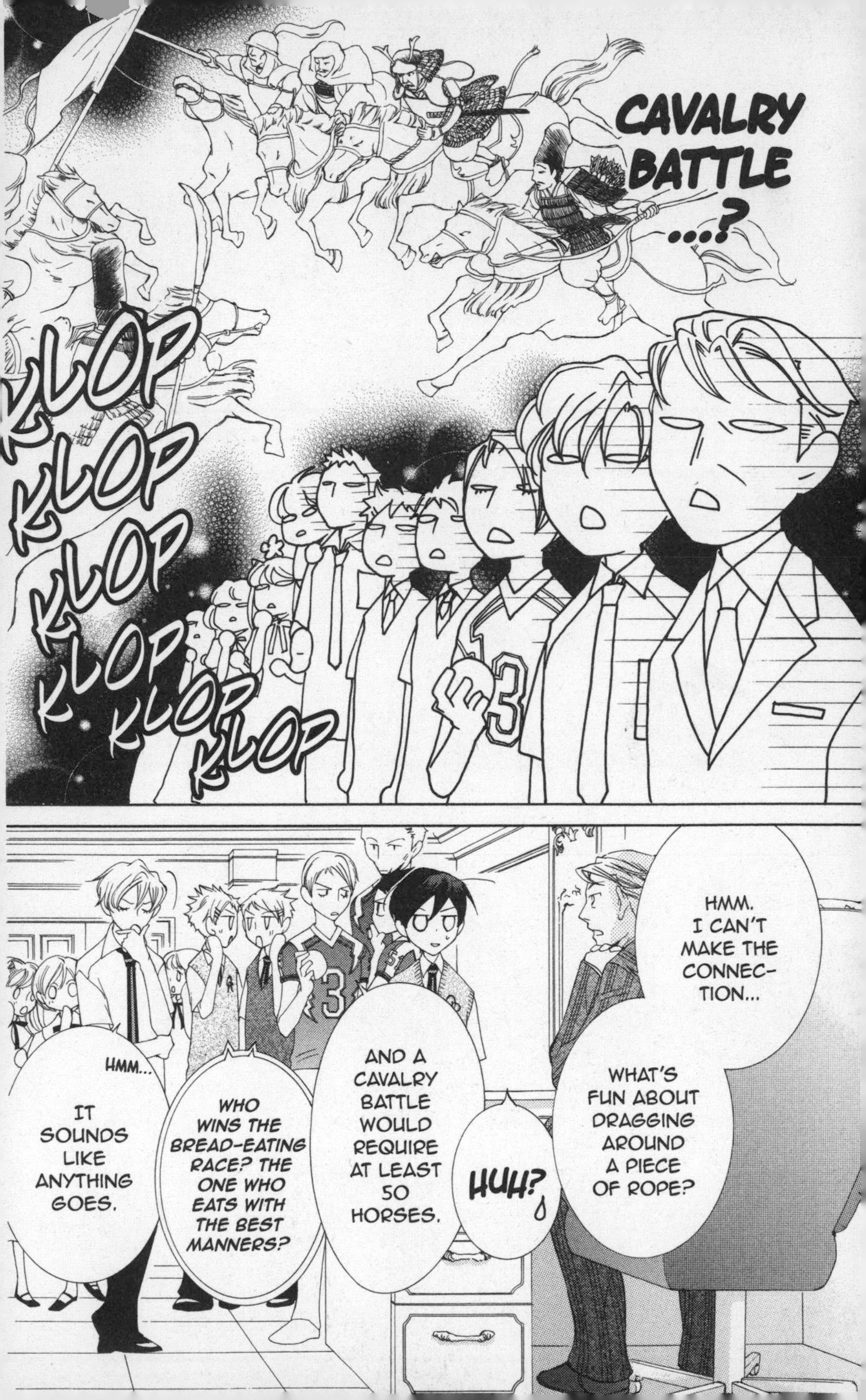
CAVALRY BATTLE ....?
KLOP KLOP KLOP KLOP KLOP KLOP
HMM. I CAN'T MAKE THE CONNECTION...
WHAT'S FUN ABOUT DRAGGING AROUND A PIECE OF ROPE?
HUH?
AND A CAVALRY BATTLE WOULD REQUIRE AT LEAST 50 HORSES.
WHO WINS THE BREAD-EATING RACE? THE ONE WHO EATS WITH THE BEST MANNERS?
HMM...
IT SOUNDS LIKE ANYTHING GOES.

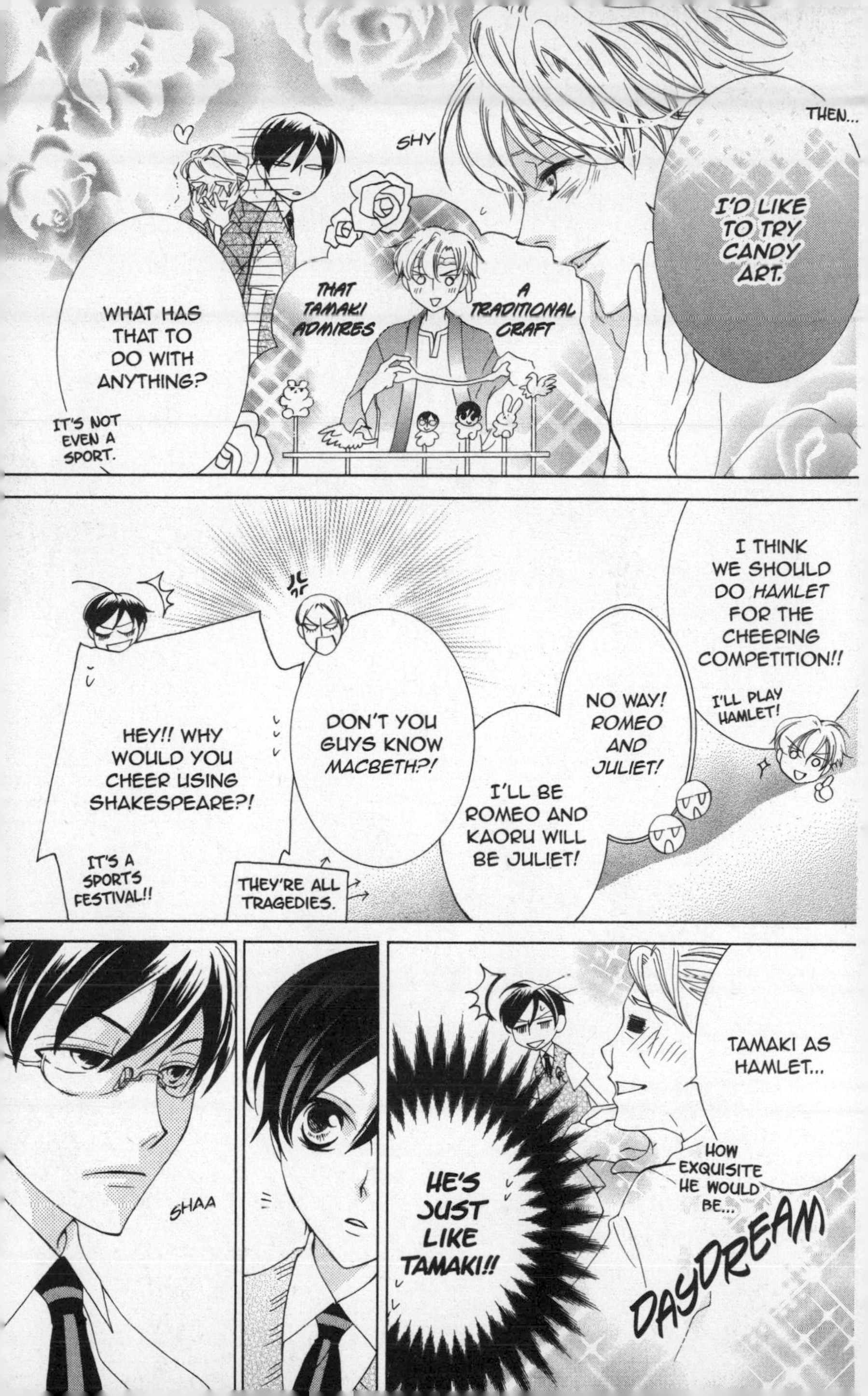
THEN...
I'D LIKE TO TRY CANDY ART.
SHY
A TRADITIONAL CRAFT
THAT TAMAKI ADMIRES
WHAT HAS THAT TO DO WITH ANYTHING?
IT'S NOT EVEN A SPORT.
I THINK WE SHOULD DO *HAMLET* FOR THE CHEERING COMPETITION!!
I'LL PLAY HAMLET!
NO WAY! *ROMEO AND JULIET!*
I'LL BE ROMEO AND KAORU WILL BE JULIET!
DON'T YOU GUYS KNOW *MACBETH?!*
THEY'RE ALL TRAGEDIES.
HEY!! WHY WOULD YOU CHEER USING SHAKESPEARE?!
IT'S A SPORTS FESTIVAL!!
TAMAKI AS HAMLET...
HOW EXQUISITE HE WOULD BE...
DAYDREAM
HE'S JUST LIKE TAMAKI!!
SHAA

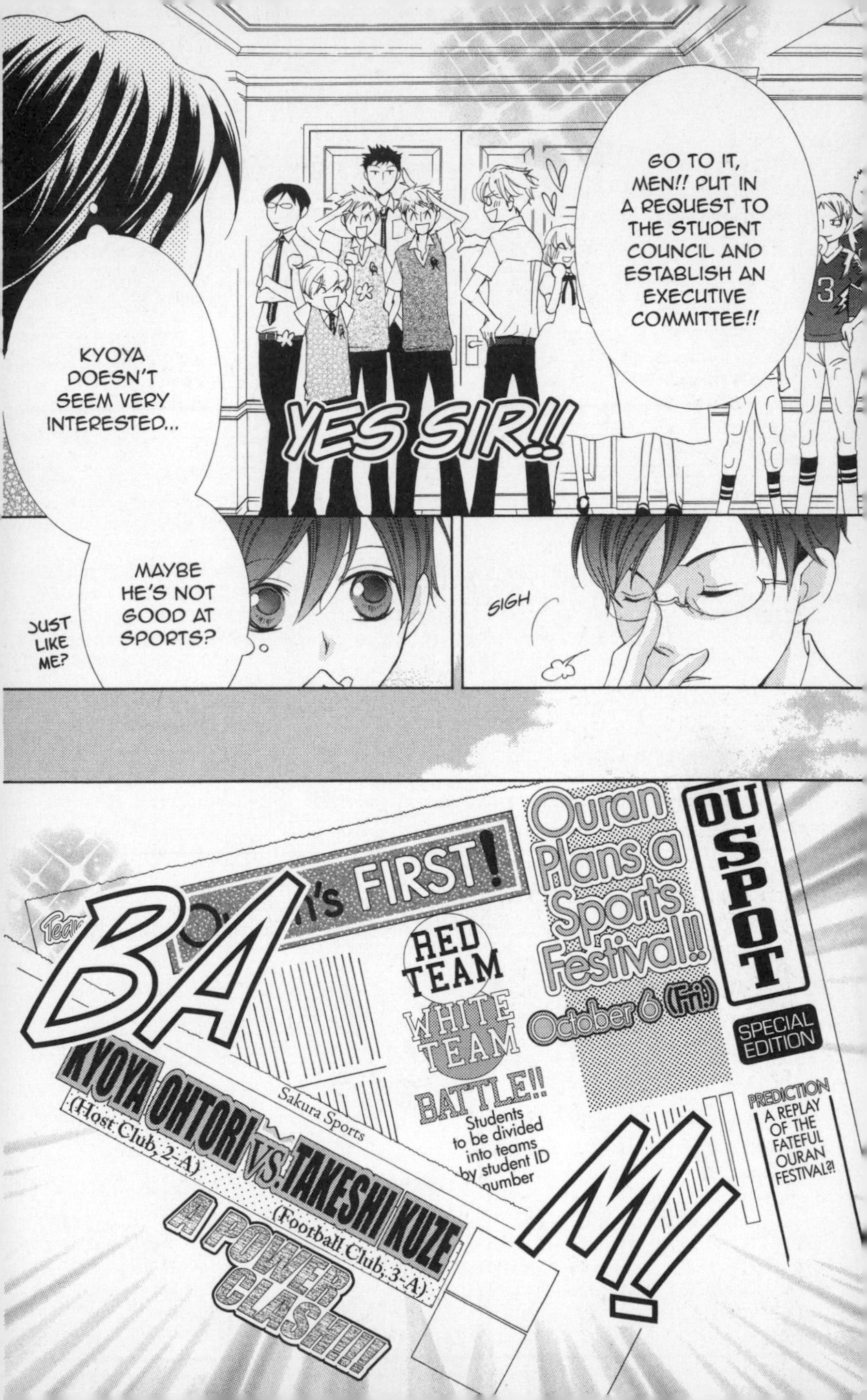
GO TO IT, MEN!! PUT IN A REQUEST TO THE STUDENT COUNCIL AND ESTABLISH AN EXECUTIVE COMMITTEE!!
YES SIR!!
KYOYA DOESN'T SEEM VERY INTERESTED...
SIGH
MAYBE HE'S NOT GOOD AT SPORTS?
JUST LIKE ME?
OU SPOT
SPECIAL EDITION
Ouran Plans a Sports Festival!!
October 6 (Fri.)
PREDICTION
A REPLAY OF THE FATEFUL OURAN FESTIVAL?!
's FIRST!
RED TEAM
WHITE TEAM
BATTLE!!
Students to be divided into teams by student ID number
Sakura Sports
KYOYA OHTORI (Host Club, 2-A) VS. TAKESHI KUZE (Football Club, 3-A)
A POWER CLASH!!!
BAM!

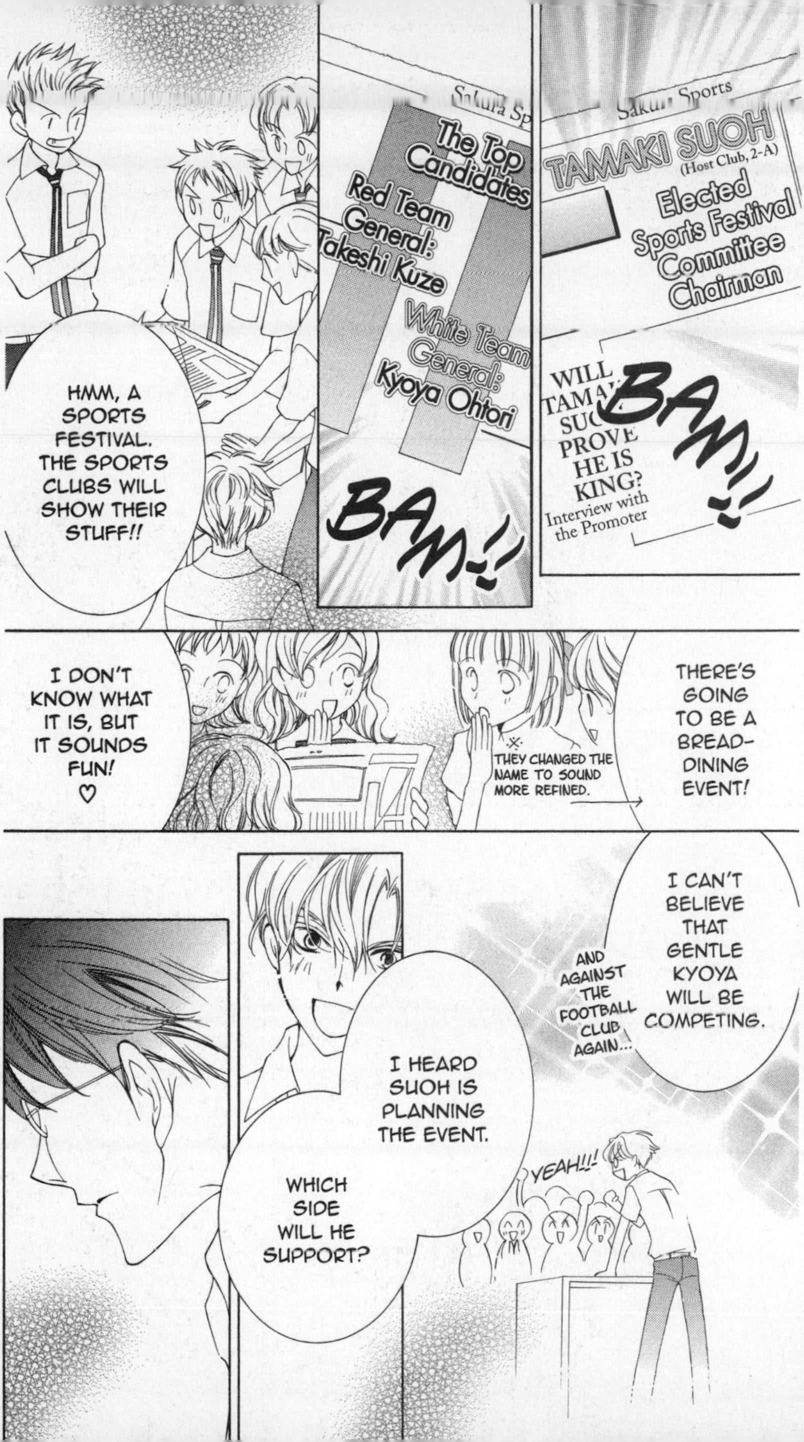
Sakura Sports
TAMAKI SUOH
(Host Club, 2-A)
Elected Sports Festival Committee Chairman
PROVE HE IS KING?
Interview with the Promoter
BAM!!
The Top Candidates
Red Team General: Takeshi Kuze
White Team General: Kyoya Ohtori
BAM!!
HMM, A SPORTS FESTIVAL. THE SPORTS CLUBS WILL SHOW THEIR STUFF!!
THERE'S GOING TO BE A BREAD-DINING EVENT!
※THEY CHANGED THE NAME TO SOUND MORE REFINED.
I DON'T KNOW WHAT IT IS, BUT IT SOUNDS FUN! ♡
I CAN'T BELIEVE THAT GENTLE KYOYA WILL BE COMPETING.
AND AGAINST THE FOOTBALL CLUB AGAIN...
YEAH!!!
I HEARD SUOH IS PLANNING THE EVENT.
WHICH SIDE WILL HE SUPPORT?

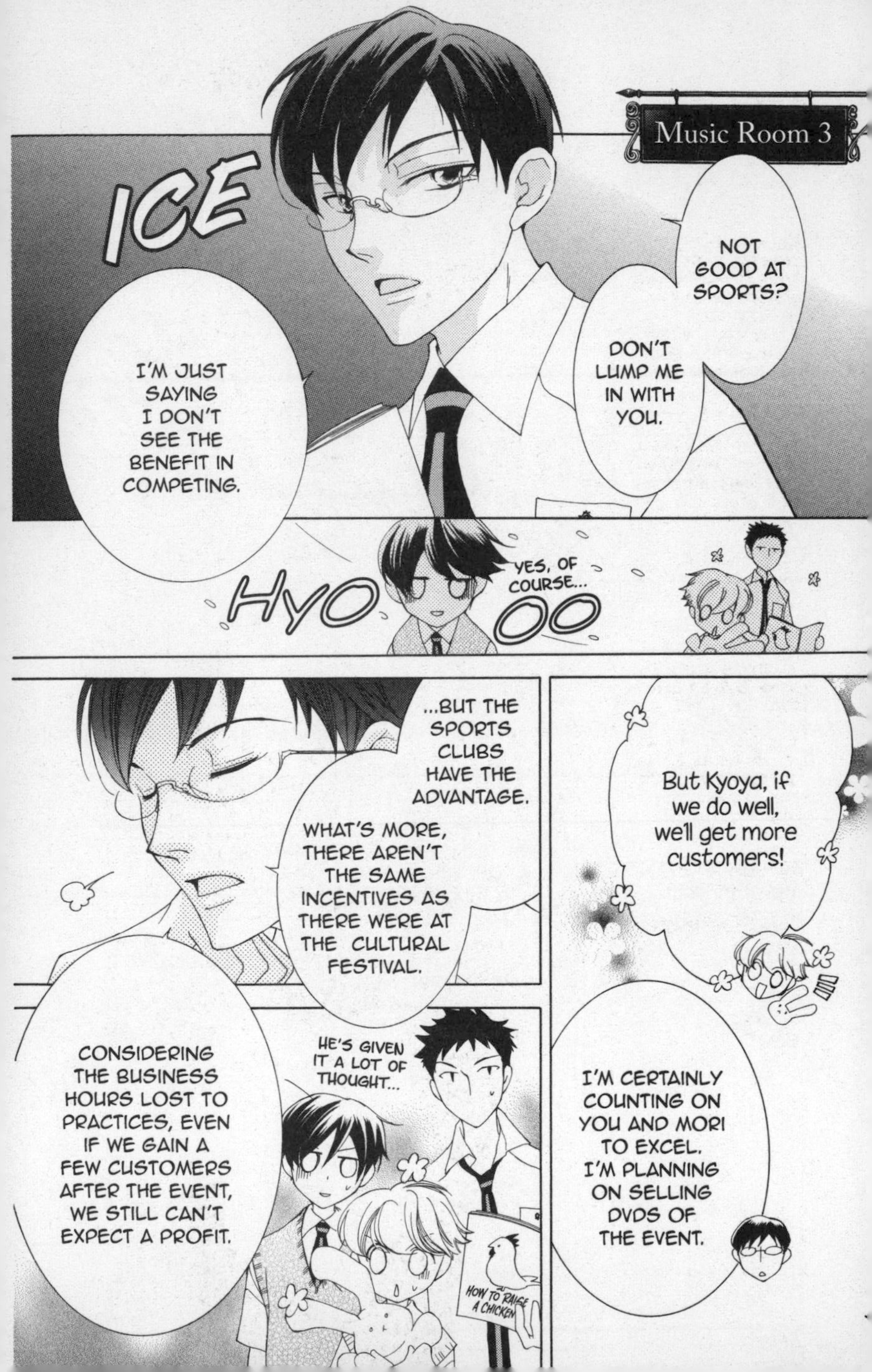
Music Room 3
NOT GOOD AT SPORTS?
DON'T LUMP ME IN WITH YOU.
ICE
I'M JUST SAYING I DON'T SEE THE BENEFIT IN COMPETING.
YES, OF COURSE...
HYOOO
But Kyoya, if we do well, we'll get more customers!
...BUT THE SPORTS CLUBS HAVE THE ADVANTAGE.
WHAT'S MORE, THERE AREN'T THE SAME INCENTIVES AS THERE WERE AT THE CULTURAL FESTIVAL.
CONSIDERING THE BUSINESS HOURS LOST TO PRACTICES, EVEN IF WE GAIN A FEW CUSTOMERS AFTER THE EVENT, WE STILL CAN'T EXPECT A PROFIT.
HE'S GIVEN IT A LOT OF THOUGHT...
HOW TO RAISE A CHICKEN
I'M CERTAINLY COUNTING ON YOU AND MORI TO EXCEL. I'M PLANNING ON SELLING DVDS OF THE EVENT.

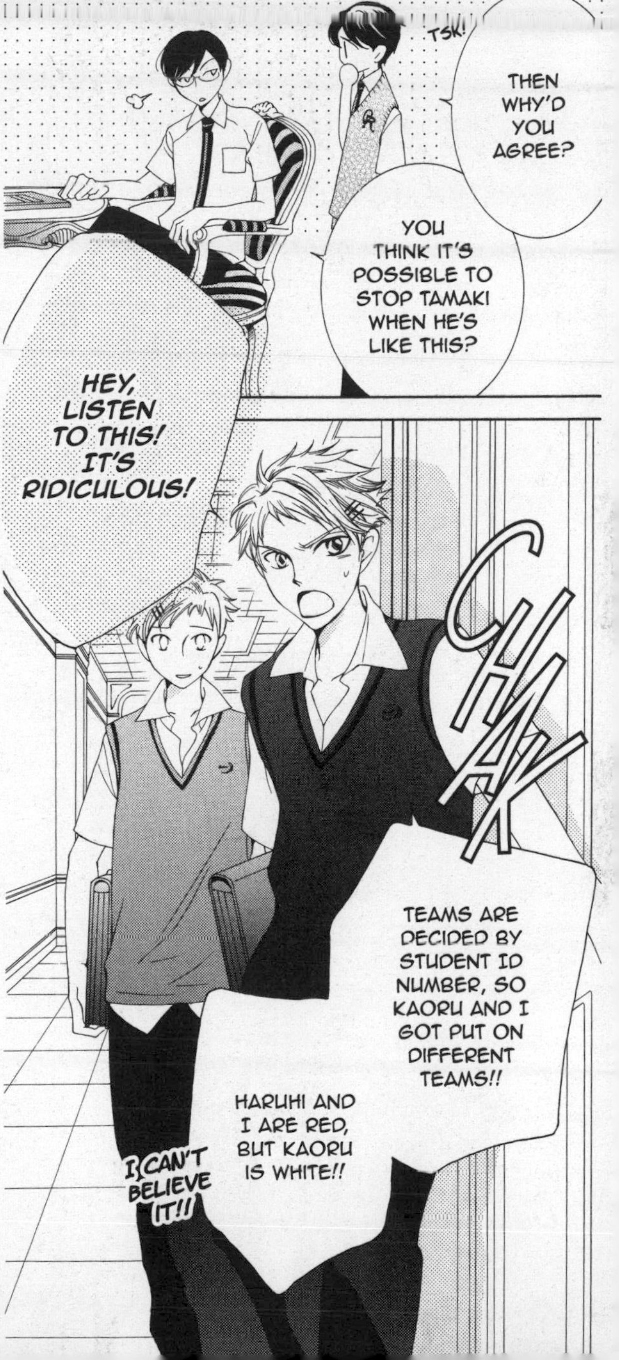
TSK!
THEN WHY'D YOU AGREE?
YOU THINK IT'S POSSIBLE TO STOP TAMAKI WHEN HE'S LIKE THIS?
HEY, LISTEN TO THIS! IT'S RIDICULOUS!
CHAK
TEAMS ARE DECIDED BY STUDENT ID NUMBER, SO KAORU AND I GOT PUT ON DIFFERENT TEAMS!!
HARUHI AND I ARE RED, BUT KAORU IS WHITE!!
I CAN'T BELIEVE IT!!

6

IGARASHI-SAN, THE DIRECTOR OF THE ANIME, TOLD ME THAT THE LAST EPISODE ON THE DVD WILL FEATURE MY FAVORITE CHARACTER SONG AS THE ENDING THEME!! I CAN'T WAIT...!!

I THINK IT WAS EITHER OHYABU-SAN OR ENOKIDO-SAN WHO SAID THAT THEY WORKED ON THAT SONG AS HARD AS THEY WOULD ON A WHOLE EPISODE OF THE ANIME.

MAAYA-SAN WAS WORRIED THAT ONE OF HER LINES MIGHT BE IN IT... (LAUGH)

I HEARD THAT ALL THE VOICE ACTORS LIKE THAT SONG. (EVERYONE SINGS TOGETHER IN IT!!)

I LOVE, LOVE, LOVE ALL THE CHARACTER SONGS, BUT I ESPECIALLY LIKE THE OVER-THE-TOP LYRICS IN TAMAKI'S SONG!!

WHY DOES HE LIKE HIMSELF SO MUCH?

I THINK WHOEVER WROTE THAT SONG IS A GENIUS.

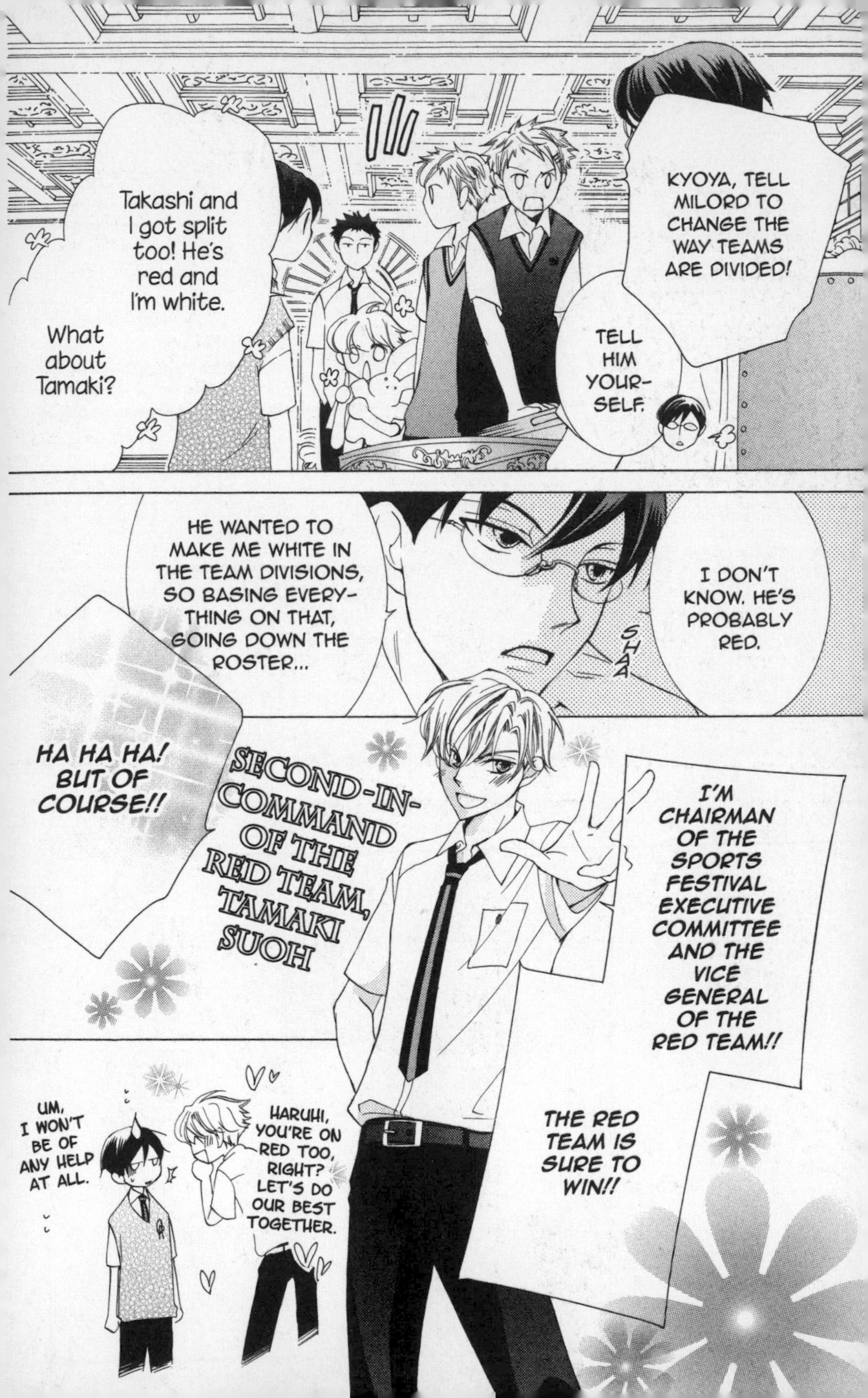
KYOYA, TELL MILORD TO CHANGE THE WAY TEAMS ARE DIVIDED!
TELL HIM YOURSELF.
Takashi and I got split too! He's red and I'm white.
What about Tamaki?
I DON'T KNOW. HE'S PROBABLY RED.
SHAA
HE WANTED TO MAKE ME WHITE IN THE TEAM DIVISIONS, SO BASING EVERYTHING ON THAT, GOING DOWN THE ROSTER...
I'M CHAIRMAN OF THE SPORTS FESTIVAL EXECUTIVE COMMITTEE AND THE VICE GENERAL OF THE RED TEAM!!
SECOND-IN-COMMAND OF THE RED TEAM, TAMAKI SUOH
HA HA HA! BUT OF COURSE!!
THE RED TEAM IS SURE TO WIN!!
HARUHI, YOU'RE ON RED TOO, RIGHT? LET'S DO OUR BEST TOGETHER.
UM, I WON'T BE OF ANY HELP AT ALL.

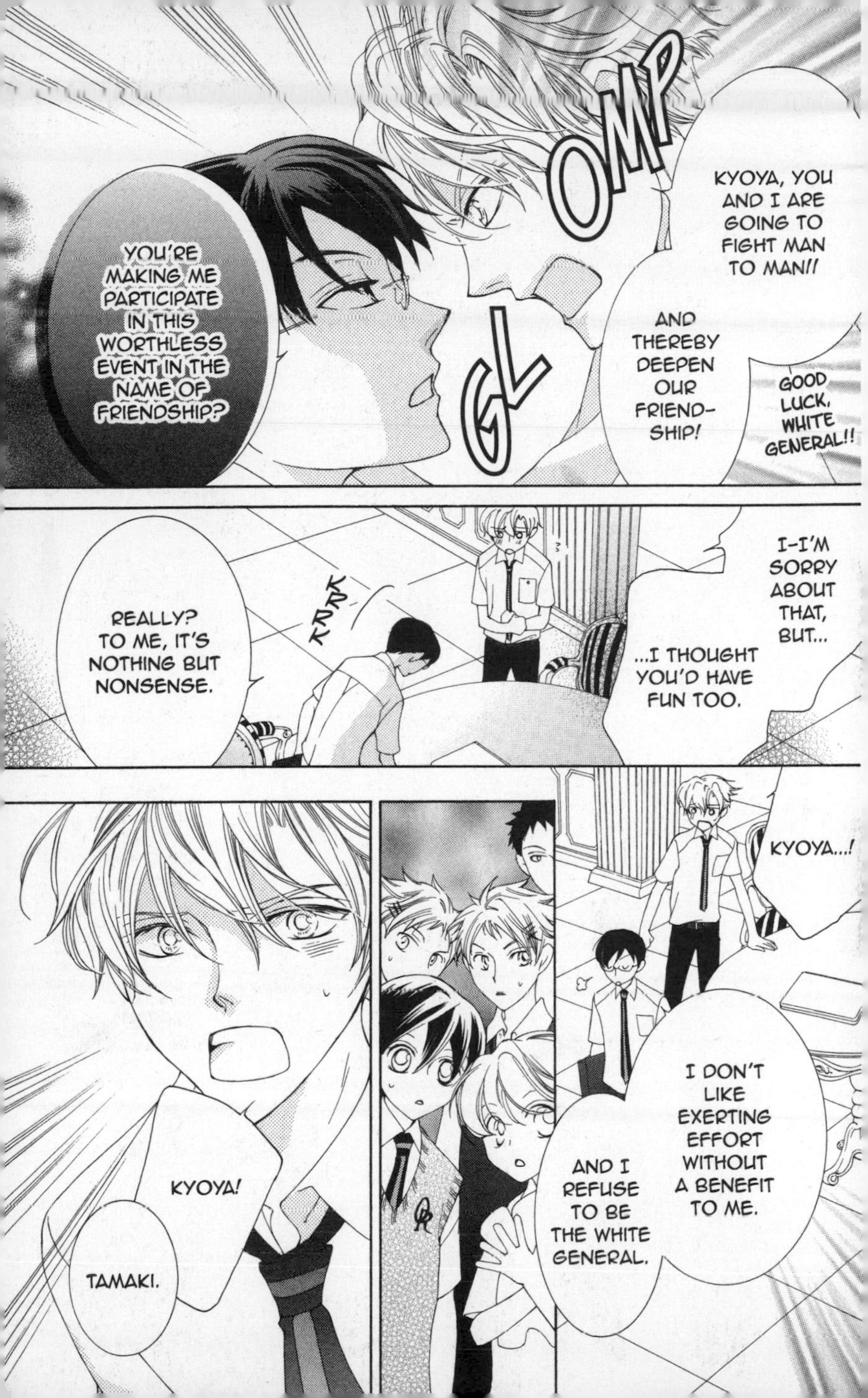
KYOYA, YOU AND I ARE GOING TO FIGHT MAN TO MAN!!
GOOD LUCK, WHITE GENERAL!!
AND THEREBY DEEPEN OUR FRIEND-SHIP!
GLOMP
YOU'RE MAKING ME PARTICIPATE IN THIS WORTHLESS EVENT IN THE NAME OF FRIENDSHIP?
I-I'M SORRY ABOUT THAT, BUT...
...I THOUGHT YOU'D HAVE FUN TOO.
KRRK
REALLY? TO ME, IT'S NOTHING BUT NONSENSE.
KYOYA...!
I DON'T LIKE EXERTING EFFORT WITHOUT A BENEFIT TO ME.
AND I REFUSE TO BE THE WHITE GENERAL.
KYOYA!
TAMAKI.

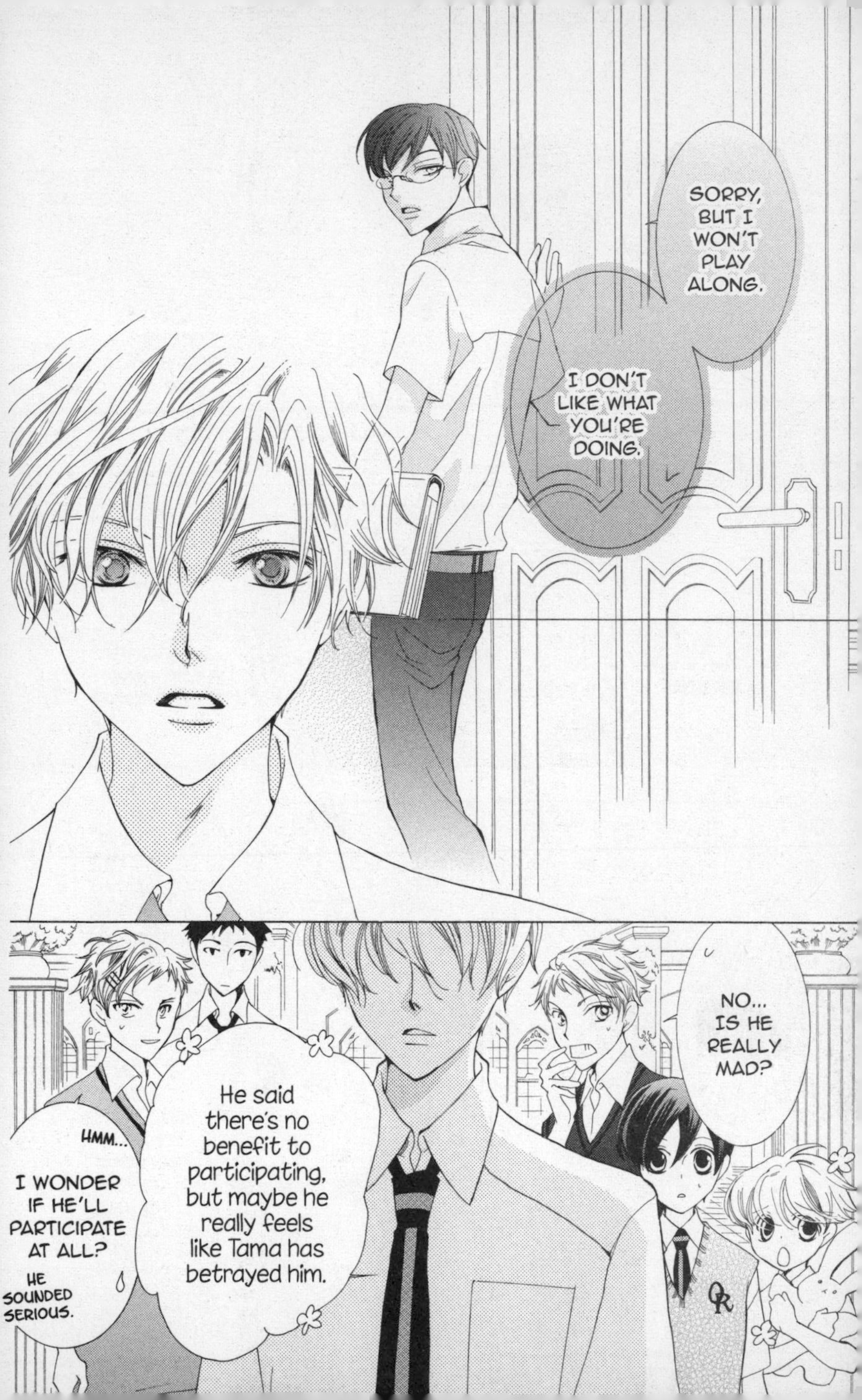
SORRY, BUT I WON'T PLAY ALONG.
I DON'T LIKE WHAT YOU'RE DOING.
NO... IS HE REALLY MAD?
He said there's no benefit to participating, but maybe he really feels like Tama has betrayed him.
HMM...
I WONDER IF HE'LL PARTICIPATE AT ALL?
HE SOUNDED SERIOUS.

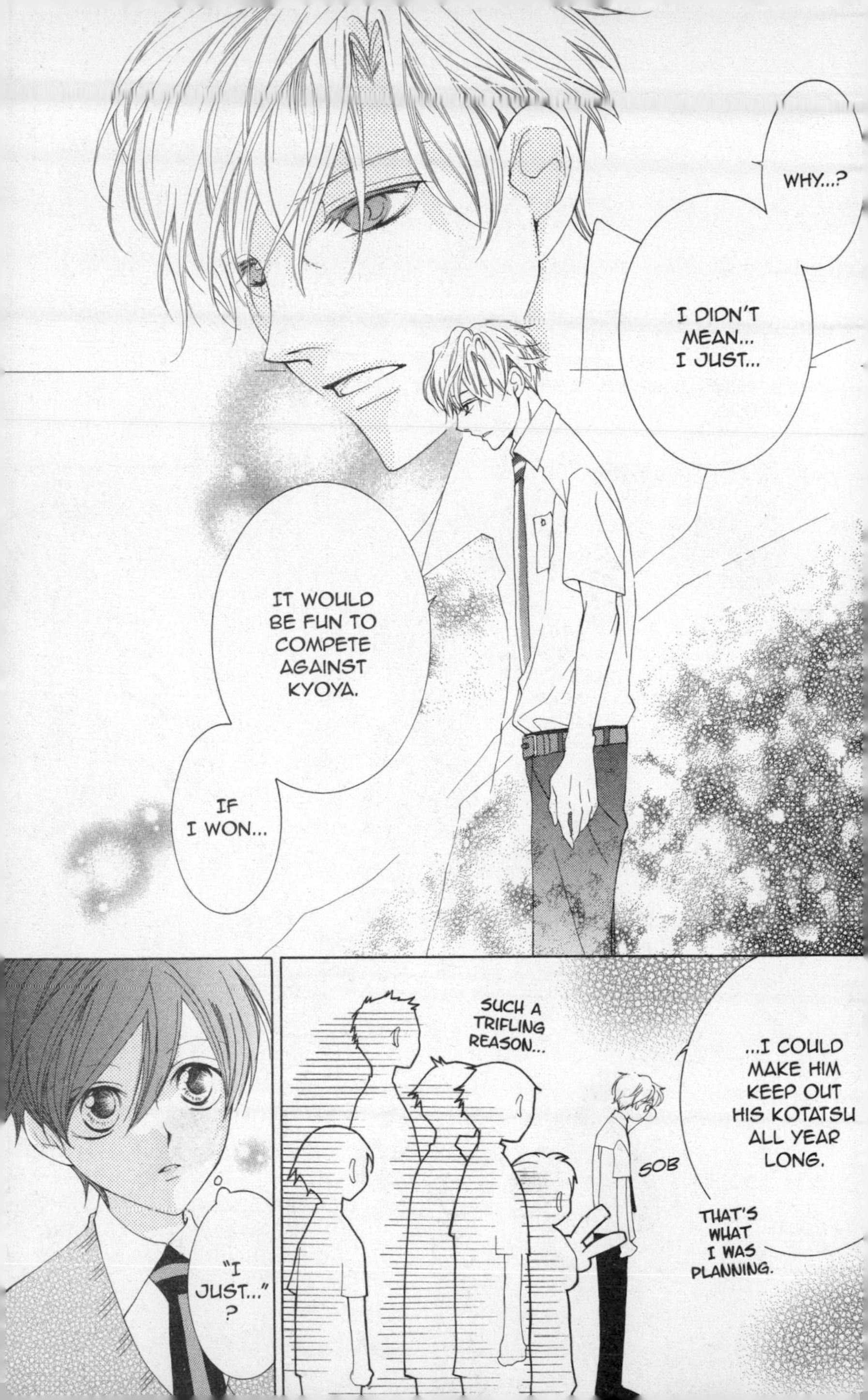
WHY...?
I DIDN'T MEAN... I JUST...
IT WOULD BE FUN TO COMPETE AGAINST KYOYA.
IF I WON...
...I COULD MAKE HIM KEEP OUT HIS KOTATSU ALL YEAR LONG.
THAT'S WHAT I WAS PLANNING.
SOB
SUCH A TRIFLING REASON...
"I JUST..." ?

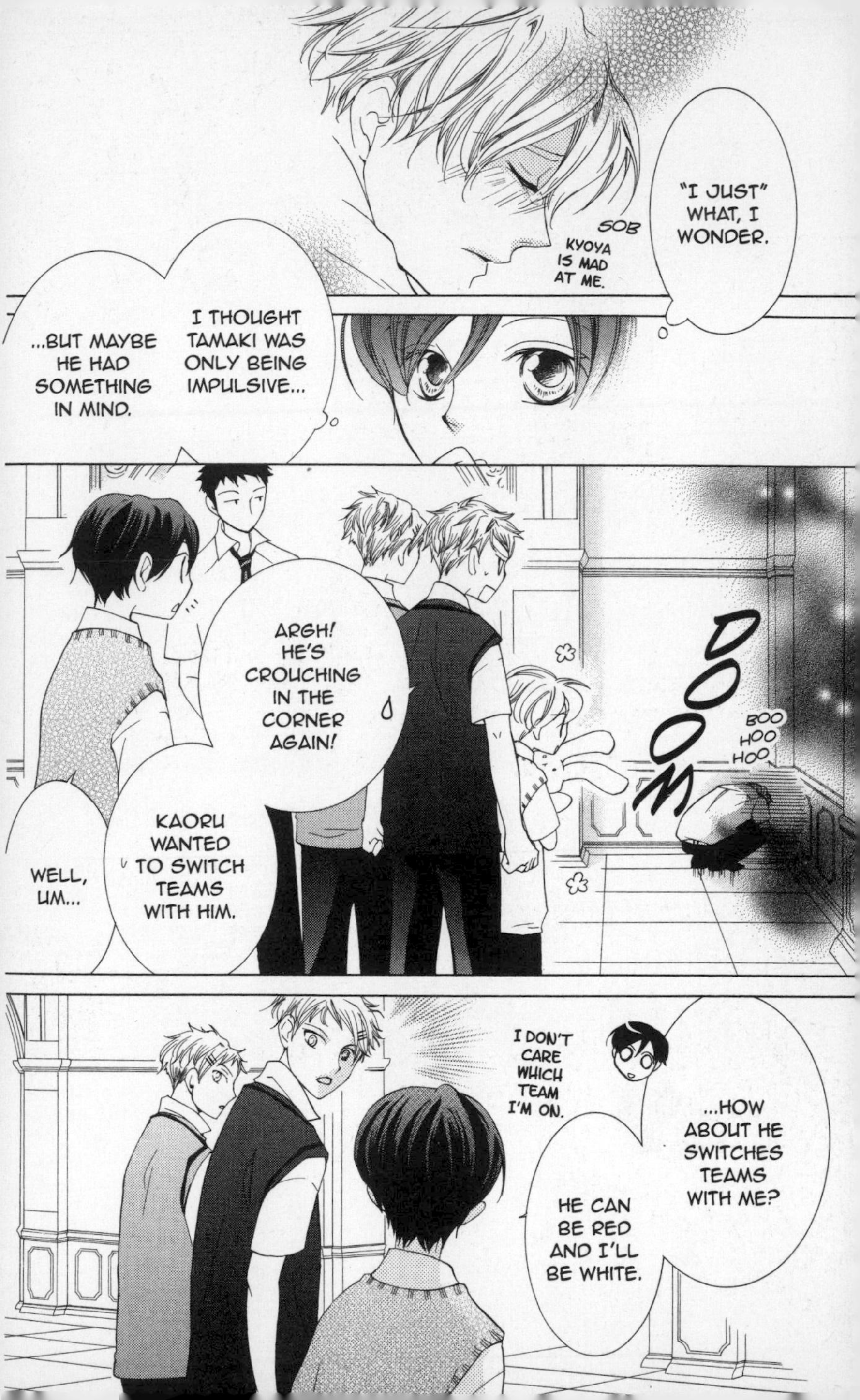
"I JUST" WHAT, I WONDER.
SOB
KYOYA IS MAD AT ME.
I THOUGHT TAMAKI WAS ONLY BEING IMPULSIVE...
...BUT MAYBE HE HAD SOMETHING IN MIND.
DOOOM
BOO HOO HOO
ARGH! HE'S CROUCHING IN THE CORNER AGAIN!
KAORU WANTED TO SWITCH TEAMS WITH HIM.
WELL, UM...
...HOW ABOUT HE SWITCHES TEAMS WITH ME?
I DON'T CARE WHICH TEAM I'M ON.
HE CAN BE RED AND I'LL BE WHITE.

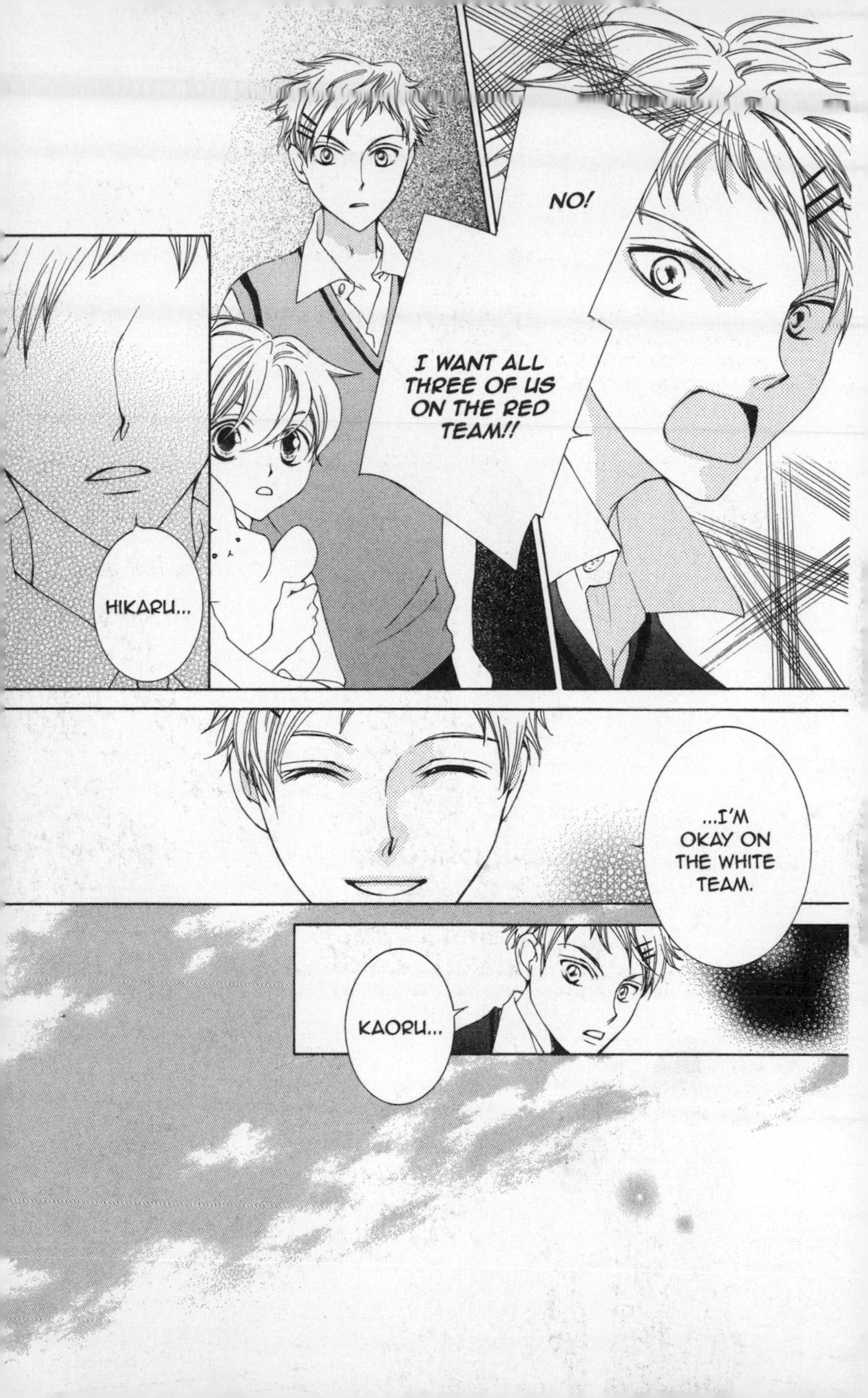
NO!
I WANT ALL THREE OF US ON THE RED TEAM!!
HIKARU...
...I'M OKAY ON THE WHITE TEAM.
KAORU...

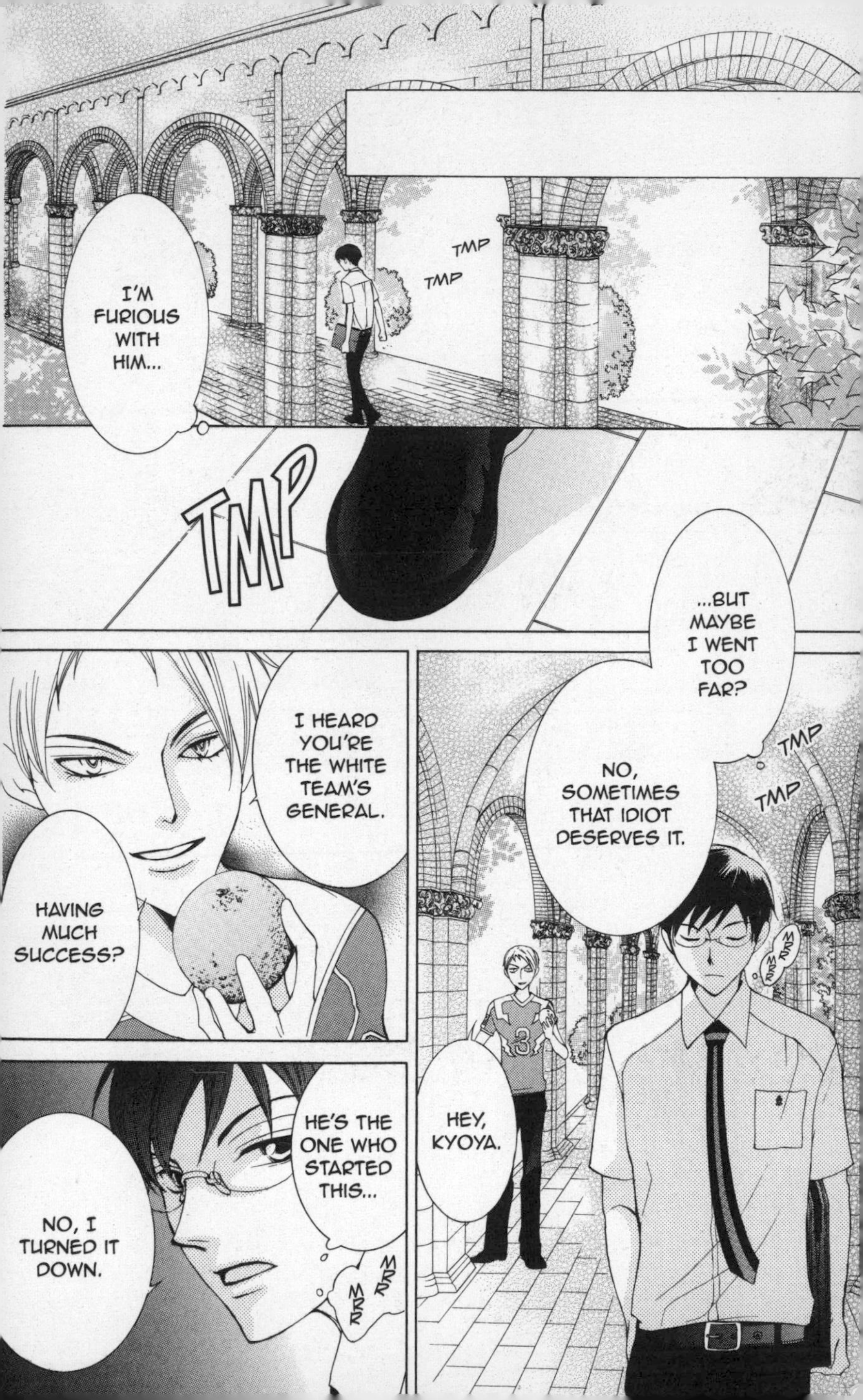
TMP
TMP
I'M FURIOUS WITH HIM...
TMP
...BUT MAYBE I WENT TOO FAR?
NO, SOMETIMES THAT IDIOT DESERVES IT.
TMP
TMP
MRR MRR
HEY, KYOYA.
I HEARD YOU'RE THE WHITE TEAM'S GENERAL.
HAVING MUCH SUCCESS?
HE'S THE ONE WHO STARTED THIS...
MRR MRR
NO, I TURNED IT DOWN.

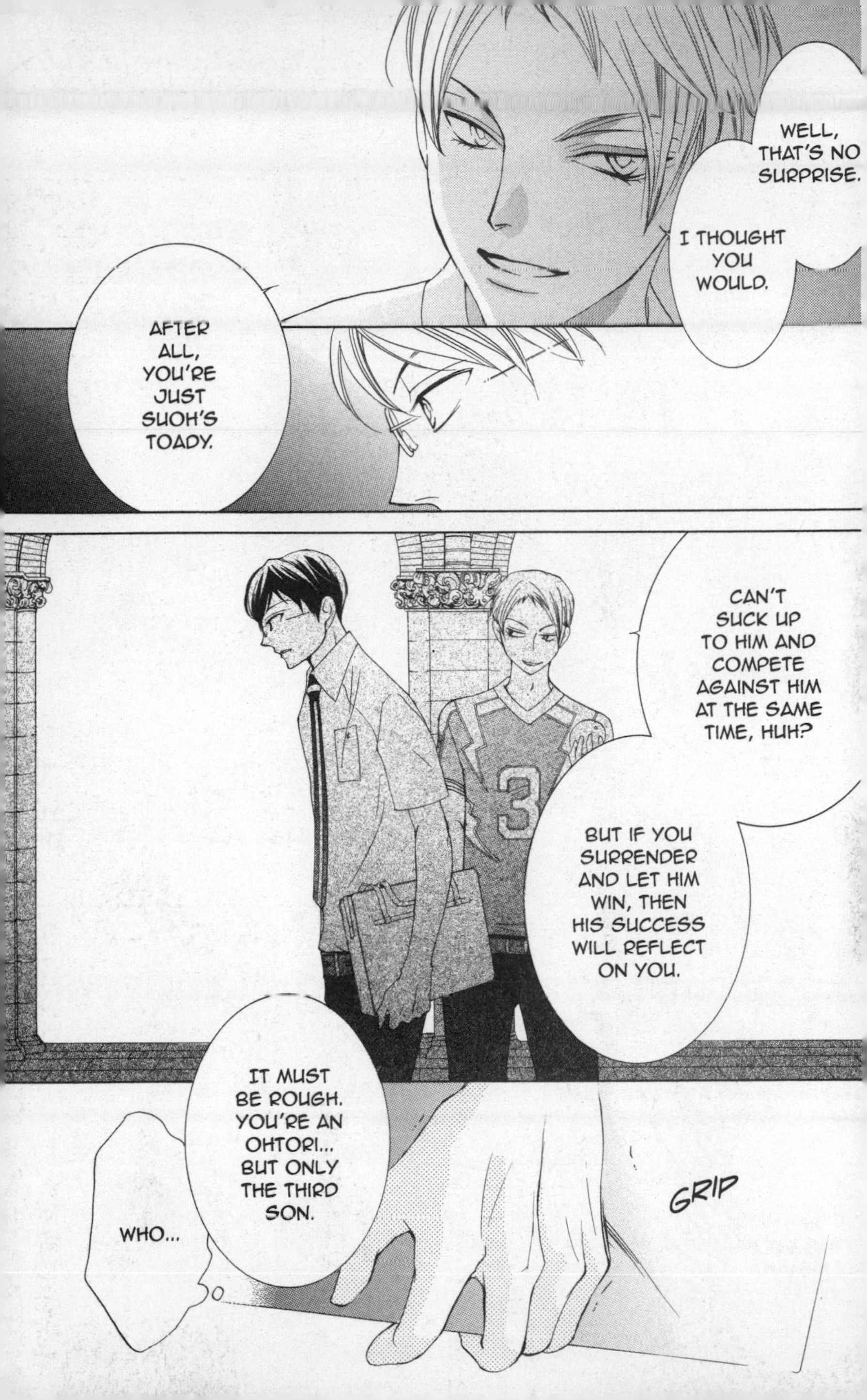
WELL, THAT'S NO SURPRISE.
I THOUGHT YOU WOULD.
AFTER ALL, YOU'RE JUST SUOH'S TOADY.
CAN'T SUCK UP TO HIM AND COMPETE AGAINST HIM AT THE SAME TIME, HUH?
BUT IF YOU SURRENDER AND LET HIM WIN, THEN HIS SUCCESS WILL REFLECT ON YOU.
IT MUST BE ROUGH. YOU'RE AN OHTORI... BUT ONLY THE THIRD SON.
GRIP
WHO...

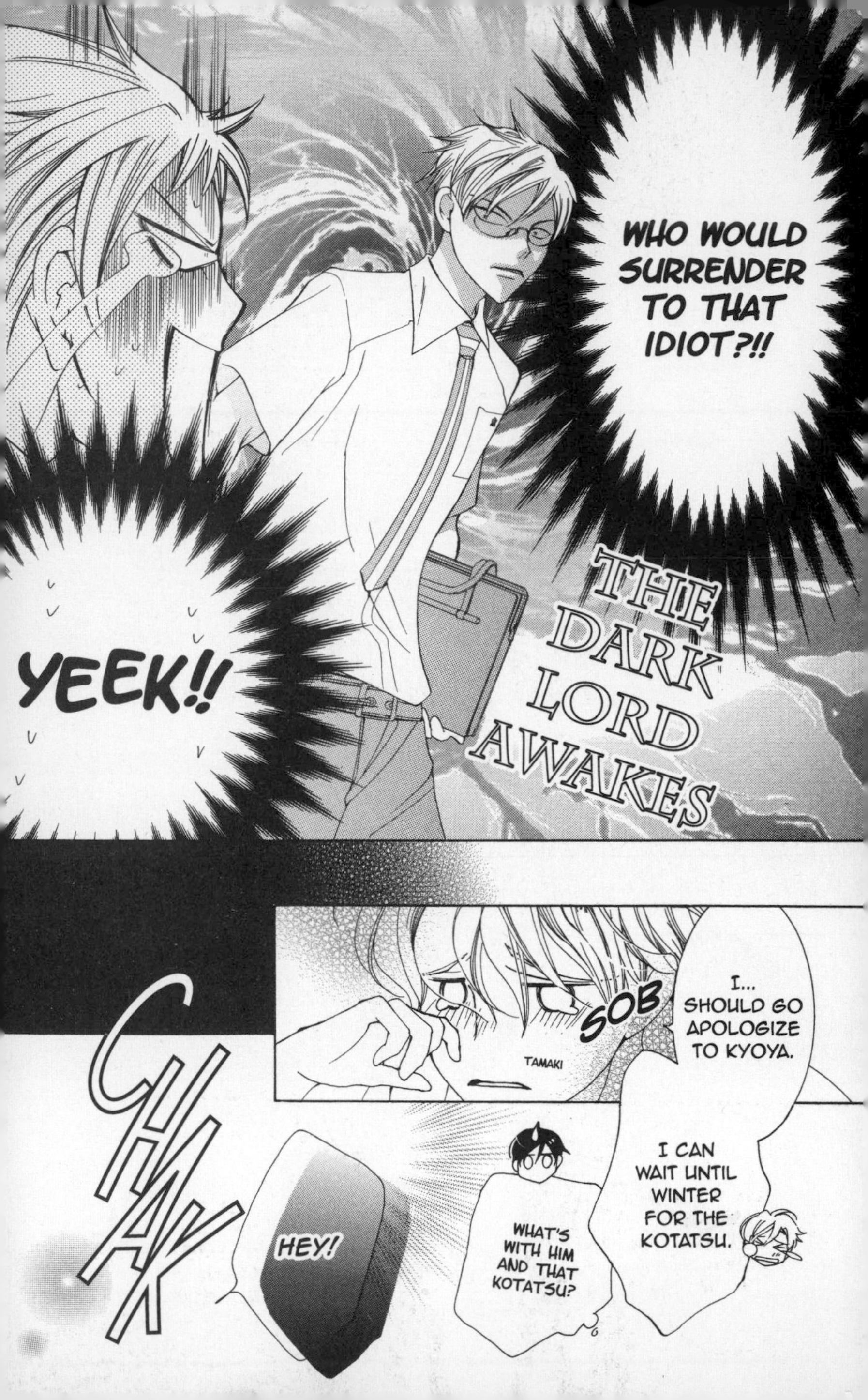
WHO WOULD SURRENDER TO THAT IDIOT?!!
THE DARK LORD AWAKES
YEEK!!
I... SHOULD GO APOLOGIZE TO KYOYA.
SOB
TAMAKI
I CAN WAIT UNTIL WINTER FOR THE KOTATSU.
WHAT'S WITH HIM AND THAT KOTATSU?
HEY!
CHAK

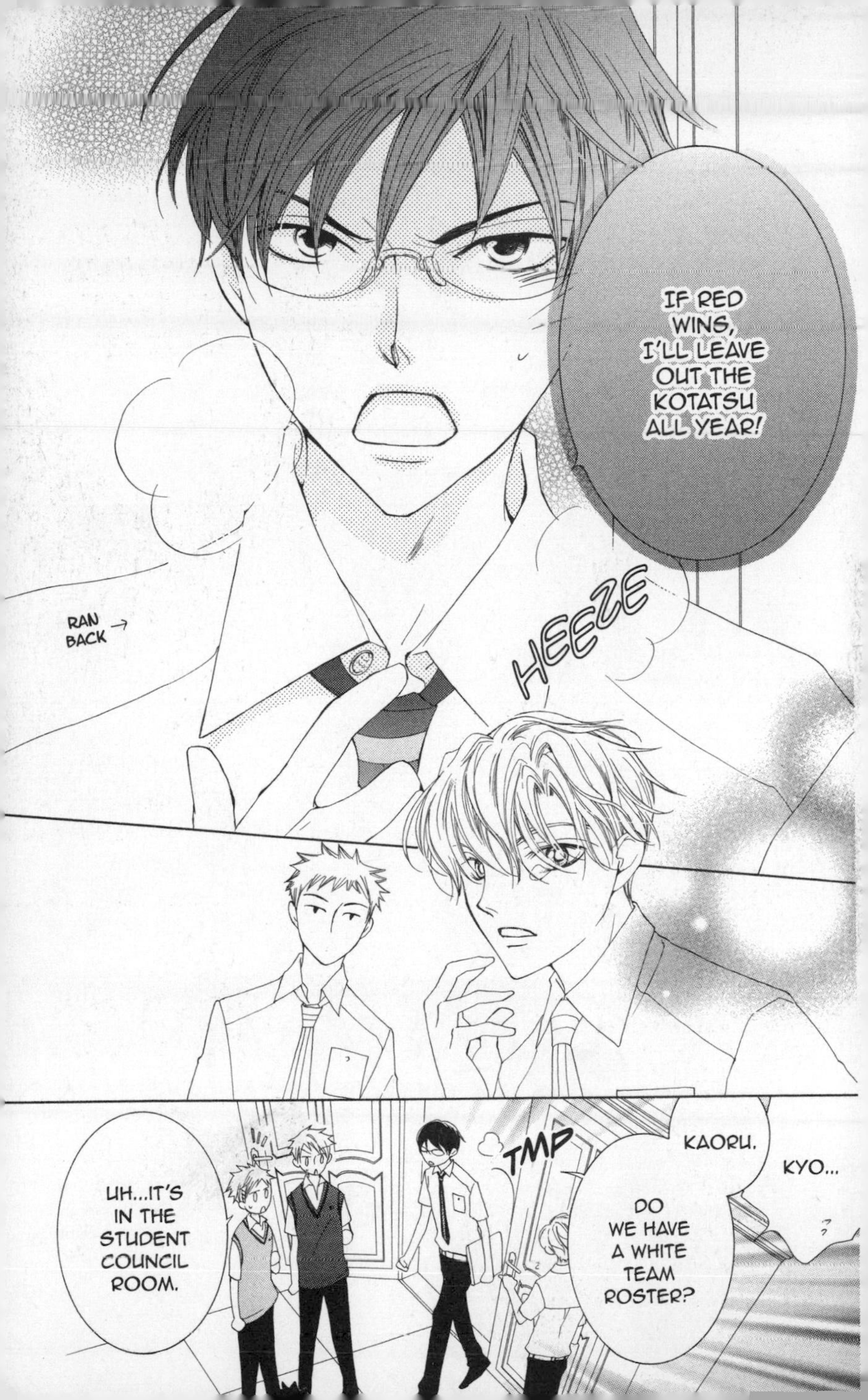
IF RED WINS, I'LL LEAVE OUT THE KOTATSU ALL YEAR!
HEEZE
RAN BACK →
KYO...
KAORU.
DO WE HAVE A WHITE TEAM ROSTER?
TMP
UH...IT'S IN THE STUDENT COUNCIL ROOM.

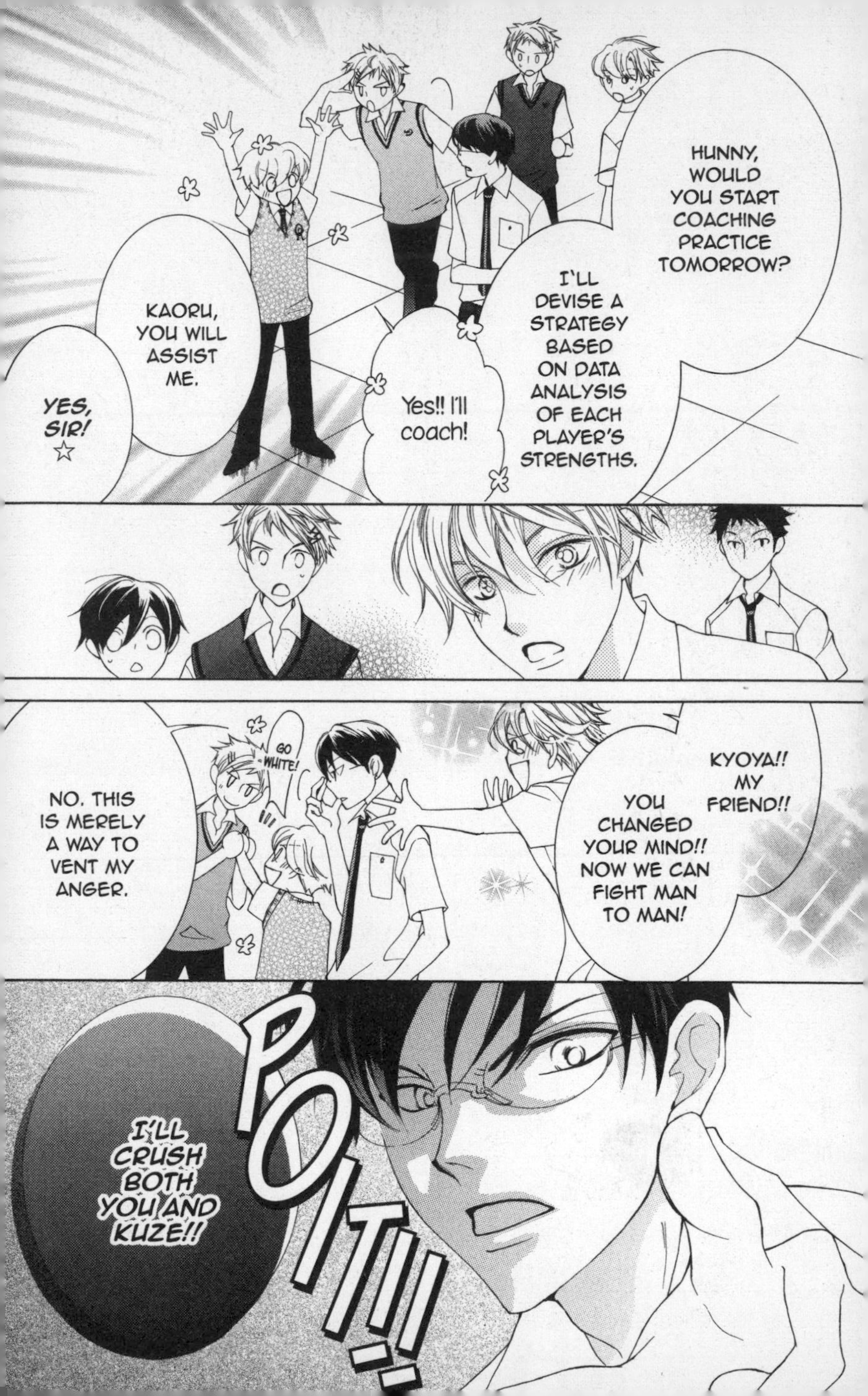
HUNNY, WOULD YOU START COACHING PRACTICE TOMORROW?
I'LL DEVISE A STRATEGY BASED ON DATA ANALYSIS OF EACH PLAYER'S STRENGTHS.
Yes!! I'll coach!
KAORU, YOU WILL ASSIST ME.
YES, SIR! ☆
KYOYA!! MY FRIEND!!
YOU CHANGED YOUR MIND!! NOW WE CAN FIGHT MAN TO MAN!
GO WHITE!
NO. THIS IS MERELY A WAY TO VENT MY ANGER.
POIT!!
I'LL CRUSH BOTH YOU AND KUZE!!

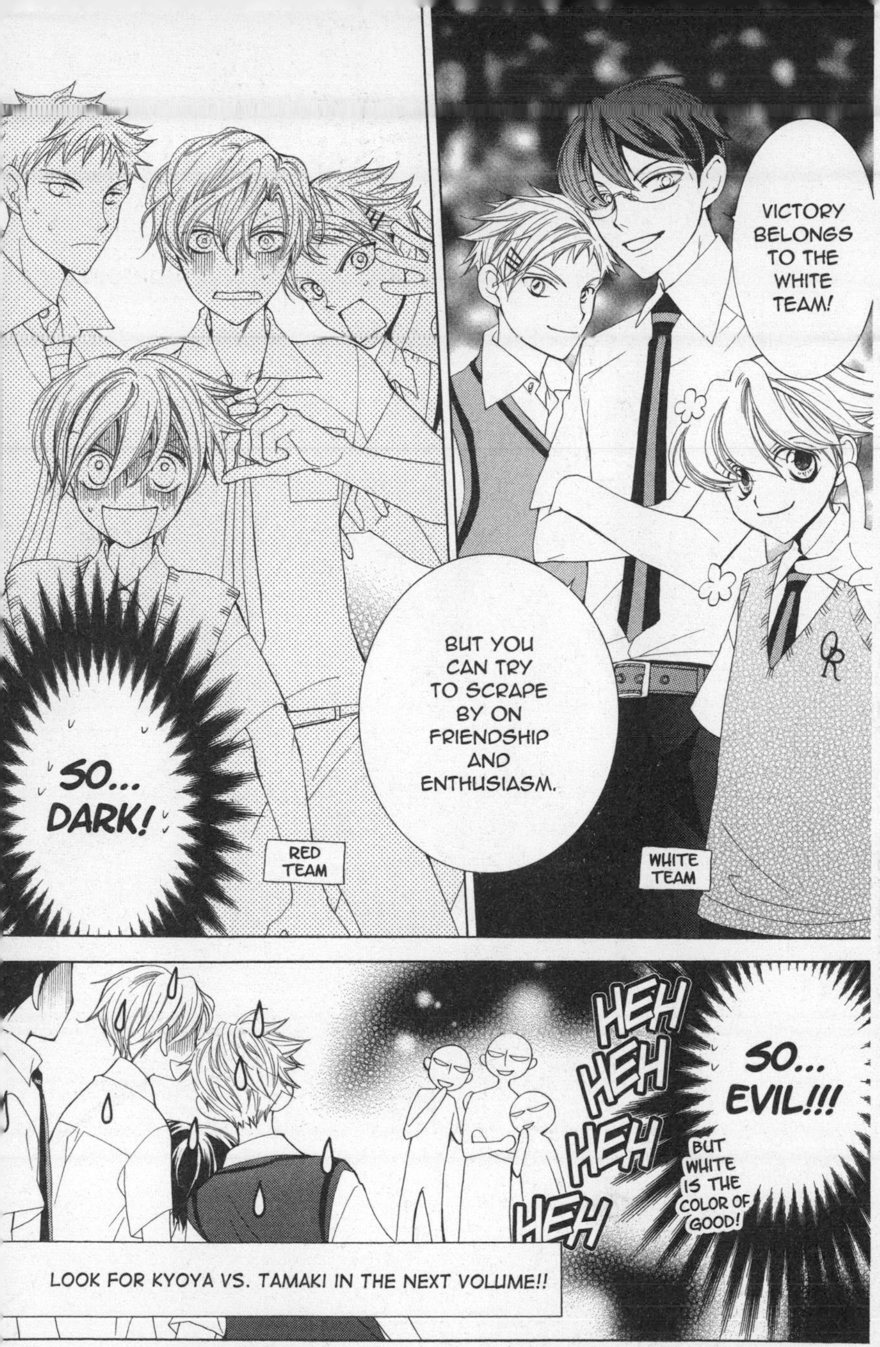
VICTORY BELONGS TO THE WHITE TEAM!
BUT YOU CAN TRY TO SCRAPE BY ON FRIENDSHIP AND ENTHUSIASM.
WHITE TEAM
RED TEAM
SO... DARK!
SO... EVIL!!!
BUT WHITE IS THE COLOR OF GOOD!
HEH HEH HEH HEH
LOOK FOR KYOYA VS. TAMAKI IN THE NEXT VOLUME!!

OURAN HIGH SCHOOL HOST CLUB, VOL. 10/THE END

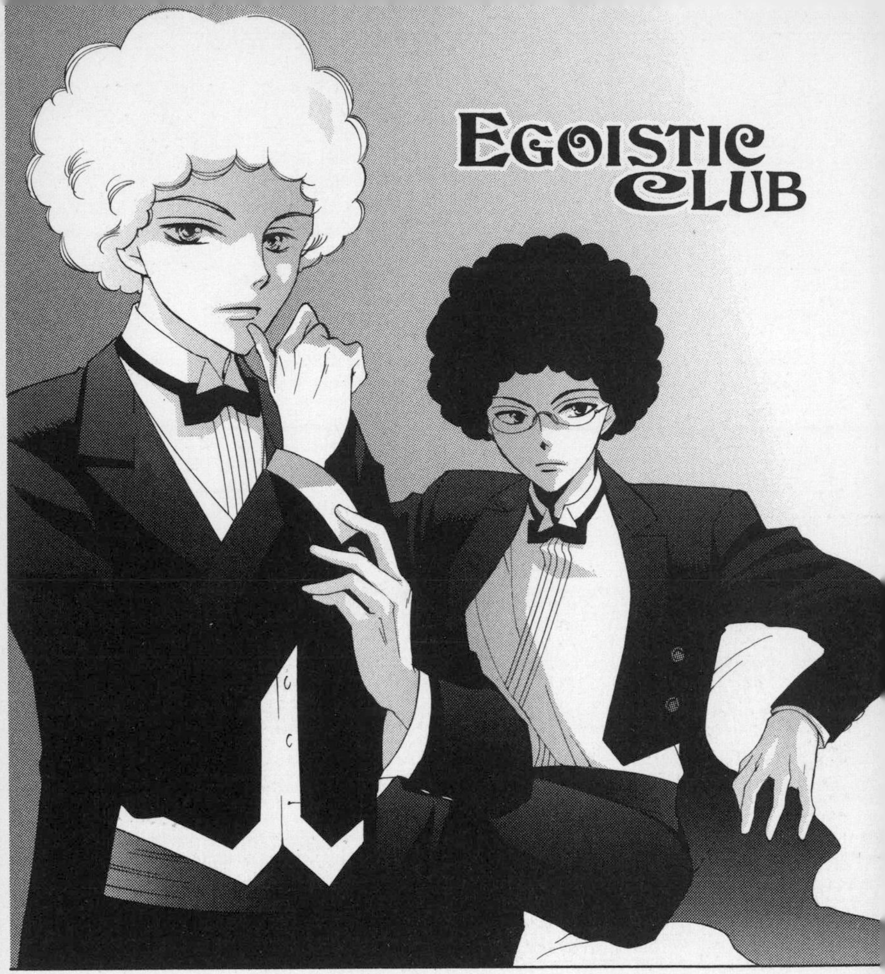
EGOISTIC CLUB

HELLO, EVERYONE!! THIS IS HATORINE.

THE PICTURE ABOVE IS OF KYOYA AND TAMAKI.

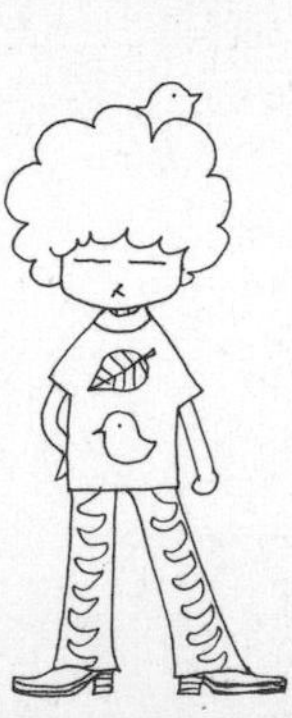

I CAN'T HELP BUT USE KYOYA FOR THIS KIND OF GAG.

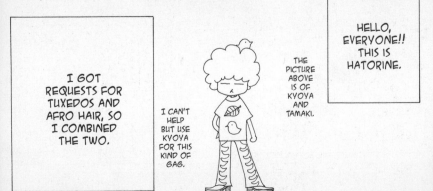

I GOT REQUESTS FOR TUXEDOS AND AFRO HAIR, SO I COMBINED THE TWO.

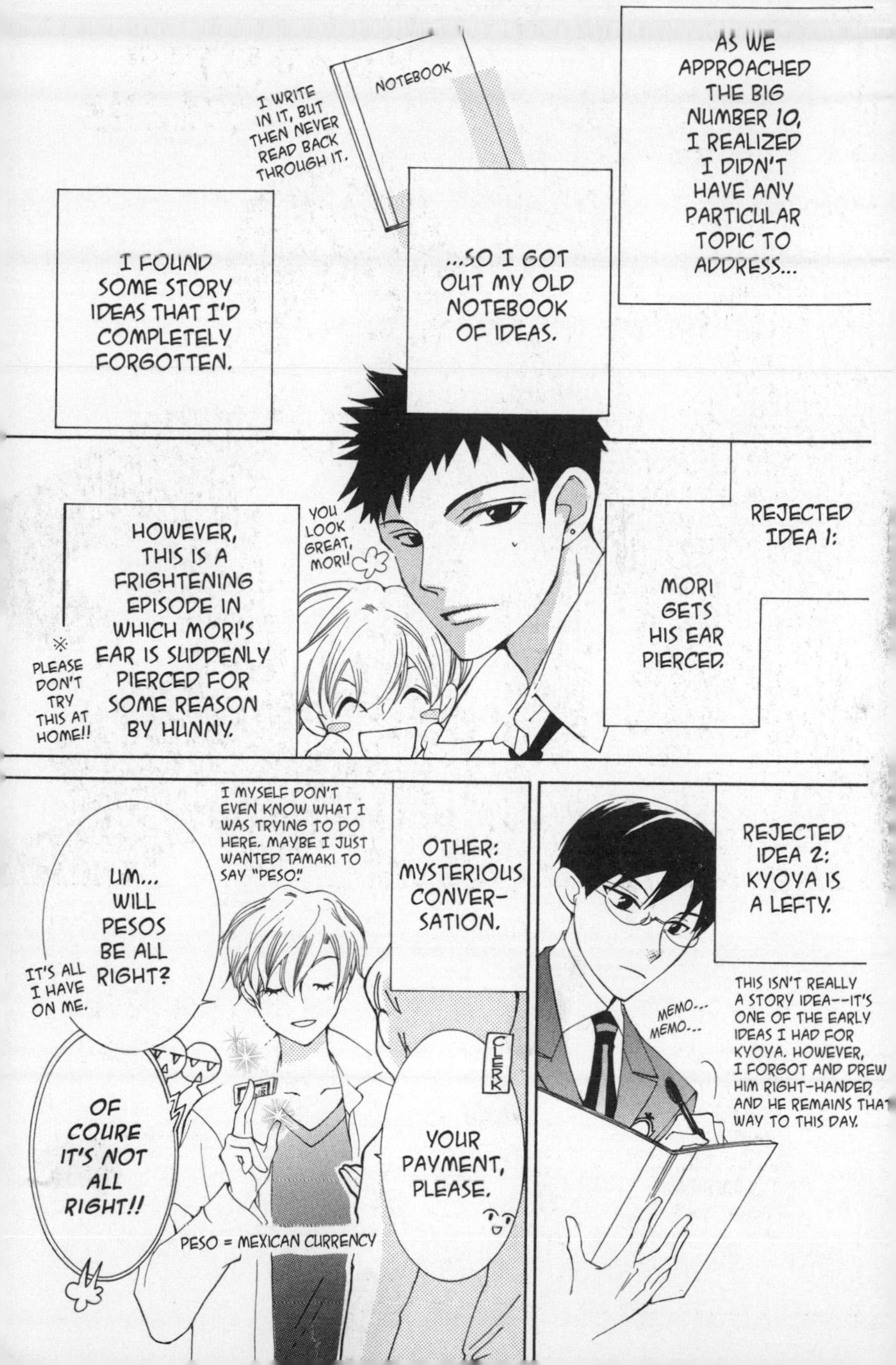

AS WE APPROACHED THE BIG NUMBER 10, I REALIZED I DIDN'T HAVE ANY PARTICULAR TOPIC TO ADDRESS...
...SO I GOT OUT MY OLD NOTEBOOK OF IDEAS.
NOTEBOOK
I WRITE IN IT, BUT THEN NEVER READ BACK THROUGH IT.
I FOUND SOME STORY IDEAS THAT I'D COMPLETELY FORGOTTEN.
REJECTED IDEA 1:
MORI GETS HIS EAR PIERCED.
YOU LOOK GREAT, MORI!
HOWEVER, THIS IS A FRIGHTENING EPISODE IN WHICH MORI'S EAR IS SUDDENLY PIERCED FOR SOME REASON BY HUNNY.
※ PLEASE DON'T TRY THIS AT HOME!!
REJECTED IDEA 2: KYOYA IS A LEFTY.
MEMO... MEMO...
THIS ISN'T REALLY A STORY IDEA--IT'S ONE OF THE EARLY IDEAS I HAD FOR KYOYA. HOWEVER, I FORGOT AND DREW HIM RIGHT-HANDED, AND HE REMAINS THAT WAY TO THIS DAY.
OTHER: MYSTERIOUS CONVERSATION.
I MYSELF DON'T EVEN KNOW WHAT I WAS TRYING TO DO HERE. MAYBE I JUST WANTED TAMAKI TO SAY "PESO."
CLERK
YOUR PAYMENT, PLEASE.
UM... WILL PESOS BE ALL RIGHT?
IT'S ALL I HAVE ON ME.
OF COURE IT'S NOT ALL RIGHT!!
PESO = MEXICAN CURRENCY

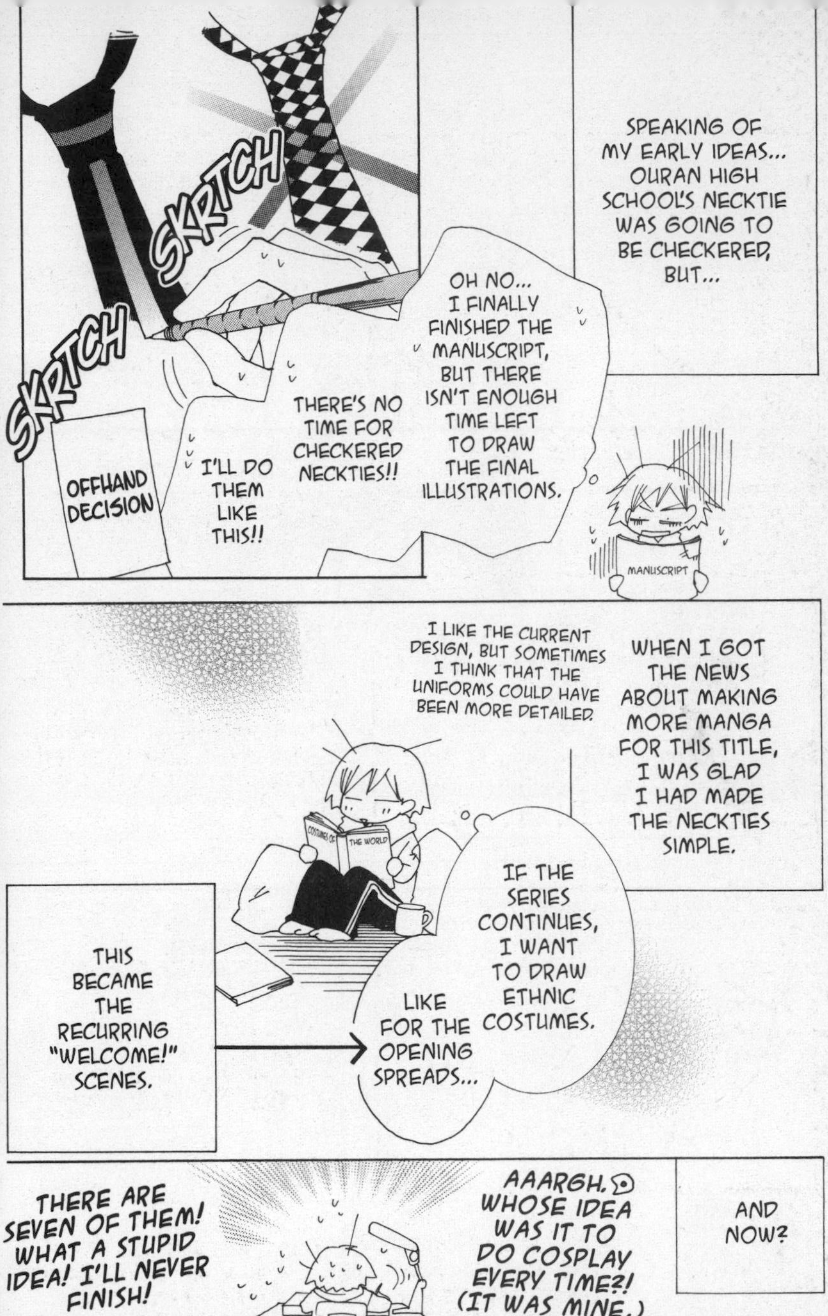

SPEAKING OF MY EARLY IDEAS... OURAN HIGH SCHOOL'S NECKTIE WAS GOING TO BE CHECKERED, BUT...
OH NO... I FINALLY FINISHED THE MANUSCRIPT, BUT THERE ISN'T ENOUGH TIME LEFT TO DRAW THE FINAL ILLUSTRATIONS.
MANUSCRIPT
THERE'S NO TIME FOR CHECKERED NECKTIES!!
I'LL DO THEM LIKE THIS!!
SKRTCH
SKRTCH
OFFHAND DECISION
WHEN I GOT THE NEWS ABOUT MAKING MORE MANGA FOR THIS TITLE, I WAS GLAD I HAD MADE THE NECKTIES SIMPLE.
I LIKE THE CURRENT DESIGN, BUT SOMETIMES I THINK THAT THE UNIFORMS COULD HAVE BEEN MORE DETAILED.
COSTUMES OF THE WORLD
IF THE SERIES CONTINUES, I WANT TO DRAW ETHNIC COSTUMES.
LIKE FOR THE OPENING SPREADS...
THIS BECAME THE RECURRING "WELCOME!" SCENES.
AND NOW?
AAARGH. WHOSE IDEA WAS IT TO DO COSPLAY EVERY TIME?! (IT WAS MINE.)
THERE ARE SEVEN OF THEM! WHAT A STUPID IDEA! I'LL NEVER FINISH!

AS I STRUGGLE THROUGH EACH DAY...THE HOST CLUB CARRIES ON.

AND NOW, FOR THOSE OF YOU WHO CAN'T DISTINGUISH BETWEEN THE TWINS...

THIS IS HOW HATORI REMEMBERS!!

THE LECTURE

1. IMAGINE SOMETHING SYMMETRIC LIKE CURTAINS TIED AT THE SIDES.

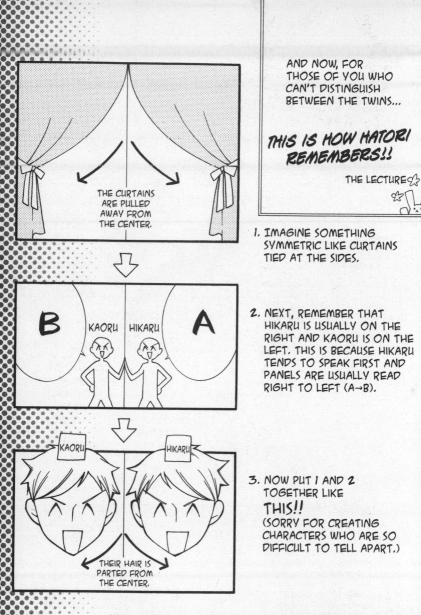

THE CURTAINS ARE PULLED AWAY FROM THE CENTER.

2. NEXT, REMEMBER THAT HIKARU IS USUALLY ON THE RIGHT AND KAORU IS ON THE LEFT. THIS IS BECAUSE HIKARU TENDS TO SPEAK FIRST AND PANELS ARE USUALLY READ RIGHT TO LEFT (A→B).

A
HIKARU
KAORU
B

3. NOW PUT 1 AND 2 TOGETHER LIKE **THIS!!** (SORRY FOR CREATING CHARACTERS WHO ARE SO DIFFICULT TO TELL APART.)

HIKARU
KAORU
THEIR HAIR IS PARTED FROM THE CENTER.

※ SO WHEN YOU DON'T KNOW WHICH IS WHICH, LOOK AT THE WAY THE HAIR IS PARTED AND IMAGINE THE CURTAINS. ONCE YOU GET USED TO IT, YOU'LL BE ABLE TO TELL THEM APART IN AN INSTANT. WELL, PROBABLY, ANYWAY.

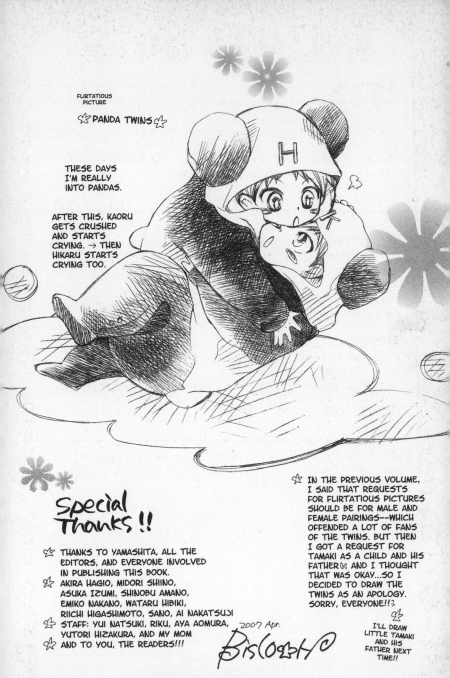

FLIRTATIOUS
PICTURE

☆PANDA TWINS☆

THESE DAYS
I'M REALLY
INTO PANDAS.

AFTER THIS, KAORU
GETS CRUSHED
AND STARTS
CRYING. → THEN
HIKARU STARTS
CRYING TOO.

Special Thanks!!

☆ THANKS TO YAMASHITA, ALL THE
   EDITORS, AND EVERYONE INVOLVED
   IN PUBLISHING THIS BOOK.
☆ AKIRA HAGIO, MIDORI SHIINO,
   ASUKA IZUMI, SHINOBU AMANO,
   EMIKO NAKANO, WATARU HIBIKI,
   RIICHI HIGASHIMOTO, SANO, AI NAKATSUJI
☆ STAFF: YUI NATSUKI, RIKU, AYA AOMURA,
   YUTORI HIZAKURA, AND MY MOM
☆ AND TO YOU, THE READERS!!!

☆ IN THE PREVIOUS VOLUME,
   I SAID THAT REQUESTS
   FOR FLIRTATIOUS PICTURES
   SHOULD BE FOR MALE AND
   FEMALE PAIRINGS--WHICH
   OFFENDED A LOT OF FANS
   OF THE TWINS. BUT THEN
   I GOT A REQUEST FOR
   TAMAKI AS A CHILD AND HIS
   FATHER♡, AND I THOUGHT
   THAT WAS OKAY...SO I
   DECIDED TO DRAW THE
   TWINS AS AN APOLOGY.
   SORRY, EVERYONE!!♬

☆ I'LL DRAW
   LITTLE TAMAKI
   AND HIS
   FATHER NEXT
   TIME!!

2007 Apr.

Bisco Hatori

EGOISTIC CLUB/THE END

EDITOR'S NOTES

EPISODE 42

Page 38: *Keba* is short for *kebai*, meaning "garish" or "gaudy."

Page 41: In Japanese lore, *kappa* are water spirits.

Page 53: *Washing potatoes*: Hunny means they're like a bunch of potatoes crammed in a bowl for washing.

Page 81: *Anmitsu* is a sweet made with jelly, red bean paste, and fruit; *senbei* are rice crackers; and *dango* are dumplings.

Page 82: *Tanuki* are usually likened to raccoons. They are mischief-makers in Japanese lore.

EPISODE 44

Page 101: A *kyoretsu* character is someone who takes things to extremes or acts in an "over the top" manner.

EPISODE 46

Page 164: *Mensore* means "welcome" in the Okinawan dialect.

Page 175: In a bread-eating race, sweet rolls are hung from above and contestants grab the bread with their mouths and race to the finish line.

Page 176: In a calvary battle, teams try to grab an item (such as a flag) from other teams. Teams are made up of three people carrying a fourth person who is trying to grab the other teams' items while protecting his own.

Author Bio

Bisco Hatori made her manga
debut with *Isshun kan no
Romance* (**A Moment of
Romance**) in *LaLa DX*
magazine. The comedy *Ouran
High School Host Club* is her
breakout hit. When she's stuck
thinking up characters' names,
she gets inspired by loud,
upbeat music (her radio is set
to NACK5 FM). She enjoys
reading all kinds of manga, but
she's especially fond of the sci-fi
drama *Please Save My Earth*
and *Slam Dunk*, a basketball
classic.

OURAN HIGH SCHOOL HOST CLUB
Vol. 10
Shojo Beat Edition

STORY AND ART BY BISCO HATORI

Translation & English Adaptation/RyoRca and John Werry
Touch-up Art & Lettering/George Caltsoudas
Graphic Design/Izumi Evers
Editor/Nancy Thistlethwaite

Ouran Koko Host Club by Bisco Hatori © Bisco Hatori 2006. All rights reserved. First
published in Japan in 2007 by HAKUSENSHA, Inc., Tokyo. English language translation
rights arranged with HAKUSENSHA, Inc., Tokyo.

Printed in Canada

Published by VIZ Media, LLC
P.O. Box 77010
San Francisco, CA 94107

10 9 8 7 6
First printing, February 2008
Sixth printing, December 2013

www.viz.com   www.shojobeat.com

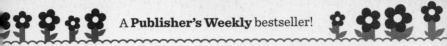

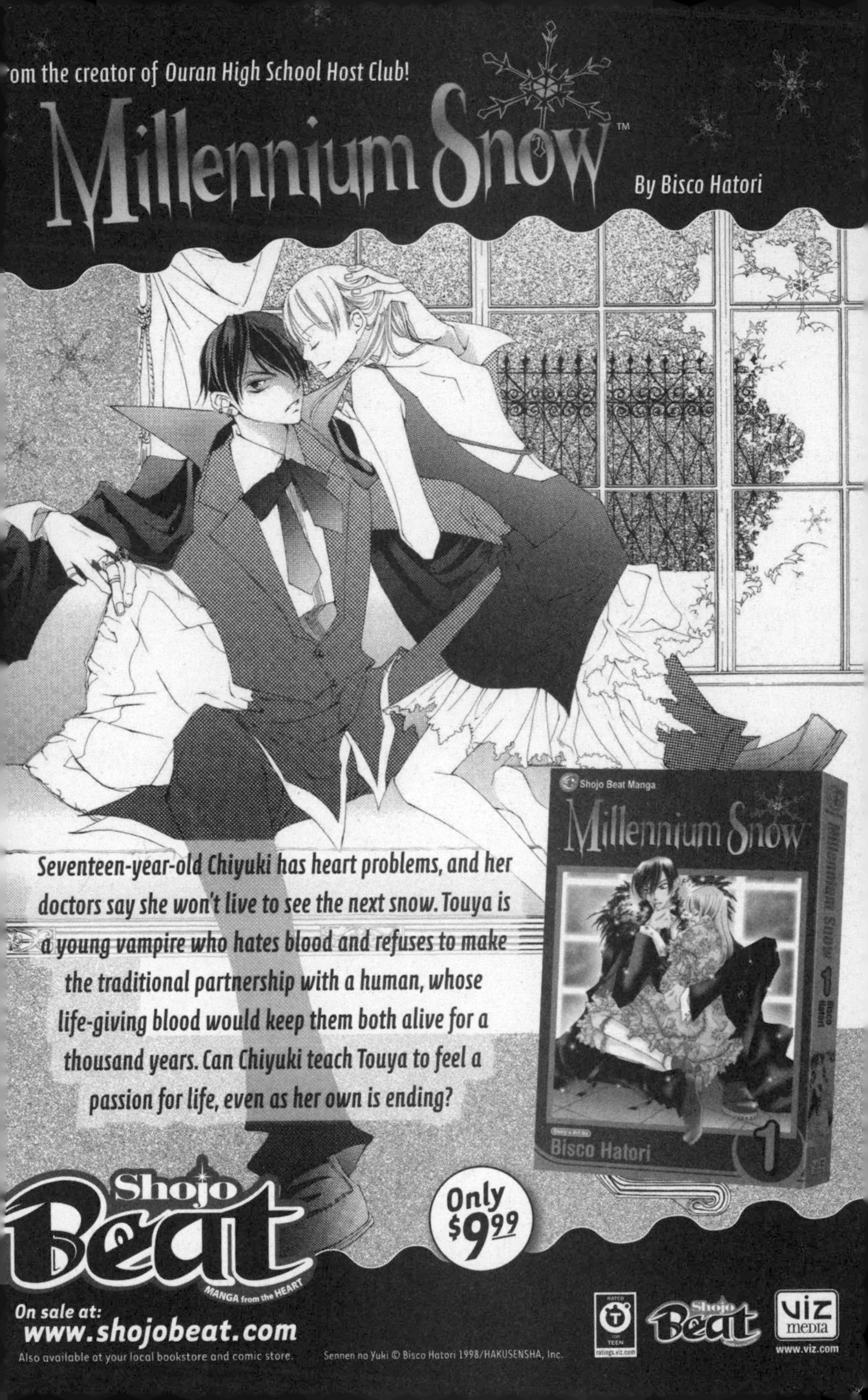

rom the creator of Ouran High School Host Club!
Millennium Snow™
By Bisco Hatori
Shojo Beat Manga
Millennium Snow
Bisco Hatori
1
Seventeen-year-old Chiyuki has heart problems, and her doctors say she won't live to see the next snow. Touya is a young vampire who hates blood and refuses to make the traditional partnership with a human, whose life-giving blood would keep them both alive for a thousand years. Can Chiyuki teach Touya to feel a passion for life, even as her own is ending?
Shojo Beat
MANGA from the HEART
Only $9.99
On sale at:
www.shojobeat.com
Also available at your local bookstore and comic store.
Sennen no Yuki © Bisco Hatori 1998/HAKUSENSHA, Inc.
RATED T FOR TEEN
ratings.viz.com
Shojo Beat
VIZ MEDIA
www.viz.com

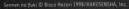

Kyoko Mogami followed her true love Sho to Tokyo to support him while he made it big as an idol! But he's casting her out now that he's famous enough! Kyoko won't suffer in silence— she's going to get her sweet revenge by beating Sho in show biz!

Vol. 1 ISBN: 978-1-4215-4226-3

Vol. 2 ISBN: 978-1-4215-4227-0

Vol. 3 ISBN: 978-1-4215-4228

Show biz is sweet...but revenge is sweeter!

Only $14.99 for each volume! ($16.99 In Canada)

Skip·Beat!

Story and Art by YOSHIKI NAKAMURA

In Stores Now!

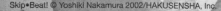

www.viz.co

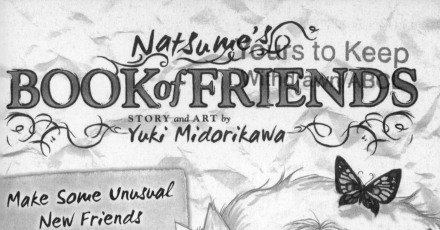

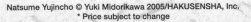

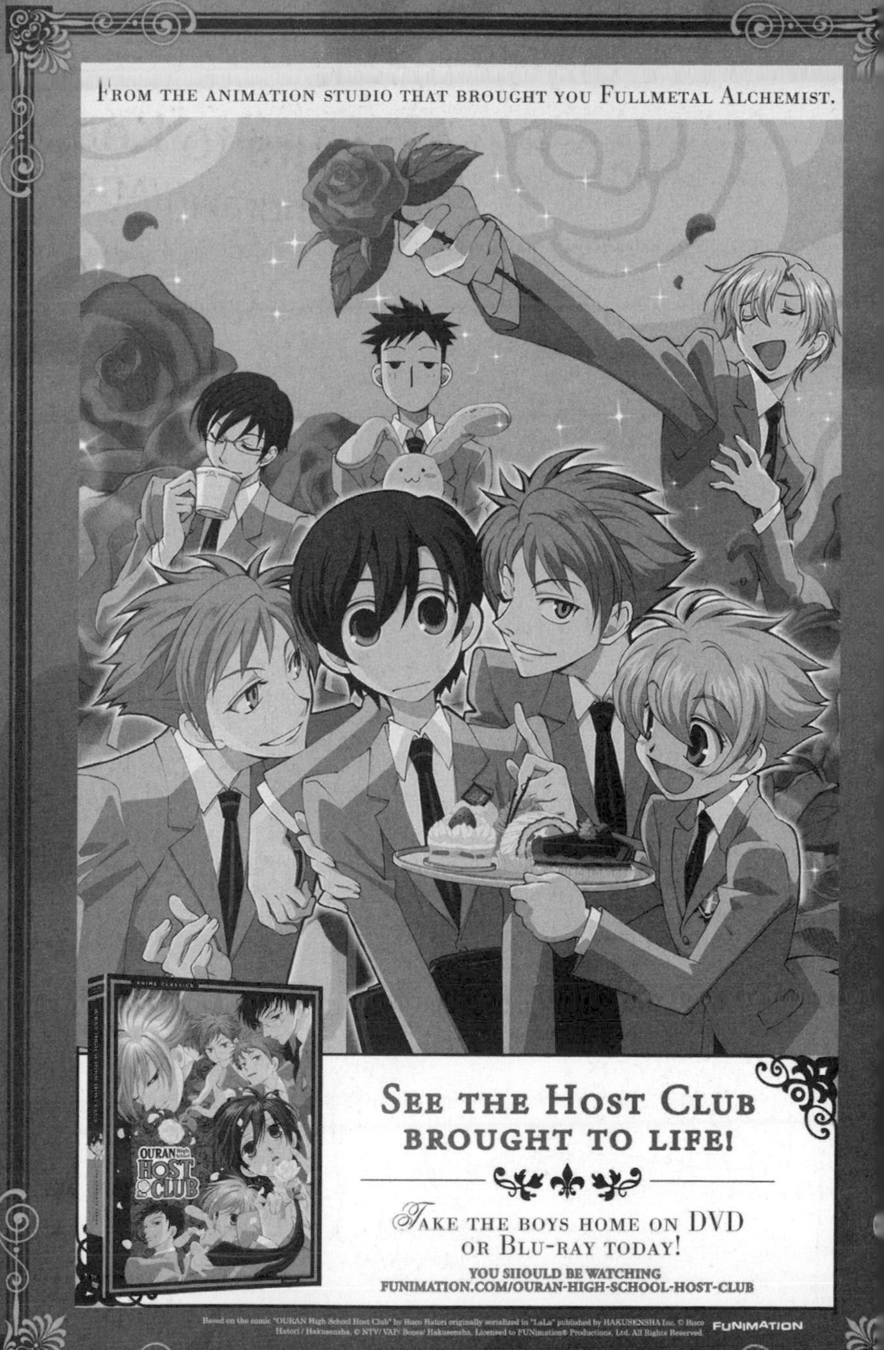

FROM THE ANIMATION STUDIO THAT BROUGHT YOU FULLMETAL ALCHEMIST.
OURAN HIGH SCHOOL HOST CLUB
SEE THE HOST CLUB BROUGHT TO LIFE!
TAKE THE BOYS HOME ON DVD OR BLU-RAY TODAY!
YOU SHOULD BE WATCHING
FUNIMATION.COM/OURAN-HIGH-SCHOOL-HOST-CLUB
Based on the comic "OURAN High School Host Club" by Bisco Hatori originally serialized in "LaLa" published by HAKUSENSHA Inc. © Bisco Hatori / Hakusensha. © NTV/ VAP/ Bones/ Hakusensha. Licensed to FUNimation® Productions, Ltd. All Rights Reserved.
FUNIMATION

SURPRISE!

You may be reading the wrong way!

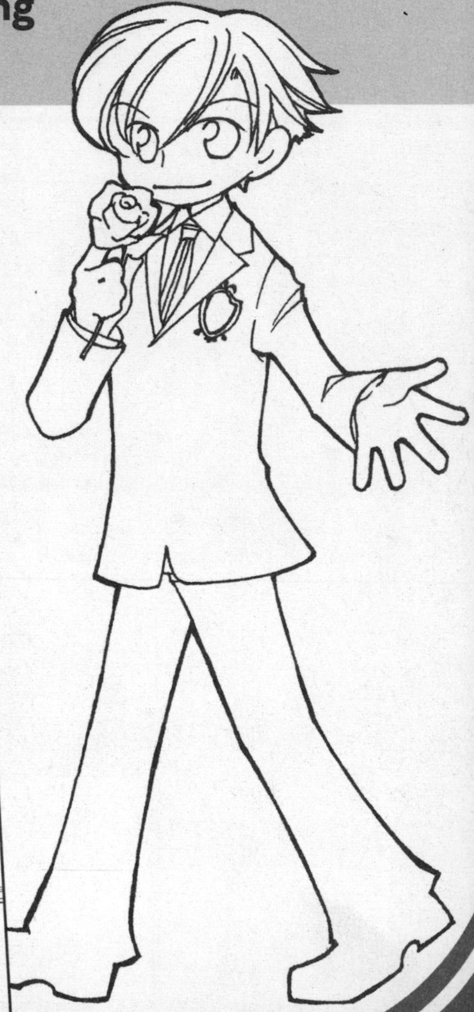

It's true: In keeping with the original Japanese comic format, this book reads from right to left—so action, sound effects, and word balloons are completely reversed. This preserves the orientation of the original artwork—plus, it's fun! Check out the diagram shown here to get the hang of things, and then turn to the other side of the book to get started!

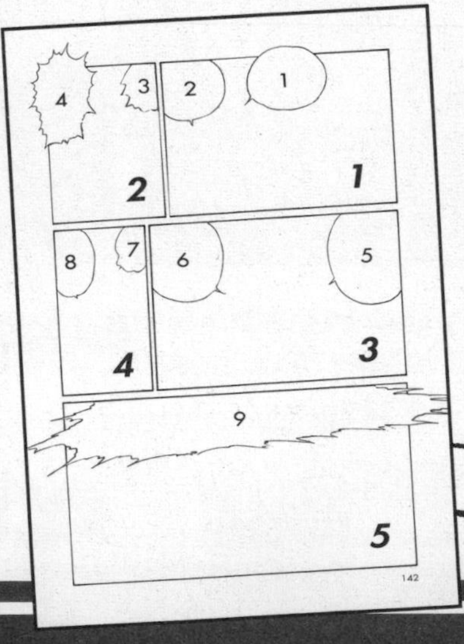
1
2
1
3
4
2
5
6
3
7
8
4
9
5
142